Politics
by
Humans

Research on
American Leadership

James David Barber

DUKE UNIVERSITY PRESS

DURHAM AND LONDON

1988

Library of Congress Cataloging-in-
Publication Data
Barber, James David.
Politics by Humans : Research on American
Leadership / James David Barber.
    p.   cm.
Bibliography: p.
Includes index.
ISBN 0–8223–0837–1
    1. Presidents—United States—History.
2. Political leadership—United States—History.
3. Political culture—United States—History.
I. Title.
JK511.B36   1988
306'.2—dc 19   87–36593 CIP

To Robert E. Lane

> . . . *Our referee,*
> *Our Host, that is, and trusted guide, who made*
> *Decisions for our happy cavalcade,*
> *Turned round and said, 'Matters, my lords, stand thus;*
> *There's but one story lacking now to us.*
> *We've carried out my sentence and decree.*
> *We've heard a tale from each in his degree,*
> *What I ordained is nearly done, I say.*
> *God send the best of fortune, so I pray,*
> *On whomsoever is last to pour the liquor.*
> *Sir Priest,' he said, 'are you by chance a vicar?*
> *Or else the parson? Tell the truth, I say;*
> *Don't spoil our sport though, be you what you may,*
> *For every man but you has told his tale.*
> *Unbuckle now and show what's in your bale,*
> *For honestly, to judge you by your looks,*
> *You could knit mighty matters out of books.*
> *So up and tell a story, by cock's bones!'*
> —CHAUCER, "THE PARSON'S TALE"

Contents

Introduction

THOSE WHO SEEK to label eras call
this one "The Age of Analysis." Problems come whole; take them
apart and attack the pieces one at a time. It works. Absent the analytic mode, nary a bridge would be built or a casserole cooked or a
treatise written. In scholarship, analysis can be a boon to creativity—
better ways of cutting the coconut. But distinctions can widen into divisions and, eventually, into "disciplines"—which is what has happened in the academic world. Ironically, the analytic framework which
once freed thought from medieval categories now operates as a drag
on progress, particularly in the social sciences.

Political science has a special bridging advantage. For the focus of
our concern is not a particular method but a particular phenomenon:
government. Thus we need not be constrained in swiping methods
from our neighbor disciplines such as history, anthropology, economics, sociology, and psychology. Whatever advances knowledge of government belongs to us. Further, the reason we study government provides a useful selective principle. Political science is a practical inquiry
aimed at bettering the world. As noted below, the word "government"

comes from the Greek for steering—a practical art if there ever was one, navigating the present toward a wanted future.

So political science burgles its neighbors selectively, to find tools for understanding how to make government better. That selectivity renders irrelevant, for our peculiar purposes, vast territories of the adjacent disciplines, occupied by those for whom truth surpasses utility as a value, for example, by those who seek betterments beyond the political, or by those who find in politics their favorite entertainment.

The course of my research (a stumbled march) has in the main explored psychology, with a view to exploiting it for political science. Within the governmental terrain, I have concentrated on leadership, not because I think other directions of inquiry useless but because leaders, positioned at the crux of the enterprise, exhibit the meaning of politics in its most significant sense. My focus has been on political leadership in the United States, a decision which reveals an initial skepticism about transcultural analogies, though I find such possibilities increasingly intriguing. Within American leadership, three classes of phenomena have caught and kept my attention.

The first is the Presidency. If a political locus can impel leadership in this nation, that is it. Given the recurrent patterns of linkage, the Presidency is not a bad place to look for the bundling together of the disparate strands of American politics. Yet history makes clear that Presidents vary in ways important to the directions of political action. True, the office makes the man; true, too, the man makes the office. To understand that interplay we need individual psychology, particularly the psychology of adaptation (or coping) and development (or biography). And because our interest is progressive, not merely retrospective, we need to look beyond the individual variations to discern types, from which are derived predictive clues applicable in the selection of Presidents yet to come.

If the Presidency is dominated by an individual, leadership in other arenas of power is more a matter of mutuality, particularly in the ways persons in positions of power perceive one another. In institutions such as legislatures, bureaucracies, town councils, and even clusters of citizens, force is rare; power is largely a matter of shaping anticipations which in turn are profoundly shaped by shared memories, myths, and expectations. Politicians, having been coached by their cultures for many a year, enter the governing process bearing with them perception-shaping mental constructs which channel not only old needs but also new hopes. So the salient features of a power system can only be understood by understanding what the participants make of it. The appropriate psychology in institutional politics, then, is more social than individual, verging on and sometimes merging with anthropology.

The third area is communication. One cannot effectively study leadership in the American democracy without searching out how public discourse works. Politics is mediated—that is, nearly all of what any citizen perceives of politics comes through journalism. So it is no surprise that who gets elected and, perhaps as important, under what assumptions and with what aspirations, depends on what the media make of candidates. As the democracy develops wider and wider circles of actual participation, the mass media gain influence and thus relevance for research. Scholars should notice how politicians themselves spend their anxiety and enthusiasm, their curiosity and defensiveness. Today the politician puts at least one of his two eyes to media. Who are these mediators? What are *their* motives, *their* aspirations, *their* professional traditions? How do their ways shape those of politicians and consequently of the state?

In the first place, then, leadership inheres in the leader—his character, his style, his worldview, in relation to political conditions. In the second place, leadership is conditioned by political culture, by institutional and social customs and expectations. In the third place, leadership is a process which, in a democracy, happens through mediated communication, so that the predilections of newspeople focus and color political life.

This book is arranged in those three parts. Reviewing my research over the past quarter century, I have picked the pieces I think illustrate most clearly my way of looking at politics, as that viewpoint has developed (and still is developing) from one project to the next. These various reports, scattered in time and place of publication, are brought together to ease access for researchers who would otherwise spend too many hours tracking them down. Then too, it may be helpful to have in one place different angles on the same basic direction.

The thread through these pieces is this: politics is a human enterprise. No mechanical metaphor or organic analogy can capture what that means to those who steer governments. Rather, politics and the human psyche must be understood as they exist: inextricably combined. Beyond analysis, that is the synthesis upon which the hope of progress rests.

I

Leader-in-Chief

The American Presidency is a unique combination of two traditions, republican and democratic, played out in three essential roles.

1

The Office

IN THE GREAT sweep of history, the American Presidency is new. Ages went by with most of humanity clear out of the picture of rulership, asleep to the affairs of state, seldom even wondering what the king was doing tonight. The United States of America was meant to be different: a people ruling ourselves by means of a government made by us. The President is our First Servant. We expect him to know what the wiser and better parts of our nature would want the government to do, and to see to getting that done. We load him with duties and then stand back and watch. Those who were for him cheer, those who were against him squint.

Harry Truman said that "most Presidents have received more advice than they can possibly use," and he was right. People who would never presume to tell an engineer how to build a bridge or a surgeon how to transplant kidneys feel free to straighten out their President. Professors and journalists have probably been the worst offenders. Professors have the leisure to smoke out the lessons of the last war and apply them to the next one—a mode of reasoning that can lead to cavalry charges against concrete bunkers. Journalists these days, let in to watch the President change his socks and comb his hair, can't help but feel the urge to supply answers to questions the President ought to ask but hasn't thought of yet. And if you stick a microphone in the face of your average American citizen, who may have trouble remembering the difference between the Declaration of Independence and the Bill of Rights, you can usually get him or her to pass on some words of counsel and advice to the Chief Executive. Many a President has found the job a lonely one—yet at the same time complained, as Warren G. Harding did, that "I can't get away from the men who dog my footsteps."

Now in these chancy times, citizens might well contemplate what a perilous course we have set for our servant and consider whether we, *with* him, might find a way to lend a hand.

The Republican Tradition: Plainness and Power

Two traditions have shaped the modern President's ways of being, a republican and a democratic tradition. The political parties with those names both aim to stand for both traditions.

The republican tradition came first. It grew out of a revolution against a meddling king and his high and mighty governors. The revolutionaries established a negative principle: no rule by a distant power in which we had no voice. The Constitution makers had the more complex task: to design a government, a "new order of the ages," strong enough to last, yet free of the terrors of tyranny. After considerable debate, they decided not to call the President "Majesty" or "Excellency" but "Mister President." He would serve not for life but for a set term, be elected not by his fellow governing leaders but by the citizenry, acting through a special electoral college. If he lurched beyond the bounds of the Constitution, he could be thrown out of office at any time. And the President was made dependent on the people's representatives for laws and money and, as it turned out, on independent judges who had the ultimate power to decide what the laws meant.

At its birth, the Constitution was a theory. Its fathers hoped, despite deep doubts, that it would last a quarter-century or so, resting that hope mainly on the idea that if part of the system went wrong, the other parts would correct it. The task of making the theory work fell to a miscellaneous band of Congressmen, judges, soldiers, clerks, and to a President who, in the early years, floated from city to city looking for a permanent home. In 1790 a wrangling Congress finally delegated the choice of a capital city to President Washington: he placed it at the southernmost extreme of the territory allowed him. Early Washington, D.C., mocked Major Pierre L'Enfant's grand plan. It was a swampy, malarial little village in the woods, where Congressmen lived in boarding houses, leaving their families safely back home, a post where foreign diplomats hustled for some more civilized assignments, a place soon peopled by "a class of swaggering sycophants . . . for[cing] themselves into the presence of distinguished and well-bred people," as one of the latter put it. And all that *talk!* "Babeltown," they called it.

So the government got under way in a frontier town rather than in the elegance of New York or Philadelphia, and the Presidency got underway with a frontiersman. George Washington, for all his natural dignity, had been a hill-hopping surveyor, a farmer, a country squire. As President he saw "the glare which hovers round the external trappings of elevated office," but wrote that "to me there is nothing in it, beyond the lustre which may be reflected from its connection with the power of promoting human felicity." Washington the town and Washington the man left lessons by example for succeeding Presidents, especially the lesson an ancient king required to be repeated to him daily: "Remember, your Majesty, that you are mortal."

That theme of republican virtue, of plainness in the Presidency, lasted past the start. We see it in just-inaugurated Thomas Jefferson waiting his turn for lunch, in Abraham Lincoln's letter to a child who wanted him to grow a beard, in Eleanor Roosevelt serving hot dogs to the King and Queen of England, in Harry Truman washing out his own socks and underwear in the White House, in Gerald Ford toasting his morning muffin. From time to time Presidents forgot their mortality and got their egos tangled in the trappings, confused themselves with the Saviour or the sovereign. Eventually, though, the Presidency gets called back to its old republican homeplace.

Not that the Presidency was or is for weaklings. The republican tradition recognized the need for positive leadership. The Presidency became an engine of enterprise, not a home for retiring glad-handers.

President Washington could be tough. He demonstrated to John Hancock, the big-signatured governor of Massachusetts, that the President of the United States took precedence over any governor, and he made the Senate understand that he, not they, would decide when he needed their advice and consent on foreign policy. Presidents henceforward, with too many sorry exceptions, have felt responsible for making the government move out to solve problems—which is, in a fast-moving world, the only way to preserve, protect, and defend the Constitution.

The Democratic Tradition: Bring in the People

What was incomplete in the republican tradition was power for the people. Only a minority of male, white, propertied people was allowed to vote in the first place, and the impact of their votes was muted and filtered through various representational indirections. Voters cast ballots for state legislators who, in turn, elected the U.S. Senators. In the first three Presidential elections, most of the electoral college was chosen by the state legislatures. The Bill of Rights— the price the founding fathers had to pay to get their Constitution accepted—inhibited abuse of power but came short of sharing power with the great body of the people.

That remained for the second of our great traditions, the democratic tradition, the impulse insisting that government "by the consent of the governed" meant more than passive approval of the best available inside deal. Jefferson was away in Paris when the Constitution was written; possibly he would have made the founders see the contradiction between the wide language of the Declaration and their narrow definitions of the franchise. It took generations and many hard, long courageous struggles to get the laws fixed so that an eighteen-year-old black working girl could walk relaxed into the court house and cast her vote.

Laws work when people want them to. The democratic tradition reached beyond the formal rules to the spirit, the nation's lifeblood and vital energy. Raucous General Andrew Jackson may not have had as wide a base of voters as was once thought, but he charged into the Presidency "like a cyclone from off the Western prairies," as Woodrow Wilson put it, and laid about him as the people's President. "His strength lay with the masses, and he knew it," his friend Martin Van Buren remembered. Let the people in—the White House furniture could be repaired. The country would never be the same. Equally important, what the country thought about the Presidency would never be the same.

Keeping the democratic tradition lively was imperative because it runs against a natural social tendency: for those in the know to get together and work things out to their own advantage. It is *so* much easier that way, so much quicker, so convenient and familiar and calming to the nerves. The President, like the rest of us, craves the surcease of anxiety. If he wants to, he can find calm in a little coterie of White House pals, spiced up from time to time by some old friend from the provinces. That is not just a Washington disease—at this moment, all over the country, cozy companionships of the powerful are cementing themselves, "successful" people are discovering that they speak the same language, and casually the deals are going down. The democratic tradition moves against this trend, urges involvement and participation and access by more people in more government decisions—not only at the finish but from the start. This is the inclusive impulse, the open government impulse, the sense that government is the community's business and that the community is everybody—not just a companionship of the powerful.

From the beginning, Presidents have hoped and claimed to speak for The People, for the nation as a whole against the special interest groups or privileged classes. The voice of the people is accepted as a secular version of the voice of God, and the President may see himself as a political John the Baptist. The President can and often does invoke The People against the conglomerate of their own representatives, against the newspapers, against the weight of informed opinion. Woodrow Wilson felt this urge most keenly: "Whatever strength I have and whatever authority I possess are mine only so long and so far as I express the spirit and purpose of the American people." But until very recently, no one had a very good way to find out what the people—the actual people as distinguished from The People as an idealized abstraction—had on their minds. Picking apart the election returns gave only the foggiest clues; for instance, we know now that a lot of voters cast their ballots *against* the Presidential candidate they dislike, leaving the winner with only a negative mandate—not to do what the other candidate would have done. Mass media and polling give the people a direct means of learning what the President is saying and doing and give a much clearer account of what we think we want. There is still a good deal of fog in the polls, but on dramatic public issues the President is constrained or empowered by what Gallup and Harris discover on the surface of the popular psyche.

The Bond of Sentiment:
Leaning on the President

The democratic tradition is loud with exhortation: people should take part in politics, vote, speak up, get involved. Leaders harangue the nation's youth with this message. The old Greek word for "idiot," they remind us, referred to people who kept to private life and failed to exercise their civic duties. All that preaching comes from a fearsome fact: there are a lot of "idiots" among us, politically lazy folk who have their own fish to fry and are prepared to let the government cook itself. We tend to look to each new President as suddenly responsible for the nation's general welfare, all by his lonesome, as Henry V's soldiers looked to him:

> Upon the king! Let us our lives, our souls,
> Our debts, our careful wives,
> Our children, and our sins, lay on the king . . .

For the democratic Presidency is, in the public eye, much more than an "executive" office. For better or worse, we tie ourselves emotionally to our Presidents, even to the ones who falter and fail. We hunger for the President to reassure us that things are going to turn out all right, to serve as an inspiring example of the nation's ideals, to march at the head of the column in the attack on our troubles. In England, the Queen is there to absorb and express those deep feelings, leaving the Prime Minister relatively free to operate as a practical politician. Here all that falls on the President—and if he fails in *that* relationship, all his other castles fall.

This mysterious bond of feeling between the people and the President shows itself whenever a President dies in office. Most Americans still remember where they were when John F. Kennedy was cut down, and the way it felt—like a blow to the solar plexus—when we lost that fresh young contender. Researchers have found that the same wave of deep sadness swept through the people at every Presidential death in office: not only for Lincoln and Roosevelt, but for James Garfield, William McKinley, and poor Harding. By contrast, when *ex*-Presidents die there is but a respectful formal mourning.

Not that we are constant worshipers at a White House shrine. A better way of putting it is that Americans feel ambivalent, divided inside, about their Presidents. We rally round the President in a crisis and in the high hope of inauguration day, but with a curious regularity we also seem to like to raise a President up and then watch him fall. His popularity declines as he moves on the hard choices. His great purposes become less newsworthy than the fits and starts of his political experiments. Maybe something in us wants our most powerful champion to turn out to have feet of clay; maybe we are simply reacting to the truth that no lone two-legged human can possibly succeed as George Washington in today's Washington, D.C. In any case, the President is the lead actor in the national political drama. His other skills, however strong, won't save him if he is a bust in that role.

The people expect the President to keep the Constitutional faith, not only to leave law and liberty intact when he moves out of the White House, but also to use the formalities with a democratic spirit.

The Great Conversation:
The Art of Honesty

Above all, the President is called upon to maintain the Great Conversation by which we discern, eventually, "ideas whose time has come." The dictators disdain chatterbox democracy, but our tradition depends on talk, on "reasoning together." When the great conversation breaks down, people fall into private dreams and public grunts, and the end of the democratic tradition is not far. If history is any guide, Presidents do their worst damage when they fall into a credibility gap—when their words no longer signify their intentions. The black lie in

Presidential politics (as distinguished from the little white lies all of us tell everyday) is a lie about where his mind is and where he is trying to take us. Theodore Roosevelt understood that well: "My value as an asset to the American People consists chiefly in the belief that I mean what I say." For all his troubles, Harry Truman left little doubt about what he was trying to say, and Dwight Eisenhower, despite his rambling rhetoric, came across as sincere—people felt they knew what he meant. Amazing but true: we speak the same language but we keep misunderstanding one another. Jefferson realized that truth-telling was not always easy. He said, "The whole of government is the art of being honest"—honesty required *art*. Given hundreds of millions of us potential misunderstanders, it also takes patience in explaining and an ear tuned in to hear the reaction.

Presidents have found need of Jefferson's art because so much of what they say is subject to selection and interpretation by other explainers. The American mass media are the envy of the world. In most nations, the press falls far short of our standard; of course, that does not mean that what we have is good enough for *us*. Presidents have seldom wound up with a favorable opinion of the press, having seen too many of their sacred cows butchered by reporters. Realistic Presidents know that while they can dominate the media (a determined President can almost always get his message out) and even bypass the reporters (as FDR did with his fireside chats), still they are very dependent on the talkers and writers who tell the story day after day. Even in the "pop-up" Presidential press conference, where the President decides whom to recognize and when to change the subject, he is vulnerable to surprise and discombobulation as he stands up there winging quick answers to questions he cannot always anticipate. He can count on this or that little frightening phrase being ripped out of context and bannered on the evening's news. And he can be sure that the columnists, whose job it is to make reality simpler and more interesting than it really is, will at times find him flabbergastingly wrong. No President since Coolidge (who loved reporters) has ended up with the warm feeling that his portrait in the press was a masterpiece.

The printing press had its first great outpouring in an age of faith, in Martin Luther's time. You can still find people who justify their political sentiments by reference to something set down in black and white, as if the printing of it made it true. Television news became popular in the 1950s; we saw the Army-McCarthy hearings and the Kefauver crime investigation with our own eyes. The public uses both media casually though not uncritically these days, but we swim in a sea of assertions beyond our power to test in any direct way. Therefore, the President we know, the only one we can know, is the President delivered to us in the morning paper and the evening news— a mediated President.

Presidents learn to use the press, to put the best face they can on the matter. Historically that has included a fair portion of fakery; the first "media event" no doubt happened long before Charlemagne crowned himself. But what tears up the President's nerves—even when he is not faking—is the double bind the press puts him in. Hard experience clarified that bind in Herbert Hoover's mentation: he saw his duty "to help the people of the United States to get along peacefully and prosperously without any undue commotion or trouble over their affairs," but the reporters kept pressuring him to "provide the press with exciting news of something about to happen." Reporters live by a cardinal rule: "Nothing is new for very long." Their pencils have to push, their cameras roll, lest we the people miss our daily dose of excitement and enlightenment.

Past Presidents have all grappled with the professional President-watchers, and sometimes won. Some reporters have let themselves be had, turned into flacks. But that goes against the H. L. Mencken tradition that the only way for a reporter to look at a politician is down. And if today's television entertainment is romantic fantasy (and what fun those wars were!), today's television news conveys a sense of suspicion, of selfish purpose behind the politician's apparent generosity, the lie behind his candid look, the blunder masked by his smooth exterior. The President has to live with a press set up to discover that he is seldom what he seems.

The trick is to give them their news, an unending parade of events, and to counteract skepticism with achievements that cannot be neglected. Modern Presidents can take comfort in the fact that they are not the first to be roasted in the press. Washington was cartooned as a strutting fop, Lincoln as a baboon, TR as a buck-toothed maniac, Franklin Roosevelt as a helpless cripple, and so it goes. The natural human reaction is to crawl back into your shell, repeating to yourself the old definition of the critic: the guy who comes down on the battle-field when the fight is over and shoots the wounded. That reaction can turn a President into a secretive sovereign, barricaded with his sycophants in the Oval Office, sucking the thumb of "public relations" as the bane and benison of his existence. Presidents who have been relatively successful with the press—and none has been wholly so—have done what they could to help reporters do their work, in the furtherance of the President's own purposes, and then let the devil take the hindmost, as President Roosevelt did, laughing over Westbrook Pegler's relentless diatribes as he read them aloud to his circle of reporters in the Rose Garden.

Presidential Progress:
Catching the Political Imagination

Woodrow Wilson, a President who wrote better than he ruled, summed up the power Presidents can achieve if they succeed in connecting with and guiding forward the mainstream of national belief:

> The President can dominate his party by being spokesman for the real sentiment and purpose of the country, by giving direction to opinion, by giving the country at once the information and the statements of policy which will enable it to form its judgments alike of parties and of men.
>
> His is the only national voice in affairs. Let him once win the admiration and confidence of the country, and no other single force can withstand him, no combination of forces will easily overpower him. His position takes the imagination of the country. He is the representative of no constituency, but of the whole people.

Finding and holding positions that will capture the imagination of the country is hard to do, because the popular imagination, and the real experiences it grows out of, are in perpetual motion. The republican and democratic traditions are enduring themes, but there is in our memory and anticipation another theme that bucks against the whole idea of tradition—the theme of progress. Our history as a democratic republic is old: our political culture values newness of life, progress if possible, change in any case. We are a people always starting over again, from the New Zion planted in Plymouth to the waves of new Americans transported here, by their will or against it, to the eventual millions fanning out across the landscape in search of a new chance, even a new identity. The cowhands used to sing "What Was Your Name in the East?" But from then to now each generation has its eyes fixed more on the future than the past.

To the President, that makes innovation a necessity. He will sink if he stands still. Born and bred in rapidly retreating days gone by, he struggles to catch up with present-day life and to lead us on into happier tomorrows. Thumbing through the history books in search of guidance, he finds tales running in every conceivable direction— how Lincoln, for instance, was tough and gentle, tragic and comic, sensitive and vulgar. If he consults the futurologists, he may find a Merlin, but is more likely to find a numerological trend-projector or a modern Delphic oracle high on gas. Part of him tries to capture the meaning of the time we are just emerging from; part of him has to lean against the "lessons" so confidently pronounced by experts in the hypothetical correction of deeds already done. They will help him see how fast the world turns; he must figure out in which directions he will try to nudge it.

John Jay, in *Federalist LXIV*, saw the opportunity hiding inside the apparent chaos:

> They who have turned their attention to the affairs of men must have perceived that there are tides in them; tides very irregular in their duration, strength, and direction, and seldom found to run twice exactly in the same manner or measure. To discern and to profit by these tides in national affairs is the business of those who preside over them; and they who have had much experience on this head inform us that there frequently are occasions when days, nay, even hours are precious.

All times try men's souls, but a President's own time will go down in history with his name on it. The popular tides seem sluggish or fickle as he ditches and dams. There was a time when the idea of votes for women was a bizarre speculation. Before this century runs out, we may well have a woman President. Successful Presidents have been midwives for such ideas whose time has come, though even the best of Presidents can radically misread the temper of his times, as Franklin D. Roosevelt did when he tried to pack the Supreme Court. That temper seems to move by action and reaction: a stolid William Howard Taft follows a vigorous TR and, in turn, gives way to a moralizing Wilson, and when Wilsonian uplift gets tiresome, it is time for an easygoing Harding. It is no accident, we can say with hindsight, that the big question Gerald Ford had to face was, is he honest? Some Presidents grasp the current mood and manage to press forward. Others, like John Quincy Adams, find being President a "harassing, wearying, teasing condition of existence," a blur of "perpetual motion and crazing cares." Or, as the President tries to listen for what's going on, he may grump with Taft: "I'll be damned if I am not getting tired of this. It seems to be the profession of a President simply to hear other people talk." Or he can switch and twitch so rapidly, with every little jiggle of opinion, that he becomes, in Hoover's disdainful phrase about FDR, "a chameleon on plaid."

Roosevelt was no chameleon, he was an experimenter. Unsure about a lot of things, he knew, "One thing is sure. We have to do something. We have to do the best we know how at the moment. . . . If it doesn't turn out right, we can modify it as we go along." Feeling for a path out of the dark of the Depression, he stepped along vigorously and tentatively, ready to change course as need be.

Government as Navigation:
Presidential Variations

"Government" comes from the Greek word for steering. To steer straight in modern politics requires feedback—monitoring the *results* of the steering, the actual effects of policies on the lives of the citizens. Hard as it is to get his program passed and beaten down into administration, the President may find it harder yet to determine what if any difference it all makes to the people. Polls help, but isolated, randomly selected pollees are themselves in a poor position to see the overall picture. It is up to The People's Choice to know what they would choose if they were he; we need the general's view, not the view from the foxhole. The war in Washington is too often a closet drama in which victory is proclaimed before the real battle is joined, out there in "the field." Congress has its hearings, for people who can take time off and get to Washington, and there are traveling Presidential commissions from time to time. But a severe and persistent problem, even today with all our sophisticated means of communication, is the President's intelligence: smart as he is, he will do dumb things if he is blind to the facts or relies on too many other second-guessers. Again, Roosevelt had it right when he told Rexford Tugwell, "Go and see what's happening. See the end product of what we are doing. Talk to people; get the wind in your nose." And the President must be prepared for bad news—not only the news of clean failure but the mushier news of maybe yes and maybe no. Being human, he would love to hear from the constituent who wrote FDR:

> Dear Mr. President:
>
> This is just to tell you that everything is all right now. The man you sent found our house all right, and we went down to the bank with him and the mortgage can go on for a while longer. You remember I wrote you about losing the furniture too. Well, your man got it back for us. I never heard of a President like you. . . .

But more important than the praise and damnation is knowledge— reliable, closely researched findings on what the input has done to the output. The big thinkers have yet to solve this one, though there is much good new research in progress. Meanwhile, the President acts on what he has.

The President. This is the point at which to say that there is no "President," only Presidents, one after another, each equipped with such ways and means as history—his and ours—hands him. What kind of person a President is is important because the "office" (another abstraction) is so loosely defined. For all the advice a President gets, there is no manual for the job. He promises to be faithful in executing the office and to keep the Constitution. That document spells out some of his powers—what he *may* do but not what he *should* do when he runs up against situations X, Y, Z. On a discouraging note, the first mention of the President tells of the Vice President taking over, followed at once by the procedure for impeachment.

The Constitution's spare provisions were written in the confidence that George Washington would be the first of the series, and that he could be counted on to set the proper precedents. He tried, but many of the precedents he dwelled upon have long since passed into the archaic. For example, "Whether it would tend to prompt impertinent applications and involve disagreeable consequences to have it known that the President will, every Morning at eight Oclock, be at leisure to give Audience to persons who may have business with him?" Washington had to invent "the Presidency" from scratch. In important and trivial ways, so has each new President down to now.

Artemus Ward admired Washington's dignity: "Washington never slopt over." But slopping over has not been the only temptation—some Presidents have tried to dignify themselves right up through the clouds.

A popular myth, born of the union of a political religiosity and the vicarious hopes of the middle-aged, has it that the White House transforms its Chief Occupant, alchemizes him from politician to statesman. Chester A. Arthur is the usual example, a shady spoilsman (Wilson called him "a nonentity with sidewhiskers"), who, as President, turned on the bosses and got the Civil Service Act passed and implemented. On the other hand, dark-minded writers dwell on Lord Acton's cautious conundrum that "power tends to corrupt, and absolute power corrupts absolutely," an opinion for which there are more examples. A better way of putting it is that the Presidency tends to exaggerate a man: If he was gnawed by self-doubt before, the Presidency will make it gnaw harder—much harder. If he was a spoiled child grown large, his Presidential nature will feed on the psychological spoils so plentifully available. Give the Presidency to an essentially pontifical character—there to do his high, disagreeable duty—and he will find it possible to rise above all those tedious political fights. Or, with some luck and calculation, we may get a President who exaggerates the office's positive possibilities: a happy warrior, confident and vigorous, searching for ways to grow toward excellence and in the habit of forgiving himself when he fails.

Such subjects are, in fact, more appropriate to election day than to inauguration day. At election time—1980, 1984—we need to take a long, close look at the candidates, not just in the artificial flurry of campaigning, but in their lives and ways before the Presidential bug fastened on them. What Presidentially relevant skills have they demonstrated? What beliefs—about people, about history, and about political morality—have they brought to bear on their experience over the years? What basic character shapes their politics? We need to get past the little campaign bloopers a candidate makes and the whoppers he tells (which feed the lazy analyst in search of a magic sign) and ask who he is—and why. The best clues to that are in what he was in the warp and woof of his life experience. And one more thing: can he laugh at himself? The public President had to be a "solemn ass," according to Coolidge, though in private he himself was the wittiest since Jefferson, and most Presidents can get a humorous kick out of the foibles of their adversaries. But humor about the self, in moderation, can give him a little distance, a little valuable detachment, and is a symptom, I think, of inner strength, as when Lincoln compared his laughter to "the neigh of a wild horse on his native prairie."

Mr. President Comes to Washington: Connecting with Congress

But of course the President is only one factor in the Presidential equation. He operates in a town full of egos with their own powers and purposes. A number of them think they could do his job better than he can. A significant few have it in mind to replace him at the first opportunity. And yet most have a strong stake in his success, not only because their political lives depend on that, but also because they care about the country and recognize how essential Presidential leadership is to national progress.

Citizens who despair over political fighting in Washington should recall that the separated powers are *supposed* to fight. The Constitution makers set it up that way, and generations of Washingtonians have fulfilled their expectation. They scattered responsibility and split up authority, so that no one power could lord it over the others for long. The sign on Harry Truman's desk—"The Buck Stops Here"—was wrong: the buck is all over town, and it moves from hand to hand. Illogical, yes. Inefficient, without a doubt. Surely *someone* has to have the last word? Not in our system: the words roll on, vibrating through a strangely sovereignless concatenation of semi-independent networks. Like kids tied together in a three-legged race, our government marches on legs from different bodies.

The system thus insures that the President will experience frustration. Congress, the major power at the other end of the street, will see to that if no one else does. Theodore Roosevelt once spoke softly of Congress: "I have a very strong feeling that it is a President's duty to get on with Congress if he possibly can, and that it is a reflection upon him if he and Congress come to a complete break." But another time TR clenched his fist and exclaimed to his cousin Franklin, "Sometimes I wish I could be President and Congress too!" Even patient Lincoln got mad at Congress: "I will show them at the other end of the Avenue whether I am President or not!" And cool John Kennedy opined that "it is much easier in many ways for me—and for other Presidents, I think, who felt the same way—when Congress is not in town."

A wag has said that Congress is composed of representatives running for reelection and Senators running for God. John Adams would have agreed:

> But is not man, in the shape of a senator or a representative, as fond of power as a president? . . . are not ambition and favoritism, and all other vicious passions and sinister interests, as strong and active in a senator or a representative as in a president? Cannot, indeed, the members of the legislature conceal their private views and improper motives more easily than a president?

Perhaps. But they are, most of them, honorable men and women, as honor goes in politics, which is a good deal farther than it goes in most endeavors. The President who wants to make the relationship work has to begin with the assumption that their intentions are at least as good as his are, and that they share allegiance to the democratic politician's code: let your word be your bond; fight hard and make up quickly; stick by your friends and be civil with your opponents; listen in the cacophony for strains of agreement; do your homework; and if you can, let everyone have one piece of cake. He learns that the best fringe benefit in politics is the benefit of the doubt, which has a way of coming back to the giver.

Congress used to be a revolving door: members met in short sessions, debated at length, and yearned to get back home and stay there. Nowadays, the sessions are nearly continuous, general debate is rare and relatively meaningless compared to committee work, and a member can make a long career at comfortable pay. Congress is elaborately organized. It seems that nearly everyone is chairman of something. Simplifying reforms, such as cutting down a forest of standing committees, gave growth to scores of subcommittees, which spring up like saplings in the sunshine. Congress is getting its own bureaucracy, its own computers, even its own polling capacity. The whole thing is vastly more complicated than when Jefferson dealt with thirty-two senators and 106 representatives. The pecking orders run up, down, and sideways, though those who handle the money—the legislature's most ancient prerogative—are usually at the top of the heap. Party organization is fluid and fragile, the minority too small to hope for much, the majority too large to control easily.

No wonder then that Presidents, particularly those coming in from out of town, need help in discovering and moving the Congressional power levers. The key to it is probably not in the mechanics—how many breakfasts with whom—but in the quality and continuity of the conversation. Genuine, regular consultation is the art to master.

Advisers: Secrecy and Mistakes

The President can expect with confidence at least one kind of counsel from Congress: "Congressmen are always advising Presidents to get rid of Presidential advisers," John Kennedy said. "That's one of the most constant threads that run through American history, and Presidents ordinarily do not pay attention." In just forty years, the White House staff has grown from thirty-seven to more than five hundred, and the "Executive Office of the President" to thousands, circles upon circles. In practical terms, however large his "personal" staff, only forty or so can sustain the coveted claim of intimacy, since the President has only two ears and two eyes and no way to be two places at once. What concerns Congressmen and other thoughtful critics are the dangers of secrecy and mistakes.

What his critics see as secrecy the President sees as privacy. No President so far has managed to get along without private discussion.

At the bare minimum, Presidents cannot go public with, say, where the hydrogen bombs are tonight. But even in his day-to-day decision making, the President needs—in the interest of all of us—talk we are not privy to. Candor is in short supply; Presidents suffer from aides hell-bent on "helping" him by nodding to his every pronouncement. He not only needs nay-sayers (ones he can't typecast as certified devil's advocates and then dismiss), he also needs independent souls whose lives would not be over if they no longer worked in the White House. And they have to be—and feel—free to bat around all sorts of damn fool ideas in case one turns out to be viable after all. That is hard to do on television.

Most people understand that. We want open covenants; we don't care too much how they are arrived at. The secrecy that hurts is secrecy about what the President is *doing*—secret wars, secret peace agreements, secret money, secret police. Let him talk to whomever; just keep us informed of the upshots.

Every President ought to have a crony or two, some old boy or girl he can unwind with, play golf, shoot craps, whatever suits his style this side of decency. Cronies' influence always gets exaggerated in the grocery-store press, as if the old friend were Mesmer the hypnotist or some mind-bending Rasputin. Surely the public's need to know stops short of prying apart those easy bonds. And we might try to leave a President's children in peace, beyond the range of the camera's bug-eyed prurience.

A more serious danger in President-adviser relations is the danger of mistakes with dreadful consequences. Close historical research from a psychological perspective reveals a weird tendency—"group-think"—for the little knot of advisers around the President to get carried away and to carry him away with them, particularly in crisis circumstances. Psychologists have known for a long time that people in groups will do the strangest things, things they would never do on their own, such as disbelieve their senses or violate their strongest values. A series of cases, including the Bay of Pigs fiasco, shows how the President and his group puffed themselves up into a sense of invulnerability, silenced reasonable doubts, grossly underestimated the opposition, celebrated their fundamentally unexamined unanimity—and were off and running toward disaster.

I think the problem there is isolation, not secrecy. The group locks itself in, locks other counselors out. The risk of leaks is worth taking in such cases, compared to the risk of groupthink. Certainly it makes sense to mix up the group's composition a bit to get some fresh vision. But only the President himself can see to that—call in the Cabinet or the key Congressmen or a maverick or so. And only the President can establish an atmosphere that blends trust and caution, confidence and skepticism, in reasonable proportions to encourage creative conflict.

Chester Cooper, who worked with a President not enthusiastic about dissent, tells how his mind would fog over with groupthink:

> During the process I would frequently fall into a Walter Mitty-like fantasy: When my turn came, I would rise to my feet slowly, look around the room and then directly at the President, and say very quietly and emphatically, 'Mr. President, gentlemen, I most definitely do *not* agree.' But I was removed from my trance when I heard the President's voice saying, 'Mr. Cooper, do you agree?' And out would come a 'Yes, Mr. President, I agree.'

There have been times when Presidents faced too much conflict in the inner circle; Lincoln's Cabinet would qualify as an example, and that problem could arise again. But the modern worry is galloping consensus in the Oval Office.

Bureaucrats and Judges:
Compounded Complexity

In the buildings up and down the street from the White House, action consensus is not the danger. In gross terms, the federal bureaucracy has not grown all that much lately (the big growth is in state and city bureaucracies), but parts of it have. The National Security Council staff, for example, a mere fraction of the White House establishment, recently exceeded in number Franklin Roosevelt's entire White House staff—experts, executives, secretaries, cooks, bakers, gardeners, and all—at the time World War II was going full blast. The sheer mass of the administrative apparatus has a way of diluting action, muting the Presidential thunder.

Complexity adds more trouble. FDR fumed at the "higgledy-piggledy patchwork of duplicate responsibilities and overlapping powers" he encountered, as had Presidents from Lincoln on. John F. Kennedy was amazed and angered to learn, in the midst of the Cuban missile crisis, that his order to negotiate American missiles out of Turkey—an order issued eighteen months previously—had never been executed. It had run out of steam in the bureaucratic pipeline.

Bureaucrats are just people, honorable men and women again, workers who hope to make a contribution. But organizationally they comprise a collection such as must be somewhere in the Patent Office—inventions old and new, active and moribund, propping each other up with paper. Old agencies die hard, long after their functions pass away. New ones proliferate like kudzu in the rainy season. The reasons are not terribly obscure: give a man a pencil and a desk and he is going to do something. Pretty soon you'll need another man to coordinate him. A committee might help. A liaison person. An executive director. A press office and a grievance office and a legal office and so on. The list of people who have, in effect, veto power over the vigorous pursuit of policy stretches down the page, and the odds of policy survival drop off.

A President can grasp this bushel of nettles at one or another handle. All try reorganization in the good old American hope that hooking up the pipes differently might make the water run. Sometimes yes, sometimes no. All times, reforms in the name of simplicity generate new complexities the reformers neglected to imagine. Along the way, though, the reorganizer tends to get some of his people better positioned, and that may help push some progress through the system.

The other handle is inspiration. Kennedy understood the bureaucracy's tired blood problem and dosed it with New Frontierism—the excitement that can lay hold of the hearts of people when hope occurs. Washington filled up with bright young things and great expectations. In the halls of the bureaucracy many a pointy-headed drone turned himself into a Camelotian go-getter fired with lust for achievement. In hindsight we can see that the results were mixed; some achieved all too well. Lincoln said, "I cannot run this thing upon the theory that every officeholder must think I am the greatest man in the nation, and I will not." But alternatives to chart-shuffling and idealistic dramatics are dim in the minds of the responsible imaginers.

Bureaucracy is meant to help the President get the laws executed.

At least since Hammurabi, laws have needed explaining as to what they mean. In a pretty little mausoleum on Capitol Hill sit the nine Solomons of the Supreme Court, the only federal officers with unlimited tenure, who, figuratively speaking, kiss the President goodbye the day their appointments go through the Senate. Normally he has little to do with them, but he feels their eyes on the back of his neck. Not only can they stay his hand or take his tapes: they symbolize The Law, the whole idea that our common life will run by written rules fairly applied, the primeval idea of our political civilization, God's gift to the Hebrew children. The Supreme Court has a better reputation than the Presidency these days. Not even Roosevelt's mighty win in 1936 could hold back the popular wrath when he trifled with the Court. They have no battalions, only legitimacy. The number of specific Presidential moves they disallow is less significant than the fact, in the President's mind, that if they will, they can.

Peace and Persuasion:
Getting with the People

The law's writ, with an exception or two, runs to the water's edge. Beyond is a lawless world, jerry-built from the scraps of a battered sense of humanity, dotted with tin-can dictators and cutthroat terrorists, short on food and shorter on the hope of peace, bullied by gigantic tyrannies too frightened to open up their gates, a world at a loss for what to do with itself. The man hired will have to look after it, that most powerful man in all the world.

In the end, what does his power amount to? If he has to shoot off the rockets we are all done for, so that's no power. Here at home, he soon discovers by how far his reach exceeds his grasp, that his so-called powers amount to little more than the chance to wheedle in the ears of the other politicians. But with a little bit of luck, he might get through by persuasion, might understand what Erasmus meant when he wrote that "it is no great feat to burn a little man. It is a wonderful achievement to persuade him." And who knows? If the rest of us were to shoulder our civic responsibilities for a change, he might wind up as President, not only of, by, and for the people, but with us.

*Andrew Johnson's
bizarre rhetoric—a
key factor in his
failure as President
—traces to his trau-
matic childhood and
emergence as a
young politician.*

2

Life History

EVERY CHIEF EXECUTIVE of a great
state is required in fact, if not in law, to make speeches to a national
audience, to receive advice and information, to represent his nation
to the world, to bargain, to exercise authority, and to manage the
ordinary business of his office. These requirements leave much room
for choice, which makes the national leader's behavior politically intriguing, psychologically interpretable, and fateful for the world's
welfare. Choices among these available emphases can amount to a
distinctive political style. In this essay I want to illustrate, by means
of a single example, how we might be able to explain—perhaps even
to anticipate—the shape and force of such a distinctive style long
before the man is a leader.

Our American predictions have so often been wrong that some
new system of prescience seems necessary.[1] One thinks of Woodrow
Wilson, the scholar in the White House who would bring reason to
politics; of Herbert Hoover, the Great Engineer who would organize
chaos into progress; of Franklin D. Roosevelt, that champion of a
balanced budget; of Harry S. Truman, whom the office would surely
overwhelm; of Dwight D. Eisenhower, a militant crusader; of John F.

Kennedy, who would produce results in place of moralisms; and of Lyndon B. Johnson, the southern conservative.

We should do better at prediction if we considered the President as a person who tries to cope with an environment by using techniques he has found effective. For all the complexities of personality, there are always regularities, habitual ways of handling similar situations, just as the demands and opportunities of the Presidency are complex but patterned. Thus the President-as-person interacts with the set of recurrent problems and opportunities presented by the Presidency; the pattern of this interaction is his political style. He copes, adapts, leads, and responds not as some shapeless organism in a flood of novelties, but as a man with a memory in a system with a history.

The main outlines of presidential style are not hard to discern. One major dimension is activity vs. passivity, the standard way of classifying our chief executives. A second dimension, which does not always coincide with the first, is the emotional flavor or flair he displays—whether he generally appears happy or depressed by what he is called upon to do. These two main clues[2] can help our understanding of many other aspects of the style of political leadership. For example, once we know that Calvin Coolidge husbanded his energies and was usually bored or depressed as President, we are not surprised to discover his emphasis on a rhetoric of high principles and his avoidance of "political" relations with Congress.[3]

Once the main features of a style are grasped, one must find out what holds the pattern together. The best way to discover that is to see how the pattern was put together in the first place—how at a critical juncture the person brought together the motives, resources, and opportunities life handed him and molded them into a distinctive shape, and how the style he adopted then presaged the main ways in which he would shape his energies as President.

I will illustrate with one case (alluding occasionally to others) how a President may select rhetoric as a major outlet for his energy. The President is Andrew Johnson. I shall try to show how his peculiar rhetorical style, which had important political consequences, can be traced directly to that critical period in his life when he made politics a major factor in his adult identity. The facts can be presented only briefly, and the theory only tentatively. My purpose is not to characterize the President Johnson of a century ago, but to suggest that a focus on the formation of adult identity provides an important clue to Presidential style.

The Man Close Up: Johnson in the White House

The first President Johnson was habitually restrained in his day-to-day relations with those who worked closely with him. Nicknamed "The Grim Presence," Andrew Johnson impressed his secretary by his "chilling manner" and "sullen fixedness of purpose." "Never once in more than two years did I see him unbend from his grim rigidity, to the flexibility of form and feature which belongs to ordinary humanity." Johnson "cracked no jokes and told no stories"; his rarely seen smile was a "grim cast-iron wrinkle on the nether half of his face at public receptions." His favorite line of poetry was from Gray's *Elegy*—"The dark, unfathomed caves of ocean bare"—a phrase he frequently recited and relished for its grandeur and solemnity. Always dressed "with extreme fastidiousness in sober black," he impressed "even those who dislike him" with "the great dignity with which he bore himself and the remarkable neat appearance of his apparel." The contrast with Lincoln's appearance may have highlighted these perceptions.

Even in crisis situations, Johnson typically retained his reserve. At the news of Lincoln's assassination, he was "grief stricken like the rest" and "oppressed by the suddenness of the call upon him to become President," but "nevertheless calm and self-possessed." With his back to the wall in the impeachment crisis, he bore himself with "dignity and forebearance"; his "mood fluctuated, from bitterness in the early days of the trial to grim and philosophic amusement as it entered its closing phases."

The Johnson biographers mention a few exceptions to his restrained, humorless, formal behavior in close relations, but their rarity only emphasizes his habitual stern self-control. With children he was sometimes relaxed and easy; he did have one long, rambling conversation with his secretary in two years; he may have been "melted by a woman's tears" when wives of imprisoned Confederates sought his pardon; he may have had "a soft spot in his heart for animals"; and in his last days in the White House he did hold several gay parties. When Johnson was a Congressman, he and a few companions "got in kind of a bust—not a big drunk," as he wrote to a friend in Tennessee, and went to Baltimore to see "The Danseuses Viennoises," who performed so enticingly "that Job in the midst of his afflictions would have rejoiced at the scenes before him."

No such relief was available to Johnson in the White House. "Devoid of outside interests, an indefatigible worker," following the same grinding schedule from day to day, Johnson plodded through his tasks and endured stoically the attacks of his enemies. Johnson worked standing up; "never free from physical pain," he sometimes endured "excruciating torture" from a kidney ailment and severe pains in his arm that made writing difficult. His wife, Eliza, "lay a constant invalid in a room across the hall from his library, where through doors ajar, her cough, her sobs and sometimes her moans of anguish summoned him to her bedside." His recourse was work—"work, work, work, with a sullen fixedness of purpose as the sole means of rendering tolerable his existence." With time out for lunch (a cup of tea and a cracker), he "worked incessantly, often making of himself for days and sometimes for weeks a prisoner in the White House."

Johnson in the White House had no close friends to whom he could unburden himself. He "gave his full confidence only to the members of his family, notably to his invalid wife and to the official White House hostess, his daughter Martha Patterson." As Gideon Welles, Secretary of the Navy, observed:

> There is a reticence on the part of the President—an apparent want of confidence in his friends—which is unfortunate, and prevents him from having intimate and warm personal friends who would relieve him in a measure. . . . It is a mistake, an infirmity, a habit fixed before he was President, to keep his own counsel.[4]

Eric L. McKitrick captures this aspect of Johnson's orientation in his chapter titled, "Andrew Johnson, Outsider." And Jefferson Davis, in what Johnson's most sympathetic biographer calls a "not unkind and in many ways acute analysis," gave this interpretation:

This pride—for it was the pride of having no pride—his associates long struggled to overcome, but without success. They respected Mr. Johnson's abilities, integrity, and greatly original force of character; but nothing could make him be, or seem to wish to feel, at home in their society. Some casual word dropped in debate, though uttered without a thought of his existence, would seem to wound him to the quick, and again he would shrink back into the self-imposed isolation of his earlier and humbler life, as if to gain strength from touching his mother earth.[5]

Andrew Johnson was rarely aggressive in his close personal relations. If he was a "hard-word, soft-deed man," his hard words seldom came out in conversation. To the importunings of the Radicals Johnson responded, shortly after assuming the Presidency, by "listening to everybody, nodding at everything and staying as far away as possible from controversial issues." Later when Thaddeus Stevens called on the President to criticize his policies and to threaten desertion by the Congressional Republicans, "Johnson gave no indication of yielding but pleaded for harmony." Beset by mobs of pardon-seeking southerners in his office, he remained "mild and subdued, and his manner kindly"—even though in 1861 a mob in Lynchburg, Virginia, had dragged him from a train and beaten him severely, and in 1862 a Confederate mob had thrown his invalid wife and family out of his Tennessee home into the street. Repeatedly his noncommittal and somewhat enigmatic responses conciliated Radical Senator Charles Sumner. Johnson tolerated Secretary of War Stanton's presence at his Cabinet meetings for more than two years, although he knew Stanton was plotting against him. "Johnson's failure to do anything about it was a topic of avid speculation." When Stanton was finally asked to resign and replied with insolent refusal, Johnson "was neither surprised nor upset"; he did not call Stanton in for a confrontation. Welles wrote of Johnson's performance with Stanton: "Few men have stronger feeling; still fewer have the power of restraining themselves when evidently excited." He was similarly conciliatory in face-to-face talks with Grant and others who let him down.

Throughout the impeachment trial, Johnson remained impassive in personal conversation, with one significant exception. He expressed considerable impatience with his team of attorneys, who had decided it would be strategically inadvisable for the President to do as he wanted to: to "march into the Senate and do a little 'plain speaking.' "[6]

For almost all of his time in the White House, in almost all of his personal relations with those with whom he had to deal as President, Andrew Johnson expressed neither affection nor antagonism, but patient consideration. These observations of others are consistent with Johnson's own self-image. He saw himself as "generally temperate in all things" and judged that "mercy and clemency have been pretty large ingredients in my composition. . . . I have been charged with going too far, being too lenient." He disliked "demagogues," such as Benjamin Butler (although he was courteous to Butler in person), braggarts like Schuyler Colfax, and those who were "all heart and no head," like Horace Greeley. "The elements of my nature," Johnson said, "the pursuits of my life have not made me either in my feelings or in my practice aggressive. My nature, on the contrary, is rather defensive." He felt he might have been a good chemist: "It would have satisfied my desire to analyze things."

The Speaker: Johnson Before Crowds

The contrast between Andrew Johnson's restrained, mild, hesitant style in conversation, and his performance in certain wider rhetorical situations can hardly be overstated. His image as just the kind of aggressive demagogue he denigrated was fixed in the public mind at his inauguration as Vice President on March 4, 1865, just forty-one days before he became President.[7] Shortly before Lincoln's brief speech ("With malice toward none, with charity for all. . . ."), Johnson delivered a defiant and muddled diatribe to the crowded assembly. Interrupting the administration of his oath of office, he launched forth in this fashion:

> I'm a-goin' for to tell you here today; yea, I'm a-goin' for to tell you all, that I'm a plebeian! I glory in it; I am a plebeian! The people—yes, the people of the United States have made me what I am; and I am a-goin' for to tell you here today—yes, today, in this place that the people are everything.[8]

Speaking without notes, "on and on he went, his voice loud and unclear, his words tumbling over one another and losing themselves in their own echoes." The Supreme Court, the senators, and in particular Mr. Seward and Mr. Stanton, he shouted, "are but the creatures of the American people. . . . I, though a plebeian boy, am authorized by the principles of the government under which I live to feel proudly conscious that I am a man, and grave dignitaries are but men."[9] Each lot of "grave dignitaries" was reminded that they were subordinate to the people Johnson personified—including, according to one account, "you, gentlemen of the Diplomatic Corps, with all your fine feathers and gewgaws." Partway through, the Vice President forgot the name of the Secretary of the Navy and stopped to ask someone sitting close by so that he could include Gideon Welles in the list of those to be put in their places.

Judging from reports of the audience's immediate reaction, Johnson's manner was even more shocking than were his words. "Senators were struck with consternation, and diplomats with difficulty restrained their laughter." Shortly after the speech began, Senator Sumner "put his hands over his face and bent his head to his desk." Lincoln came in during Johnson's speech and, perceiving the situation, sat quietly through it with an expression of "unutterable sorrow," his "head drooping in the deepest humiliation." As he walked out to the Capitol steps to deliver his address, Lincoln told the marshal: "Do not let Johnson speak outside."

A reporter summed up the event in a private letter:

> The second official of the Nation—drunk—*drunk*—when about to take his oath of office, bellowing and ranting and shaking his fists at Judges, Cabinet and Diplomats, and making a fool of himself to such a degree that indignation is almost compelled to pity.[10]

In the next few days "Andy the Sot" was derided throughout Washington and celebrated in song at Grover's Theater on E Street. A few days later a senatorial caucus "seriously considered the propriety of asking him to resign as their presiding officer"; the Senate voted to exclude liquor from the Senate wing of the Capitol; and two Senators were dropped from all standing committees, "because of their habitual inebriety and incapacity for business." Lincoln quickly passed over Johnson's inaugural performance: "I have known Andy for many years; he made a bad slip the other day, but you need not be scared. Andy ain't a drunkard." The Cabinet, however, discussed the affair at length the following week in an atmosphere of grave concern. Gideon Welles noted that Secretary of State Seward's "tone and opinion were much changed since Saturday. He seems to have given Johnson up now." The Democratic press reviled Johnson editorially, pleased to denounce the supposedly Radical Vice President; the New York *World* called him "an insolent drunken brute, in comparison with whom Caligula's horse was respectable." And the Radical press hit him from the other side: "It is the plain duty of Mr. Johnson either to apologize for his conduct, or to resign his office." Johnson retreated to the Blair family estate in Silver Springs to recuperate. On March 9, 1865, he wrote to the Senate reporter, requesting "an accurate copy of what I said on that occasion."

Johnson's biographies have worked and reworked the explanations for this remarkable speech that brought him national disgrace as he assumed national office. A combination of illness, fatigue, and anxiety affected him that morning, and he took too much brandy. Clearly he was not (as were both his sons) an alcoholic. Nor do we need to rely on the immediate details to explain his behavior; he was displaying a pattern, not an exception. Johnson's speaking style, under certain special conditions, continually subverted his reputation as a steady, stern, and reliable leader.

During the campaign of 1865, Johnson had made a less widely publicized but equally revealing speech to a large crowd of Negroes in Nashville. On the night of October 24 he faced "a mass of human beings, so closely compacted together that they seemed to compose one vast body, no part of which could move without moving the whole," over which "torches and transparencies . . . cast a ruddy glow."

Johnson began by reviewing Lincoln's Emancipation Proclamation, put into effect the year before. He pointed out that for "certain reasons" the Proclamation's benefits "were not applied to the Negroes of Tennessee."[11] He then proceeded, entirely on his own, to announce: "I, Andrew Johnson, do hereby proclaim freedom, full, broad and unconditional, to every man in Tennessee." This amazing statement stimulated great applause. Thus urged on, Johnson launched into an attack on the local aristocrats and concluded:

> Colored men of Tennessee! This, too, shall cease! Your wives and daughters shall no longer be dragged into a concubinage . . . to satisfy the brutal lust of slaveholders and overseers! Henceforth the sanctity of God's holy law of marriage shall be respected in your persons, and the great state of Tennessee shall no more give her sanction to your degradation and your shame![12]

The crowd was ecstatic: " 'Thank God,' 'Thank God' came from the lips of a thousand women." Johnson was carried away by their response. Before "this vast throng of colored people," he said, he was "almost induced to wish that, as in the days of old, a Moses might arise who should lead them safely to their promised land of freedom and happiness." At which point someone shouted, "You are our Moses!"—a cry echoed again and again by the crowd.

On taking the Presidential oath of office on April 15, 1865, the day after Lincoln was shot, Johnson delivered a brief, calm address, stressing continuity. But the next day, meeting with the Congressional Committee on the Conduct of the War, he responded to Senator Ben Wade's comment—"Johnson, we have faith in you. By the gods, there will be no trouble now in running the government"—with a sentiment he had earlier expressed in various speeches, one which would completely mislead the Radicals as to Johnson's intentions: "I hold that robbery is a crime, rape is a crime; murder is a crime; treason is a crime and must be punished. Treason must be made infamous, and traitors must be impoverished." He repeated these phrases on April 18 and 21, in nearly the same words, to delegations from Illinois and Indiana—on both occasions as an "impromptu response" to expressions of support. Johnson was misunderstood, as he was at other times, because he made ringing general statements subject to opposing interpretations.

By December 2, 1865, his relations with the Radicals had deteriorated, and his patience with Senator Sumner had given out in an interview marked by Johnson's "caustic" questions.

On December 5, Johnson's son Robert read to the new Congress the President's message, composed by the historian and writer

George Bancroft. Johnson had sent Bancroft only two suggestions: passages from Thomas Jefferson's inaugural and from a speech by Charles James Fox. The result was a "lofty," "cogent," and "restrained" message, generally well received. On December 18, he sent another report, calmly advising a reconstruction policy less stringent than that of Thadeus Stevens. He discussed dispassionately with the Cabinet his veto of the Freedman's Bill in February 1866, an event which created a national sensation and clearly divided Johnson's supporters from the Radicals.

Three days later, on Washington's Birthday, a crowd of well-wishers who had been celebrating Johnson's veto at a Washington theater came to the White House and called for the President to greet them. Earlier in the day, friends had urged him not to speak, and Johnson had replied: "I have not thought of making a speech, and I shan't make one. If my friends come to see me, I shall thank them, and that's all." But he gave in at last to the crowd's importuning, climbed onto a low wall, and, as the day darkened, delivered a diatribe by the light of a guttering candle. When he referred indefinitely to leaders opposed to the Union, a voice called out—"Give us the names." Johnson responded:

> A gentleman calls for their names. Well, suppose I should give them. . . . *I say Thaddeus Stevens of Pennsylvania* (tremendous applause)—*I say Charles Sumner* (great appaluse)—*I say Wendell Phillips and others of the same stripe are among them.* . . . Some gentleman in the crowd says, "Give it to Forney." I have only just to say: That *I do not waste my ammunition upon dead ducks* (Laughter and applause).[13]

Johnson went on and on, reiterating for an hour and ten minutes the old themes of his personal life history, the false accusations against him, and his similarity to Christ. Johnson asked:

> Are those who want to destroy our institutions not satisfied with one martyr? . . . If my blood is to be shed because I vindicate the Union . . . let an altar of the Union be erected, and then if necessary lay me upon it, and the blood that now animates my frame shall be poured out in a last libation as a tribute to the Union; and let the opponents of this government remember that

when it is poured out the blood of the martyr will be the seed of the church.[14]

Several weeks later Thaddeus Stevens entertained the Senate by mockingly denying that this speech had ever been made. The affair "gave rise to a wave of wonder and dismay" throughout the country.

The suspicions that the President was a drunkard were revived. The hands of Thaddeus Stevens and the other Radicals in Congress were strengthened. Senator John Sherman, who tried valiantly to patch up relations between Johnson and the Congress, deeply regretted the Washington's Birthday speech: "I think there is no true friend of Andrew Johnson who would not be willing to wipe that speech from the pages of history." On April 18, 1866, Johnson repeated this performance at a soldiers' and sailors' serenade, in a speech that "resembled the other in all particulars, with the possible exception that this time the personal note, the sense of persecution, was even less controlled than before."

President Johnson's disastrous rhetoric reached its culmination in his famous "Swing Around the Circle" in August and September 1866. Convinced that he could win the people if only he could address enough of them in person, Johnson was repeatedly drawn by a crowd's reaction to extreme flights of vituperation. Apparently unmindful that his speeches were being reported by the press throughout the nation, the President followed the same course time and again, first denying he would make a speech, then delivering a harangue full of blood and religion, and ending by leaving "the Constitution and the Union of these States in your hands." At St. Louis on September 8, 1866, he complained that he had been called a Judas.

> Judas Iscariot! Judas! There was a Judas once, one of the twelve apostles. Oh yes; the twelve apostles had a Christ. . . . The twelve apostles had a Christ, and he could never have had a Judas unless he had had twelve apostles. If I have played the Judas, who has been my Christ that I have played Judas with? Was it Thad Stevens? Was it Wendell Phillips? Was it Charles Sumner?[15]

In a nineteen-day tour, during which he traveled some two thousand miles and delivered eleven major and twenty-two minor speeches,

Johnson was repeatedly harassed by hecklers and wildly enthusiastic supporters, both stimulating his angry rhetoric. As an observer recalled: "Whenever cheers on the route would be proposed for Congress, he would stop and argue the case between himself and Congress. . . . It is mortifying to see a man occupying the lofty position of President of the United States descend from that position and join issue with those who are dragging their garments in the muddy gutters of vituperation."

Again and again, Johnson's friends warned him against extemporaneous speaking. Senator Doolittle of Wisconsin wrote to say:

> I hope you will not allow the excitement of the moment to draw from you any extemporaneous speeches. You are followed by the reporters of a hundred presses who do nothing but misrepresent. I would say nothing which had not been most carefully prepared, beyond a simple acknowledgment for their cordial reception. Our enemies, your enemies, have never been able to get any advantage from anything you ever wrote. But what you have said extemporaneously in answer to some questions has given them a handle to use against us.[16]

When Gideon Welles advised him similarly, "President Johnson always heard my brief suggestions quietly, but manifestly thought I did not know his power as a speaker." Repeatedly he tried to resist giving speeches, but then gave in and delivered another highly emotional diatribe. As Johnson himself put it in a speech on the "Swing": "I tell you, my countrymen, that though the power of hell, death, and Stevens . . . combined, there is no power that can control me save you . . . and the God that spoke me into existence. . . . I have been drawn into this long speech, while I intended simply to make acknowledgments for the cordial welcome."

There can be no doubt that Johnson's speaking style had important effects on his Presidential power, although it was only one of many elements in that equation. As McKitrick sums up the effect of the "Swing Around the Circle":

> It is probably fair to say that few truly confirmed Johnson partisans were likely to have changed their minds as a result of it, dignity or no dignity. Yet the problem for Johnson was not

simply that of keeping what following he had, but also of persuading large numbers of not yet fully hardened Unionists to make the decision of deserting to him. Not only did the tour fail in this function for the doubtfuls; but for great numbers of those that remained, it seemed to have provided the perfect excuse to throw away all lingering reservations and to do what they were already on the point of doing—return to the Republican fold for good. It was then that they could insist, while having no more use for Thad Stevens than ever, that they could not support a man who had so debased the dignity of the presidency as had Andrew Johnson.[17]

At his impeachment in early 1868, the first nine articles referred to his supposed violations of the Tenure of Office Act (which severely restricted the power of the President to control his Cabinet) and the tenth accused him of making "scandalous harangues." Clearly the man's reputation had undermined the President's authority, and his performances on the stump had contributed heavily to that decline. He left the Presidency to return to Tennessee for another speaking tour, to devote "the remainder of his life to a vindication of his character and that of his State." Despite the disastrous effects of his impromptu speeches, he intended to "indulge in no set speeches, but [to] have a few simple conversations with the people here and there." He toured Tennessee delivering unrehearsed speeches to large crowds. He was defeated for the Senate in 1869, but returned there in 1875. Johnson died on July 31 of that year. He is buried in Greeneville, Tennessee, his body wrapped in an American flag and his head resting on his copy of the Constitution.

The Rhetorical Emphasis

Words can trap thought, and speech can subvert action. Johnson's words—indeed, his way of saying words—came close to doing what the Civil War did not do: altering the fundamental structure of the American Presidency. His rhetoric was clearly patterned, and he exhibited a strong consistency of style which can be discerned in the midst of the many inconsistencies of policy. The examples refer to

Johnson and rhetoric, but the applicable analytic distinctions have more general significance to Presidents and their styles.

From the full repertoire of Presidential roles, Johnson selected speaking and detailed office work as channels for his immense emotional force. We cannot imagine him operating as his namesake of a century later does, devoting endless hours to negotiation in search of consensus. Johnson spent himself in work and words. Sometimes he could give a calm address; most of his speeches in the Senate, for example, were reasoned arguments, more like a lawyer's brief than a stump harangue. But as his performance on the Swing Around the Circle made clear, he repeatedly—almost uniformly—burst forth in fiery rhetoric whenever he faced a crowd of partisans. Had he learned from the reactions to his inaugural disaster to rely on written speeches, his reputation probably could have been salvaged. But he never learned that lesson. Again and again, he repeated the same performance, illustrating how a particular strategy can become a permanent feature of Presidential style. His friends implored him to restrain himself; his enemies gave him unmistakable evidence that he could only harm himself by continuing. Johnson recognized the problem and repeatedly resolved to change. The impulsive character of his blurted pronouncements testifies to the compulsive element in his rhetoric.

Johnson had an exaggerated faith in the efficacy of his rhetoric. Although he "knew" or saw the destructive effects of his speeches, he believed that he had extraordinary power as a speaker. He felt that he would succeed if only he could speak his heart to those on whom his power depended. In a sense, he was right: Success in terms of audience responsiveness, success in the immediate environment, was often his. He won applause and (perhaps equally important to him) challenge from the crowds. He would not or could not, however, make a balanced assessment of his impact as a speaker. Even as he was being impeached, in part because of his wild speeches, he had to be restrained from addressing the Senate. At the extreme, he shows how a political leader may come to believe that he has a magic strategy, a way of acting that is not subject to the ordinary rules of political evaluation, one that is bound to work if rightly performed.

Johnson was wild on the stump, but subdued in the office; he, like Moses, called for action, but was beset by the vice of procrastination; he was generous and patient with Stanton and Sumner in person, but damned them in his speeches. These contradictions demand explanation. Johnson's obvious feelings of elation in the exercise of rhetoric, his reiteration of personal history and status, and the highly symbolic language he used—all point to the expressive, tension-releasing importance he found in speaking.

If one proposed to explain Andrew Johnson's particular rhetorical style, many other significant elements could be noted even at this descriptive level. The major themes of his speeches, his rhetorical reactions to contemporary political conflicts, and the relations between the symbols and values he expressed and those of the particular historical-cultural environment of the 1860s could be analyzed. But I am concerned here not with the flesh and blood of individual political psychology, but rather with the extent to which a rhetorical specialist like Johnson may share a skeletal structure with other Presidents who emphasize their own strategies. For example, Woodrow Wilson trusted that he could personally persuade the American people to adopt his version of the League of Nations; Herbert Hoover demonstrated a strange disparity between private works and public words; and Calvin Coolidge combined dinner-party acerbity, good-natured banter with reporters, and the preaching of moralistic platitudes over the radio.

The Springs of Political Energy:
Motives and the Self

Intense political activity may represent either compensation for low self-esteem, usually resulting from severe deprivations in early life, or a specialized extension of high self-esteem, but seldom does it represent an ordinary or normal adaptation to one's culture.[18] In analyzing the development of a distinctive style that emerges in the adult identity crisis, the style's genesis is of less interest than are its structural and dynamic properties at a particular critical period. In order to understand the background against which the distinctive style emerged and to estimate the degree to which the style was compensatory or extensive, however, one must first trace the deeper and older dimensions of personality.

This is not difficult to do in Johnson's case. He reached late adolescence with a long heritage of deprivations and assaults on the self, and no clear success other than success in survival. His father, a genial handyman at a Raleigh, North Carolina, tavern, died when Andrew Jackson Johnson (named after General Jackson) was three, leaving the family destitute and completely dependent on the mother's drudgery in washing and sewing. The Johnsons were "mudsills," landless poor whites, in constant contact with the privileged guests at the tavern. His mother, an ineffectual woman nicknamed "Aunt Polly," later took up with a ne'er-do-well drifter; Andrew had to care for both of them throughout his late teens. At the age of fourteen, just at the time when noise and movement and a certain graceful clumsiness are natural, he was bound as an apprentice tailor, made to sit quietly and be still, and thrown prematurely into adulthood and enforced concentration. At sixteen, this "exceedingly restless" and "wild, harum-scarum boy" ran away from home and work for about a year to escape prosecution for stoning the house of some local girls. The tailor offered a reward for his arrest and return. Wandering to South Carolina, he fell in love with a Sarah Word, but his suit was rejected. On his return home the tailor refused to take him back, and Johnson began at sixteen a two-year trek, wandering through western North Carolina and eastern Tennessee looking for work, with his mother and impecunious "stepfather" in tow. When Andrew was eighteen, the family finally settled in Greeneville, Tennessee.

Childhood had left him hurt and nearly helpless, but he had a skill— tailoring—which would sustain him while he found himself. Undoubtedly Johnson's lifelong detestation of aristocrats, his championing of the Homestead Bill, his extreme independence, and many other themes in his adult personality can be traced to these early years. But the scant evidence available can be interpreted with fair confidence in a simpler and more general way. The pattern is one of severe deprivation, which roused in Johnson strong needs for enhancing self-esteem. While it is difficult to explain precisely why and how this energizing force was channeled into a distinctively rhetorical style, the force was clearly there to be channeled.

The School of Life:
What Johnson Learned

Andrew Johnson had no formal schooling, but from an early age (perhaps ten) he hung around the local tailor shop and listened to what
went on there. To palliate the tedium, the tailors hired someone to
read aloud to them. They worked in silence, listening to the spoken
word. Later Andy was apprenticed: "Many hours a day, shut out from
fresh air, crouched down over a needle and thread, deprived of the
joys of childhood, the lad bent to his tasks; the inside of a school-
house he never saw."

His mother could not read or write. The foreman in the tailor shop
later recalled teaching the boy how to read, but most probably Andy
devoted little if any time to reading in his early teens, particularly in
comparison with the long hours spent listening to the tailor's reader.
Thus, for Johnson, words came late and in the spoken form. The
newspapers, possibly some novels and poems, but particularly political speeches were read. A special favorite of Andy's was a volume of
the orations by British statesmen.[19] In somewhat overdrawn terms
L. P. Stryker recounts the effect of the reading of these speeches:

> To Johnson it was like a torch to tinder. It lighted in his soul the
> fire of high resolve. . . . Painfully and slowly from these
> classics of the forensic art he learned to spell and to read. A new
> and undiscovered country lay before him. Cross-legged, he plied
> with his fingers his busy tailor's needle, while his mind, white
> hot with a new hope, was far away within the English Parlia-
> ment. And at night he found and pursued the company of books
> and stayed with them until, worn down from the long day's toil,
> he fell asleep.[20]

Or as his contemporary biographer John Savage put it: "This volume [of orations] molded into form and inspired into suitable action
the elements of his mental character, and thus laid the foundation of
his fame and fortune"; in hearing the speeches, "his own thoughts
struggling through took form and color from their influence." Johnson
told Savage that his favorite speeches were those of Pitt and Fox,
both vehement orators and champions of democracy, whose words—

thick with wit and studied insult, and aggressive in tone—were meant to wilt the opposition.

Johnson's running away and subsequent wandering interrupted his rhetorical education, though he kept the book of speeches until his library was destroyed in the Civil War. In Greeneville his young wife, Eliza, whom he married in 1827 when he was nineteen, taught him to write and read to him in the tailor shop, again a learning experience in a context of high emotional involvement. Johnson borrowed books from the few Greeneville collections and began to attend the Polemic Society, a debating group, at Greeneville College. He may also have read a number of books from the college library, a collection of three thousand volumes which "came chiefly from the private libraries of the Mathers, Jonathan Edwards and other New England theologians of the day" and was composed "mainly [of] volumes of sermons and theological discussions."

Every week he walked four miles each way to the college. Memories of his participation, mostly gathered much later, vary from references to his "natural talent for oratory" to his being "a very timid speaker, afraid of his own voice." Sometime in 1829 he was part of a separately organized debating society of Greeneville youth.

Students from the local colleges habitually gathered at his tailor shop during this period, because, as one of them remembered: "One lived here whom we know outside of school, and made us welcome; one who would amuse us by his social good nature, one who took more than ordinary interest in catering to our pleasure." He and Eliza lived in the back room—the only other one—and the students and other casual visitors sat around in the front room while he worked. In 1831 he moved the family, now Eliza and their two boys, into a new house and purchased a separate tailor shop. He hired a schoolboy to read, "not the novels of Jane Austen and Maria Edgeworth, but Eliot's debates, Jefferson's messages, and over and over again the Constitution of the United States."

Johnson's biographers make much of his earliest political ventures, but these were probably little more than extensions of his role as owner and operator of a convenient gathering place for townsmen and students interested in politics. It is not clear that he "organized" the Greeneville debating group, except by providing a place for it to meet, or that he was the leading light in forming a "Worker's Party" in town. He was first elected alderman in 1829. The ticket of nominees was put together on the Saturday night before the election on Monday. Johnson's name appeared first on the ballot, but despite this favored position he received the lowest vote of the seven elected—eighteen votes, as compared to thirty-one for the front-runner. Johnson was elected alderman again the next year and was mayor for the following three years. In 1832 the county appointed him a trustee of the Rhea Academy.

These early political experiences did not represent a marked deviation from Johnson's regular round of life. The duties of alderman and mayor could not have been onerous in a town of about seven hundred people whose electorate was unable to muster more than thirty-one votes for the leading aldermanic candidate. The idea that he conducted a hard campaign for alderman against the town aristocrats is hardly believable—surely most of them were in church on the intervening Sunday before his first election. The flavor of Johnson's participation is probably best caught by one of the young men of Greeneville, who later recalled that despite the boisterousness of his visitors in the tailor shop:

> Andy neither lost his temper nor suspended his twofold employment of reading and sewing. The moment the needle passed through the cloth, his eye would return to the book, and anon to the needle again; and so, enter when you would, it was ever the same determined read and sew, and sew and read. His sober industry and intelligence won the favor of the grave and sedate, and his genial tolerance of the jovial groups which frequented his shop secured him unbounded popularity with the young men of the place.[21]

In other words, Johnson let them use his shop, did not interfere with them, and out of gratitude and affection they put him up for office and elected him. Like his father, Andrew was tolerant; unlike his stepfather, he applied himself with extraordinary diligence to his work. His friends were men of his own class who gathered around him mainly for reasons other than his friendship. There is no clear evidence that Johnson was an active leader of the tailor-shop caucus. Johnson at this point was a localist, a figure well known to the Greeneville working class, a businessman whose occupation naturally brought him into the circle of the town's political actors and talkers. In 1834, probably because he was mayor and a trustee of Rhea Academy, he joined in the call for a new Tennessee constitution, but whether his participation went beyond a signature is uncertain. In the following year Johnson's horizons underwent a radical expansion.

The Rehearsal: Gathering Resources

Johnson's childhood left him with a need to cure the pain of deprivation and with a way of sustaining himself until he found the right medicine. In many cases men who become Presidents have gone through what Erik Erikson calls a moratorium, "a span of time after they have ceased being children, but before their deeds and works count toward a future identity." In retrospect such a period may be seen as a preparation for the full use of an important political strategy, a free rehearsal—free in the sense of not being counted at the time in the calculus of success. The rehearsal is a learning time, but much of the learning is latent, even playful, and its significance may not be evident until much later. Learning in such a rehearsal period may be passive or active; usually it is both. The typical pattern may begin with the passive collection of images or impressions, often at the periphery of attention, and progress slowly through a series of apparently unrelated experiments in action. Some of the features of this process in Johnson's life have wider applications.

In many cases the *timing* or phasing of learning in relation to a normal set of life stages is important. For example, each of the rhetorically peculiar Presidents previously mentioned was slow to catch on to the written word. Wilson could not read well until he was eleven; Coolidge failed his first set of entrance examinations at Amherst; Hoover was unable to pass his English courses at Stanford. Such retardation may be only one aspect of a more general phenomenon: the special importance of out-of-phase learning for the development of distinctive strategies. Perhaps learning that comes "too early," as well as learning that comes "too late," acquires a particular significance because it offers a way of resolving conflicts before they have become severe or after their severity has accumulated to a disproportionate degree. In any case, learning appropriate to the grammar-school age may take on immense personal importance if postponed until adolescence, when all the emotional conflicts of the earliest years come back again. Most generally, one would want to know whether a period of intensive learning relevant to strategy distinctiveness occurred, in what period of life it took place, and what major conflicts accompanied this learning. Johnson first heard great oratory while passively immobilized on his tailor's table; he first began to read with one of the few kind adults he knew as tutor; he first learned to write from his new bride; and he first began to speak in the need-supplying society of younger friends. At each stage, the *learning* took place *in an atmosphere of emotional intensity*, during which Johnson was working on some fundamental problems of his own.

Similarly, the *sequence* of learning may shape distinctive strategies, particularly in terms of the form of earliest exposure. Johnson began with the spoken word. He heard much oratory *before* he could read; messages came to him in an oral medium *first* and then in writings about speeches. Early lessons in the strategies of action set a context into which subsequent lessons must fit. Sequence is also important in understanding how the learner shapes a cumulative development from a stream of individual lessons.[22] For Johnson the talent for oratory grew step by step, in large part because of a series of lucky connections.

Johnson received a double introduction to oratory: he heard it, and it was about speeches. The *character* of the material learned obviously influences the development of skills relevant to strategy, although there is rarely a simple correspondence between what is purveyed and what is perceived and retained. The character of the material is a variable in learning many different kinds of skills—from bargaining to dominating—but it has a special significance in rhetoric, because the word form allows so many different types of representations. For Johnson the curriculum was first the aggressive oratory of the parliamentarians and then the fiery biblicism of New England divines. In neither case did the material itself have much to do with Tennessee in the mid-nineteenth century, but Johnson later found that he could draw on it for many a speech. In tracing the roots of a rhetorical style, one wants to keep an eye out for the man more interested in speeches than in facts, more imitative of styles than insightful of content.

Johnson as President has frequently been described as a scholar rather than a doer, a theorist rather than a political operator. The *degree of abstraction* of learned material—in the sense of its direct applicability in the immediate environment—may be an important factor here. The historical movement of Johnson's intellective process, insofar as his rhetorical development is concerned, was from far away (England and God) to near at hand (Jackson and Tennessee). Abstract thought, particularly in a context of passive reception and no responsibility for consequences, is freely available for need-fulfilling purposes and for all varieties of vicarious experimentation in fantasy. Strong emotional linkages can develop in such a context precisely because the matter is removed from the restraints of compromise and calculation inherent in practical affairs. Johnson's school was in this sense a totally permissive one: no one would give him a failing mark or an honors grade for what he thought of Pitt and Fox and Jonathan Edwards. Surely a special clue to watch for in tracing the rehearsal for a particular type of political strategy is *the interplay between the abstract and the voluntary in the learning process.*

To the way in which words came to Johnson must be added the way he found to turn them back on the world. In his early teens, his activity was intense, but not in speaking. Slowly the distant and the impersonal had to be linked with the close and the personal in order for what was passively learned to acquire relevance for action. No simple formula can encompass the complexity of those steps, but at least two features are common to this and other cases.

Johnson's active learning of oratory began only after he located in Greeneville, when a particular combination of personal successes and community opportunities made possible his political emergence. Johnson's shop in Greeneville was a place for conversation, for clubhouse talk about the issues of the day. There he heard and began to join in words closely related to the local political situation, to the possibilities and probabilities of organization, action, and achievement by those present. Politics took on a new dimension for him; to Pitt and Fox were added Andrew Jackson and his national enemies (still relatively distant), the local aristocrats and speakers (close but absent), and the leading conversationalists in the room (at hand). He began to see, one supposes, how a person like him might play a part, how the gap between himself-as-auditor and himself-as-orator might be bridged. His early trials in the debating societies, pursued with diligence, gave him a chance to experiment with his voice without committing his future or risking his present. And the nominations, campaigns, and elections in Greeneville, as small steps beyond a secure station, taught him that some form of political life was not impossible for him, that he could perform as acceptably as the others he knew. The linkage here is through persons. The lesson was I *can* learn, *am* learning, *know* how, as well as or better than others do. The mechanisms are *identification with a group in which the strategy is practiced, experimentation without risk, and minor gambles in commitment.*

Issues as well as persons provide linkage. Johnson could "remember" when he listened to the tailor-shop conversations about the aristocrats and the other themes of the "Greeneville Democracy" what he had heard before from the young English orators of a previous generation. He could see, or at least feel, the connection between the injustice to his namesake Andrew Jackson in the 1824 election and the thunderings of the New England divines. An ideology of sorts—one that fitted his own history, the myths he had imbibed, and the situation in which he found himself—began to form in his mind. Learning came to encompass a set of ideas in addition to the set of techniques he had started to master. His experience and his anticipations began to take on expressible meanings, made explicit at last in a speech in which he conjured up a path from obscurity and degradation, through effort, to a grand achievement: the joining of godliness and government. In terms of rhetorical strategy, he had found what to say. In terms of distinctive strategies in general, he exemplified *the significance of rationalization for action and the ways in which available rationalizations can speed or delay cumulative individual development.*[23]

The Man Becomes a Politician

On another Saturday night, in the spring of 1835 when Johnson was twenty-six, he nominated himself for the state legislature. Johnson was there when conversation at Jones's store was interrupted by someone bearing news from a "muster" a few miles away at which Major Matthew Stephenson and Major James Britton had been entered in the race for the Tennessee lower house. Stephenson, from neighboring Washington County, was a Whig who had performed effectively at the constitutional convention the previous year. He was also, by east Tennessee standards at least, an aristocrat, "a wealthy citizen of character and social position." After listening for a while to the discussion of this news, Johnson "sprang from his seat to say: 'I, too, am in the fight.'" Like any other uninvited volunteer, Johnson had only to follow this statement with a formal public announcement to get on the ballot. Several of his friends coached him for his first meeting with Stephenson, to be held in the latter's territory at Boon's Creek in Washington County. Stephenson "was thought to await an easy victory." Johnson's friends researched his political record and otherwise prepared carefully. Stephenson began by expounding various Whig doctrines. Johnson, the "audacious youngster," then "hacked and arraigned" the aristocratic major, challenging his claims for Whiggism in Tennessee. He dealt with several issues and gave a preview of a lifelong theme: "He assured the boys that he was neither a lawyer, a major or a colonel, but a plain man laboring with his hands, for his daily bread, that he knew what they wanted and would carry out their wishes." Johnson was elected by a small margin.

Johnson had thus nominated himself in response to the news that an aristocrat was in the race, had set out to attack his enemy personally, and had found the weapon—spoken words—to succeed. The rehearsal was over; Andrew Johnson had entered a new and much broader arena of action equipped with a strategy for success: in close interpersonal relations (as with the politicos of the tailor shop), restraint; with enemies at a distance (as with the "aristocratic" Major Stephenson), attack. He had found not only the place in which speech could serve his needs for vindication: political oratory; but also the themes which would serve him the rest of his life: self-justification and righteous indignation against the privileged. And he had discovered the language with which to express these themes—that of principles and abstractions and personal allusion. His school had done its work. One can hear in nearly all his speeches the words of the New England divines and Old England parliamentarians, transformed to bear on his cause and reflect his high purposes, particularly in those peculiar diatribes which marred his Presidency.

One other feature of his strategy for success seems to have been critical: his identification with Andrew Jackson. Part of the development of identity is the imitation of models, done with or without awareness. Such models link the person to something beyond himself. Arising from the past, they point the way to the future. The passionless abstract ideal is translated to human form, to an embodiment not so impossible to achieve.

Johnson's very name—Andrew Jackson Johnson—gave him an original connection with a defiant fighter who became President. Jackson's followers felt he had been cheated of the Presidency in 1824, when, despite receiving the largest popular vote, he was defeated after the election was thrown into the House of Representatives. His followers were organizing vigorously in the years leading up to 1828, and Jackson must have been a frequent topic of conversation in Johnson's tailor shop just as he was taking his first political steps. In his maiden speech against Stephenson, Johnson invoked "Old Hickory"; his first speech in Congress was a defense of Andrew Jackson. He helped institute an annual Jackson-Jefferson celebration in Greeneville, ran on a ballot headed with Jackson's picture, and heard again and again almost from the time he began in politics: "You are a second Andrew Jackson"; "You are a man, every inch of you, standing in the shoes of 'Old Hickory'"; or you are "trying to ape Andrew Jackson but cannot make the grade." At least "from 1840 onward, 'Old Hickory' was Andrew Johnson's political pilot, the model of his conduct and the idol of his heart." The roots of the connection with Jackson were personal and local: the name and the particular significance Jackson had for politics in East Tennessee just as Johnson was emerging to the state arena. The idol who was there at one's birth and reappears as one is forging an identity has an immense advantage over competing symbols.

Andrew Jackson was in many ways different from Andrew Johnson. As one sympathetic account says: "Externally, of course, no two men were more unlike, Jackson being a rollicking fellow, fond of horseracing and cockfighting, and more fond of sports than books; Johnson, caring nothing for sports, too serious-minded, and always plugging away at some problem of government." But these were not the features Johnson's early companions and supporters stressed when they constantly reiterated the Jackson-Johnson similarities. Friends would point out: "They came from the same stock; they had both hewed their fortunes from the rough rock of adversity; both were of the people and knew their hopes and fears; both were men of physical as well as intellectual courage; both hated sham and both were passionate lovers of the Union." The identification persisted; as President, Johnson refused to allow Jackson's desk to be moved, despite its inconvenient location. "I love the memory of General Jackson," he said. "Whatever was Old Hickory's I revere."

The Breakout: Confluence of Motives, Resources, and Opportunities

Andrew Johnson's campaign against Major Stephenson seems to mark a turning point in his life. At that time, he brought together the motives from his childhood, the skills from his period of rehearsal, and the political opportunities in the close environment to form a distinctive political strategy that would serve him for the rest of his life. His emergence does not have the same clarity and concentration of development that we find in some other cases.[24] But if one had been able to observe Johnson closely in 1835, had analyzed his life situation in relation to his history with careful attention to the elements of Presidential leadership style, at least the following generalizable elements would have emerged.

Perhaps the most important feature of the breakout phase is the marked *infusion of confidence*. Deprivation may so damage self-esteem that success is incapable of rescuing it, or strategies of adaptation developed to meet extreme emergencies of deprivation may be fixed too early to be much affected by later experience. In Johnson's case, however, as in many others, the breakout period was one in which the achievement of success coincided with the culmination of the development of skill and the community's readiness to respond in such a way as to fix a political style.

As is evident from the account of Johnson's success in Greeneville, his fortunes changed rapidly for the better, contrasting markedly with his situation of only a few years before. This picture is efficiently clarified in the following table based on Harold D. Lasswell's well-known formulation of values,[25] noting the degree and character of Johnson's attainment in each of his pre-Greeneville years and at the time of his candidacy for the state legislature.

The *rapid pace* of these changes, their *simultaneous* development, and particularly the *contrast* with his previous fortunes made this period a special time of growth and increasing self-esteem such as Johnson had never known. Aside from some primitive learning (on which he could build) and his skill at his trade (which he could perfect and which taught him that he could develop a skill), he brought to early adulthood very little. Within a few years he had attained success and adopted a style. The two are closely related: to discover the critical period of commitment to a set of distinctive strategies, one must watch for massive increases in supplies of confidence.

Johnson's breakthrough period shows two other features of particular significance for distinctive political strategies: a special kind of relatedness to a close group and a sudden, radical expansion of the politician's "field of power."[26] Johnson, like others with pronounced

Table 1   Changes in Value Attainments in Johnson's Critical Period

Value	Pre-Greeneville (1808–26)	At time of candidacy for state legislature (1835)
Power	None except in family	Public official
Wealth	Extreme poverty	Moderate means
Enlightenment	No formal schooling; heard oratory and learned reading late	Much learning; Academy official
Skill	Dependent on single skill: tailoring	Expert in his trade; developing speaking skill
Respect	Very low; a homeless "mud-sill"	Host to students; nominations and elections
Well-Being	Fatherless; ineffective mother; much discomfort and insecurity	Stable family; own home; relative ease and happiness
Affection	No male or female friends among peers; rejected by home-town adults	Wife, children; surrounded by friendly group
Rectitude	Runaway lawbreaker; no religious life	Decent achievement; developing ideology; attached to religious colleges

emotional conflicts, probably experienced strong tendencies to withdraw from society, to escape into a kinder internal world. Such a person may find communication difficult and communion impossible, because he has meanings a common language cannot express and feelings he can hardly formulate, much less share. But thrown, by occupational or other necessity, into continual company, a person cannot avoid talk and may slowly learn, as Johnson did, to be *at once one with and slightly apart from a band of brothers*. This closeness can meet important needs. People learn to rate themselves in part by the ways others react to them, and one such reaction is simply acceptance as a member of the group. Young people, like old people, come together at times not to accomplish anything in particular or even to talk, but simply by their physical togetherness to "say" to one another "we are not alone." When much talk—talk about politics, in particular—is added to this simple juxtaposition, the context is arranged for powerful combinations of affection, experiments in expression, and linkage to broader social arenas. Johnson was surrounded with friends—representing the local working class, intelligentsia, and out-of-office politicians—whose whole entertainment was conversation.

There was in Johnson's case, again as in many others, a *relatively radical expansion of his "field of power"* at the time he adopted a distinctive strategy. His focus of attention shifted from a narrow to a broad arena of action. The hometown politician considering a relatively big-time candidacy thus comes to see his present place in a new perspective. Johnson's candidacy for the state legislature represented to him a significant leap beyond the arena of power he had mastered. Yesterday's inadvertently accumulated resources suddenly appeared in a new and larger context.

The Explanation of Presidential Styles

Johnson's success was incomplete; no amount of success could fully compensate for the needs left from his traumatic childhood. For the rest of his life, he would struggle to make up for what he had suffered. His habit of restraint at work and at close quarters with others continued to serve as a maintenance technique, a way of surviving a chaotic future. But oratory offered him much more: power to control a crowd and, at last, a country; respect, even from the aristocrats; rectitude, as vindication; affection, in the applause; pleasure in the effective use of skill; well-being, in that calm of the soul which follows speaking his mind and heart. And in a more complex and indirect way, oratory gave Andrew Johnson a way of setting the world at odds, of putting the others in their place and thus confirming his own place of defeat and failure.

Johnson's distinctive political style, formed in late adolescence and early adulthood, presaged his style in the Presidency. Much intervened between this early coalescing of disparate elements into a structured identity and the exercise of his Presidential style. The backings and fillings of his career on the way to the nation's highest office present a confused picture, in contrast to the clear connections between these two widely separated life stages. Any moderately attentive person could have predicted, in 1865, that Johnson would be an outsider, that he would not be socially lionized by the Washington elite, that he would have difficulty coping with the violent political forces in that age of hate and sentimentality. But how would he react to these challenges? How might his ways of approaching and dealing with them have been foreseen?

I have suggested one analytic system for tracing the roots of Presidential style. There are many uncertainties in it; one would especially want to see it applied to more Presidents, including some not yet elected. But in most biographical accounts, the period during which an adult identity was forged can be readily isolated, particularly when one is sensitive to marked infusions of confidence, coming fast, simultaneously, and in contrast to a deprived past; to a special kind of relationship to a close and supportive group life; and to a relatively sudden expansion of the "field of power." Once located, this period can be surveyed in the light of a short list of requirements for a Presidential role. Those particularly emphasized can be traced back into the learning process, viewed as a rehearsal for the emergence of the distinctive style. Together with a general assessment of self-evaluation gathered from accounts of early life, these explorations may reveal, in clearer form than they would in later adulthood, the fundamental shape of a potential President's strategies for adapting to the challenges he will confront.

When a man is chosen to lead a great nation, he stands in a uniquely high and lonely place, one not much like the steps he has recently been climbing. But in his memory is another time when he came out of relative smallness into relative greatness. Then he had tried a style, and it worked. What would be more natural than for him to feel that it might work again?[27]

3

*Coolidge and
Hoover lacked "per-
sonality" in the pop-
ular sense. But their
biographical dramas
(and particularly
their "first indepen-
dent political suc-
cesses")* explain
*their Presidential
peculiarities.*

Hard Cases

IN THE UNITED STATES, no one
can be President but the President. If he withholds his energies or
fritters them away ineffectively, we endure or enjoy a period of national stalemate. So we need to know as much about why some Presidents fail to lead as about why others succeed. Indeed, it can be argued that our periods of political drift have been as fateful for the
nation as our eras of New Freedom, New Deal, and New Frontier.

But the dull Presidents are a trial for the political analyst, particularly for the student of personality and political leadership. It is not
just that they sap one's intellectual verve, but that their personality
configurations are, on the surface, indistinct. They thus provide "hard-
case" tests for the supposition that personality helps shape a President's politics. If a personality approach can work with Coolidge and
Hoover, it can work with any chief executive. I mean to show here
how these two men illustrate some recurrent dynamics of Presidential
style and how these dynamics can be caught in a theory with predictive possibilities.

The following pages take up these themes in order. First, I shall set
forth a scheme for classifying Presidents according to the major di-

mensions of their political styles and demonstrate the applicability of the classification scheme to Coolidge and Hoover. The purpose of this section is to define and apply concepts potentially useful for classifying political leaders in terms of patterned regularities in political styles, not simply to describe each President as a unique case. The data I shall use are biographical; their presentation in small space requires radical summarization.

The second section poses a theory, focusing primarily on the President's first independent political success, of the development of a political style. In brief, I argue that a President's style is a reflection of the ways of performing which brought him success at the time, usually in late adolescence or early adulthood, when he emerged as a personality distinctive from his family heritage, in a role involving relatively intensive participation in a socially organized setting. It is at this point that the argument moves from classification to prediction, from an emphasis on naming to an emphasis on explaining. Biographical materials are then treated in a more dynamic fashion, in an effort to reveal the psychological functioning which sustains an integrated pattern of behavior, that is, a distinctive and consistent political style.

"Style"

"Style"* in this context means a collection of habitual action patterns in meeting role demands. Viewed from outside, a man's style is the observed quality and character of his performance. Viewed from inside, it is his bundle of strategies for adapting, for protecting and enhancing self-esteem. The main outlines of a political style can be usefully delineated, I have argued, by the interaction of two main dimensions.[1] The first is *activity-passivity* in performing the role. Presidents have often been typed in this way. The question here is not one of effectiveness but of effort. Political roles, including the Presidency, allow for wide variation in the amount of energy the person invests in his work. Such investment has a large voluntary component and typically reflects to a high degree the man's personal habits

* (1988: Later in the development of research on Presidents, I distinguished "character" from "style." See below, chapter 4.)

as these interact with the demands of the situation. The second dimension is *positive-negative affect* toward his activity. Action per se tells us nothing of affect. The way one feels about his work—specifically, whether he goes about his tasks reasonably happily or with an air of discouragement and sadness—tells much about the fit between his needs and his duties. His affect toward his work represents the self's way of registering that fit. Like activity-passivity, the affect dimension links personality with political leadership.

Put together, these two crude and simple variables delineate four political types. Briefly, the active-positive shows a style oriented primarily toward productiveness; the active-negative toward personal ambition; the passive-positive toward affection; and the passive-negative toward (minimal) performance of duty. Within these general nuclear types, a series of personality dynamics relate the self-system, reactions to political experience, strategies of adaptation to political roles, types of vulnerability to political persuasion, and effectiveness in performing political tasks. In psychological terms, activity and affect interact to give, respectively, generally adjusted, compulsive, compliant, and withdrawn types. There is no one "political man," no universal pattern of leadership performance.

For the analysis of political behavior in collegial bodies such as legislatures, this classificatory scheme may capture the main comparisons. For the Presidency, an office of immense individual power, we need more precise characterizations. I propose here to deepen the analysis within each category by elaborating three subcategories. These subcategories emerge when we ask (extending the major dimensions of activity and affect) to what extent and with what adjustive purpose the President takes advantage of the main opportunities the role affords him. Specifically, how does he integrate his personal style with the role's opportunities for:

> *Rhetoric:* A leader may accentuate certain kinds of expressiveness to audiences, ranging from the world audience to his companions at dinner.
>
> *Business:* He may or may not concentrate on managing the endless flow of details that flood onto his desk, the studying and budget calculations, the reviewing of memoranda, the personnel problems, etc.

Personal Relations: A president may concentrate in various ways on bargaining with, dominating, combating, and depending on the political elite close around him.

Obviously, all Presidents do all of these things. But equally obviously, they vary in their devotion to each and in their style of performance in each. The first task in analyzing a Presidential style, then, is to characterize, within the general framework of activity and affect, the way the man habitually meets the role's demands that he speak, that he manage ordinary business, and that he operate with others at close range. The examples presented—and they are only that—show how these style elements can be distinctive and habitual for the man and politically significant for the nation.

Once the styles are understood, we move to an even more difficult question: how might they have been predicted? How might we have supposed, on the basis of the man's known history, what he would do with the office?

The Coolidge Style

Calvin Coolidge as President fits the passive-negative, or withdrawn, type. Of the three main dimensions of style he emphasized rhetoric. His rhetorical style was sharply compartmentalized according to the audience: witty banter with reporters, high-minded addresses to the nation, silence at social occasions. He avoided detailed work on presidential business. His personal relations were coolly detached. These patterns are evident as the main themes of the Coolidge Presidency.[2]

Rhetoric

Coolidge complained that "one of the most appalling trials which confront a President is the perpetual clamor for public utterances." But this "foster-child of silence" was anything but quiet in public. In office sixty-seven months, he held 520 press conferences, an average of 7.8 per month, compared with Franklin Roosevelt's 6.9. He gave radio addresses about once a month. He got off to an excellent start with the reporters, cracking jokes at this first conference; their "hearty applause" on that occasion made it "one of my most pleasant memories." They were "the boys" who came along on his vacations. Clearly he enjoyed their enjoyment, particularly when he could surprise or titillate them with Yankee humor. He carefully stage-managed his "I do not choose to run for President in nineteen twenty-eight" statement, releasing the news at noon on the fourth anniversary of taking office, grinning broadly. His wife was as surprised as the reporters were. He let himself be photographed in full Indian headdress, cowboy chaps and hat, overalls, and any number of other outfits; there is a picture of him presenting a sap bucket to Henry Ford. When a friend protested that his antics made people laugh, Coolidge said, "Well, it's good for people to laugh."

His formal addresses had a completely different tone. They were sermons from the church of New England idealism. "When the President speaks," he wrote, "it ought to be an event," by which he meant a serious and dignified and uplifting event. He spoke on "Education: the Cornerstone of Self-Government," "The High Place of Labor," "Ordered Liberty and World Peace," "Authority and Religious Liberty," "Religion and the Republic," "The Genius of America." "Destiny is in you," "Do the day's work," "The things of the spirit come first," and "The chief ideal of the American people is idealism"—this was Coolidge in the Presidential pulpit. And he was quite serious. When Will Rogers imitated his nasal twang and penchant for clichés, he was much offended and refused Rogers's apology.

Business

Coolidge sincerely believed in hard work. He felt busy, even rushed, but his constant routine included a daily nap and often eleven hours of sleep in twenty-four. Often tired and bored, he gradually abandoned all physical exercise except for brief walks and spent much time in silent contemplation, gazing out his office window. His strength was not effort but patience. "Let well enough alone," was his motto. He was the "provincial who refuses to become excited over events for which he has no direct responsibility." He kept Harding's cabinet, let Daugherty hang on for a long time, tried to delay his friends' efforts to boost him in 1924. Asked how he kept fit he said, "By avoiding the big problems." Most of the time Coolidge simply did not want to be bothered.

Underneath these tactics, supporting and justifying them, was a strain of mystical resignation. "I am only in the clutch of forces that are greater than I am," he wrote, despite being "the most powerful man in the world." He bore his young son's death with Roman stoicism: "The ways of Providence are beyond our understanding." The dedicated man, he wrote in his newspaper column, "finds that in the time of need some power outside himself directs his course." Coolidge could wait, storing up his meager energies with a feeling of rightness in entrusting himself to fate. "Government is growth," he said, and added: "—slow growth." He and Providence presided while the rate slowed down.

Personal relations

Coolidge got rid of much work by giving it to others, and he believed in doing just that. "One rule of action more important than all others consists in never doing anything that some one else can do for you." He appointed or retained "men of sufficient ability so that they can solve all the problems that arise under their jurisdiction." He rarely interfered and he resented others interfering with him. His loyal helper, Frank Stearns, got repeated rebuffs for his trouble. Coolidge seldom discussed political matters with his wife. He complained of Hoover as Secretary of Commerce (Coolidge called him "the wonder boy" or "the miracle worker"): "That man has offered me unsolicited advice for six years, all of it bad!"

Yet he was always surrounded by people. He and Grace entertained more than any previous family in the White House. Alone, he said, he got "a sort of naked feeling." His poker face, his long impenetrable silences at social affairs were known to all Washington and gave rise to scores of anecdotes as matron after matron tried to pry a few words from him. Occasionally he could be induced to talk about Vermont. More often, he simply sat. This was "a form of defense," his biographer says. "Can't hang you for what you don't say," said Coolidge. "In order to function at all," he warned his successors, the President "has to be surrounded by many safeguards. If these were removed for only a short time, he would be overwhelmed by the people who would surge in upon him." He learned not to smile, as smiling encouraged longer office visits. He had very little interest in women and was, his biographer says, "embarrassed when left for even a short period in the company of the other sex." Undoubtedly much of Coolidge's acerbity at dinner parties was a reaction to intensified shyness at having to cope with the matrons to his left and right. When he did speak, it was some tart, pithy puckishness, mildly aggressive, disconcerting, with a quality of surprise in a conventional conversational setting. In a rare and revealing confession, he once told Frank Stearns why:

> Do you know, I've never really grown up? It's a hard thing for me to play this game. In politics, one must meet people, and that's not easy for me . . . When I was a little fellow, as long ago as I can remember, I would go into a panic if I heard strange voices in the kitchen. I felt I just couldn't meet the people and shake hands with them. Most of the visitors would sit with Father and Mother in the kitchen, and the hardest thing in the world was to have to go through the kitchen door and give them a greeting. I was almost ten before I realized I couldn't go on that way. And by fighting hard I used to manage to get through that door. I'm all right with old friends, but every time I meet a stranger, I've got to go through the old kitchen door, back home, and it's not easy. (Fuess, 1965, p. 25).

Coolidge "tried deliberately to suppress 'aggressive wittiness,'" but "it broke out repeatedly in quaint comments."

Even this brief account shows the main features of the Coolidge style. Clearly he belongs in the withdrawn type. Aside from his banter with reporters, he did not particularly enjoy being President, given all the demands that made on him, and he conserved his energies stingily. Many of his characteristics—his rural Yankee background; his persistent turning back to his past, his father, his homeplace; his avoidance of controversy and patient faith in Providence; his penchant for reverie and retreat; his sense of strangeness in a cosmopolitan environment ("Puritan in Babylon")—concord with empirical findings on this type in a very different environment. His style within that type is also clear. Words for Coolidge were shaped heavily by his relations to different audiences. The "serious" audience was the nation, to which he addressed sermons on common virtue, purveying the illusion of specificity through epigram. In fact, his abstract pseudo-Hegelian fatalism had little clear connection with the political issues of the day. His humor at news conferences was badinage with the boys, a show with much audience participation, full of little surprises. There as in his dinner table silences and mild insults, the focus was on Coolidge as a clown, one who could touch the heart but leave the political brain and brawn of the nation relaxed.

His philosophy helped him rationalize his leisurely pace. His method was to concentrate on matters only the President had to decide, and to define that category as narrowly as possible. Most everything could wait. And Coolidge himself could wait, with utter, unflappable calm, for longer than the last of his advisors. He also managed to rationalize his independence of others; clearly his style in close interpersonal relations cut him off effectively from much of the Washington conversational froth—but also from any effective political bargaining with administrative or legislative or party leaders. He was a loner who endured in order to serve, while the nation drifted.

The Hoover Style

Hoover belongs in the active-negative category, the compulsive type. He emphasized hard work on detail and endless conferences behind the scenes. He avoided and detested the rhetorical demands of the office. In personal relations his was a stance of highly restrained aggression. Again, some illustrative evidence is necessary to make this pattern clear.[3]

Rhetoric

The rise of Herbert Hoover coincided with an immense expansion in the mass media, particularly newspapers and radio. Hoover was a genuine hero; his remarkable effectiveness in European relief activities cannot be seriously questioned. He was the subject, not the instigator, of a vast public relations buildup largely due to increased media demands for news and to the drama and success of his works. But Hoover in the Presidency "transmuted all adventure into business," as

Arthur Schlesinger (1957) complains. He detested the office's demands for dramatization. "The presidency is more than an executive responsibility," he wrote; "it is an inspiring symbol of all that is highest in American purpose and ideals." Yet he could not bring himself to practice the pretense such inspiration requires. "This is not a showman's job," he said, "I will not step out of character," and "You can't make a Teddy Roosevelt out of me." He felt uncomfortable when forced to perform in public: "I have never liked the clamor of crowds. I intensely dislike superficial social contacts. I made no pretensions to oratory and I was terrorized at the opening of every speech." The "miracle worker" disdained "the crowd" which "only feels: it has no mind of its own which can plan. The crowd is credulous, it destroys, it hates and it dreams—but it never builds."

Extremely sensitive to criticism, Hoover reacted to personal abuse with "hurt contempt." He was rarely aggressive, normally suffering in silence with only an occasional private complaint. He got off to a good start with the press, setting more liberal rules for the conference, but even before the stock market crash he began to restrict the reporters, became more secretive, and admonished them for the error of their ways. Often he withdrew to his forest camp in Virginia without notice to the press; there he set up guards to keep the newsmen away. He began to play favorites among them and to go over their heads to editors and publishers. He cancelled conferences on short notice, ignored questions, and took to reading prepared statements. Eventually, most of the White House reporters turned against him. He met them less and less frequently and virtually eliminated conferences near the end of his term.

Hoover's public addresses rarely discussed specific policies in detail. His twenty-one radio addresses were mainly "greetings" to specific groups, full of vague moral precepts. Speechwriting was as hard for him as speechmaking. He drafted each one in longhand, went through a dozen or more drafts, and heavily edited proofs to produce a labored and ordinary address. But perhaps the most peculiar feature of the tone of Hoover's Presidential statements was their public optimism in the midst of social disaster. As the Depression deepened, again and again he found business fundamentally sound, the worst of the crisis over, employment gradually increasing, government efforts remarkably successful, no one actually starving—or so he said, giving rise to a "credibility gap" of modern proportions. His pollyanna reassurances stand in stark relief against both the condition of the country and the character of the man. His secretary put it more kindly: "Figuratively, he was the father protecting his family against the troubles impending, shouldering their burdens for them, keeping the 'bad news' to himself, outwardly trying to be as smiling and cheerful as possible."

Business

Meanwhile, he slaved and suffered in silence. Long before the Depression Hoover was frequently discouraged. At the Paris Peace Conference in 1919, Colonel House found him "simply reveling in gloom"; Ike Hoover remembered that in the White House he "never laughed aloud" and "always had a frown on his face," and his secretary recalls that "he worried as have few Presidents in our history, with discouragement at his lot most of the time." He was glad when it was all over: "All the money in the world could not induce me to live over the last nine months. The conditions we have experienced make this office a compound hell." He worked as hard as he worried. Even before the crash his routine was a rigorous one, beginning with an energetic medicine ball game first thing in the morning. After his inauguration he immediately set about a series of programs for change and reform. Then when the panic hit, "he began that grinding, brutal, self-lacerating labor, often eighteen or twenty hours a day or clear around the clock, which would continue unbroken until the blessed hour of release more than three years later. No galley slave of old was more firmly riveted to his drudgery, for he was chained by his surpassing sense of duty." "So tired that every bone in my body aches," Hoover trudged on. Near the close of his tenure he allowed himself one bitter outburst in public, significantly in reply to charges that he had "done nothing." In "the one harsh word that I have uttered in public office," he called such charges "deliberate, intolerable falsehoods."

And so they were. He had done plenty, but to little effect. Hoover was immersed in detail. As Bernard Baruch put it, "To Hoover's brain facts are as water to a sponge. They are absorbed into every tiny interstice." He had a "card index" mind which could grasp and retain details and figures without notes. He commissioned endless policy studies to produce the facts on which to base programs. His whole orientation, in other words, was away from the vagaries of opinion and toward the hard precision of fact.

Much of his energy went into an endless round of conferences. Hoover appeared to believe that if only he could bring the right people together and give them the right proposal, they would agree and march off to execute his plan. John Kenneth Galbraith called these "no-business meetings," designed to accomplish nothing, but there is little doubt Hoover had high hopes for this technique of "coordination." In almost all such encounters he had more pertinent information and had worried through a more thoroughly organized proposal than any other participant. And he was President of the United States. The others he expected to behave as had his subordinates in business, in the European relief organization, and in the Department of Commerce: as willing endorsers and enforcers. When Cabinet members and Congressmen failed to respond in this way, Hoover's gloom deepened. His personal discouragement proved contagious; to Henry L. Stimson, his Secretary of State, a private conversation with Hoover was "like sitting in a bath of ink."

Personal relations

Hoover kept his aggressive feelings tightly controlled in close relations as in public ones. At a time when, as he complained, "My men are dropping around me," when H. G. Wells found him a "sickly, overworked and overwhelmed man," Hoover was often tempted to lash out. Deep inside he may have been, as his apologist Lyons believed, "a sensitive, soft-hearted person who craves affection, enjoys congenial company, and suffers under the slings of malice," but he could also feel intense anger. "I'll rattle his bones" was his typical expression when thwarted by some obstructionist. In 1932 he meant to "carry the fight right to Roosevelt. . . . We have got to crack him every time he opens his mouth." But he would quickly rein in these feelings:

> He was almost always the master of his emotions, however provoked he might be. If something went wrong, if some individual really aroused him he would, in common parlance, "blow off

steam." But it was only for a moment. The next minute he would be pressing his buzzer. When the stenographer was seated beside his desk, instead of telling Mr. Blank cryptically what he thought, he dictated a most diplomatic communication. There was never a barb in it. Rather, it represented earnest and skillful effort to induce that individual to see eye to eye with him. (Joslin, 1934, p. 19)

With his immediate staff "there were no cross words if a subordinate made an error." Nor would he "let himself be baited into a controversy if he could possibly avoid it." Many a time it was tried out on him. His usual comment, made with supreme contempt, was: "A man should not become embroiled with his inferior." His expression was one of "pained disbelief" when other political and congressional leaders failed to keep their commitments.

Of course, his demeanor affected his political relations. His inability to enter into genuinely cooperative relations with others, relations involving compromise, an appreciation for the irrational in politics, a sense for the other man's position, meant that his endeavors to induce an enthusiastic response were doomed to failure. He could lead an organization of committed subordinates, but he could not create that commitment among leaders with their own bases of power and their own overriding purposes.

Hoover did accept renomination in 1932, but reluctantly. He "had no overpowering desire to run again," expressed his indifference to the subject, anticipated defeat, and found the campaign a "miserable experience." But he "felt that he must follow through to the end of the struggle. Be that as it may, he had a desperate desire for vindication of himself and his policies." The purpose was defensive, not for any positive achievement. The expected defeat brought relief, not despair.

No brief account can do justice to a complex character, but it seems clear that Hoover belongs in the compulsive type of political leader, outlined by much activity and much unhappiness in the role. Many themes fit this pattern: his struggles with the "exposure" element of the public figure role, resulting in the adoption of a propagandistic orientation; his history as a rapidly upward mobile young man whose links to politics developed out of his nonpolitical occupation; his feelings of frustration and powerlessness in the face of an unresponsive or hostile environment; his anxious, unremitting labor; his suffering and struggle to restrain his aggression. Deeper analysis, one would predict, would reveal a self dominated by the conflict between conscience and ambition, alternating between feelings of guilt and feelings of impotence.

The main distinctive elements in Hoover's style can also be readily summarized. Words were difficult for him; he resisted expression and fell back on a rhetoric of exaggeration when forced into the limelight. Work was his main strategy for success, intensely compulsive work on detail. And in his relations with others he stressed restraint of aggression, an anticipation that his plan would win and succeed in execution. These strategies failed. That Hoover sustained them in the face of repeated negative messages from the environment attests to their rootedness in his personality. The office no more made the man than it made his successor.

Toward a Predictive Theory

Where did these styles come from? Our problem is not to discover why Coolidge and Hoover became Presidents while others with similar background took different paths, but to find out why, being Presidents, they acted as they did. Furthermore, we want an *economical* method for answering that question, a method amenable to *generalization* to other cases, and a method which produces *predictive* statements. That requires a theory. Let me set mine out as starkly as I can.

First independent political success

In the lives of most political leaders there is a clearly discernible period, usually in late adolescence or early adulthood, in which a style is adopted. Typically that period can be identified (a) by marked infusions of confidence from relative success, (b) by a relatively new and special relationship to group life, and (c) by a relatively sudden emergence from obscurity to wider attention. The way in which the man finds words to relate himself to an expanded audience, the role of work in bringing him new success, and the mode of his more intimate links with others around him presage his style in the presidency. If we can discover how future Presidents met and resolved these fundamental problems in their own critical periods, we should be able to predict how they are likely to attempt (not necessarily successfully) to solve similar problems as chief executives.[4]

Motives

How can one understand this formative period? First one must view it against the background of compensatory needs inherited from childhood. It is important to highlight the significance of change in the person's life situation. We want the meanings his new development had for him, and that requires knowledge of what he was before. A style's staying power, its persistence and resurgence, depends on its rootedness in strong motives. Viewed retrospectively, a style offers important compensations; viewed prospectively, it promises the continuation and extension of rewards. There is a turning away from an unsatisfactory prior condition to a possibly more satisfactory condition for the future. These satisfactions, and the anticipation of them, are the motive forces which energize the new system.

Resources

Second, the formative period can only be discerned in the light of the resources a man brings to it. The condition of one's body is a simple example of personal resource. The condition of one's mind is a subtler case, depending as it does on learning and on the collection of relevant experiences and perceptions a person brings to the formative period. These constitute a repertoire of potential style elements upon which he can draw when his time comes. His learning until then can be considered as a rehearsal, though rarely in any conscious sense, for a decisive commitment to a particular style. His experiments in self-definition, real and vicarious, set out boundaries and pathways for his map of the future.

Opportunities

And last, a style is not formed in a vacuum but in a context of opportunities. Just as we do not expect a person who has always had all the affection he has wanted to seek an unending succession of affection in adulthood, and just as we do not expect an illiterate to adopt an identity as a writer, so not every environment available at the time offers the same chances for personal development. These constraints and stimuli in the immediate culture may have a great deal to do with the kinds of strategies one translates into part of his personal identity.[5]

As a beginning test, then, the following pages examine Coolidge and Hoover at the time of their first independent political success, introduced in each case by a radically summarized account of the needs and resources brought from childhood. A final section draws together these themes with the conclusions derived from the material on their Presidential styles.

Coolidge: Needs from Childhood

John Calvin Coolidge, Jr., was born in Plymouth, Vermont, on the Fourth of July 1872, the first child, after four years of marriage, of John Calvin Coolidge and Victoria Josephine Coolidge, nephew of Julius Caesar Coolidge, grandson of Calvin Galusha Coolidge, descendant of five generations of his family in a Vermont village. His mother was a quiet, delicately beautiful person, a chronic invalid since shortly after her marriage. Coolidge remembered "a touch of mysticism and poetry in her nature." His father was a big, stern-visaged man, a storekeeper and pillar of the community who had held many town offices and went to the state legislature. His son admired him for "qualities that were greater than any I possess," and accepted much paternal admonition without complaint.

Calvin's early hero was his grandfather "Galoosh," tall, spare, and handsome, an expert horseman and practical joker, said to have a trace of Indian blood, who raised colts and puppies and peacocks and taught the boy to ride standing up behind him. His grandmother ("The Puritan severity of her convictions was tempered by the sweetness of womanly charity") read the Bible to him and when he misbehaved shut him up in the dark, windowless attic, "dusty with cobwebs."

Calvin's younger sister Abbie, his constant playmate, was "a lively affectionate girl, with flaming red hair, who was full of energy and impressed everybody by her personality"—almost the exact opposite of her shy brother. Calvin himself was small and frail, with his mother's features, punctual and methodical, only occasionally joining in the schoolyard teasing.

So much for the cast of characters. Life began its hammer blows at this shy boy when he was six. His hero Galusha died as Calvin read to him from the Bible. Six years later his invalid mother, "who used what strength she had to lavish care upon me and my sister," died as a result of an accident with a runaway horse. Her passing left an indelible mark on him:

> In an hour she was gone. It was her thirty-ninth birthday. I was twelve years old. We laid her away in the blustering snows of March. The greatest grief that can come to a boy came to me. Life was never to seem the same again. (Coolidge, 1929, p. 13)

Calvin was despondent too long. His family became concerned; but he kept up his school work "with no tardy marks and good deportment."

Later at the nearby Black River Academy, where his parents and grandmother had gone to school, he was unhappy and homesick, though his father brought him home nearly every weekend. In his third year Abbie joined him there; Calvin had written he hoped she could come. A year and a half later, at age fifteen, she was dead of appendicitis. Calvin came home to be with her in her last hours.

There was another unsettled time for Calvin, like that following his mother's death. He failed the entrance examinations for Amherst College. He had caught cold and stayed home "for a considerable time." In late winter he went back to Black River Academy to get "certified" for Amherst. There he worked hard, "made almost no acquaintances," and in two months was approved for Amherst. In September his father married a Plymouth neighbor, a spinster Calvin had known all his life. "For thirty years," Coolidge wrote much later, "she watched over and loved me." They corresponded regularly until her death in 1920.

Amherst was an all-male place where three-quarters or more of the students belonged to fraternities, "the most unique feature of Amherst life . . . strongly recommended by the members of the faculty," as the *Students' Handbook* said. Calvin needed no urging. He had written his father from school that he and a friend should visit the college "to see about getting me into a society there." But the scheme did not work. Calvin moved into a boardinghouse. The others there were quickly pledged. He remained an "Ouden," an outsider in a small community of clans. "I don't seem to get acquainted very fast," he wrote home in October. After Christmas he wrote that "Every time I get home I hate to go away worse than before and I don't feel so well here now as the first day I came here last fall but suppose I will be all right in a day or two." Two days later: "I feel quite reconciled to being here tonight but felt awful mean yesterday and the day before. I don't know why, I never was homesick any before." In his first two years at Amherst Coolidge was "to say the least, an inconspicuous member of the class." He faithfully attended class meetings, but did not join in the myriad activities, formal and informal, scholarly and athletic, religious and amorous, going on around him. He took long walks in the woods.

Nor was his social isolation balanced with scholarly achievement; his first term marks averaged 2 on a scale of 5. "The marks seem pretty low, don't they?" he wrote his father. He remembered much later that "It needed some encouragement from my father for me to continue." He had begun with the hope that he could do well in his courses with plenty of time to spare.

Thus at twenty-one Calvin Coolidge was an indistinct personality, inarticulate, ineffective, alone. Particularly in affection and achievement he stood on the threshold of adulthood much deprived.

Coolidge: Resources from Childhood

In his mind he had been gathering impressions and registering experiences which would later be useful. He had known his father and grandfather as political leaders in the community. He saw how his father made decisions—"painstaking, precise, and very accurate"—and came to understand government as "restraints which the people had imposed upon themselves in order to promote the common welfare." In the summer before he entered Amherst his father took him to a gathering in Bennington to hear President Benjamin Harrison;

there he heard much high oratory about the "high consecration to liberty."

As a boy he had taken a minor part in speaking "pieces," acting in amateur plays, and was even an "end man" once in a local minstrel show. Cicero's orations stuck with him from Latin classes. At graduation from Black River Academy, in a class of five boys and four girls, he delivered an address on "Oratory in History;" the newspaper called it "masterly" and his teacher said his speech was "the best one he had seen." After his freshman year at Amherst, at the Independence Day celebration in Plymouth—"Of course, the Fourth of July meant a good deal to me, because it was my birthday"—he delivered a speech on "Freedom," "burning with fervor, replete with denunciation of Proud Albion, and rich with the glorification of our Revolutionary heroes." Perhaps inspired by his freshman rhetoric teacher, this was his last experiment in the florid style of oratory.

Had Coolidge's life taken a different turn, other events, other impressions would have lasted into his autobiographical years. As it was, he had in his mind a number of important images: of small-scale Yankee democracy, of his mother reading the Romantic poets, of his father succeeding by being careful, of the familial legitimacy of politics, and of himself surviving before audiences. So far he had made nothing of these resources. But they were waiting.

Coolidge: First Independent Political Success

Of the events in his first two years at Amherst, Coolidge wrote:

> In the development of every boy who is going to amount to anything there comes a time when he emerges from his immature ways and by the greater precision of his thoughts and action realizes that he has begun to find himself. Such a transition finally came to me. It was not accidental but the result of hard work. If I had permitted my failure, or what seemed to me at the time a lack of success to discourage me, I cannot see any way in which I would ever have made progress. If we keep our faith in ourselves, and what is even more important, keep our faith in regular and persistent application to hard work, we need not worry about the outcome. (Coolidge, 1929, p. 60)

As a matter of fact, what he calls his "transition" was triggered by events nearly "accidental"; his success did not result primarily from "hard work"; and he was, as we have seen, "discouraged" by his earlier lack of success. (Perhaps every autobiography is a mixture of real memories and new meanings, a last attempt to join together life and belief.) In any case, Coolidge did begin his junior year an isolated boy with no real achievements and left Amherst as a young man with a distinctive style of action. In between the whole intensity of his experience, its pace and significance were revolutionized.

Amherst upperclassmen could wear high derbies and carry canes. Each fall the members of the junior class raced from one end of the athletic field to the other, clad in "topper" and stick. The last seven across the line had to provide dinner and entertainment for the rest. Coolidge was not last, but was one of the losers. His assignment was a speech on "Why I Got Stuck." He began in silence by turning his pockets inside out to show that he had lost all his money on the race. Then: "You wouldn't expect a plow horse to make time on the race track or a follower of the plow to be a Mercury," he said. Pitching hay didn't fit one as a sprinter. And other such comments. Then, in conclusion: "Remember, boys, the Good Book says that the first shall be last and the last shall be first." The speech was a success—the whole class laughed and gave him an ovation. It was his first such appearance and it brought him more attention and notoriety than anything he had done at Amherst so far. He began to emerge as a character, although the incident is not mentioned in his *Autobiography*.

That same year he began to attract attention as a debater. Public speaking and debating were compulsory parts of the curriculum. One of his classmates wrote: "It was in his junior year that we discovered Coolidge. In that year we began debating, and in the debates we found that he could talk. It was as if a new and gifted man had joined the class." Coolidge now became more and more adept at brief and direct statement. He won frequently in debating, perhaps every time in the junior debates. In November of that year he wrote his father proudly: "In view of the fact that yesterday I put up a debate said to be the best heard on the floor of the chapel this term . . . can you send me $25?" In January he wrote home another glowing report of a successful debate. At the end of his junior year the students in the public speaking class voted to split the prize between Coolidge and another speaker. He continued debating in his senior year. In September he was elected to present the "Grove Oration" at the graduation exercises the following June. This was meant to be a humorous speech following the ponderousness of more formal addresses. In June, after a long series of indoor sermons and addresses, the students went to the College Grove, lit up their corncob pipes, and settled back on the grass. Coolidge began this way: "The mantle of truth falls upon the Grove Orator on condition he wear it wrong side out," and went on through a series of in-house jokes, continually interrupted by hecklers and shouts of laughter. "The oration was packed with what today would be called 'wisecracks,'" his biographer says, "many of them sarcastic observations on members of the faculty—remarks which, although good-natured in tone and intention, had nevertheless something of a bite." The speech was a smashing success.

In parallel with these oratorical victories, Coolidge achieved social ones. He was elected a member of Phi Gamma Delta on January 15 of his senior year. This began a lifelong active tie, his only fraternal connection. From the start he entered into the group's affairs; a classmate recalls that

> He took a deep interest in the chapter, was most faithful in attending "goat" and committee meetings, and while he did not live at the house, he passed considerable time there. We soon began to rely upon his counsel and judgment, and he was a distinct help to us in many serious problems we had to meet at that time. (Fuess, 1965, p. 54)

He wrote his father that "being in a society" would cost a little more money. From that time on, Coolidge was a faithful "Fiji," raising money, acting as the chapter's lawyer, returning to inspect the house carefully from cellar to garret, organizing (while he was President) the "Fiji Sires and Sons." His role in his brief membership as a student was that of the faithful attender and business helper; he skipped the dances and card games and "wild parties." At long last he had found a band of brothers. He was not a central figure in this group, but it is obvious that his membership meant a great deal to him after years of being left out. The moral he draws from this in the *Auto-*

biography is touching: "It has been my observation in life that, if one will only exercise the patience to wait, his wants are likely to be filled."

Garman's influence

He had found a voice and developed a relationship to his audience; he had a club of friends. At the same time, Coolidge found a model, an idol with whom to identify and a set of philosophical beliefs to guide him. This was Charles E. Garman, professor of philosophy, whose course, as Coolidge took it, ran from the spring term of junior year through senior year, moving from psychology to philosophy to ethics. "It always seemed to me that all our other studies were in the nature of a preparation for the course in philosophy," Coolidge remembered. Garman, a tall, cadaverous man with piercing black eyes, was a dramatic character, "a middle-aged Hamlet," extremely popular among the students.

Garman was in reality "a devout and rather orthodox New England Congregationalist" with a strong neo-Hegelian bent. Our interest is less in what he taught than in what Coolidge carried away from him and retained for thirty-five years. Garman did not carry his question-raising method to the point of not providing answers. Coolidge recalled his emphasis on rational judgment in ethical matters, the existence of a personal God and of "the complete dependence of all the universe on Him," man as set "off in a separate kingdom from all other creatures," the "spiritual appeal" of art as Divine revelation, the essential quality of men, the dignity of work and industry's right to work's rewards, "that might does not make right, that the end does not justify the means, and that expediency as a working principle is bound to fail." All of this Coolidge lays out in an unusually lengthy passage of his memoirs. Garman posted aphorisms on the walls of his classroom—"Carry all questions back to fundamental principles," "Weigh the evidence," "The question *how* answers the question *what*," "Process not product," and so forth. But perhaps the key lesson Coolidge retained is found later in the *Autobiography* in the context of his early steps in politics, when he was elected mayor of Northampton, Massachusetts:

Ever since I was in Amherst College I have remembered how Garman told his class in philosophy that if they would go along with events and hold to the main stream, without being washed ashore by the immaterial cross currents, they would some day be men of power. (Coolidge, 1929, pp. 99–100)

Already the echoes of Coolidge as President are apparent.

Coolidge remembered that "We looked upon Garman as a remarkable man who walked with God," and that he was "one of the most remarkable men with whom I ever came in contact," a man who "was given a power which took his class up into a high mountain of spiritual life and left them alone with God," who had "no pride of opinion, no atom of selfishness," "a follower of the truth, a disciple of the Cross, who bore the infirmities of us all." Coolidge did not try to defend Garman's position theoretically. But

I knew that in experience it has worked. In time of crisis my belief that people can know the truth, that when it is presented to them they must accept it, has saved me from many of the counsels of expediency. (Coolidge, 1929, p. 67)

He had found a rule of life, and the words to express it with.

The break with his past

Coolidge had written a romantic story for the Amherst *Literary Monthly* in the summer between his junior and senior years. In his senior year he tried his hand at a very different literary task, undertaken in secret: an essay for a national contest on "The Principles Fought for in the War of the American Revolution." The Amherst history department awarded his piece a silver medal; the following December when he was working in a law office in Northampton, Coolidge learned he was also the national winner. One of the partners asked him, "Have you told your father?" To which he replied, "No, do you think I'd better?" In his *Autobiography* Coolidge recalled that

I had a little vanity in wishing my father to learn about it first from the press, which he did. He had questioned some whether I was really making anything of my education, in pretense I now think, not because he doubted it but because he wished to impress me with the desirability of demonstrating it. (Coolidge, 1929, p. 74)

Coolidge had moved from an emotional psychology, a sentimental dramatism in his story ("Margaret's Mist"), to the logic of principles, the metier of ethical philosophy which he would continue to emphasize all his life. But his "No, do you think I'd better?" also represented a change. Right after graduation he returned to the farm for a summer's work and then went to Northampton to learn law. As late as January of his senior year he had not yet decided whether the law or storekeeping would be his profession. He wrote his father then, "You will have to decide." He did know that he wanted "to live where I can be of some use to the world and not simply where I should get a few dollars together." By graduation he had decided that the law was "the highest of the professions." On his own, Coolidge sought a place, and in September 1895 he went to work in a law office in Northampton. When he joined the law office Coolidge made a break with his past. The boy whose name had been recorded in various forms now discarded the "John" and became plain Calvin Coolidge. And "during these first years he worked so hard that for three years he did not find time to go back to Plymouth." The distance was about a hundred miles.

"That I was now engaged in a serious enterprise of life I so fully realized that I went to the barber shop and divested myself of the college fashion of long hair." He who had so often written home of his successes kept the largest one a secret. He found a job without his father's help. None of the Coolidges had been lawyers. Calvin had formed his style and begun his own life. He had found a way to be; he was not entirely certain where he was going.

As we have seen, Coolidge himself attributed to his experience in the last two years at Amherst a shaping influence on his mind and heart. His biographers agree. Fuess is convinced that "he was, during his first two years at Amherst, acutely conscious of his slow progress. His ambitions had been thwarted; he failed to make a fraternity, he was unnoticed by those around him, his marks were only mediocre, and he had no compensating successes." Then "perhaps his entire political philosophy" was shaped by his junior and senior teachers as he combined a spurt of learning with social success. William Allen White goes further: his "spirit awoke in Amherst," Garman "unlocked for him the philosophic mysteries of life," he was "baptized for life," "this reborn spirit whom Garman begot," and "Body and mind and spirit were cast into the iron mold of a fate which guided him through life."

Clearly Coolidge had found at Amherst the major features of the style that served him as President. The similarity in his rhetoric, business management, and personal relations habits in these widely separate periods of his life are striking.

Hoover: Needs from Childhood

Five generations of Coolidges lived in the confining culture of a small New England town; five generations of Hoovers lived in the confining culture of Quakerism, moving about from time to time but retaining their religion and its peculiar community practices. Gentle and free in ideology, Quakerism was often harsh and repressive in practice. Quaker meetings left Hoover with a sense of "the intense repression upon a ten-year-old who might not even count his toes."

Herbert Clark Hoover was born on August 10, 1874, in West Branch, Iowa, two and a half years after his brother, Theodore, and two years before his sister, May, to Jesse Clark Hoover, a blacksmith and farm implement salesman of twenty-seven and Huldah Minthorn Hoover, a seminary-educated lady of twenty-six. An aunt present at his birth wrote that "Jesse and Huldah always made much of thee because thee represented the little girl they hoped soon to have." Hoover remembered his mother vaguely as "a sweet-faced woman." She was very religious, spoke often in meeting, an efficient and serious-minded person. His father had a teasing humor, but was capable of punishing Herbert severely.

A plump baby, Herbert nearly died of croup in his second winter and suffered many other illnesses and accidents. But as he grew stronger and older he became a healthy, outdoor-loving boy.

His father died unexpectedly in the summer of Herbert's sixth year. His mother became "less and less a creature of this world after her husband died," leaving the children for long periods while she travelled about preaching. Herbert was passed around from uncle to uncle, each of whom worked him hard but also let him play in the woods and fields. In the winter after his eighth birthday his mother died of pneumonia. "Bereavement put a sudden end to his little-boyhood, as it had to his babyhood," Will Irwin writes.

Separated from his brother and sister and sent to an uncle's farm, Herbert "took it hard—but with his mouth shut and grief showing only in his eyes." At age ten he was again uprooted and sent to Oregon to live with his mother's brother, Henry John Minthorn, whose only son had just died. "Thee is going to Oregon," he was told, and "his lips closed very tight." Minthorn put him to school and chores, for a time of "sober routine." His uncle was a severe taskmaster; once Herbert "stalked out in anger and boarded with other relatives." At fifteen he was taken with his uncle to open a "Quaker land-settlement business" in Salem. A visitor told him of opportunities for engineering education at the newly opening Stanford University. Over the family's objection—and this is the first report of Herbert arguing—he took the Stanford entrance examinations, failed them, but was admitted for special tutoring in the summer.

Hoover thus left home and childhood with understandable enthusiasm. The major deprivations are clear: he lost both his parents, suddenly and unexpectedly, by the age of eight—a severe loss of affection and stability—and he had been shuffled about, against his will, from one stern relative to another, separated from his brother and sister, powerless to shape any segment of his own life. He needed others, and he needed to get his own place in the world and hold it. All his work so far had brought him nothing but more work. Words were not yet part of his equipment; he had kept a tight-lipped sense of humiliation as person after person he relied on had agreed to abandon him to others.

Hoover: Resources from Childhood

Neither the political nor the rhetorical emphasis in Coolidge's upbringing were there for Hoover. His Uncle Laban was an Indian agent and his Uncle Henry Minthorn had been one; Hoover vaguely remembered the Garfield campaign of 1880 and the lone (and drunken)

Democrat in West Branch. That appears to have been the extent of his political exposure. Nor is there any record of early appearances before an audience. He did not like school: years later, asked to name his favorite study, he replied, "None. They were something to race through—so I could get out of doors." He remembered some of his teachers with affection, but their lessons appear to have made no substantive impression on him. At home there were no novels, "save those with Total Abstinence as hero and Rum as villain." He and his brother read—surreptitiously—"Youth's Companion," a mild thriller of the day, and with their cousin George acted out the parts. At first "Bertie" acted as lookout in case someone should discover this sinful behavior; then he was promoted to "super parts":

> When Tad commanded the Colonial army, Bertie was that army; he was also the white maiden bound to the stake, while George as the Indian Chief tortured her and Tad as the *Deerslayer* came to the rescue. (Irwin, 1928, p. 15)

Not even at play, then, did he take the lead.

But these indoor intellectual forays never compared in Hoover's experience or memory with the outdoors and the physical. The early pages of his *Memoirs* read like a nature book, full of owls and rabbits and fish. He and his cousins played with machinery and put an old thresher back together; in Oregon he and another office boy tried to repair sewing machines for sale. The heritage was much stronger from the males of his line—the farmers and blacksmith—than from his mother's religiousness. In the office he was efficient in detail, learned to run a typewriter, and spent as much time as he could in the hills. The focus was on things, not words. He recalls a kind teacher who got him started on *Ivanhoe*, an "opening of the door to a great imaginative world" which "led me promptly through much of Scott and Dickens, often at the cost of sleep," but "Oregon lives in my mind for its gleaming wheat fields, its abundant fruit, its luxuriant forest vegetation, and the fish in the mountain streams." On Sunday evening he was allowed to read "an improving book," but one wonders how much of that there was after the Sabbath routine:

> On Sunday mornings, when work of necessity was done, came Sabbath school; then the long meeting; then dinner; then a pe-

riod of sluggish rest followed by a Band of Hope meeting, where the lecturer or teacher displayed colored prints of the drunkard's dreadful interior on each stage of his downward path, with corresponding illustrations of his demeanor and conduct. (Irwin, 1928, p. 30)

Unlike most men who have become President, Hoover had in his background virtually nothing of legitimating family example, identification with political figures, or practice in expressing ideas to audiences.

Hoover: First Independent Political Success

The same September that Coolidge entered Amherst, Hoover entered Stanford. At seventeen he was the youngest and, reportedly, the youngest-looking student in the first class at that new university. Will Irwin describes the effect the next four years had on Herbert Hoover:

He had lived, so far as he was aware, a happy childhood. But after all, that sympathetic brooding which makes childhood supremely happy had been lacking to his life since he was nine (sic) years old; for the greater part of another seven years a repressed atmosphere, wherein his extraordinary intelligence had no proper soil for growth; and hard work at menial or mechanical tasks. The atmosphere of freedom, of high animal spirits, the intellectual stimulus of those original young professors who went adventuring to Stanford—these struck in. Here he knew his first joy of the intellect, here he felt the initial stirring of his higher powers, here he found his wife. Stanford became a kind of complex with Herbert Hoover. Within fifteen years his interests and his wanderings were to embrace the globe; but those golden hills above Palo Alto were always the pole to his compass. (Irwin, 1928, pp. 33–34)

Hoover came to Stanford early in the summer of 1891 to be tutored. Still one subject short of the number required at the end of the summer, he studied a couple of physiology textbooks for two straight nights and passed an examination. He was admitted "conditioned in English"—the language came hard for him, "then and for many years he was impatient with words." He took English examinations twice a year for the next several years without success. In his senior year he failed German. The English "condition" was finally removed to allow him to graduate, when two of his engineering professors argued that his technical reports showed sufficient literary skill. In class and out of class he "said little and listened a lot; there was a wordless eagerness about him," as Lyons puts it. As a sophomore he was "shy to the point of timidity—rarely spoke unless spoken to," his classmate Lester Hinsdale recalled from their lunches together. Irwin remembers Hoover visiting him in the infirmary when Hoover was a senior.

> He did not say a word of sympathy for me—in pain and forever out of football—but I felt it nevertheless. Then, at the door he turned for an instant and jerked out: "I'm sorry." Just that; but it was as though another man had burst into maudlin tears. (Irwin, 1928, p. 60)

When he met his future wife in geological laboratory—he was a senior, she a freshman—he was tongue-tied and red-faced. No other girls were among his close friends at Stanford, nor were there any "frivolous flirtations." It is important to note, then, that verbal expressiveness had no part in Hoover's success at Stanford. He never found there a way to attract attention or to achieve his goals through speech-making or even facile conversation. That mouth so tightly shut at critical moments in his childhood symbolized his verbal restraint at Stanford and as President (though not as Secretary of Commerce). Typically, Hoover talked haltingly, rarely looking the other in the eye, with one foot thrust forward as he jingled the keys in his pocket.

Success came from systematic and ordered work

Hoover's success at Stanford came from work, not words, and from a way of relating to others. He began his extracurricular working career at college by hiring on as a clerk in the registration of the new class. The skill exercised was meticulous attention to detail. Later in his freshman year Professor Branner employed him to do typing, again a matter of careful mechanical work. Then he branched out; he and two partners established a newspaper route and a laundry service for the students. These were soon sublet to other students, providing a small but regular income for Hoover. His entrepreneurial talents were beginning to emerge. Later he sold out the laundry for $40 and he and a new friend started a cooperative residence for students in Palo Alto, a project he dropped soon because it kept him away from the campus.

In the summer after Hoover's freshman year Professor Branner got him a job with the Geological Survey of Arkansas, of which Branner had been state geologist, at $60 a month and expenses. In his two subsequent Stanford summers he worked for the United States Geological Survey in California and in Nevada. That first summer, "I did my job on foot, mostly alone, stopping at nights at the nearest cabin," in the Ozarks, making systematic notes, gathering and filing away facts, observations. The mountaineers were suspicious of traveling inquirers: "I finally gave up trying to explain." In the subsequent summers Hoover was "far happier," he writes. He worked as a "cub assistant" to Dr. Waldemar Lindgren, riding a horse all day and camping out with the survey team at night. Hoover very much wanted this job. At the first of the post-sophomore summer he was not yet employed, so he and a friend canvassed San Francisco for contacts for putting up billboard advertising. They signed up "a few hundred dollars" worth of contracts and went to work. Then Hoover heard of the geological survey and that there was a place for him with it. He walked eighty miles in three days to take it on.

Hoover's exact role in these two latter summers needs specification. He was, "as the youngest member of the Geological party," the disbursing officer: "I had to buy supplies and keep the accounts according to an elaborate book of regulations which provided wondrous safeguards for the public treasury." Carefulness by the book again, combined with outdoor energy and listening to the experts around the campfire.

Hoover returned to Stanford and extended his business enterprises. For a brief time he was a shortstop on the baseball team but soon became manager, "arranging games, collecting the gate money and otherwise finding cash for equipment and uniforms." He did so well that he was advanced to manager of the football team. One game produced $30,018. Hoover was acquiring a reputation for management. Operating in a new and developing environment without precedents he was under demand as the man who could—and would—take care of a wide variety of chores and enterprises for his fellows. Branner knew him for his efficiency; when other students complained that Hoover seemed to have too much pull with the famous geologist, he replied "But I can tell Hoover to do a thing and never think of it again." These talents also gave him his start in campus politics.

His start in campus politics

Like Coolidge, Hoover was a "Barbarian" at Stanford. Fraternities developed quickly among the richer students interested in social prominence. He was not one of those. Sam Collins, one of the oldest members of Hoover's class, had proposed the cooperative rooming house at the beginning of their sophomore year. Collins was impressed with Hoover's system and order in straightening out the finances. Under Collin's tutelage Hoover first got involved in college politics when he was brought in with a group of "Barbarians" that organized to overthrow fraternity control of the student offices and activities. A zealot named "Sosh" (for "socialist") Zion declared his candidacy for student body president; "Collins swung in behind him in this campaign, and Hoover followed." He was assigned to canvass the "camp," the students who lived in rough shacks left over by the workers constructing the new college. Still he was "rather inarticulate—this repressed boy of eighteen," but he did what he could and the Barbs won, in a close vote.

The next summer Hoover worked for Dr. Lindgren, but he also thought about ways of organizing the many student activities at Stanford, some of which had been very sloppily run and one of which had had a scandal. Hoover returned in the fall with a draft of a new constitution in which student activities would be brought together under the control of the student body. In addition to a president and a football manager, a treasurer, bonded and double-audited, would handle the finances. Hoover's plan was modified in some detail in bull sessions with Collins and others; they decided to put off a move for it until electing, under the existing rules, a student government sympathetic to the plan the following spring.

In the spring term this group gathered again and developed a ticket, with Lester Hinsdale as candidate for president, Herbert Hicks for football manager, and Herbert Hoover for treasurer. Hoover was reluctant. He thought the treasurer, who would collect a salary, should be a graduate student.

> "But there's the salary," they said: "you can drop your work for Doc Branner and your laundry agency. The job will support you."
>
> "No, sir!" responded Hoover, emphatically. "If I accept this nomination and get elected, there's one thing sure. I take no salary. Otherwise, they'll say I'm backing the new constitution just to get a paid job!" (Irwin, 1928, p. 54)

The "3-H" ticket won. Sosh Zion opposed the salary. Hoover refused to take it, though he worked like a demon for the remaining two years at Stanford as treasurer. The new student government got the student body to pass the new constitution.

Hoover spent the following summer working again for Dr. Lindgren, who put Hoover's name with his own on the various maps and reports. "Years later, Hoover confessed to a friend that no subsequent honor had puffed him up so much as this."

The next autumn, Hoover's junior year, he was busy running a lecture series, keeping the records and accounts for athletic events, and generally making himself useful. As Will Irwin recalled,

> In the conferences over this or that problem of our bijou party in a toy state he seemed hesitant of advancing an opinion. Then, when everyone else had expressed himself, he would come in with the final wise word . . . After all, ours was the world in miniature. I lived to see him in councils whose decisions meant life or death for millions; yet it was always the same mind and the same method. (Irwin, 1928, p. 62)

Hoover, in other words, was one of the boys, but at the edges of the group in most of their activities. He was the reliable treasurer, the arranger of meetings, the hard-working but shy and restrained person. He was valued for his virtues, particularly his energy and carefulness, his thoroughgoing honesty. He was never a charismatic leader at Stanford. In nearly all of his activities someone else—usually someone older like Professor Branner or Professor Lindgren or Sam Collins or Lester Hinsdale—took the lead, and Hoover followed and served. Things got solved at Stanford in the caucus, and Hoover took his part there. But there is not, in all of this student political and business activity, any record of his ever having spoken to a large gathering of his classmates. He was the man behind the scenes. He made friends, but many were the sort of friends whose respect is stronger than their affection.

In words, then, Hoover was restrained and not very expressive. In work he devoted all his energies to concentrated effort. In his personal relations he was a quiet, behind-the-scenes coordinator, not a leader. And so he was as President of the United States.

A Summary of Main Themes

The links between each style at the time of first independent political success and in the Presidency are clear in these two cases. Briefly put:

For Coolidge, *rhetoric* in the presidency consisted of (a) serious, abstract, epigramatic addresses, full of themes from Garman, delivered much like his serious debates and speeches at Amherst, and (b) witty banter with reporters, much like his funny speeches to his fellow undergraduates. As President he avoided as much of the *business* of the office as he could; work on detail had played little or no part in his Amherst success. As President he avoided close personal relationships, keeping others at a distance with mildly aggressive wit; at Amherst intimate friendship or close cooperation had never been his style.

For Hoover, *rhetoric* was impossibly hard, and he failed at it, as words had so often failed him at Stanford. Forced to speak, he fell back on his mother's Quaker mysticism and his uncle's phony advertising. His whole soul was poured into the *business* of the office, meticulous attention to detail, and careful designs for the arrangement of things. At Stanford very similar efforts had brought him money, independence, respect, and acceptance. In *personal relations* President Hoover tried desperately, in conference after conference, to repeat his success at Stanford in gaining cooperation by mastering details and presenting his plan.

The similarities are evident. Analyzed retrospectively here, they seem amenable to discernment in their earlier forms by an analyst attuned to the role demands of the Presidency.

Presidential Style and First Independent Political Success

There are fundamentally three steps in this argument. One is that there is such a thing as Presidential style, in the sense of habitual patterns of performance in response to recurrent role demands. I have tried to illustrate how the flow of energy and affect in three channels captures, within a broader typological framework, the major dimensions of such styles. Presidents tend to solve their rhetorical problems, their problems of managing business, and their problems of adapting in close personal relations in characteristic, patterned ways, not randomly or simply as flexible, rational responses to historical events.

Second, there is an identifiable formative period, that of first independent political success, in which the major elements of presidential style are exhibited. Personality formation is a long developmental process, subject to change before and after this period. But the *main, adaptively strategic, politically relevant action patterns* are evidenced most clearly when a young man, drawing together themes from his past, present, and anticipated future, answers for himself the question, "What works for me?" The fit between Presidential style and the style of the formative period is not vague or mysterious, but direct: in rhetoric, business management, and personal relations Presidents tend to behave as they did when they first found a way to succeed with these tools.

The third step in the argument is less clear. Why does this congruence occur? The answers are speculative. Most probably, the strength of the adaptive pattern derives from the confluence, in its original formation, of (a) satisfaction of strong needs for compensation for earlier deprivations, (b) at least some resources from the past applicable to present achievement, and (c) a favorable set of opportunities. At a deeper level of analysis this pattern's staying power derives from a solution to the Eriksonian identity crisis; it may represent the behavioral manifestation of an intensely emotional late-adolescent trial and victory. The outward signs of the formative period are a new surge of success on one's own, a new way of linking oneself to others and a new fame. To the psychoanalyst these may be signs only, referents to much deeper developments in the meanings of work and luck, love and hate, thought and word. Psychoanalytic data would reveal, one suspects, such factors contributing strongly to habit formation in this critical period.

At an even more speculative level the analogy between being President and emerging as a successful young adult with an individual style can be posed. Both are in some sense culminations of preparatory stages, modes in the curve of life, high points of achievement beyond which one may never go. Both are unique experiences, in the double sense that neither ever happens twice in the same life and that no two persons work them out in the same ways. Both highlight the lone individual discovering what he can make of a situation in which a great deal depends on his personal choices. A new President, scanning (though seldom consciously) his life's repertoire of successful strategies, might well turn to those which had worked so well for him as he became a man.

A few cases plus speculation do not make a theory. Yet as these ideas are refined they may find application in stylistic analysis not only of past Presidents but also of men yet to be Presidents. At that point we may be able to move beyond some of the many uncertainties of prediction, to guess better than we have, and before the fact, what the most powerful politician in the world will do with that power.

Following "A General Mapping Scheme for Understanding Presidential Behavior," the distinction between and linkage of character and style are illustrated in the cases of Taft, Truman, Eisenhower, Lyndon Johnson, and Nixon.

4

Character and Style

THE PRESIDENT IS a lonely figure in the midst of a crowd of helpers. He must share the work; he cannot share the core responsibility. He may try, as Harding did, to escape this tension by surrounding himself with advisers he can give in to, but he finds in that strategy no way out when their counsel is divided. He may, as Wilson did, seek escape by turning inward, with a private declaration of independence, but only at the risk of mistake and failure in ventures where cooperation is essential. The endless speculation about who has the President's confidence—and who is losing it and who is gaining it as issues shift—reflects a general recognition that the way a President defines and relates to his close circle of confidants has significance for policy. Detailed studies tend to confirm this general opinion, in such relationships as Wilson with House, Franklin Roosevelt with Howe and Hopkins, and Eisenhower with Sherman Adams. Obviously, important policy choices involve several major factors; this is one of them.

The variations suggest that designing advice-making machinery for the President—that is, the right system for all future Presidents—may be beside the point. For example, a system which mobilizes intellectuals through ad hoc commissions will not work for a President who is disdainful of intellectuals and suspicious of commissions. The structure must fit the man if it is to be effective. The hard question is how to produce that fit. That requires a way of anticipating the ways a President's needs, values, and habits are likely to connect with alternative advisory relationships. In turn, that calls for concepts which will highlight, amidst the flux of individual idiosyncrasies, those characteristics most relevant for discerning regularities in the man's links with his friends at the office.

In this chapter I will first suggest a general mapping scheme for successive approximations to understanding Presidential behavior. This is advanced very tentatively as a framework to be corrected and supplemented as individual cases are analyzed. Second, I will concentrate on one area of the map: the relations between character and style in the President's adaptation to the interpersonal aspects of his role. Four cases will be reviewed briefly. Third, I will present an estimate of President Nixon's performance in this area, with attention to the possibilities for attenuating the dangers inherent in his character-style combination.

The ultimate purposes of these explorations are to develop an explanatory theory of Presidential behavior and to use that theory for assessing candidates in the future.

A General Mapping Scheme for Understanding Presidential Behavior

The scheme outlined below is best considered as a paradigm of accentuations, in this sense of Harold Lasswell's:

> We note first the importance of recognizing what is meant by the *accentuation* of power. Accentuation is a conception of cultural relativity, and it implies that the political type developed in one setting may attach very different importance to power from that given to it by the political type elsewhere. . . . [R]elative stress on power is what we mean by its accentuation.[1]

In this setting—within a given political culture and a given political role—we are interested in identifying the kinds of accentuations most

Figure 1 A Paradigm of Accentuations

Stages of definition	Factors in experience and performance			Key developmental/indicative phase
	(A) Words	(B) Work	(C) Persons	(D)
1. Character	Criteria of self-judgment	Orientation toward action	Affective response to self and others	Childhood
2. Worldview	Ideological investments	View of social causality	View of human nature, loyalties	Adolescence
3. Style	Rhetoric	Decision management	Personal relations	Early adulthood
4. Climate of expectations	Legitimizing	Politicizing	Normalizing	Nomination and campaign
5. Power situation	Public support	Washington support	White House support	Election and inauguration

likely to be important for the man's performance as President. So it is not a matter of some qualities being present and others absent, but of the relative strength of and the balance among the relevant qualities. Furthermore this scheme is, at this stage, closer to Lasswell's ideas of a "developmental construct" than to his characterization of "scientific propositions." That is, it projects probable trends and continuities as they develop in the life history and points to possible indicators of those trends. From these initial posings we may be able to move on to explanatory hypotheses, suggesting why certain continuities occur.

"Factors in Experience and Performance" refers to three broad dimensions of life as an enterprise in which the individual receives from and acts upon his world. In analyzing the opportunities the Presidential role affords, I found it useful to focus on the President's rhetoric—his relating to public audiences, on decision management—his relating to the flow of details and demands for choice he encounters, and on personal relations—his relating to the close circle of advisors and opponents who surround him. Identification of these simple parts of the President's role led into explorations of the larger dimensions of words, work, and persons in pre-Presidential life histories. By that route I began to see how the President's rhetoric, for example, traced back to the meanings public expressiveness had had in the development of his style as he emerged from relative obscurity to relative prominence, usually in early adulthood; how that in turn drew content from the ideological investments he had developed as he learned a way of connecting his beliefs with those of his culture, particularly in adolescence; and how these beliefs had grown out of an even earlier set of learnings about who one is and ought to be.

Similarly, the dimension I call "work" sensitizes the observer to connections among all the ways an individual relates to action and effort: most basically whether his fundamental character tends toward making his environment, or complying with its demands, or withdrawing from adaptive effort, or some relatively more flexible combination and alternation of these stances. In terms of the worldview, the question translates into how he comes to view the pace and development of change in the larger world and how he relates his sense of his own development to that. Is it that life rolls on from age to age the same, as it seemed to Coolidge? Or is all flux and confusion and fad as Harding appears to have felt? Or is there some mysterious key to grace, some magic moment when the right move will shake the world? These assumptions about social causality tend to reinforce or conflict with the practical habits a man pursues as he learns what kind of work succeeds for him.

Similarly the "persons" factor embraces one's core appreciation of oneself and significant others as fundamentally lovable or not; one's connection of these feelings with a view of human nature as various or unitary, attractive or repulsive, trustworthy or devious, and with one's special loyalties, memberships, and identifications; and one's style of behavior in dealing with the human environment.

Freud said that to be happy is to love and to work, to which must be added: to believe. Somehow every man answers these questions in his life: What is worth believing? What is worth trying? Who is worth loving? More concretely: Presidents must adapt to intense role demands that they communicate guidance, operate productively, and cooperate closely with others. These adaptive opportunities represent parts of larger contexts in which the search for meaning and purpose, the discovery of a style of acting, and the extension of personal trust and affection are critical.

The "Stages of Definition" refer to an additive sequence by which progressive clarifications of behavior can be obtained. Thus character is seen as a general stance toward the self and the environment; worldview adds the content of differentiated beliefs about reality; and style focuses on the processes by which character and worldview are translated into patterns of activity. Empirical variations show the indeterminacies in this sequence—there are compulsive liberals and compulsive conservatives, hopeful and skeptical rhetoricians, specialists in personal relations who are deeply aggressive and those who are deeply loving, etc. Isolating these stages analytically is meant to simplify actual complexity without falling into the trap of a characterological reductionism. Furthermore they enable one to grasp the importance of learning and habit development without losing sight of the more fundamental character forces which energize these life-historical accretions.

The right-hand column, "Key Developmental/Indicative Phase," suggests (somewhat ambiguously) a dynamic and an evidential proposition. Dynamically, the *primary* life-stage in which character is formed is childhood, the *primary* time of focusing on an identity which links one with larger social meanings is adolescence, and the *primary* stage for adopting lasting habit patterns for success in a particular arena of life is early adulthood. The emphases expresses my awareness that these developmental stages are times of special accentuation, not final, isolated freezings. Cases will differ in the sharpness with which development occurs. For example, it now seems to me that the President with compulsive tendencies is far more likely to have developed a political style in some relatively short, dramatic period of compensation than is the President with tendencies toward a pattern of compliance. Nevertheless, it remains to be seen how widely the hypothesized linkage between life-stages and personal development holds.

The "Indicative" element suggests a different, evidential proposition. Leaving aside when a stage of personal definition may in fact develop, we are also interested in economical ways to draw together the evidence for comparisons among cases. The question is one of the clarity of our vision as observers rather than the reality of the process being observed. For example, a person's propensity for perceiving the world as a jungle may have been growing in him for a long time, but may emerge with special vividness in adolescence, making the theme much more visible (in biographies, for instance) than it was or will be later in his story.

I have said nothing yet of the fourth and fifth rows in this paradigm of accentuations, "Climate of Expectations" and "Power Situation." These represent far leaps in time beyond the first three and even farther leaps in terms of my own understanding; they are preliminary guesses about distinctions that may turn out to be important. They refer to the President's perceptions of the basic state of the political environment as he moves into office. I think every Presidential election year defines a climate of expectations, a widely shared sense of the time's most critical needs. This climate tends to stress some combination of three themes. In a "legitimizing" period, the attentive public shows a central concern for morality in politics, for cleansing the government, for reversing trends toward deteriorations of trust. Often this concern takes a nonpartisan or antipartisan thrust: the need is for good character in the Presidency, for a man who will rise above politics, a man of all the people, a Solomon, an Eisenhower. But much of the energy behind this theme is reactive; there is a sense that politicians have poisoned the well of national loyalty (1952?), that immorality threatens the national conscience (1928?), that some bizarre distortion of values may lead the nation away from its established traditions (1964?). The answer is a man of high principle who will restore respect and confidence in the fundamental moral rightness of democratic leadership. (Such a man is not always available.)

Alternatively, the climate of expectations may stress changes or confirmations of policy trends, demands to politicize the nation in the sense of emphasizing a programmatic direction. The question at the forefront of public attention is, "Which way for America?" The President is made to think he has a mandate to implement a partisan program. He is expected to perform as a representative of his party or faction, whether that means expanding the role of the government in meeting human needs or removing deadening government restrictions on the nation's energies. The emphasis is less on virtue, more on power. Such elections (1912, 1924, 1936, 1948, 1960?) tend to polarize the electorate along partisan, programmatic lines. In such elections, about half the people lose. The President is apt to enter (or reenter) office ready to implement a "mandate."

A third type of climatic emphasis is the appeal for rest, the desire for a breathing space, a peaceable time, an end to troubles and conflicts. The stress is on well-being as a value. In memory of 1920, I call this theme "normalizing." The appeal is for relief from the worries, the social anxieties, the unwanted uncertainties the nation has been experiencing, not on moral uplift or partisan programs. There was much of this *dona-nobis-pacem* feeling about 1968—and in 1932.

For legitimizing, the people want father; the election should be a coronation. For politicizing, big brother, empowered in a victory celebration. For normalizing, mother and Thanksgiving dinner.[2] The columnar placement of these climate of expectation themes should be obvious by this point.

A President's character, worldview, and style may or may not fit well with the climate of expectations he confronts. Similarly the power situation he faces has different implications for different Presidents. For example, an activist President bent on redirecting the nation's course cares much more about the shape of power than does a President who intends to change little or nothing. The alignment of political forces a President encounters as he moves into office—the structure of power opportunities—breaks down conveniently into the public arena in which his rhetoric plays the main part, the Washington community of Congress, the Court, the bureaucracy, the lobbies, etc., in which he may struggle for favorable decisions, and the close crew of assistants in and around the White House with whom he interacts intimately. A survey of the power situation would acquire explanatory meaning only in the light of the President's style and purpose. The usual mistake is to think that every President is hungry for all the power he can get.

We reach for a map when we want to get somewhere. Until some question of relationship among or configurations within some locale is defined, the above map is useful only to highlight important factors which might otherwise be forgotten. So far, I have explored the functioning and formation of a highly distinctive rhetorical style,[3] developed a similar but comparative analysis of the styles of two "weak" Presidents,[4] and prepared a short study of direct resonances between character and political events—direct in the sense that the usual mediating function of style is bypassed.[5] Throughout these studies I am trying to maintain a focus on possibilities for prediction (so that, eventually, candidates can be assessed) and on the significant political consequences of various Presidential performances. In this chapter I want to look at interactions of character and style—ways in which a set of politically relevant adaptive habit patterns (style) many conflict or concord with a President's basic character orientation. As mentioned previously, style adoptions in early adulthood occur in a context where character comes together with a particular set of historical circumstances which may or may not facilitate a style consonant with all aspects of that character. For instance, Hoover clearly belongs among the compulsive characters in the Presidency; there is much evidence of his driving energy, depressed mood, orientation toward manipulating his environment, his ambition, and his problems with controlling aggression. These forces fed his conscious desire to use the Presidency for positive achievement, for reshaping his environment. The Hoover character was in these ways similar to the Andrew and Lyndon Johnson characters, for example. But Hoover's style, developed when he emerged as a campus political leader at Stanford, was centered in the management of decisions (through careful work on details) and personal relations (gaining acceptance for prepackaged proposals in small groups). Rhetoric played virtually no part in his first independent political success at Stanford, where he failed English four years running and was famous for his shyness. In the Presidency, Hoover had to speak, though he hated the office's demands for dramatization. His driving ambitions ran head-on into his rhetorical blankness and he had to invent some way to reach beyond this stylistic gap to get at the public. Lacking the guidance of successful experience in rhetoric, he drew upon his character-rooted sense that words are essentially devices for persuasion—propaganda weapons rather than symbols for realities or terms of commitment. The result was a rhetoric of reassurance, a pollyana optimism so obviously out of line with national conditions that its main effect was to increase, not allay, national anxieties. In this case, then, a marked imbalance in style opened the way for the emergence of character forces. Forced to perform, but lacking habits, the President fell back on character.

"Character" comes from the Greek word for engraving; it is what life has marked into a man's being. "Style" is the stylus or instrumentation by which a man marks his environment. A complete character and style analysis for any individual political leader requires a close examination of his life history, with special attention to periods in which self-esteem is linked with experiments in adaptation. For comparative purposes, however, it is useful to begin with cruder first approximations, sorting the Presidents into rough types as tending to accentuate certain broad character and style features.

The general character tendencies are indicated by a combination of two simple dimensions, activity-passivity and positive-negative affect toward one's activity. These are independent dimensions; they interact to produce four types:[6]

Active-positive. The combination represents a congruence between action and affect typically based on relatively high self-esteem and relative success in relating to the environment. There is an orientation toward productiveness as a value and an ability to move flexibly among various orientations toward action as rational adaptation to opportunities and demands. The self is seen as developing over time toward relatively well-defined personal goals. The emphasis on rational mastery in this pattern can lead to mistakes in appreciating important political irrationalities.

Active-negative. The basic contradiction is between relatively intense effort and relatively low personal reward for that effort. The activity has a compulsive quality; politics appears as a means for compensating for power deprivations through ambitious striving. The stance toward the environment is aggressive and the problem of managing aggressive feelings is persistent. The self-image is typically vague and temporally discontinuous. Life is a hard struggle to achieve and hold power, hampered by the condemnations of a perfectionistic conscience.

Passive-positive. This is the receptive, compliant, other-directed character whose life is a search for affection as a reward for being agreeable and cooperative rather than personally assertive. The contradiction is between low self-esteem (on grounds of feeling unlovable, unattractive) and a superficial optimism. A hopeful attitude helps the person deny inferiority and elicit encouragement from others. The dependence and fragility of this character orientation make disappointment in politics likely.

Passive-negative. The factors are consistent but do not account for the presence of the person in a political role. That is explained by a character-rooted orientation toward doing dutiful service; the compensation is for low self-esteem based on a sense of uselessness. Typically the person is relatively well-adapted to certain nonpolitical roles, but lacks the experience and flexibility to perform effectively as a political leader. The tendency is to withdraw from the conflict and uncertainty of politics to an emphasis on vague principles (particularly prohibitions) and procedural arrangements.

A first approximation to a President's style is simply the configuration of energy investments among rhetoric, decision management, and personal relations. The emphasis is captured crudely in the way he allocates his time, and somewhat more precisely in the way he allocates his attention and emotion. Beyond such allocations are the accentuations within each style area. A rhetorical specialist like Woodrow Wilson, for example, may shape his sermons quite differently from other rhetoricians like Andrew Johnson or John F. Kennedy. These variants are likely to be linked to the experience in early adulthood of the man's first independent political success, that period of style adoption in which he found marked infusions of confidence from relative success, a relatively new and special relationship to group

Figure 2   Typology of Presidential Character

Level of activity

		Active	Passive
Affect toward his activity	positive	Truman	Taft
	negative	L. Johnson (Nixon)	Eisenhower

life, and a relatively sudden emergence from obscurity to wider attention. A scanning of the life-historical context in which these early changes occurred, and of the ways they got worked out in subsequent political situations adds closer approximations.

Enough conceptualizing. I want to turn now to the four cases, noted in figure 2, of Taft, Truman, Eisenhower, and Johnson, with a provisional set of observations on Nixon in order to illustrate how character and style interactions help to explain peculiarities in the President's personal relations.

Some Presidential Cases

William Howard Taft: passive-positive

What lends drama to Presidential performances is the interplay of character and style. Consider William Howard Taft. In character, Taft was from the beginning a genial, agreeable, friendly, compliant person, much in need of affection from wife, family, and friends. He fits the passive-positive category most closely, with his slow-moving pace and his optimistic grin. Taft endured several illnesses and a severe accident during childhood. His family was remarkable for its close, affectionate relationships. I think he was spoiled. His father expected his children to do well in school, and Will did. By his Yale days he was a big, handsome campus favorite, with many friends but no really intimate ones. By his twenties he was a fat man. Always sensitive to criticism and anxious for approval, he repeatedly entered new offices with a feeling of personal inadequacy to the tasks before him. He was a humane friend of the men and women around him. His mother often said that "the love of approval was Will's besetting fault." As Secretary of War under Theodore Roosevelt, he won the President's approval by complying willingly with every assignment and by repeatedly expressing his devotion to him.

Taft's political style developed in his career as a lawyer and judge. By a series of family connections and historical accidents (Taft said he always had his plate turned right side up when offices were being handed out), he found his way into the judiciary and adopted the style of the legalist, the law-worshipper. He found the bench comfortable and secure, stable and safe, honorable and respected. He developed a decision-management style based firmly in a narrow, literal, conservative concept of a judge's relationship to the law. Principles were applied to cases to give verdicts, period.

The conflict between Taft's character and style was largely latent until after he became President in 1909. In the White House he had to choose between loyalty and law. His biographer, Henry F. Pringle, wrote:

> Indeed, one of the astonishing things about Taft's four years in the White House was the almost total lack of men, related or otherwise, upon whom he could lean. He had no Cabot Lodge. He had no Colonel House. For the most part he faced his troubles alone.

Again there is the pattern of his earlier years: many friends, no intimates. And from his character came also his worshipful, submissive orientation toward Theodore Roosevelt, which he continued to express in letters and conversation as President. "I can never forget," he wrote to Roosevelt from the White House, "that the power that I now exercise was a voluntary transfer from you to me, and that I am under obligation to you to see to it that your judgment in selecting me as your successor and in bringing about the succession shall be vindicated according to the standards which you and I in conversation have always formulated."

Taft saw himself as a follower of TR—but not as an imitator of the TR style. "There is no use trying to be William Howard Taft with Roosevelt's ways," he wrote. Taft had learned, as a lawyer and judge, to manage decisions by the application of legal principles: "Our President has no initiative in respect to legislation given to him by law except that of mere recommendation, and no legal or formal method of entering into argument and discussion of the proposed legislation while pending in Congress," Taft said in a post-Presidential lecture in which he disagreed explicitly with Roosevelt's view that the "executive power was limited only by specific restrictions and prohibitions appearing in the Constitution." This was more than a matter of intellectual principle. Taft's judicial stance worked—as long he was in judicial roles—to protect him from the fires of controversy. But in the White House, he abhorred the heat of the kitchen. As his Presidential aid wrote, "I have never known a man to dislike discord as much as the President. He wants every man's approval, and a row of any kind is repugnant to him."

President Taft had once told an aide that "if I only knew what the President [i.e., Roosevelt—for a long time Taft referred to TR this way] wanted . . . I would do it, but you know he has held himself so aloof that I am absolutely in the dark. I am deeply wounded." But Taft's character-rooted affectionate loyalty to Roosevelt inevitably came into conflict with Taft's legalistic style. The initial issue was the Ballinger-Pinchot controversy over conservation policy. The details are not important here. What is significant to this discussion is that Taft attempted to solve a broad but intensely political conflict within his administration through a strict application of the law. As he wrote of the controversy at the time: "I get very impatient at criticism by men who do not know what the law is, who have not looked it up, and yet ascribe all sorts of motives to those who live within it."

Slowly he began to see the Roosevelt Presidency as less than perfection, flawed by irregular procedures. He tried to find a way out which would not offend TR. But as criticisms from TR's followers mounted, negative references to Roosevelt crept into Taft's correspondence. The two managed to maintain a surface amiability in their meeting when Roosevelt returned from Africa, but as Roosevelt began making speeches, Taft found more and more cause for Constitutional alarm. When Roosevelt attacked property rights and then the Supreme Court, Taft became edgy and nervous. He lost his temper on the golf links. He began criticizing Roosevelt in less and less private circles. The man who had written in 1909 that "my coming into office was exactly as if Roosevelt had succeeded himself," wrote in 1912 of "facing as I do a crisis with Mr. Roosevelt."

The crisis came a piece at a time. In 1911 Taft still hoped to avoid a fight, though he saw Roosevelt as "so lacking in legal knowledge that his reasoning is just as deficient as Lodge's." Roosevelt continued to criticize. Taft stuck by his legal guns. However, he confided to his chief aide, Archie Butt: "It is hard, very hard, Archie, to see a devoted friendship going to pieces like a rope of sand."

By the end of 1911 it was clear that TR would not support Taft for relection. As Pringle says of Taft's mood:

> He was heartsick and unhappy. "If I am defeated," he wrote, "I hope that somebody, sometime, will recognize the agony of spirit that I have undergone." Yet Taft remained in the contest. He fought to the limit of his too-tranquil nature because he envisioned the issue as more than a personal one. The "whole fate of constitutional government," he said, was at stake.

Roosevelt attacked "legalistic justice" as "a dead thing" and called on the people to "never forget that the judge is as much a servant of the people as any other official." At first Taft refrained from answering what he privately called TR's "lies and unblushing misrepresentations," but in April of 1913, confessing that "this wrenches my soul" and "I do not want to fight Theodore Roosevelt," he defended himself in public:

> Neither in thought nor word nor action have I been disloyal to the friendship I owe Theodore Roosevelt. . . . I propose to examine the charges he makes against me, and to ask you whether in making them he is giving me a square deal.

Taft's nerves were shattered by the ordeal of attacking TR, that man "who so lightly regards constitutional principles, and especially the independence of the judiciary, one who is so naturally impatient of legal restraints, and of due legal procedure, and who has so misunderstood what liberty regulated by law is. . . ." Exhausted, depressed and shaken, Taft was found by a reporter with his head in his hands. He looked up to say, "Roosevelt was my closest friend," and began to weep.

In 1912 the Republican party split apart and the Democrats captured the government.

The break between Taft and Roosevelt had numerous levels and dimensions; one of those was clearly the conflict within Taft between his legalistic style and his submissive character. Taft's decision-management approach—the application of principles to cases—served him well, both before and after he was President. It failed him as President. If he had had a different character, he might have pushed Roosevelt aside as soon as he won the Presidency, as Woodrow Wilson did the New Jersey bosses when he won his governorship. As it was, Taft nearly tore himself apart—and did help tear his party apart—by hanging onto his leader long after Roosevelt had, in Taft's eyes, broken the law.

Harry S. Truman: active-positive

Harry S. Truman belongs among the active-positive Presidents. His activity is evident; beginning with a brisk walk early in the morning, he went at the job with all his might. And despite occasional discouragement, he relished his experience. His first memory was of his laughter while chasing a frog across the backyard; his grandmother said, "It's very strange that a two-year-old has such a sense of humor." When Democratic spirits hit the bottom in the 1948 campaign, Truman said, "Everybody around here seems to be nervous but me." And he played the piano.

Although he was in his sixties throughout his long stay in the White House, he put in sixteen to eighteen hours a day at Presidenting, but "was fresher at the end than I was at the beginning," according to Charles Ross. Truman often got angry but rarely depressed. Once he compared the criticism he got with the "vicious slanders" against Washington, Lincoln, and Andrew Johnson. Truman expressed his buoyancy under attack in these words (quoted in William Hillman's *Mr. President*):

> So I don't let these things bother me for the simple reason that I know that I am trying to do the right thing and eventually the facts will come out. I'll probably be holding a conference with Saint Peter when that happens. I never give much weight or attention to the brickbats that are thrown my way. The people

that cause me trouble are the good men who have to take these brickbats for me.

And then there is that ultimate, almost implausible indication of persistent optimism: he is said to have enjoyed being Vice President (for eighty-two days). The White House staff called him "Billie Spunk."

Truman had a strong father (nicknamed "Peanuts" for his short stature) and an affectionate mother. The family had more than its share of difficulties, especially financial ones. They moved several times in Harry's early years. His severe vision problem kept him out of school until he was eight, and at nine he nearly died of diphtheria. But he appears to have come through it with an unusually strong store of self-confidence, ready to endure what had to be, ready to reach out when opportunities presented themselves. He drew on a home in which the rules said: Do the right thing, Love one another, and By their fruits shall ye know them. When he telephoned his mother to ask if she had listened to his inauguration as Vice President on the radio, she answered: "Yes. I heard it all. Now you behave yourself up there, Harry. You behave yourself!"

Truman's drive for decisions, his emphasis on results, his faith in rational persuasion, his confidence in his own values, his humor about himself, and his ability to grow into responsibility all fit the active-positive character. The character shows itself as an orientation, a broad direction of energy and affect, a tendency to experience self and others in a certain way. Truman attacked life; he was not withdrawn. He emphasized his independence; he was not compliant. He laughed at himself; he was not compulsive (though he showed some tendencies in that direction). His character thus provided a foundation for the transcendence of his defenses, for devoting his attention to the realities beyond himself.

Style is what he built on those foundations. Truman's style developed in two main spurts. "So far as its effect on Harry Truman was concerned," his biographer writes, "World War I released the genie from the bottle." He had worked in a bank, farmed, taken a flier on an oil-drilling enterprise, joined the Masons, and fallen in love with Bess Wallace. The family was having financial difficulties again. His father died in 1914, when Harry was thirty. At the outbreak of the war he joined the National Guard and was elected lieutenant by his friends. Sent away from home to Oklahoma, he became regimental canteen officer, with Eddie Jacobson as his assistant. The other Fort Sill canteens had heavy losses, but the Truman-Jacobson enterprise returned 666 percent on the initial investment in six months. In charge for the first time, Truman had shown that he could succeed through careful management. Later, in France, he was put in charge of a rowdy flock of Irish pranksters loosely organized as a field-artillery battery. One former officer who could not control the men had been thrown out of the Army; another had broken down under the strain. Upon assuming command, Truman recalled later, "I was the most thoroughly scared individual in that camp. Never on the front or anywhere else have I been so nervous." Alfred Steinberg, in *The Man from Missouri*, gives this account of how Truman handled himself:

> "Men," he told the sergeants and corporals, "I know you're been making trouble for your previous commanders. From now on, you're going to be responsible for maintaining discipline in your squads and sections. And if there are any of you who can't, speak up right now and I'll bust you back right now."

Truman did his own reconnaissance at the front, to get his information first-hand. When his troops broke and ran under fire in "The Battle of Who Run":

> "I got up and called them everything I knew," said Truman. The curses that poured out contained some of the vilest four-letter words heard on the Western Front. Said Father Curtis Tiernan, the regiment's Catholic chaplain, who was on the scene, "It took the skin off the ears of those boys." The effect was amazing, Padre Tiernan recalled with pleasure. "It turned those boys right around."

"Captain Harry" came out of the war with the respect and admiration of his men. He had learned that his angry voice could turn the tide and that he could decide what to do if he got the facts himself and paid attention to the details. Most important, his style developed around intense loyalty in personal relations: everything depended on the stick-togetherness of imperfect allies.

After the war, Truman and Jacobson opened their famous haberdashery, serving mostly old Army buddies. An Army friend who happened to be a Missouri Pendergast got him into politics—not against his will. He ran for county judge and won; his performance in that office reconfirmed his faith in hard personal campaigning and in careful, honest business practice. During the campaign he was charged with voting for a member of the other party and he answered with his speech:

> You have heard it said that I voted for John Miles for county marshal. I'll have to plead guilty to that charge, along with 5,000 ex-soldiers. I was closer to John Miles than a brother. I have seen him in places that made hell look like a playground. I have seen him stick to his guns when Frenchmen were falling back. I have seen him hold the American line when only John Miles and his three batteries were between the Germans and a successful counterattack. He was of the right stuff, and a man who wouldn't vote for his comrade under circumstances such as these would be untrue to his country. I know that every soldier understands it. I have no apology to make for it.

These experiences reinforced and confirmed an emphasis Truman had grown up with. "If Mamma Truman was for you," he said, "she was for you, and as long as she lived I always knew there was one person who was in my corner." Throughout his political life Truman reiterated this for-me-or-against-me theme:

> "We don't play halfway politics in Missouri. When we start out with a man, if he is any good at all, we always stay with him to the end. Sometimes people quit me but I never quit people when I start to back them up."
>
> [To Admiral Leahy:] "Of course, I will make the decisions, and after a decision is made, I will expect you to be loyal."
>
> [Margaret Truman, on her father's philosophy:] ". . . 'the friends thou hast and their adoption tried, grapple them to thy soul with hoops of steel'. . . ."
>
> [From Truman's own memoirs:] "Vinson was gifted with a sense of personal and political loyalty seldom found among the top men in Washington. Too often loyalties are breached in Washington in the rivalries for political advantage."

[Truman on Tom Pendergast:] "I never deserted him when he needed friends. Many for whom he'd done much more than he ever did for me ran out on him when the going was rough. I didn't do that—and I am President of the United States in my own right!"

[Truman to Harry Vaughn:] "Harry, they're just trying to use you to embarrass me. You go up there, and tell 'em to go to hell. We came in here together and, God damn it, we're going out together!"

[Of Eisenhower's refusal to stand up for Marshall:] "You don't kick the man who made you."

What did this emphasis on loyalty mean for the Truman Presidency? The story of Truman's wrangles with aides high and low is well known. Conflicts, misunderstandings, scandals, and dismissals piled up: Byrnes, Wallace, Ickes, Louis Johnson, J. Howard McGrath, Morgenthau, MacArthur, Baruch, Clifford vs. Steelman, and the rag-tag crew of cronies and influenceables typified by Harry Vaughan. The landscape of the Truman administration was littered with political corpses. Both Presidential candidates in 1952 promised to clean up what Eisenhower called "the mess in Washington."

I think Patrick Anderson, in *The President's Men*,[7] is right when he sees the key to Truman's loyalty troubles "in the man himself, not in those who so poorly served him." Anderson continues:

Truman once said that his entire political career was based upon his World War I experience, upon the friends he made and the lessons he learned. It was as an army captain under fire in France that Harry Truman first learned that he was as brave and as capable as the next man. He learned, too, the rule that says an officer must always stand by his men. Perhaps he learned that rule too well; in later years he seemed to confuse standing by Harry Vaughan when he was under fire from Drew Pearson with standing by the men of the 35th Division when they were under fire from the Germans at Meuse-Argonne and Verdun.

After the war, he was a failure as a businessman; his success came in politics. It must have galled Truman that he owed his political success to the corruption-ridden Pendergast machine.

But he kept quiet, he kept his hands clean, he learned to mind his own business. That may be another lesson he learned too well. The most simple, most harsh explanation of Truman's tolerance is just this: You can take the politician out of the county courthouse, but you can't take the county courthouse out of the politician.

But it is not that simple. Another reason Truman stood by Vaughan and the others was no doubt simple political tactics: If you fire a man, you in effect admit wrongdoing; if you keep him, you can continue to deny it. More than by politics, however, Truman seems to have been motivated by stubborn loyalty to his friends. It was a sadly misguided loyalty, for Presidents owe a loyalty to the nation that transcends any allegiance to erring friends. Roosevelt understood this instinctively; Truman would not recognize it. Truman's dilemma was complicated by the fact that his nature was more sentimental than that of the other recent Presidents. It is often helpful for a President to be a ruthless son-of-a-bitch, particularly in his personal relationships; this, for better or worse, Truman was not.

There appears to have been a lapse in communication in each of Truman's "breaks" with such high-level personages as Wallace, Byrnes, Baruch, and MacArthur. Truman believed that he had made clear to the other fellow just how he must change his behavior; each of the others believed that Truman had endorsed him in the course he was pursuing. Truman seems to have been slowly, and then radically, disillusioned with men in whom he had placed his trust. He was not able to realize that the loyalties around a President are not black and white—as they are in battle or in a Missouri political campaign—but rather shade off from Vaughan-like sycophancy at one end of the spectrum to MacArthur-like independence at the other. For Truman, loyalties were hard and brittle; when they broke they broke. Before he became President, he had, after all, been the chief of loyal subordinates only twice: in the Army and as a "judge" in Missouri. It was natural for him to revert back to those times when he was again in charge.

In terms of our character and style analysis Truman shows one form of danger inherent in the political adaptation of the active-positive type. To oversimplify what is really much more complicated: the character who has overcome his own hang-ups, who has leaped over the barriers between himself and the real world, whose bent is toward rational mastery of the environment, is likely to forget, from time to time, that other persons, publics, and institutions maintain themselves in rather messier ways. In another context I have said this type may want a political institution "to deliberate like Plato's Academy and then take action like Caesar's army," neglecting the necessities of emotional inspiration and peaceful procedure. The type is also vulnerable to betrayal when he assumes that others who seem to share his purposes will see those purposes precisely as he does and govern their actions accordingly. He is especially prone to this mistake with respect to the active-negative type who is, on the surface, like him in many ways.

Truman's style exaggerated these characteristic vulnerabilities. What he had learned of himself when he was under twenty was shaped and channeled by what he learned of life when he was over thirty. Character fed style, style digested character. Amid many Presidential successes, most of his failures can be traced to a particular way in which style reinforced character trends.

Dwight D. Eisenhower: passive-negative

Eisenhower as President is best approximated in the passive-negative category, in which tendencies to withdraw predominate. On a great many occasions in the biographies Eisenhower is found asserting himself by denying himself; that is, by taking a strong stand against the suggestion that he take a strong stand.

No, he would not get down in the gutter with Joseph McCarthy; no, he would not stop the Cohn and Schine high jinks. Franklin Roosevelt had usurped Congressional powers, he thought, and he would not do that: "I want to say with all the emphasis at my command that this administration has absolutely *no* personal choice for a new Majority Leader. *We* are not going to get into *their* business." When "those damn monkeys on the Hill" acted up, he would stay out of it. Press conferences were another Rooseveltian mistake: "I keep telling you fellows I don't like to do this sort of thing." Was he under attack in the press? "Listen," Eisenhower said, "anyone who has time to listen to commentators or read columnists obviously doesn't have enough work to do." Should he engage in personal summitry on the international front? "This idea of the President of the United States going personally abroad to negotiate—it's just damn stupid."

With a new Cabinet, wouldn't it make sense to oversee them rather carefully? "I guess you know about as much about the job as I do," he told George Humphrey. His friend Arthur Larson wrote that Eisenhower found patronage "nauseating" and "partisan political effect was not only at the bottom of the list—indeed, it did not exist as a motive at all." In 1958 the President said, "Frankly, I don't care too much about the Congressional elections." Eisenhower disliked speechmaking (he had once been struck by lightning while delivering a lecture). Urged to address some meeting, he would typically say, "Well, all right, but not over twenty minutes." Sherman Adams writes that Eisenhower "focused his mind completely on the big and important aspects of the questions we discussed, shutting out with a strongly self-disciplined firmness the smaller and petty side issues when they crept into the conversation." In other words, he did not so much select problems upon which to concentrate as he selected an *aspect* of all problems—the aspect of principle.

When someone aggravated Eisenhower, he would write his "name on a piece of paper, put it in my lower desk drawer, and shut the drawer." When it came time to end his four-pack-a-day cigarette habit, "I found that the easiest way was just to put it out of your mind."

Eisenhower's tendency to move away from involvements, to avoid personal commitments, was supported by belief: "My personal convictions, no matter how strong, cannot be the final answer," he said. The definition of democracy he liked best was "simply the opportunity for self-discipline." As a military man he had detested and avoided politics at least since his first command, when a Congressman had pressed him for a favor. His beliefs were carved into epigrams:

> He that conquereth his own soul is greater than he who taketh a city.
> Forget yourself and personal fortunes.
> Belligerence is the hallmark of insecurity.
> Never lose your temper except intentionally.

It is the tone, the flavor, the aura of self-denial and refusal that counts in these comments. Eisenhower is not attacking or rejecting others; he is simply turning away from them, leaving them alone, refusing to interfere.

His character is further illuminated by his complaints, which cluster around the theme of being bothered. His temper flared whenever he felt that he was either being imposed upon or interfered with on matters he wanted others to handle. He "heatedly gave the Cabinet to understand that he was sick and tired of being bothered about patronage." "When does anybody get any time to think around here?" he complained to Adams. Robert Donovan said of Eisenhower: "Nothing gets him out of sorts faster than for a subordinate to come in and start to hem and haw about a decision. He wants the decision and not the thinking out loud." Eisenhower felt that his 1955 heart attack was triggered when he was repeatedly interrupted on the golf links by unnecessary phone calls from the State Department. In 1948, when he finally managed to stop the boomlet for his nomination, he said he felt "as if I've had an abscessed tooth pulled." He told a persistent reporter as the 1948 speculations continued: "Look, son, I cannot conceive of any circumstance that could drag out of me permission to consider me for any political post from dogcatcher to Grand High Supreme King of the Universe."

Why, then, did Eisenhower bother to become President? Why did he answer those phone calls on the golf links? Because he thought he ought to. He was a sucker for duty and always had been. Sentiments which would sound false for most political leaders ring true for Eisenhower:

> My only satisfaction in life is to hope that my effort means something to the other fellow. What can I do to repay society for the wonderful opportunities it has given me? . . . a decision that I have never recanted or regretted [was the decision] to perform every duty given me in the Army to the best of my ability and to do the best I could to make a creditable record, no matter what the nature of the duty. . . . in trying to explain to you a situation that has been tossed in my teeth more than once (my lack of extended troop duty in recent years), all I

accomplished was to pass up something I *wanted* to do, in favor of something I thought I *ought* to do.

He did not feel a duty to save the world or to become a great hero, but simply to contribute what he could, in the best way he was able. From the family Bible readings, from the sportsmanship of a boy who wanted nothing more than to be a first-rate athlete, from the West Point creed, Eisenhower felt, amid questions about many other things, that duty was a certainty.

In all these respects, and also in his personal comradeliness, Eisenhower fits the passive-negative (or "reluctant") type. The orientation is toward performing duty with modesty; the political adaptation is characterized by protective retreats to principle, ritual, and personal virtue. The political strength of this character is its legitimacy. It inspires trust in the incorruptibility and the good intentions of the man. Its political weakness is its inability to produce, though it may contribute by preventing. Typically, the passive-negative character presides over drift and confusion, partially concealed by the apparent orderliness of the formalities. Samuel Lubell caught the crux of this character when he saw in Eisenhower "one man's struggle between a passion for active duty and a dream of quiet retirement."

Eisenhower's political style, particularly his style in personal relations, channeled these character forces in an interesting way. At West Point he was a minor hell-raiser (eventually ranking 125th in a class of 164 in "conduct") and a dedicated athlete until an injury, incurred because he would not tell a sadistic riding instructor that he had a weak knee, removed him from competition. He missed combat in World War I and kicked around for a good many years in staff jobs and football coaching; he served seven years on the staff of that flamboyant self-dramatist, Douglas MacArthur, for whom Eisenhower learned to make a newly developing kind of military administration work.

The old structure of military command—the hierarchy—was giving way to a system less like a pyramid, more like a floating crap game, a system of interdependent functional specialties—teams—that had to be brought together around new technological and strategic concepts. Eisenhower mastered the skills this system increasingly demanded, particularly the ability to coordinate, to gather together the right threads into the right knot. It was *this* style, the style of the modern administrative team-coordinator, that stuck with Eisenhower on into his White House years. The danger of his "military mind" was not that he would be a martinet, a MacArthur; here Harry Truman misestimated him. It was Eisenhower's command habit of central coordination that shaped his behavior. The President, he said,

> must know the general purpose of everything that is going on, the general problem that is there, whether or not it is being solved or the solution is going ahead according to principles in which he believes and which he has promulgated; and, finally, he must say "yes" or "no."

The well-known staff system Eisenhower put into the Presidency was designed to leave him free to coordinate at the highest level. The trouble was that the level got higher and higher, more and more removed from the political battlefield, until, in his second term, Eisenhower had to break through a good many layers and circles to get at the controls of policy.

In the Army, Eisenhower's brand of coordination went forward in a context of command; the colonels were dependent on the generals. An order announced (after however much coordination) was an order to be executed. Not so in politics, where promulgation is just the beginning. In an Army at war, coordination takes place behind the advancing flag: the overriding purposes are not in question. Not so in the political "order," where the national purpose is continually questioned and redefined.

When Eisenhower had to deal with military matters as President, such as Lebanon and the Suez crisis, he could act with celerity and precision. He took his greatest pride in the fact that there had been eight years of peace during his administration. But at the same time his character and style fit together to contribute—along with many external factors—to a long list of less happy incidents and trends (Dixon-Yates, Dullesian brinksmanship, the Faubus and U-2 bumbles, the McCarthy contagion). He didn't mean it this way, but when Eisenhower said that "our system demands the Supreme Being," he was probably right.

Lyndon B. Johnson: active-negative

For this generation of President-watchers, it would be tedious to document President Lyndon B. Johnson's difficulties in personal relations. The bullyragging, the humiliations visited upon the men around him, are nearly as familiar as his rages against the Kennedy clan. By mid-1966 it was hard to find an independent voice among his intimate advisers. What had happened to a political style whose cornerstone was the expert manipulation of personal relations?

Johnson experienced his first independent political success as a student at Southwest Texas State Teachers College. Lyndon's mother pushed the boy to get an education; when he was four years old she persuaded the local schoolteacher to let him attend classes. In 1924 he graduated from high school at fifteen, the youngest of the six-member senior class as well as its president. That year he had lost an important debating contest ("I was so disappointed I went right into the bathroom and was sick"). The year before the family had moved back to a farm in Johnson City and stayed "just long enough for Daddy to go broke," Lyndon's sister recalled.

After high school Lyndon told all his friends he was through with school forever, despite his mother's urgings to go on. That summer he tried a clerical job for a few weeks but got discouraged and came home. Then Lyndon and two friends left home for California in an old car. A year and a half later, thin, broke, and hungry, he came back and found a job on a road gang for a dollar a day. There was some beer and girls and fights; once his mother looked at his bloodied face and said, "To think that my eldest-born should turn out like this." By February 1927, Lyndon had had enough: "I'm sick of working with just my hands, and I'm ready to try working with my brain. If you and Daddy can get me into a college, I'll go as soon as I can." On borrowed money, he set off for San Marcos.

Johnson's intense ambition—and his style in personal relations, rhetoric, and decision management—took shape in his college years. The academic side of life did not trouble him much at unaccredited Southwest Texas Teachers; he attacked his courses "with an intensity he had never before revealed." But his main energies went into operating, getting on top of the institution. President Evans got him a job collecting trash, but Lyndon soon cajoled his way into a position as assistant to the president's secretary, with a desk in the outer office. In *Sam Johnson's Boy*, Alfred Steinberg continues the story:

> According to Nichols [the secretary], what next unfolded was flabbergasting. Lyndon jumped up to talk to everyone who came to the office to see Evans, and before days passed, he was asking the purpose of the visit and offering solutions to problems. The notion soon spread that it was necessary to get Lyndon's approval first in order to see Dr. Evans. At the same time, faculty members came to the conclusion that it was essential for them to be friendly to Lyndon, for they believed he could influence the president on their behalf. This erroneous idea developed because the school lacked a telephone system tying President Evans' office with those of department heads, and when the president wanted to send a message to a department head or a professor, he asked his part-time aide, rather than Nichols, to run with a note. Lyndon's tone and attitude somehow gave the impression he was far more than a messenger.

Soon this student assistant was slapping the president on the back, accompanying him to the state capitol, answering mail, and writing reports to state agencies. "Lyndon," President Evans said, "I declare you hadn't been in my office a month before I could hardly tell who was president of the school—you or me."

Johnson was off and running. Blackballed by the dominant fraternity, he helped start a rival one, the White Stars, who won campus elections in part by Johnson's energetic behind-the-scenes campaigning and in part by fancy parliamentary tactics. Johnson sold more Real Silk socks than his customers had use for. He became a star debater, significantly in a system where he and his partner had to prepare both sides of each question because the assignment of negative or affirmative turned on the flip of a coin just before the debate. Johnson's strength was in finding the opponents' key weakness, and then exploiting it to the hilt. Later, he began to win office: president of the press club, senior legislator of his class, student council member, secretary of the Schoolmakers Club, editor of the newspaper. His editorials were full of positive thinking. They came out for courtesy, "honesty of soul," and the Fourth of July, along with some more personal sentiments:

> Personality is power; the man with a striking personality can accomplish greater deeds in life than a man of equal abilities but less personality.

> The great men of the world are those who have never faltered. They had the glowing vision of a noble work to inspire them to press forward, but they also had the inflexible will, the resolute determination, the perfectly attuned spiritual forces for the execution of the work planned.

> The successful man has a well-trained will. He has under absolute control his passions and desires, his habits and his deeds.

> There are no tyrannies like those that human passions and weaknesses exercise. No master is so cruelly exacting as an indulged appetite. To govern self is a greater feat than to control armies and forces.

> Ambition is an uncomfortable companion many times. He creates discontent with present surroundings and achievements; he is never satisfied but always pressing forward to better things in the future. Restless, energetic, purposeful, it is ambition that makes of a creature a real man.

In 1928 Johnson left college with a two-year teaching certificate. He returned a year later after having served, at the age of twenty, as principal of an elementary school in Cotulla, Texas. As principal (over five teachers and a janitor), Lyndon was in his first chief executive position. His friendly biographers report he was "a firm administrator, a strict disciplinarian, and a good teacher." He insisted that Mexican children speak only English, and he required his teachers to keep constant supervision of the students. Laziness or misbehavior "was likely to bring some form of punishment. A hard worker himself, Johnson expected others to work with equal energy and determination. He was persistent, sometimes high-tempered, energetic, aggressive and creative." His march into the classroom each morning was the signal for the students to sing out:

How do you do, Mr. Johnson,
How do you do?
How do you do, Mr. Johnson,
How are you?
We'll do it if we can,
We'll stand by you to a man.
How do you do, Mr. Johnson,
How are you?

Mr. Johnson spanked at least one boy who ridiculed his walk. His energy was incredible. He introduced school assemblies, interschool public speaking contests, spelldowns, baseball games, track meets, parental car pools for transporting children; he coached debating and basketball at the high school, organized a literary society, courted a girl who taught thirty-five miles away, and took courses at the Cotulla extension center.

Enough. Johnson's style—the whirlwind energy, the operator-dominator personal relations, the idealistic rhetoric, the use of information as an instrument—all of it was there when he emerged from road gang bum to big wheel in the world of San Marcos and Cotulla. Obviously personal relations was at the core of his style. It displayed itself in two interesting variations: Johnson on the make, and Johnson in charge. In the first he was the operator who repeated, as secretary to a conservative congressman and as Senate party leader, the story of his San Marcos takeover, showing a remarkable ability to expand his roles—and his influence—through energetic social manipulation. Johnson in charge used domination successfully, forcing subordinates into conformity.

I think Johnson's character infused this stylistic pattern with a compulsive quality, so that he was virtually unable to alter it when it proved unproductive. Clearly, Johnson belongs among the active-negative characters. His fantastic pace of action in the Presidency was obvious. He was also characteristically discouraged much of the time. On the wall of his Senate office he hung this quotation from Edmund Burke:

Those who would carry on great public schemes must be proof against the worst fatiguing delays, the most mortifying disappointments, the most shocking insults, and worst of all, the presumptuous judgment of the ignorant upon their designs.

He was, he said, "the loneliest man in the world," "the most denounced man in the world," for whom "nothing really seems to go right from early in the morning until late at night," who was "not sure whether I can lead this country and keep it together, with my background." Even at the height of his success—at the close of the remarkable first session of the 89th Congress—Johnson, convalescing from a gallstone operation, complained:

> What do they want—what *really* do they want? I am giving them boom times and more good legislation than anybody else did, and what do they do—attack and sneer! Could FDR do better? Could anybody do better? What *do* they want?

Johnson's remarkable effectiveness *in situations where the social environment provided direction* is not to be doubted. As Senate Democratic leader he reached the high point of success in consensus-building by catching issues at the right stage of development, mapping the terrain of Senatorial opinion, and manipulating members' perceptions and expectations to get bills passed. The raw materials were given: Johnson did not take a stand, he worked with the range of stands he found among other members, pushing here, pulling there, until he had a workable configuration of votes. "I have always thought of myself as one who has been moderate in approaching problems," he said. But "moderation"—like Eisenhower's middle-of-the-road—is a relational concept definable only in terms of the positions others take. In the legislative setting, Johnson *had* to work that way. In the Presidency, Johnson had around him, not a circle of Senatorial barons, each with his own independence and authority, but a circle of subordinates. There his beseeching for knowledge of "what they *really* want," his feeling that "no President ever had a problem of doing what is right; the big problem is knowing what is right," and especially his plea to his advisors that "all you fellows must be prudent about what you encourage me to go for," indicated the disorientation of an expert middleman elevated above the ordinary political marketplace.

Put crudely: Johnson's style failed him, so he fell back on character. There he found no clear-cut ideology, no particular direction other than the compulsion to secure and enhance his personal power. As his real troubles mounted, he compounded them by so dominating his advisers that he was eventually left even more alone, even more vulnerable to the exaggerations of his inner dramas, until he took to wondering aloud: "Why don't people like me?" "Why do you want to destroy me?" "I can't trust anybody!" "What are you trying to do to me? Everybody is trying to cut me down, destroy me!"

Richard Nixon: active-negative*

The description accompanying Richard Nixon's figure at the Fisherman's Wharf Wax Museum in San Francisco calls the President "industrious and persistent," "ambitious and dedicated from childhood." Like Woodrow Wilson, Herbert Hoover, and Lyndon B. Johnson, Nixon in the early months of his Presidency seemed happy in his work.

He began cautiously. Recognizing the national mood as calling for peace and quiet, empowered by a narrow, minority victory in the election, and confronting a Congress and a bureaucracy dominated by Democrats, he opted for an undramatic beginning. He devoted much of his attention in these early days to gathering around him the men who would help him shape a program, and in arranging them in relation to his own style of operation.

The recruitment process had its difficulties—Nixon received refusals from his first choices for Secretaries of State, Defense, and Treasury, and Attorney General; his friend Finch had decided not to accept the Vice Presidential nomination; Warren Burger was at least fifth on his list of candidates for Chief Justice. But it was probably Nixon's own preference which brought together in the Cabinet a collection of

* I have not changed the following speculations to reflect events after September 1969. The subsequent Carswell and Haynesworth cases, Nixon's reactions to the Vietnam Moratoria, his much noticed isolation in 1970, the invasion of Cambodia, and his continuing conflict with the Senate do not, in July 1970, seem inconsistent with this interpretation. [1988: Predictions of Nixon's Presidential rigidification, etc., were subsequently developed at length in The Presidential Character: Predicting Performance in the White House (Englewood Cliffs, N.J.: Prentice-Hall, 1972), before the Watergate crisis confirmed the pattern. See subsequent analyses in the second (1977) and third (1985) editions of The Presidential Character.]

competent, quiet, relatively obscure men whose "extra dimensions" he had to describe to the unknowing national audience, and in the White House a crew of younger lieutenant-colonel types leavened with two brilliant Harvardians. He intended to disperse power in his administration. In 1968 he had said: "Publicity would not center at the White House alone. Every key official would have the opportunity to be a big man in his field." If so, their reputations would be made, largely, within and through the Nixon administration.

Nixon's Presidential style was not entirely clear as of September 1969; he had not yet been through the fires of large-scale political crisis. But a few features emerged that seemed likely to persist. In several ways, Nixon appeared to have adopted a judge-like stance:

–He takes up one case at a time and tries to dispose of it before moving on to the next case.

–He relies on formal, official channels for information and advice. In his ABM decision, for example, "Although he instructed his aides to seek out all sides of the argument, the President appears to have had little direct contact with opponents or advocates of the missile system outside his own circle." Senators and scientists opposed to the ABM sought out Kissinger, who prepared a "devil's advocate" paper.

–At official meetings, Nixon is the presider, the listener who keeps his own counsel while other members of the group present their cases and options and briefs, like lawyers in a court. He asks questions; he himself rarely tosses out suggestions for critical comment.

–Evidence in hand, he retires to his chambers (usually a small room off the Lincoln bedroom), where he may spend hours in complete solitude reaching his decision.

–He emerges and pronounces the verdict.

By September 1969 this system had already produced some Presidential stumbles. Decisions or near-decisions taken in this fashion had to be reversed or abruptly modified as they set off political alarms. There was the $30,000 job for Nixon's brother Edward; Franklin Long and the National Science Foundation directorship; Willie Mae Rogers's appointment as consumer consultant; the Knowles appointment; the nomination and then withdrawal of Peter Bove to be governor of the Virgin Islands; the shelving and then unshelving of the "hunger" question; the backing and filling regarding desegregation guidelines; and the various changes in the Job Corps. In these cases "decisions" came unglued in the face of indignant and surprised reactions from the press, interest groups, and Congress. The resignation of Clifford Alexander and the appointment of Senator Strom Thurmond's protégé as chief White House political troubleshooter seemed to indicate inadequate consultation, as did certain exaggerations by Secretary Laird on defense and Attorney General Mitchell on "preventive detention." On the ABM, Nixon emerged, despite his victory, with about half the Senate confirmed in opposition. These bobbles may be seen, some years hence, as nothing more than the inevitable trials of shaking down a new crew. Through them all, Nixon's popularity with the public rose.

It is the isolation, the lonely seclusion adopted consciously as a way of deciding, that stands out in Nixon's personal-relations style. That style was defined, in its main configurations, at the time of his first independent political success in 1946.

Following a childhood marred by accident, severe illness, the deaths of two brothers, and much family financial insecurity, Richard Nixon made his way to the law school of Duke University, where he succeeded as a student but failed in his fervent desire to land a position in New York or Washington upon his graduation in 1937. Instead, his mother arranged a place for him in a small Whittier firm, where he spent the late 1930s in a practice featuring a good deal of divorce and criminal law, holding the town attorney office, and serving as a trustee of Whittier College. He and "a group of local plungers" gambled $10,000 to start a frozen orange juice company which went broke after a year and a half. In 1938 he proposed to Pat Ryan; they were married in 1940 and took an apartment over a garage.

After Pearl Harbor he worked briefly in the OPA tire-rationing office in Washington before entering the Navy as a lieutenant junior grade—at which, Nixon remembered in 1968, his "gentle, Quaker mother . . . quietly wept." He met William P. Rogers in the Navy. He served as a supply officer in the South Pacific, where he ran a kind of commissary, called "Nixon's Hamburger Stand." When he returned from the war, he struck acquaintances as unusually contemplative, "dreaming about some new world order," possibly feeling guilty about his " 'sin' of serving in the armed forces." Then there was an unexpected outburst: at a homecoming luncheon for some thirty family and friends, an elderly cousin gave an armchair analysis of the war. Suddenly Richard leaned across the table and cursed the old man out. Talk stopped. His folks were amazed. Nixon thought no one there would ever forget this uncharacteristic outburst.

He was returning to be, in his own words, "Nothing . . . a small-time lawyer just out of the Navy." Then, as he was winding up his service in Baltimore, he received a call from a Whittier banker asking if he would run for Congress against Jerry Voorhis. He accepted almost immediately. The year was 1945; Nixon was thirty-two. He flew back to California and appeared in his uniform before the Republican group; he brought along a collection of pictures he had had taken, in his lieutenant commander's uniform, for use in the campaign. He impressed the group with his calm, crisp answers. They took him as their candidate in what seemed like a hopeless campaign against the popular Voorhis. In his letter of acceptance he said he planned to stress "a group of speeches." Voorhis's "conservative reputation must be blasted," he said. His campaign became an aggressive rhetorical performance in which he won with little help from anyone else.

Nixon's success at this period was independent of his parents; it was his first clearly political commitment in a personal sense; it was then, he wrote later, that "the meaning of crisis [took] on sharply expanded dimensions"—a fine paraphrase of Alexander George's concept of the expansion of one's "field of power." Perhaps most important is the independence dimension: he had tried several times to make it into the big time in a big city away from home and now he had achieved that.

The shape of Nixon's style, confirmed in his subsequent success with the Hiss case, was clear in its general outline at this point. Close interpersonal relations were simply not very important to his success. He was, and remained, a loner. His style was centered in speaking and in hard work getting ready to speak. Later he attributed his victory over Voorhis to three factors: "intensive campaigning; doing my homework; and participating in debates with my better-known opponent." From then on, Nixon was primarily a man on his own—a hardworking, careful student of one issue or case at a time, continually preparing for a public presentation, highly sensitive to his rhetorical style and the reactions of audiences to him. Throughout his career, including his stint with Eisenhower, Nixon was never a full-fledged member of a cooperative team or an administrator used to overseeing the work of such a team. He stood apart, made his own judgments, relied on his own decisions.

All this should have made it evident that Nixon in the Presidency would (a) develop a rhetorical stance carefully attuned to his reading of the temper of the times (and of the public's reaction to him), (b) work very hard at building a detailed case to back up each of his positions, and (c) maintain a stance of interpersonal independence and individual final authority with respect to his Cabinet and his White House staff.

It is the way this style interacts with Nixon's character which is of interest here. Despite his current air of happy calm, similar in many ways to the early Presidential experience of others of his type, Nixon belongs, I think, among the active-negative Presidents. On the activity side there is little doubt. Nixon has always been a striver, an energetic doer who attacks his tasks vigorously and aggressively. He has often driven himself to gray-faced exhaustion. But even the less demanding 1968–69 Nixon schedules leave him on the side of activists, in contrast, to, say, Taft, Harding, Coolidge, and Eisenhower.

As for his affect toward his experience, I would put more stock in the way he has typically felt about what he was doing over a lifetime than I would put in his current euphoria. Over more than twenty political years, Nixon has seen himself repeatedly as being just on the verge of quitting. Furthermore, on many occasions he has experienced profound depression and disappointment, even when he was succeeding. As a new Congressman, he said he had "the same lost feeling I had when I went into military service." With the Hiss case victory, "I should have felt elated. . . . However, I experienced a sense of letdown which is difficult to describe or even to understand." Running for the Senate in 1950 he was a "sad but earnest underdog." The Nixon Fund episode in 1952 left him "gloomy and angry;" after the Checkers speech, he said, "I loused it up, and I am sorry. . . . It was a flop," and then he cried. He was "dissatisfied" and "disappointed" in his Vice Presidency; in "semi-shock" at Eisenhower's heart attack; he found the President's 1956 hesitations about him "an emotional ordeal"; he was "grim and nervous" in 1960, and he exploded bitterly and publicly after his 1962 defeat.

There have been a few piano-thumping exceptions, but the general tone of Nixon in politics—even when he has not been in a crisis—has been the doing of the unpleasant but necessary. It is this lifelong sense that the burdens outweigh the pleasures which must be set up against the prospect of a new Nixon continuing to find the White House a fun place. In the introduction to *Six Crises* Nixon writes, "I find it especially difficult to answer the question, does a man 'enjoy' crises?" He goes on to say that he had not found his "fun," but that "surely there is more to life than the search for enjoyment in the popular sense." Crisis engages all a man's talents; he loses himself in a larger cause. Nixon contrasts enjoyment with "life's mountaintop experiences"—what he calls the "exquisite agony" of crisis. When Nixon begins to feel pleasantly relaxed, or playfully enjoying, I think, some danger sign goes up, some inner commandment says no, and he feels called back into the quest for worlds to conquer.

There are many more aspects of Nixon's character that fit the active-negative type: the unclear and discontinuous self-image; the continual self-examination and effort to construct a "Richard Nixon"; the fatalism and pessimism; the substitution of technique for value; the energies devoted to controlling aggressive feelings; the distrust of political allies; and, most of all, the perpetual sensitivity to the power dimensions of situations. I think that if Nixon is ever threatened simultaneously with public disdain and loss of power, he may move into a crisis syndrome. In that case, the important resonances will be direct ones between character and the political environment; style would play a secondary part. But in the ordinary conduct of the Presidency (and there are long stretches of that), Nixon's personal-relations style may interact with his character to produce a different kind of danger, a kind the President and his friends could, I think, steer away from.

The danger is that Nixon will commit himself irrevocably to some disastrous course of action, as, indeed, his predecessor did. This is precisely the possibility against which Nixon could defend himself by a stylistic adjustment in his relations with his White House friends. Yet it is made more likely than it need be by the way he appears to be designing his decision-making process in the critical early period of definition.

It may seem that the danger of the Nixon Presidency lies not in exaggeration but in timidity, that his administration will turn out to be more Coolidgean than Johnsonian. Yet unless there has been a fundamental change in his personality (as Theodore White and others think there has been), Nixon has within him a very strong drive for personal power—especially *independent* power—which pushes him away from reliance on anyone else and pulls him toward stubborn insistence on showing everyone that he can win out on his own. Throughout his life he has experienced sharp alternations between periods of quiet and periods of crisis. These discontinuities in his experience have contributed to the uncertainties nearly all observers have felt in interpreting the "real" Nixon. On the one hand, he is a shrewd, calm, careful, proper, almost fussily conventional man of moderation, a mildly self-deprecating common-sense burgher. On the other hand, he has been a fighter, a rip-snorting indignant, a dramatic contender for his own moral vision. To say that the first theme traces to his mother and the second to his father is but the beginning of an explanation of a pattern in which alternation has substituted for resolution. The temptation for one of his character type is to follow a period of self-sacrificing service with a declaration of independence, a move which is necessary exactly because it breaks through the web of dependencies he feels gathering around him.

Add to this character a style in which intimacy and consultation have never been easy and in which isolated soul-searching is habitual. Add to that an explicit theory and system of decision-making in which the President listens inquiringly to his committees of officials (who have been encouraged in their own independence), then retires to make his personal choice, then emerges to announce that choice. The temptation to surprise them all and, when the issue is defined as critically important, to adhere to it adamantly is exacerbated by the mechanisms of decision. Add also hostile reporters given unusual access, an increasingly independent Senate, a generationally polarized nation, and a set of substantive problems nearly impossible to "solve," and the stage is set for tragic drama.

Another President once dismissed Nixon as a "chronic campaigner." In a campaign, day by day, the product is a speech or other public appearance. The big decisions are what to say. In the Presidency, rhetoric is immensely important, but preliminary: the product is a movement by the government. To bring that about Nixon needs to succeed not only with the national audience (where the danger of impromptu, "sincere" commitment is already great) and with the audience of himself alone (where the danger of self-deception is evident), but also with that middle range of professional President-watchers in Washington. Managing their anticipated reactions requires not only the development of "options," but widening circles of consultation around a tentative Presidential decision—in other words, consultation *after* the President has reached a course of action satisfactory to him. It is at that point that the President's friends can help him most. For it is not true in the Presidency that, as Nixon wrote of 1960: "In the final analysis I knew that what was most important was that I must be myself."

Concluding Remarks

Lives are complicated. In the hope of improving our predictions about Presidents, it is worth trying to discern the key regularities. This may bring us to the point where we can look over a field of candidates and say, with a confidence beyond common sense, where the main problems and possibilities are likely to lie. I think the way to get to that point is by broad, comparative categorization and the slow work of filling in the connections among factors.

In this essay I have concentrated on relations between two factors, character and style, focusing on the personal relations aspect of style. In discussing character I have said little of its deeper dimensions, of the innermost meanings of words, work, and persons. I believe it would (and may) be possible to show how early experience shapes political character. For example, it seems likely that the power-oriented, compulsive character grows out of early power deprivations, particularly a helpless vulnerability to erratic external forces, while the compliant, affection-oriented character may develop from early experience in which unrealistically high expectations of affectionate nurturance are established. But the origins are both less certain and less important than the result, and the result—the political character—can be discerned in its main features by the relatively simple scheme described above. In this sense, the research is behavorial, not psychoanalytic.

Style, as in the cases summarized, confronts character on the one side and the Presidency on the other, with a set of habits anchored in early adult success. The early congruences in adapting to other political (in the widest sense) roles push the new President to try again what worked for him before. But the new role is unique; the old combination may add up in a different way. The main disparities are definable, probably predictable, and possibly preventable.

Character plus style is only a slice of the problem. In the larger map sketched earlier, there are many other combinations that need exploring, both in the realm of theory and down below in the messier search for similarities in real experience.

How the research for The Presidential Character *was conducted, primarily through the experiential coding of biographies.*

5

Strategy for Research

POLITICAL SCIENCE can be improved by analytical prediction, in contrast to dissecting the present. Theorizing as an activity which begins with awareness of a puzzle or paradox (particularly typological explorations) can generate testable predictions. Applying such ideas to the behavior of politicians (such as Presidents of the United States) leads to curiosities about the interplay of political personalities with situations and roles, and suggests the most fruitful forms of psychology to exploit.

It all seems so much clearer in retrospect. What appears, during research, as a stumble in roughly the right direction, begins to look, after the research, like a "strategy." But just possibly, by focusing strongly on what those choices were and what they came to mean for the progress of the inquiry, one might help the next fellow to an easier way—make hindsight serve foresight. Therefore these confessions, true ones as far as I can tell, as to larger choices I made in the line of research that reached its culmination (for the time being) in *The Presidential Character: Predicting Performance in the White House.*[1]

On Predicting

Shaw's play *The Apple Cart*, dated March 1930, has a character named Magnus who is king of England and remarkably like Franklin D. Roosevelt. "Even political science," Magnus says, "the science by which civilization must live or die, is busy explaining the past while we have to grapple with the present; it leaves the ground before our feet in black darkness whilst it lights up every corner of the landscape behind us."[2]

The *American Political Science Review* for 1930 pretty much bears out Shaw's accusation. There are calm articles on Fascism and economic change and "pragmatic" voting behavior. The association president predicted "continued life, with an expanding field of usefulness" for that body; as for real politics, he rightly foresaw that "the top-heavy stage coach of dynastic rule has about disappeared, and that the new political vehicles have a more extended basis of popular support, greater power of action, and more concentrated control at the steering wheel."[3] And "as to the final outcome of political development, we may indulge in speculations for the distant future with as much, and no more, certainty than the physical and biological scientists."[4] There is more straight-out wisdom than we are used to, as when George H. Sabine says plainly that "the discussion of methods at large hardly ever leads to much. A method is good for just what it does, and its uses must be apparent just in the science where it is used."[5] But for all that—well, Shaw had it about right for the year of *The Apple Cart* as for the 1970s. Most of the time we don't predict, we dissect. Who now is trying to reach out beyond the relative certainties of the past to throw some light on "the ground before our feet"? Some do. More should, I think, and can, so that future readers of old political science journals might see their history anticipated.

What distinguishes the political science I am interested in from history is this: we generalize. Most historians, more attuned to history as literature, as art, want to let their stories speak for themselves. They do not want to state their theories baldly, though of course all of them have theories. I wish more historians would follow the lead of, say, C. Vann Woodward and tell us outright what their data add up to, not just as explanation of the past but as probabilities for the future. Then we could test them. But in a different sense, this series holds:

All theories are predictions.
All generalizations are theories.
All concepts are generalizations.
All words are concepts.
Therefore all words are predictions.

Here I would concentrate on the first of these propositions—not that the others are uninteresting. Theories are predictions because they specify causes and effects and therefore imply that when the causes are the same the effects will be the same. Know it or not, every time we theorize we predict.

Now of course the causes are never "the same." If they were, our task would be trivial. Since they're not, we speak in terms of probabilities in at least two senses. We may say that such and such a set of effects is in some degree probable, like the weather forecast. For example, I have argued that demythologizing the Presidency is unlikely—I would say there is about an 80 percent chance of reign. A more interesting form of prediction is the contingent variety, as when I argue in *The Presidential Character* that active-negative Presidents are most likely to go into a pattern of rigidification if and when there is a simultaneous public threat to their power and their righteousness. We need to explore the historical triggers, the conditions giving rise to high probabilities of a given outcome. All cause-effect propositions can be recast in such predictive form—an exercise which would, I think, lend political science a good deal more relevance and rigor, because we could see more clearly what actually happens and use that intelligence to improve the theories.

That improvement will come, not through general methodological preachments or unanchored speculations drifting through the sky, but by demonstration. Science marches on (when it does) by progressive approximation: X's theory about Y fits the data better than Z's, and so on. In the long run that is what counts in political science too—not the massive effluvia of appreciation and deprecation, deductive model-making, or "suggestions for further research," but the slow experience of *doing it*, of actually producing new and better combinations of theory and data that can be further improved by the test of prediction.

Besides the if-then form of prediction—relatively tight hypothe-sizing in propositional form—there is what I would call where-to-look prediction, a form in many ways more modest and more fascinating. Where-to-look prediction says: "If you want to understand and an-ticipate the basic motion of such-and-such political phenomena, look here, not there." This, not that, is going to turn out to be the most important focus of attention. For example, I predict that you will make the best sense out of the regime of a passive-positive President (the Taft-Harding variety) by concentrating on the affectional aspects of interpersonal relations surrounding the President, better sense than if you were to spend your attention on, say, his ideology or formal administrative system or policy stands. Another example is the pre-diction that a President's style can best be predicted from a close analysis of his first independent political success. That was fun to find out. I was puzzled by the lack of fit between the styles of Presi-dents and their immediately pre-Presidential styles. Of course, there were some continuities, but they were very uneven and in some cases downright obscure. Tracing back in the life histories, it turned out that a much earlier set of experiences, usually in early adulthood, when the President-to-be "emerged" politically, gave a far clearer de-lineation of the style he would practice in the White House. Taft as a young judge; Wilson, Coolidge, Hoover, and Johnson as college leaders; Harding the youthful editor; FDR as Assistant Secretary of the Navy; Truman in World War I; Eisenhower starting his Army ca-reer; and Kennedy and Nixon making their first runs for Congress— each previewed a political style he would return to as President. That, then, was the place to look in assessing the style part of Presidential performance from the biographies of future Presidents and candi-dates. I tried that for Nixon just before his first inauguration and in a series of papers and articles thereafter.[6] The Nixon case, extended in *The Presidential Character*, continues to confirm those early expec-tations. Where-to-look prediction, then, can be done and can result in strong reality testing as actual history unfolds. To stretch the hu-bristic analogy to its uttermost: that's what Marx, Freud, and Darwin were all about.

Those who think scholars should stay away from prediction pose a flock of objections. Predicting is too uncertain to be scientific; the political scientist should wait until he has a thoroughly validated theory before venturing to predict. Or our predictions may be taken far too seriously by a naive public who, incompetent to assess the evidence, will take what we say as authoritative. Or we will confuse people's thinking by mixing up what we say is *likely* to happen under given circumstances with what we think *should* happen. Such worries are based, it seems to me, on several misconceptions. Of course we should recognize the tentativeness of any prediction in social science, and of course any individual scholar ought to do his best to base his predictions on the solidest ground possible. But private cogitation is not the only way to improve our theories. Social science is in important respects a social enterprise. We move it forward by debate about successive approximations—by displaying evidence and inference and inviting alternative explanations. That is done in the hope that others will join in the work of improvement, not in the expectation that all will merely applaud and conform. Given the real state of our discipline (as distinct from various perfectionist ideals easier to pronounce than to perform) political scientists who do research (as distinct from those who advise others on how to do research) should keep doing what they do: publish their tentative findings as they go along, humbly inviting the correction of their colleagues.[7]

But won't the public be misled? Probably not for long. There is no convincing evidence that the public is overly impressed with the dicta of political science. Furthermore, in the public arena, nonprediction is not an option. In choosing Presidents, for example, the press and public *inevitably* predict, as they assess candidates and platforms and parties. The real question, then, is whether political scientists might help improve those predictions, too, by entering into the wider public debate. I think so. For example, in every Presidential campaign there is a great deal of writing about the candidates' stands on particular issues, debate which assumes that the man is likely to do what he says he will do. But in the past decade's Presidential elections, such criteria of choice have been wildly misleading. Briefly put, a public which voted for peace in 1964, for domestic tranquility in 1968, and for competence in the Presidency in 1972 has had a disappointing time of it. At the very least, there is room for improvement and no reason to think political scientists will do worse than the journalists. We can count on the press for skepticism and on the public for appropriate hesitations.

As for the confusion of *is* and *ought*, scholars are as vulnerable as others. The point is to make clear, as best one can, when he is analyzing and when he is preaching. I see no a priori responsibility for the scholar—as such—to recommend reforms. Indeed there is plenty of room in our sprawling discipline for researchers who don't give a hang about translating their findings into recommendations. But there are satisfactions for those who do: the sense of wholeness that can come from linking one's scholarly work, one's teaching (in the widest sense) and one's role as citizen interested in the advancement of values. Political activity always leads one beyond the tentativeness of his findings to choice and risk. The alternative is too often a kind of paralysis: such an awareness of uncertainty and complexity that a permanent hesitation takes over. My own unsteady resolution has been to do what I could, politically, about certain issues that seemed ethically most clear (particularly civil rights and opposition to the war in Vietnam) and to support candidates who, by the dim light of my researches, seemed the best available alternatives. But I have tried to remind myself and my readers, from time to time, that a hypothesis is not an iron law and that a scientific conclusion may not impel a particular political action.

On Theorizing

Yes, but where is the *theory* in all this? What distinguishes it from astrology or luck or guessing? There is no room here to go far into the specifics, but at least I can try to show some of the decisions I struggled with (and still do).

Theorizing usually begins for me with puzzlement. I read or hear or think about some contradiction and try to figure out how research might resolve it. Theory is thus not a thing but an activity. For instance, I started out on the first of my four books in the general "political psychology" area with a feeling that much of what was going on in political science (back then in the late fifties) was missing a point. In those days voting and public opinion—highly significant topics for political scientists to study—were all the rage, and yet many such studies were demonstrating (a) that the public was, by and large, pretty apathetic and uninformed about politics, and (b) that a great deal of public opinion was in a sense reactive: people were responding to messages from leaders. Therefore (with some in-between logic), I focused on a middling group of public-to-leader transitional people, freshman state legislators, and studied those in Connecticut close at hand in 1958–59. The initial substantive focus also grew out of a puzzlement: there was apparently (from the statistics and the language of politics) a good deal of competition for these offices, yet droves of legislators left after one or two sessions. Many fought to get in and then got out at the first opportunity. I wondered why. The answers as I found them are part of the analysis in *The Lawmakers.*[8] After I got into the research I ran into another puzzle: in the data I had, passive legislators were just about as likely to intend to return to the assembly as active legislators were; that seemed strange— wouldn't one expect the activists to be happier in their work and want to continue it? The data said no. Again, I wondered why and eventually developed a scheme for understanding the main variants of legislative joy and pain: the spectator-advertiser-reluctant-law-maker typology elaborated in the same book.

It would be easy enough, but redundant, to recount the puzzles which led on into *Power in Committees,*[9] *Citizen Politics,*[10] and *The Presidential Character.* The point is that for me at least, theory (as activity) begins with a question, a contradiction, a paradox, a puzzle— not with an answer. Nor has it generally been enough to have a generalized curiosity in some topical area. When a student tells me he wants to write about Presidents, I ask "Why? What question about Presidents (or whatever) do you have?" Inquiry really gets off the ground when one moves from topic to question. The step tends to cut away, for example, all kinds of research embroidering the obvious.

The necessity for theory is easy to propound theoretically; it needs emphasis in the kinds of studies I have been doing because of a special temptation. Thinking how to predict Presidential performance, one can all too easily drift into the myth that you should study everything about each President. This myth of completeness is, in execution, paralyzing: you can't know everything. There is no such thing as discerning the "full life" of a person. He himself could talk into your tape recorder from now till doomsday and you still wouldn't know it, because he, like you and every biographer, historian, and reporter, uses his mind interpretatively. He forgets. He misremembers. He lies.

He exaggerates. In short, both the observed and the observer are for-ever selecting from the stream of experience those items that bear on a "theory," be it your scientific concept or his need to make his life meaningful. The same for "personality"; personality is an abstrac-tion, not a totality. One never knows the whole of it. Faced with the corpus of writing by and about, say, Franklin Delano Roosevelt, that lesson can be a comfort. But it means you have to decide, hopefully consciously and defensibly, where to look for what.

So give up the quest for understanding the "whole man." Those who preach that cannot do it. And anyway, conscious choice is a lot more fun than the sleep of endless, wandering research.

Theorizing with prediction in mind also means (requires, needs) more than one case. The single case study of a particular President can be extraordinarily useful—even crucial—as raw material for the building of generalizations. And you might be able to predict what a particular President X is going to do on the basis of his individual life history. But prediction for the longer run—the run in which we do not yet know the Presidents or candidates—can only move by analogy. That is, we will want to know what to watch for in the way of *similarities* between past and future Presidents. At a minimum, the single case study acquires relevance for the future if (and only if) it makes it possible to predict the conditions for another single case study yet to be. Woodrow Wilson, for example, is dead; but there might come along another President who shares critical, theoretically discerned characteristics with Wilson and thus might be expected to perform in significant ways as Wilson did. The first Secretary of De-fense committed suicide. It would be comforting to believe that a strong understanding of Forrestal will help us spot that danger for the future, when another "Forrestal" comes along.

Obviously the inference is strengthened when we have more than one case to base a generalization-prediction on. Even two historical cases is a big advantage because you can, in a sense, go through the exercise of "predicting" the one from the other. The fewer the cases under close examination, the more necessary to import, vicariously as it were, other "cases" by the route of theory. Because, of course, the-ories grow out of cases and get applied to other ones.

Having decided on a collection of cases (defined by sampling or, as in *The Presidential Character*, by choosing a more or less arbitrary historical cutoff point and dealing with all subsequent incumbents), gathering and ordering data depend on the research strategy, and thus on the substance of the theory, and thus on one's political philosophy. I think Presidents are important mainly because of the effects they have on the actual human beings who make up polities. Not their "greatness" (or lack of it) per se, not their fascination as men in dramatic roles, not their availability as mediums for working out our own hang-ups, not their morals or intellectual talents—none of those, except in and as they bear on how these topmost leaders make for happiness or sadness for the citizenries who rely on them. Presidents in my scheme of values are overwhelmingly more important as political forces than as individuals. Presidents are *dangerous:* they can and do hurt people, just as they can and do contribute to social progress. Therefore, a minimum requirement for the kind of research I want to do on any President is that it encompass his social impact, that it include evidence and inference about how he affected life and death way out beyond the Washington machine. Lyndon Johnson, for example, was "a fascinatingly rousing bastard,"[11] as Robert Sherill put it—one could write fascinating novels about his personal doings, as William Brammer did in *The Gay Place*.[12] Or one could concentrate on his administration's ideology or his budget practices or whatever. But no account I would want to write about Johnson as President could dodge the flood of gore he spilled all over Vietnam.

What I wanted to find out about Presidents was how and why they did what they did to people. To get across briefly the way I approached that task, I cannot do better than to quote a bit from a "Coding Scheme for Presidential Biographies" I gave my student assistants in January 1968.[13] I think the mode of analysis has been improved and deepened since then, particularly in the following year's work at the Center for Advanced Study in the Behavioral Sciences. This earlier exploration, for example, was pretty much focused on style, which turned out to be one of five important dimensions of predicting Presidents. But let it be as it was in January 1968.

> Of course, coding is intimately related to the focus of the research. Theoretically, every sentence in the biography could yield content more or less illuminating about Presidential leadership styles. The present research has as its major focus the descrip-

tion, classification, and explanation of patterns of Presidential behavior. The emphasis is on patterns. We want to find concepts applicable beyond the single case, beyond a short historical era, beyond actions to meet particular temporary political crises or issues. We are particularly interested in three dimensions of Presidential styles:

Integrated habit patterns. No President deals in exactly the same way with every new problem he encounters; no President completely changes his way of solving problems with each new event. In between these extremes there are habitual responses to recurrent, similar role demands. There are the individual adaptive strategies for surviving and succeeding in a stressful environment. The person conserves physical and emotional energy and maximizes the effectiveness of such energies in meeting his needs, by adopting certain habits of action. These habits free him from the necessity to invent and apply a completely new approach every time he confronts a problem or opportunity similar to what he has previously experienced. Such habits may or may not be productive (i.e., good). At this first level of analysis, we simply want to know: What are the major habit patterns the President practices in response to the demands and opportunities the role affords him? For example, in the article on Andrew Johnson it is clear that the President repeatedly responded to a certain recurring situation—a large and excited audience—with wild flights of rhetoric. In response to the problems of managing the office work of the Presidency, Andrew Johnson habitually worked extremely hard, long hours, and alone. Thus the first and simplest dimension of style is the man's collection of habits cued by recurrent situations.

Second, we do not confront a miscellaneous disconnected set of habit items. A President is a person, and as such he has a *personality* which tends toward integration. His habits bear upon one another. They relate to one another functionally, dynamically, in a complementary way. Part of this is a simple matter of energy: no President can habitually devote intense effort to *all* of the role demands he encounters. He is inevitably selective. Part of this selectivity is imposed upon him by external events. When the Bay of Pigs came up, Kennedy could not devote much attention to Laos. But there are deeper strains. Habits tend to be integrated by the *self*. Of particular importance in this integration are the *criteria by which one judges himself* and *the results of that judging in terms of positive and negative self-images.* (More on this later.) Thus a second way of considering the patterning of behavior is to look at the patterner, the self, and the needs and values by which habitual behavior patterns are linked with one another.

Third, there are individual life–historical roots of both the self and the style of action. All we have been talking about so far concerns the President's performance in office. But it would be particularly valuable for political scientists to be able to *predict*, before the fact, at the time of nomination, how a person is most likely to perform in the Presidential office. Obviously, this is another place at which extreme interpretations do not hold water. No President comes to the office like a newborn babe without any predispositions or lessons of experience; every President is affected by the assumption of that office. He changes his behavior in certain ways. In between these extremes we may be able to discern, out of the plethora of his life experience, certain strong links between Presidential and pre-Presidential style. The problem of generalization, and the simplification that imposes, is extremely severe.

What is deemphasized in this scheme? Everything which does not lend itself to the production of potentially testable *generalizations* about Presidential behavior. Thus we shall be less concerned with the substance or content of particular political issues. We will be standing relatively close to a President as an individual, which means less concern for distant phenomena, such as relationships among other political actors effecting events without much reference to the President, public opinion, broad economic or historical trends, etc.—except insofar as these enter into the President's own approach to decision-making.

We shall be coding specifics. Part of the problem is placing events (actions, expressions) in meaningful (i.e., potentially generalizable) categories. The events which interest us are those bearing on the President's political actions. We are not concerned with how many times he brushes his teeth unless that datum illuminates some facet of his Presidential performance. For each event, at least ideally, we would want to have three bits of information. We want to know *what he did*. We want to know *how he felt* about what he did. We want to know *how he rationalized* what he did. As a practical matter, reports of actions, feelings, and justifications will not present themselves in neat packages in the biographies. But we should be alert to data of all three varieties. Confronted with an expression of feeling, we should ask, is this linked with any action? Similarly, we should ask of any statement of philosophical principle what its connection is with actual behavior. And we should try to find out, for any important action, what it meant in terms of feeling and self-justification for the person who is President. It is in the interplay of these behavioral, emotional, and ideological scenes that we are likely to discern most clearly the dynamics which will eventually enable us to explain more comprehensive patterns.

Procedures. The notes will be taken on 5 x 8 cards, with a new card for every subheading. The first card. . . .

As it turned out, a lot of the cards wound up in the discard pile because they did not take us anywhere theoretically. Others, however, added whole new dimensions to the analysis: style turned out to be only part of the story. But I do not think we would have been able to see the new distinctions—at least not as clearly—had we neglected the patient labor of cataloguing Presidential incidents as to "what he did . . . how he felt . . . how he rationalized." In turn, these initial labors led me (the students graduated) back into the biographies to reexplore, test, confirm, deny, and to take notice of evidence we had missed before. I think this is the way 99 percent of political science works: theorizing and data-digging go forward (or backward) together, in a continual round of imagination and perception as one plants ten delicate ideas, watches nine of them wither, and cultivates the surviving bloom.

On Types

Theophrastus (that ninety-nine-year-old third century B.C. Greek) asked, "Why is it that while all Greece lies under the same sky and all the Greeks are educated alike, it has befallen us to have characters variously constituted?"[14] His book *Characters* did not take the answer much beyond noting individual differences among selected Greeks, but his question is the starting point for all kinds of efforts to discern types. In modern political science Lasswell took the lead in seeing that not all politicians were alike (there is no one "political man") in any very significant sense, and in naming clusters of qualities characterizing sets of politicians. The typing enterprise can be a powerful aid to theorizing, though it has its pitfalls.

First, one has to get rid of a basically silly criticism of typing: the charge that human beings are too complex to be categorized, that it's all a matter of degree, that typologies are not hard and fast but continua, etc. The quick and correct answer is: of course. I say that again and again in *The Presidential Character*, which has not stopped some critics from beating the dead horse of an absolutism they imagine I propose. For example, every President is to some degree compliant *and* compulsive *and* withdrawn *and* adapted. The question is what he is predominantly. In the chapters on active-positive Presidents, for instance, I try to show how Franklin Roosevelt had tendencies in the passive-positive (compliant) direction, Harry Truman in the active-negative (compulsive) direction, and John Kennedy in the passive-negative (withdrawn) direction. Those tendencies toward other types are specially interesting, because the way each President dealt with them (in these cases, overcame them) helps us see the interplay of his *main* character with subthemes potentially very important for policy. Furthermore, simple honesty compels any researcher to recognize uncertainty in assigning an individual to a type. More than that: a researcher can, if he's not careful, forget too quickly the fogs which separate him from perceiving reality. As I said in *The Lawmakers*,

> At a certain stage in the development of a typology, one experiences a peculiar intellectual seduction. The world begins to arrange itself in fourfold tables. The lines separating the categories get blacker and thicker, the objects near the margins move quietly

toward the centers of the cells or fade into invisibility. Particularly in the speculative interpretation of interviews, the most resolute resistance to the wiles of simplicity is required.[15]

But as I see it now there is a worse one. Too many political scientists think they have said something meaningful when they call attention to complexity. Now if there were in our field some regnant theoretical orthodoxy, some oppressive paradigm in need of iconoclasm, it might make sense to suggest complexities uncaptured in its canons. Such is not the case. We have instead theories upon theories of all sorts to explain the same data—surely in itself sufficient evidence of complexity. The recognition that an alternative theory fails to account for important data is but a prologue (worth, perhaps, a paragraph or so) to the announcement of one that does *not* so fail.

Typological research has at least two promising payoffs. First, a typology can be used to organize evidence and thus to generate hypotheses. A list is not a very useful type: that is, arraying all the discernible characteristics of one type against those of another type takes the researcher only the first inch. One goes on to structure the data on the supposition that some characteristics are likely to be either indicators of, or determinants of, other characteristics—for example, activity and affect as baselines for organizing data on character patterns among politicians. These two dimensions (there may be others) run through the enormous literatures of psychology and political science. In political science we are forever talking about the activists and the apathetics, about active minorities, about participants and nonparticipants. In psychology such terms as ascendance, dominance, initiative, dramatizing, gregariousness, aggressiveness, exhibitionism, striving, achieving, manipulating, and the like have an obvious activity component. Activity is behavior; affect is sentiment. Again, much of political science deals with preferences, with how and why political actors like or dislike alternative policies, places, experiences. Fundamental to psychology also is the pleasure and pain dimension, the positive or negative feelings people have about what they and others are doing.

An obvious question is whether these two dimensions go along together. Are all (or nearly all) the active leaders also happy ones? Do negative sentiments impel passivity? There are theoretical reasons for supposing so, but as it turns out when the data are arrayed this way, the dimensions are independent. There are plenty of complaining activists and enjoying inactivists. Here is a reminder, if we needed one, that behavior in the strict sense of observable action is a highly uncertain indicator of psychological meanings. The facts of political action do not speak for themselves. We cannot read why from what. We have to find out sentiments more directly, by listening to what leaders themselves say about their experience in politics.

This particular typology, then, produces four cells. It immediately raises the question why the theoretically "deviant" cases exist—that is, why some relatively passive leaders seem happy and why some relatively active ones are sad. Hypotheses follow from the questions. Maybe the passive-positives derive rewards other than the rewards of activity. Maybe the active-negatives have strong motives other than enjoying what they do. And maybe the other types display nonobvious patterns of action and feeling. Without going into the whole analysis here, it is evident that hypotheses can be made to grow out of typological soil.

A second large payoff is the way typologies can help uncover causal dynamics and developmental patterns. Once the main defining dimensions are clear for an individual leader—that on balance, his predominant characteristics place him in one or another cell—the researcher can begin systematically exploring what other characteristics are common to the cellmates and how these might help to explain one another. For example, passive-positives keep stressing the affectional side of politics; at the same time they express many doubts about their ability to do the leadership job. That may suggest a dynamic explanation—that they seek to allay the doubts by concentrating on the affection they receive. Similarly, one can bring time into the picture: when the data are arrayed temporally, what patterns of development emerge? For example, passive-positives seem to have been heavily indulged in affection when they were children. What might that have done to their habits of self-evaluation and to their expectations about affection in political life?

Such questions can be explored in any system of research, but the typological mode has some advantages. It includes all the subjects but does not assume they are all alike. It allows for variation without lapsing into useless complexity. It sensitizes the researcher to the possibility that leaders in roughly the same role may display a few major, different patterns of cognition, motivation, and behavior. It reminds us that not all variables are created equal and it enhances the odds that we will be able to see how, amid the apparent flux of reality, there is a series of enduring themes and structures.[16]

Let me illustrate from the argument in *The Presidential Character* how one typology can lead into others at different levels and stages, and thus uncover possible causal connections. Character (which I use as the most important of five major elements for understanding Presidential behavior) is viewed at first *descriptively* (or, if you will, phenomenologically). Step one is therefore a review of all the avaliable data on how the person reacts to situations—the qualities of his experience. A simple scheme for arraying such data asks what he does, how he feels about what he does, and how he explains (justifies, gives meaning to) both. In step two, one views these data *symptomatically;* a symptom is a sign or clue which stands for or indicates other characteristics, as when a physician hypothesizes that fever indicates infection. In this case activity and affect are hypothesized as the main symptoms. Ordering the data along these baselines reveals clusters of similar actions, reactions, and rationalizations that are not immediately obvious—for example, the central concern with "principles" displayed by passive-negatives. At this point, then, one has moved beyond the collection of bits of experience to a theoretical structure, in which some types of variables are more usefully indicative than others.

The next step (three) is to look again at this (now ordered) evidence *dynamically.* What does the pattern suggest in terms of causal relations among its elements? Obviously activity and affect are not causes in any important psychological sense; they are symptoms; they can now be viewed, along with the experience patterns they stand for, as "dependent" variables to be explained. Here I hypothesize the self as the most significant generator of experience (insofar as, and only so far as, experience depends on character). The regnant motive is the protection and enhancement of self-esteem. The person behaves (physically and psychologically) in such a way as to keep and improve a favorable image of himself. The important variants in experience are caused by differences in (a) one's level of self-esteem and, even more significantly, by (b) the criteria by which one judges himself. Thus the dynamic reason why active-negatives concentrate on keeping and getting power, for example, is that their self-esteem is based heavily upon feeling powerful. That is why their attention is so taken up with the power aspects of situations, why they struggle for power in their situations, why they react so negatively to threats against their power. Dynamic analysis thus orders the data in yet another way, suggesting how the threads and themes in the pattern move one another.

Step four is to stand back yet another yard and try to see the data *developmentally*. One asks where did this self come from in the person's life history? The general supposition is that character is learned; at its center, a person learns how to define and evaluate himself. If we are to believe a long Freudian tradition, the early years are likely to be most important in shaping character. The child sees and hears and feels how his parents treat him, and then how they react to his experiments in adaptation. Later comes learning from peers and teachers. These minicultures (refracted versions of larger cultures) get into his psyche, tell him what he is like and what he must do to be liked. The scientific advantage of developmental analysis is that it enables the researcher to see character under construction—a piece at a time. The dynamic relationships unfold historically. Thus, for example, the initially obscure Nixon character becomes much clearer when we see how, as a child, he had to work out a way to relate to his mother's restraint and his father's vociferousness.

These steps, if we're lucky, produce a much more clearly patterned vision of the adult politician in action. There remains one more typological step (number five): considering the data *predictively*. With respect to character, for example, one asks first what the odds are that the person's basic self-image and adaptive orientation are likely to persist. Explorations at the margins help with this. What would it take, for example, for a (passive-positive) William Howard Taft to move over across the boundary into active-positive territory? Or an (active-negative) Lyndon Johnson to withdraw into Coolidgean (passive-negative) escapism? As in the simpler version I developed in *The Lawmakers*, one assesses, roughly to be sure, the costs and benefits of such hypothetical moves. In pseudoprediction, where one already knows the character displayed in a Presidential history, careful attention should be paid to veerings outward, away from the supposed main type toward alternative types. That can be a test, of sorts, of the initial placement. A second predictive substep is more important: to put the character back into the larger context, including not only his own style and worldview but also the power situation and climate of expectations he confronts (or might confront). The purpose at this stage is to think through types of resonance: what particular features of the situations he may face are likely to elicit what particular types of responses from him? I will say some more about that later. It is by all odds the most difficult stage of typing, because it is a try at relating relationships—a deutero or secondary process of abstraction. But it can clarify; by that route I came to suppose that the pattern of rigidification is most likely to be set off by simultaneous threats to the active-negative President's sense of power and sense of virtue. Such suppositions, then, lend themselves to tests ranging from broad assessments (e.g., that the main problem with an active-negative President will be stubbornness) to more precise propositions (e.g., the triggering of rigidification by this double threat). Thus in the end the focus moves from typing to testing, from naming to predictive propositions.[17]

Now if I were to start all over again, those are the steps I hope I would follow. But of course real research never marches along in such neat cadences. The way most social science findings are presented— in slick, tight, logical order—obscures the fits and starts, the blank walls, the sudden openings, the pathways lost and found, the long climbs through forests of fact, by which flesh and blood researchers arrive at their (never conclusive) conclusions. Checklists and models are most useful in reminding one not to forget certain possibilities. Probably far more important to success in research, however, is a hard-to-define attitude: a genuine curiosity, a readiness to listen to the data, an intense desire to wring from the flux of experience the knowledge of theory. I do not know how to describe that better. I strongly suspect it gets diverted, too often, by too much concentration on "publishing" (something, anything), by an excess of concern for what various audiences will think, and by the temptations of moralism.

On Situations

There is no need to enter into sterile arguments about whether it is the person or the situation that engenders political action and thus moves history. Obviously it is both. More important, it is the interplay of the two; the significant research payoffs come from understanding how the inhibitions and reinforcements work as people deal with their environments. History is not anonymous, not some mighty, undirected, Hegelian tide sweeping along little bubbles named Jesus and Gandhi and Lenin. Nor is it a random Hericlitean flux. Nor, on the other hand, is history merely biography, the lives of kings writ large. Man makes history and then has to cope with what he has made. For any particular man, history is an inheritance, not all of which he welcomes, a gift and a burden, an opportunity and a durance vile.

For political leaders like Presidents, I hypothesize, the critical situational elements are the power situation and the climate of expectations. In a democracy (and, to a surprising degree in totalitarian politics), large-scale social action depends on consent. The processes of consent-making tend to be regularized and formalized in institutions. At any given time, these processes confront the policymaker with configurations of power, that is, with specific demands for *his* consent and specific alignments of institutionally organized opinion which must be brought into agreement if action is to result. (Here, of course, the definition of action must include stopping things as well as starting them.)

The need to focus on the relationship between a leader and the power situation is easily illustrated. In 1933 activist FDR could hardly deliver bills to Congress fast enough to keep up with their rate of passage. In 1961 activist JFK could count on initial skepticism, if not downright opposition, to almost anything he wanted to propose to Congress. But the power situation is never all-determinative: not all Presidents are activists. To a Calvin Coolidge more or less satisfied with the Old Deal, Congressional reluctance to consent to Presidential initiatives was not much of a problem. Here as in any power relationship, we cannot see clearly or predict accurately unless we know what the actors *want* to happen. Therefore both sides of the relationship must be taken account of.

Similarly with the climate of expectations. If the power situation is

best conceived in structural terms, best analyzed by methods of institutional sociology, the climate of expectations is cultural and historical—mythic, if you will. It too sets parameters of consent; at any
given time the climate of expectations delivers up to the President his
prime problems of persuasion. There are two important components:
the persisting myth of his office and the immediate collection of expectations focused on him, now. Thus Henry V sees how his kingli-
ness must reach beyond his humanity:

> I think the king is but a man, as I am; the violet smells to him
> as it doth to me; the element shows to him as it does to me; all
> his senses have but human conditions: his ceremonies laid by, in
> his nakedness he appears but a man; and though his affections
> are higher mounted than ours, yet, when they stoop, they stoop
> with the like wing; therefore, when he sees reason of fears, as
> we do, his fears, out of doubt, be of the same relish as ours are:
> Yet in reason, no man should possess him of any reason of fear,
> lest he, by showing it, should dishearten his army.[18]

The burden of mythic expectations weighs heavily:

> Upon the king! let us our lives, our souls,
> Our debts, our careful wives,
> Our children, and our sins, lay on the king:
> We must bear all.
> O hard condition! twin-born with greatness. . . .[19]

And Fluellen reminds him that special expectations surround a king
in the instant circumstances of battle—"no tiddle taddle, nor pibble
pabble" but "the ceremonies of the wars, and the cares of it, and the
forms of it, and the sobriety of it, and the modesty of it."[20]

The same (in kind) for Presidents, or indeed, with varying content,
for the judge in his robes, the ambassador, the sergeant, and the
local justice of the peace. The American culture, I suggest, looks to
Presidents for cognitive guidance (a personal perspective on events),
and for emotional sustenance of strong needs for reassurance, a sense
of action, and legitimacy. Those are continuing needs but differently
emphasized from time to time. After the "Truman scandals," for
example, the public looked to General Eisenhower as a restorer of
legitimacy; no wonder he took pains to keep his government "clean

as a hound's tooth." The 1973 emphasis on Gerald Ford's simple republican virtues owed much to the contrast with the political ground against which they appeared—Nixonian hyperpolitics.

What is most interesting about this emotional surround is the ways it can resonate with the President's own character, worldview, and style.[21] He perceives the climate of expectations in his own way, restrained, to be sure, in perceptual manipulation by the known objective characterics of the situation. Particularly with the advent and systematization of public opinion polling, Presidents are no longer free to project their preferences on an unasked public, as Woodrow Wilson could, for example. Therefore Presidents at odds with national opinion must come to grips with it or deny it, as by inventing a "Silent Majority." This process is invariably selective: an activist President will tune his attention to popular demands for activity; a specialist in rhetoric will hear best those voices pleading for instruction and inspiration; a President who believes that heroes make history will listen out for worshipful sounds. How he makes these connections will shape his part of the action. And at some times and in some respects, mutually reinforcing resonances may reach fortissimo, as when a President deeply doubtful of his personal powerfulness hears the public glamoring for arms and a high cause. As recent history makes clear, what a President chooses *not* to listen to may be equally important.

One other cloud in the climate of expectations deserves special mention: the continually repeated poll on how the President is doing at "his job." The rating is vague but general and comprehensive—not how is he doing at this or that, but overall. Thus when his job-performance standing declines the President cannot say (to himself, to others) that his successes compensate for his failures in the public mind. His temptation then is to find some other basis for self-evaluation, in the support he got in the past (e.g., his electoral "mandate"), the appreciation future publics will accord him, or in the hope of better verdicts from God or "History." The public's temptation (as we, too, get the news of our growing disdain) is to move from disagreement to disbelief. Add to the mix a defensive, rhetorical campaign of "explanation" by the President and you have the basis for a credibility gap, a fundamental weakening of the bonds of trust between President and people. This is a qualitative change, not a mere matter of degree. When trust breaks, argument ceases. The downward spiral drops faster. Judging from twentieth-century history only one President, Harry Truman, has managed to recover from this political malady. Wilson, Hoover, and Johnson (active-negatives all) each finally succumbed as each tried to talk his way out with increasingly unbelievable rhetoric.

We may yet see this scenario played through again and again in the Presidency. Already there is evidence suggesting that future Presidents will be elected by landslides and then buried in avalanches of mistrust. The evidence is new; the phenomenon may be old, in a Western culture in which the hero is so often portrayed as a *tragic* hero, elevated by fate and destroyed by hubris.[22] Publics may use Presidents as tragedians to produce the attendant catharsis. Presidents whose characters contain a hunger for martyrdom, learned in the same cultural school of life, may cooperate in the production.

Situations, then, must first be ripped theoretically from the actors in them, moved apart so we can see what is going on in the space between. The relationships—the resonances—can then be analyzed to reestablish the reality of their connectedness.

From Role to Style

All these steps move toward explanation (making plain) and prediction (saying before). But of what? Of why leaders behave as they do. All of their behavior? No, their important behavior. Which is? That which affects significantly the public welfare. Thus the rule of relevance requires linking Presidential behavior to public outcomes—at a minimum, not neglecting those Presidential actions which are thought to have the most significant impact on people's lives and fortunes.

A similar approach helps cut away a good deal of the underbrush obscuring leadership roles. "Role" is a word lifted from the theater. But when an actor plays a role on the stage, he has a script and he has a director. In a great many political roles, there is neither. Roles in politics are exceedingly ill-defined, much less clearly circumscribed, than roles in business or professional life. Consider the role of Senate party leader: Lyndon Johnson found that a near nothing and made it a crux of power. Consider two "Secretaries of State"—Dulles and

Rogers—to see the vast variations possible in a political role. Beyond such variations are the complexities in the concept itself: does role mean permitted behavior, expected behavior, valued behavior, or typical behavior? A President, for example, *may* "wear many hats," from his chief of state hat to his hat as legislative leader.

I think a way out of such scatterations of attention is to ask what arenas of action a President *must* enter, what roles (if you like) he must play. That minimal approach tends to isolate the bedrock role imposed on occupants of a political position. The list will differ for judges, Congressmen, party leaders, etc. I concluded for Presidents that every one must do at least some of at least three things: address the national audience, negotiate in relative privacy with other leaders, and study the myriad pieces of paper that come across his desk. No President I know of has managed to get away without doing some of each. If he tried to dodge any one entirely, he would wind up baffling his most ardent admirers. Whatever else may be included in "the role of the President," these things are.

Role gets defined from the perspective of the office. Style is his way of coping with role demands—his collection of habits for performing to meet the demands. Style is evident in his action; only when one wants to understand why it works as it does is it necessary to delve behind the obvious. Thus, whatever else one might note about Mr. Nixon's style, there is no trouble seeing that he invests great quantities of energy in managing his image with the public at large and in close study of details. By contrast, he is not at all given to jawboning sessions with Congressmen or Cabinet members. A simple definition of style emphases can be followed, then, with a survey of how a President habitually performs in each—comparing, say, the Nixon rhetoric with that of Kennedy. One begins to see the whole performance: how Hoover fled from public speaking into an endless round of small-group conferences, how Harding's rhetorical success masked his near-total inability at Presidential homework. But beyond these details is the larger methodological point: to begin modestly with the minimum, necessary role requirements, and to define both role and style in terms of action, of performance.

From the actor's viewpoint, style is habit. The role is new, he is old. The roles he has been in may not be much like the new one, but he will proceed, as all of us do, consciously or not, by analogy. How has he met similar situations in the past? Of course, his intentions also enter into it—he wants to do better than he did before, may even have profound hopes for revolutionizing his modes of operation. He may, like Nixon, keep preaching at himself as to what one ought to do in the role. But alas, it is far easier to scan one's history and, in the mind, derive "lessons" for a hoped-for future than it is actually to change one's basic coping habits. That must remain a hypothesis, though there is a good deal of evidence to support it, as many a middle-aged cigarette-smoker and exercise-avoider can attest.

On Stealing from Psychology

No, the grass is not necessarily greener over there. Wandering in the chaos of our own discipline, political scientists are forever turning to some other one—history, economics, philosophy or what have you— in the hope that their ordered ways can be adapted to the study of politics. Most often, it does not take long to learn that each scholarly body has disorders of its own, that the list of fundamental, demon-strated, hard-core propositions is as short there as here, while theories abound. Perhaps the fun of political science is partly that we are in a fine position to borrow from neighboring disciplines. For ours is not a methodology, nor even a single methodological approach, but a subject matter. To be sure, many political science concepts are hy-pothetically extendable along many fronts, but in fact the great majority of us are mainly concerned with the doings of specific insti-tutions called governments. This gives enormous flexibility—we can take from where we will to clarify our phenomenal focus. But only the inexperienced in such scholarly burglary suppose that all would be well if only one could get a grip on, say, sociology.

Psychology has advantages. All explanation involves the search for continuities, and one important continuity is the person and his ex-perience. Politics is a response to human needs: "the state comes into existence," quoth Aristotle, "originating in the bare needs of life, and continuing in existence for the sake of a good life."[23] Nearly all politi-cal phenomena can be interpreted psychologically, and most are. There are probably more political scientists unawarely writing psy-chology than prose.

The choice for the student of leadership is what *kind* of psychology to steal. I think there are two kinds less helpful than a third.

First, the straight-out analysis of the content of the reasons the actor offers for his actions is of limited utility. The leader explains himself purposefully—politically—not scientifically. That is, the reasons he advances are themselves political acts meant to have a persuasive impact on publics and other politicians. This introduces a good deal of static into the task of understanding why he acted as he did on objective grounds. *His* explanation will nearly always be too simple: that he did what any reasonable and good-hearted person would do in similar circumstances, an analysis which leaves out important variations in behavior among reasonable and good-hearted persons of different dispositions. In effect it leaves *him* out. We know too much about the impact of personality on politics to buy that. Most significant political circumstances are full of ambiguity—particularly the kinds of questions that reach a President. Variations in the actual responses of political leaders to roughly the same circumstances warn against relying too much on the leader's plainspoken explanation. Nor are his expressed intentions much help. It is not that Presidents habitually lie, it is that they (like us) hope for more than they can get or do. Surely a strong part of John Kennedy really wanted to move quickly on civil rights, of Lyndon Johnson to bring peace to Vietnam, of Richard Nixon to run an open government. But it didn't work out those ways. Nor have Presidents' ideologies—left or right—helped much in explaining what they did.

Systematic cognitive psychology can, I think, help in a slightly different way. By moving a step up the ladder of abstraction, from particular issue stands and standardized ideological expressions to the leader's worldview, we begin to get at themes at once more persistent and more significant in shaping action. A close review of what he has said over the years may reveal a fairly consistent set of assumptions—about how history works, what people are like, what the main purposes of politics are (to use the three I have found most useful). The product is a cognitive operational code of sorts, a set of politically relevant perceptual habits, hardly ever put together in a systematic way by the leader himself but derivable from his many comments as he experiences practical problems. FDR's penchant for experiment, for example, or Harry Truman's conclusion from his reading that "a leader is a man who has the ability to get other people to do what they don't want to do, and like it"[24] represent lasting, politically relevant ways of seeing.

At the other end of the scale from taking the politician's words at face value is psychoanalytic interpretation. There are numerous forms of this; I am thinking of the technique of interpreting a subject's expressions as symbols of or clues to unconscious processes. As Freud's marvelous first introductory lecture on psychoanalysis puts it, those mental processes "which are conscious are merely isolated acts and parts of the whole psychic entity."[25] In that same lecture Freud warns his students against undertaking careers like his (but in such an intriguing and challenging way as to win them over). There are good reasons for hesitating. Psychoanalysis is an extraordinarily delicate and difficult art-science, probably best left to those with long and intensive training. It is primarily a medical technique for the treatment of patients who are in extraordinarily dire straits and thus very highly motivated toward finding relief. While Freud himself and such brilliant analysts as Erik Erikson have contributed insightful studies of individual historical leaders, your average psychoanalyst has not yet demonstrated either consensus with his copractitioners nor specially helpful judgment about political leaders. The fact that psychoanalysis developed its conceptual apparatus in the treatment of sick people lends its language a pejorative cast, encourages the assumption that there is something haywire with the subject. There are interesting arguments against all these objections and empirically there are a few inspiring examples, such as Arnold Rogow's chilling account of why the first Secretary of Defense committed suicide.[26] I think the stronger arguments concern evidence and the special needs of political science.

The kind of evidence a psychoanalyst would like to have is often very hard to get for political leaders. Their free associations are simply not available. Instead there are fragments of biography, occasional peeks into the unconscious, as in young Wilson's fantasies about being a great sea captain. Thorough psychoanalytic exploration would require a great deal more, the building up of a whole symbolic context for interpretation. Once at a conference, Erik Erikson was patient enough to listen through my presentation about Hoover and Coolidge. In the Coolidge part was a very unusual bit of self-revelation (unusual for Coolidge, that is), in which Coolidge confessed that as a child he would "go into a panic if I heard strange voices in the kitchen," because he had such a struggle with shyness and knew he would have to go in and be introduced.[27] Erikson thought that if we could just understand that one passage, a great deal would be clear about Silent Cal. Another time I asked Michael Maccoby, also a gifted psychoanalyst (who happened to be my neighbor at the Center for Advanced Study in the Behavioral Sciences), to comment on a letter Richard Nixon wrote to his mother at age ten. The letter, signed "Your good dog RICHARD," features Richard the dog in the woods with some other dogs.[28] Richard gets hurt and ends with the wish that his mother "would come home right now." The little story is full of symbols: an old dog, a boy who trips and falls on him, biting and kicking, "a black round thing in a tree," a pond, and so forth. I supposed Dr. Maccoby would tell me all about what these symbols meant. Instead, he said that the letter meant Richard was sad.

Given the evidence we've got and can get, I think that is about what we can make of such tales. Coolidge's adds to the evidence of his shyness; Nixon's is congruent with numerous reports through his life of sad feelings. Perhaps more could be made of such glimpses into the unconscious, but lacking a larger context of evidence political scientists might best hold back—at least until some analysts do it better.

Further, it is not totally clear that we would find useful, for *our* purposes, the deepest data on political figures. The linkages between the deepest drives and political behavior may be indirect and uncertain. For instance, it may be very important for a psychoanalyst treating a patient to delve down below the defenses to get at Oedipal conflicts; that may vastly improve the chances for cure. But as is well known, patients who share deep Oedipal problems may resolve or manage them in vastly different ways, such as becoming extra effeminate or extra tough. These defenses may be very important in politics. But once the pattern of defenses is clear, political science purposes may not require uncovering their deepest roots.

An alternative psychological approach is a good deal simpler, requiring only a modicum of subsurface inference. Drawing on those aspects of psychoanalytic theory that deal with ego functioning (cf. Karen Horney, Harry Stack Sullivan, and David Shapiro), on social psychology insofar as that has room for individual variations (cf.

Tamotsu Shibutani, M. Brewster Smith, and David Krech), and especially on psychologies which stress the development of the person (cf. Robert White, Gordon W. Allport, Theodore Lidz, and Irving L. Janis), one can move into the psychology of experience—of how persons *adapt* to their successive environments, how they *perceive* those environments and themselves in relation to them, and how they *evaluate* themselves in the course of these activities. Or as the original coding scheme put it, "We want to know *what he did*. We want to know *how he felt* about what he did. We want to know *how he rationalized* what he did." In all three areas the person is viewed as *purposeful*, his primary purpose being to enhance and maintain self-esteem, and as *learning*, as he moves out of a remembered past into an anticipated future. Whether or not you buy my character-world-view-style formulation for understanding the personality of political leaders, this slice of psychology, focusing on the person coping with his environments and judging himself as he goes, is likely to help your scheme along. It lends itself readily to practical research; biographical accounts, for example, are rich with reports of our hero reacting to events, assaying himself, and developing strategies for coping. Evidentially, the approach helps cull the data; consequently, one is less interested in the author's broad generalizations than in the incidents of experience he portrays. These can be accumulated carefully, over a long life-period, to build a composite, balanced picture of what the man in fact does with his life. And the evidence can be presented—and therefore argued with and countered and checked by other evidence—rather than relying on one's force or elegance of assertion. For example, a researcher who believes I have misplaced a President or so on the active-passive or positive-negative dimensions (or both), or that the derivative characteristics (e.g., compulsion, compliance, withdrawal, adaptation) are exaggerated, need not be satisfied with general castigations; he can present his own array of facts which tip the balance in another direction.

On Concluding

There is no real end to understanding politicians, no comfortable Q.E.D. to rest in. The case is forever being reopened. The matter is worth attending to because, for better or for worse, we are married to politics. Politics is a restless groping after the conditions for a decent life—a discipline of the second-best. There is no salvation in it. What politics can do (one continues to hope) is at least prevent suffering, at most make human fulfillment possible. In simple, politics is politicians; there is no way to understand it without understanding them. Essays like this one answer nothing—Sabine was right: "A method is good for just what it does." Yet it is worth thinking, as one goes along, how one is doing it. The tactics will fall into place when the strategies are clear, so I have tried to focus on the larger choices. But a general can ponder too long; the real proofs are out there in the fog of battle, where the data are.

*FDR was neither a
brilliant student
nor an exemplar of
personal virtue, but
he was a political
genius. How did
his early life help
shape his political
artistry?*

6

Roots of Genius

BIOGRAPHY IS AT the heart of democracy. Democracy's main feature is election: the people pick the rulers. Therefore the citizen is of necessity put in the role of a person-picker. To do that well demands biographical judgment. Considering how often bad leaders win elections, popular judgment of political life-histories needs improvement. In turn, those responsible for supplying the electorate with the information they need to choose among candidates ought to think through more thoroughly how to find and tell the right stuff. That responsibility falls most heavily on the political journalist who, unlike his academic counterpart, has the ear of the general public.

With the journalist in mind, I take up here one of the hardest political biography questions: what to do when important background information is missing. Three illustrations from the life of Franklin Delano Roosevelt are analyzed: his long experience with his father, James Roosevelt, his more than two years of six-hours-a-day work on the *Harvard Crimson*, and his traumatic attack of poliomyelitis. In each case important information is missing. How should the journalist covering a candidate's background deal with such hiatuses? Professional biographers have developed sophisticated answers. As the argument progresses, my preference for simplicity will be clear.

I

James MacGregor Burns moved understanding beyond the useless finding that FDR was complex by applying a typology: Machiavelli's image of the lion and the fox. Roosevelt the lion brought to politics a muscular Victorianism: steady values energetically advanced. But then "Roosevelt was projected out of this world into bizarre and unanticipated phases of the twentieth century."[1] Unlike many men of his generation, Roosevelt took a fox-like leap into the new age, retaining his basic beliefs but dashing down whatever trail of policy looked most effective in implementing them. Roosevelt-haters saw his opportunism; Roosevelt-lovers saw his idealism. Both were right. Burns, a Roosevelt scholar, eloquently depicted the combination—at its best, but also at its worst, as when, in his second term, "the defects of Roosevelt's political virtues" nearly wrecked his leadership.[2]

Roosevelt's energizing joy in Presidenting, Burns believed, owed much to his pleasure in White House theatrics. He had fun acting the part—talking, pausing, gesturing, lifting his eyebrows as he lowered his voice. But beyond the surface dramatics, "He was a superb actor in the far more significant sense that he was responding in each of his roles not merely to an assigned script but to something within himself."[3]

Burns's perception rings true. But in spite of book after book about Roosevelt, the shape of the "something within himself" still fluctuates fuzzily on the biographic screen. Where did he get the extraordinary qualities which enabled him not only to lead the nation through a wild variety of challenges but also to work his way out of the political quagmires he himself created?

The question has significance. No President since Roosevelt has come close to his achievements in domestic and foreign policy. We would do well to find and advance to the Presidency another Roosevelt, another President who combines his vigor, his values, and his political competence. Yet the story of Roosevelt's nomination and election gives little encouragement. The nation lucked out, thanks in the nomination phase to the sweat and brains of Louis Howe and James Farley, and in the election phase to Hoover's rigidification in the face of economic tragedy. To the larger public, Roosevelt's appeal probably consisted almost entirely of the fact that he was not Hoover and not a Republican. A good many of the professional President-watchers read him wrong: "Feather Duster" Roosevelt, "the cork-screw candidate," "not a strong character himself," "a highly impressionable person . . . an amiable man . . . too eager to please . . . a pleasant man who, without any important qualifications for the office, would very much like to be President"—in modern parlance, a wimp.[4] A major source of that warped judgment was no doubt Roosevelt himself. Campaigning in the midst of rapidly escalating social chaos, he wiggled his policies from speech to speech and, sensing the public's growing desperation, put on the persona of William Howard Taft: "Roosevelt smiles and smiles and smiles and it doesn't get tiresome," wrote one reporter.[5] Then as now, campaigning was to Presidenting as checkers is to tennis.

To figure out what kind of President Roosevelt would be, the President-watchers should have reached back behind his cavorting on the campaign trail to his life history. Had they been able to apply even a rough comparison of Presidential character, worldview, and style, they would have done better than the campaign-watchers. But beyond that kind of crude typological estimation, they might also have delved into the FDR biography to search out the particular self-images, orientations, and habits his experience had composed into that "something within himself" with which the roles later handed him would resonate. Had they attempted to do so, though, they no doubt would have encountered the problem which torments every serious biographer, the problem of gaps. The mystery of Franklin Roosevelt's inner dynamic continues because so much of the story of its genesis stands unknown. Had he kept a reliable daily diary, his story might be different. Instead, we must seek alternatives to the straightforward account of what he thought as he did what he did.

II

"When biographers talk shop among themselves," reports Paul Kendall, "you will hear animated discussions of a problem rarely mentioned by reviewers: the problem of gaps." Kendall explains:

> That paper trail, extending from the birth certificate to the death certificate, is never continuous or complete. The more remote in time the man is, the more gaps there will be. These gaps occur at all stages in the trail but are very likely to come during the childhood and adolescence of the subject.[6]

This is clearly the case in political biography. To piece together the story of Andrew Johnson's childhood and adolescence, for example, required drawing inferences about long times from short facts.[7] Even today, politicians' mothers, harassed by reporters to come up with interesting anecdotes about early life and times, eventually oblige—but not without the inward recognition that long gaps stretched out between the minidramas of childhood. They raised their children a day at a time, rarely anticipating that someday a writer, or a nominating committee, would want to transform their passing impressions into stories. Like the mothers, the biographers must also deal with gaps, and, as Kendall puts it,

> It is gaps that tempt the fledgling biographer to speculate, the "artistic" biographer to invent, the scholarly biographer to give a lecture on history. To fill gaps by wondering aloud, lying, padding—or simply to leave them for the reader to rumble into—is not to fill the shoes of the true biographer.[8]

Franklin Delano Roosevelt's life history illustrates the problem in several varieties. His mother, Sara Delano Roosevelt, eventually put out a book called *My Boy Franklin*[9] which is full of nicely rounded anecdotes of dramatic events in young Franklin's life, just the kinds of stories a biographer or a journalist wants, to fill in the gaps of a vaguely remembered childhood. Published in 1933, just at the time the nation was bubbling with curiosity about the Unknown Quantity they had just elected, the book has continued to fill gaps. As biographer Geoffrey Ward explains, "Franklin Roosevelt's boyhood has received little attention from his biographers, in part because many family papers have only recently been opened but also, I believe, because its serene surface seems to reveal so few telling incidents."[10] In *My Boy Franklin*, his mother supplies moments of tragedy (her wrapping a coat around him as she thought their ship was sinking into the Atlantic) and comedy (his day of "freedom" from parental supervision)—dramas nearly irresistible to the gap-confronting biographer.

III

But even with such stories plugged into the narrative, large gaps remain. One I think of considerable importance both for the Roosevelt story and predictive biography more generally is the relationship of youthful Franklin to his father. James Roosevelt's photographs exude Victorian dignity and solidity; he is not smiling even as he poses with Baby Franklin perched on his shoulder.[11] Himself an "elusive figure" who was "persuaded that a gentleman's duty was to stay out of the newspapers,"[12] James Roosevelt left behind only one miniadventure, later garbled and inflated by President FDR, that he had joined Garibaldi's army briefly while on a walking tour in Italy.[13] Such papers as he had produced and received were lost in a fire in 1866 (he was born in 1828).[14] His first wife kept a lively and revealing journal, but Sara Delano's accounts, while full of affection and respect, furnish sparse details of what his father meant to little Franklin.[15] Long after her son grew up, she said her early ambition for him had been "very simple"—"to grow to be like his father, straight and honorable, just and kind, an outstanding American."[16] His father had repeatedly refused political nominations, but when Franklin, about to be elected to the state senate, addressed "my friends" in the neighborhood, he said, "You have known what my father stood for before me, you have known how close he was to the life of this town, and I do not need to tell you that it is my desire always to follow in his footsteps."[17]

What footsteps? Certain analogic leaps are easy enough. James did his duty in his church and community, impressing on Franklin a message later reinforced by Endicott Peabody at Groton and by Franklin's cousin Theodore: that the privileged need not sell everything they have and give it to the poor, but that they had better make an active contribution to the betterment of the world around them. James and Sara were also determined optimists, bent on "keeping Franklin's mind on nice things, on a high level," a seeding which took root in the boy's happy disposition.[18] James had "a striking capacity to compartmentalize his life," as Burns notes,[19] a capacity his son would inherit or imitate. And though he never discussed business at home, James was a plunger in business, as Franklin later became a plunger in politics. According to Sara, James laughed with, but never at, little Franklin,[20] freeing humor from its negative implication, and he left discipline to others: assigned by Sara to paddle the boy, James took him aside and said, "Consider yourself spanked,"[21] much as Franklin, years later, would deal with various deviating officials. Especially in retrospect, such direct and relatively simple links are drawable; even in prospect, they might have been extractable from the multitude of available similarities. The rule of interpretation could not be plainer: like father, like son.

But in Franklin Roosevelt's case the influence of his father surely went beyond the standard identifications. Consider the amount of time they spent together. James did business in New York City a day or two a week and in the evenings; he was semi-retired, in his fifties.[22] The rest of his time he spent with Sara and Franklin on his Hudson River estate, at their summer place at Campobello, or traveling, to Europe or in the states and Canada in his private railway car.[23] He was Franklin's close companion for fourteen years. From age three on, Franklin spent nearly every summer at Campobello, where his father taught him—hour after hour—to swim, fish, and sail. As a little boy he was photographed steering James's fifty-one-foot schooner; at sixteen he got a sailboat of his own.[24] James took him to Europe, to the Chicago World's Fair, to the White House for a visit with President Cleveland.[25] Back home on the Hudson, James coached his son in sledding (from age two), rowing, skating, iceboating, shooting, and horseback riding. And "from the time that he could perch on his father's shoulder," according to one biographer,[26] Franklin rode with James on his daily round of the estate. At four he got his own chubby Welsh pony, "Debby," to ride beside his father as he checked the work of the place—on what needed to be done with the dairy cattle, poultry, horses, trees, grain fields, stables, gardens, walls, and fences, stopping to receive the reports of the hired hands along the way and issuing the appropriate orders.[27] This routine went on for at least ten years of Franklin Delano Roosevelt's life.

Neither James nor Franklin wrote up observations or reactions when they returned from these rounds. Sara took note from time to time that they had gone sledding or sailing together, but what they talked about, what they made of it, what young FDR carried away from those thousands of hours of being and doing with his father remains obscure. To suppose that those times meant nothing to him is absurd, but to infer from the fact of these interactions what they signified to the interactors is of necessity an act of interpretation, not reportage.

IV

It is just this type of hiatus the psychologist Robert White had in mind as the "gap at the center of our knowledge about personality," that is, the neglect of "continuous development over periods of time amid natural circumstances."[28] Only dynamic psychology, White thinks, has focused on individual development, "but dynamic psychology had its origin in the attempt to treat neurotic patients; it is still largely based on the study of blocked and disordered behavior. Thus it comes about that the searching eye of scientific research has barely glanced at everyday lives in progress, to say nothing of lives marked by unusual happiness or major social contributions."[29] Similarly in biography, the " 'buzz and hum' of daily life"[30] seem hardly worth recording. Even the autobiographer, Herbert Spencer wrote, "is obliged to omit from his narrative the commonplaces of daily life and to limit himself almost exclusively to salient events, actions and traits. . . . But by leaving out the humdrum part of the life, forming that immensely larger part which it has in common with other lives, and by setting forth only the striking things, he produces the impression that it differed from other lives more than it really did. This defect is inevitable."[31]

"There are no rules for handling gaps," wrote biographer Paul Murray Kendall.[32] With or without rules, though, the biographer must handle them somehow. A comically misleading solution is for the biographer to go explore in person the scene where the "buzz and hum" once sounded, hoping to pick up instructive leftover harmonics. But strolling around the field of the Battle of Gettysburg, as the birds sing and the sun shines, hardly brings home what those terrified, smoke-blinded, bomb-deafened boys went through. All of us tourists and travel-grant applicants would like to think otherwise, but, in fact, climbing Shakespeare's stairs helps little in probing Shakespeare's mind.

Another solution is the literary invention of whatever one imagines the hero may have had in his mind, as when Carl Sandburg supposes that Abe Lincoln's desire for "a little streak of honest glory . . . still lived in him, lived far under in him, in the deeper blue pools of him. It was one of his secrets as he touched elbows with people in Diller's drug store, in Canedy's, and mixed with men in shirt-sleeves around the public square in Springfield."[33] Lincoln's "deeper blue pools" may have floated that "secret"—or not; only Sandburg knows, and the link between the surround and Lincoln's ambition remains obscure.

A third solution is to elide the time, to simply skip through long periods such as FDR's time with James by supplying a paragraph of description or some illustrative anecdote, or even by shuffling sequences in such a way as to cover over the disparity between numbers of pages and numbers of years. Biographer Leon Edel, for example, says he sticks to the facts but feels no inhibition in altering their temporal sequence: "I do this in violation of all chronology. . . . By weaving backward and forward in time and even dipping into the future . . . I reckon with time, as it really exists, as something fluid and irregular and with memory as something alive and flickering and evanescent. I refuse to be fettered by the clock and the calendar."[34] Kendall calls that sort of thing "gelding the lily"—"What the novelist does with time to make an imaginary person seem real may very well tend to make a real person seem imaginary."[35] The gap remains, but it is transformed into an insignificant nap of the soul or slivered among its past and future until it virtually disappears.

The worst solution is to make it up. For ages past, and long after the invention of history, reality gaps have been filled with fiction, from imagined conversations to events thought plausible, given what one knows of the facts. The seduction begins with the obvious fact that authors select from a potentially enormous store of information what to put in and what to leave out. If there were but one historian or biographer in the field, that would make the reader heavily dependent on the author's own mind-set. At least with famous figures that isolation rarely exists, so that biographers resist the temptation to diddle with the facts. Or to invent them. Like the responsible journalist,[36] the responsible biographer has little interest in drifting over into "docudrama" or the "nonfiction novel." Kendall puts it eloquently:

> At best, fact is harsh, recalcitrant matter, as tangible as the hunk of rusty iron one trips over and yet as shapeless as a paper hat in the rain. Fact is a cold stone, an inarticulate thing, dumb until something happens to it; and there is no use the biographer waiting for spontaneous combustion or miraculous alchemy. Fact must be rubbed up in the mind, until it begins to glow, to give off that radiance we call meaning. Fact is a biographer's only friend, and worst enemy.[37]

Especially in this period in which literary criticism is floating through a phase of indifference to—even disdain for—factuality,[38] biography remains an island of stability in a sea of symbolism.

V

What then might we make of the long, long times Franklin Roosevelt spent with his father, James? I think the answer lies in the purpose of political biography. If that purpose is to develop increasingly reliable estimates, before the fact, of how leaders will behave in office, on the ground that democracy lives or dies by such judgments, then the various literary problems take a backseat to the problem of political judgment. Our concern is not entertainment but prediction, not plumbing the soul but assessing the stability of its surface, not exemplifying some philosophy or theology or spirit of the age, but learning how to see in the information available today those patterns most likely to give shape to what this particular person will do tomorrow and in the years after. We should not mind, then, being simple, even dull, even explicit about our ignorance. And we should not trade in our awkward facts for graceful fictions.

That Roosevelt turned out to be a nontheorist was, it seems to me, readily predictable from his background, particularly from what it lacked. His childhood lacked much exposure to the troubles which engender contemplation: business was not discussed, or other potential unpleasantries, such as politics. He grew up in a religious environment, but not a theologically inquiring one: his Christianity was believed in, not mulled over. That perspective was reinforced at Groton, where Endicott Peabody did not think boys should think too much, and at Harvard, where young Roosevelt reacted negatively to the theoretical bent of his professors. He rejected deep or disturbing psychologies as well, as evidenced by his glossing-over attitude toward Eleanor Roosevelt's personal crises.

But Roosevelt was more than a nontheorist; he was a pragmatist. He was a fixer. He was a politician far more interested in making things work than in understanding their deeper meanings. I think the fourteen years he spent with James confirmed the positive aspect of the Rooseveltian worldview: the sense that whatever was out of kilter could be put back together again. That is the attitude and mode of thinking he most likely derived from all those long years, in childhood and youth, of practical coaching by his father. Season after season, James taught Franklin how to handle his sled in the snow, his horse in the field, his boat in the sea. Day after day—for years—Franklin rode around the estate with his father as James dealt with one down-to-earth problem after another, such as where to plant trees, how to graze the cattle, when to fix the fences, what to say to a delinquent field hand, and so on ad infinitum. For at least a crucial decade of his early life, young Franklin Roosevelt had a practical, paternal education unlike the experience of the modern child of suburbia. If the lack of theoretical concerns left a gap in his life, he filled it by learning to address and resolve problems of practical existence.

Roosevelt went on to many another preparatory phase, bringing to bear on all sorts of issues this fundamental approach. His readiness to take on a new problem, examine what it was, figure out the practical possibilities, and act to put the most likely solution into effect—that readiness, far from common in politicians, he brought to adulthood from his peculiar childhood. To reach that conclusion requires no high-flown speculation or deep-delving insight, but a direct and simple interpretation of how this politician-to-be was spending his time and how those activities bore on what his role as President would entail.

VI

James Roosevelt died on December 8, 1900. Franklin was a freshman at Harvard. He had got through the discipline of Groton, with its rigorous schedule, cell-like rooms, and daily cold showers, confirming his independence of the luxury at home. But socially Groton had been a wounding experience for him. He entered at age fourteen, two years after his classmates, thus encountering a band of adolescents who had already worked out their cliques and manners, their gestures and codes and pecking orders. Ward explains:

> It had been the natural order of his childhood world that he be liked by everyone, and he worked almost desperately to replicate that world at Groton. His inevitable failure to do so confused and frustrated him. "I always felt entirely out of things," he admitted to one close friend many years later, and to his wife he would confess that something had gone "sadly wrong" at Groton.[39]

Thus Franklin entered Harvard with strong and special motives "to triumph where he felt he had failed at Groton, in the athletic and social standings that mattered most to him and to his peers."[40] He flung his 146-pound frame into Harvard football, but wound up on one of the eight freshman scrub teams. He went out for crew but again was relegated to intramurals. He got into the Freshman Glee Club but did not make the varsity. He did get himself elected captain of his football team and of his crew, and secretary of the Freshman Glee Club; perhaps that supplied a clue to his future political genius, but the arenas he won in were out at the margins of the Harvard scene.[41]

On the social front, Franklin duded himself up with fashionable new clothes and plunged into that even more competitive arena in the fall of his sophomore year. His letters to his mother recounted how he "ran" for the top clubs, where he ranked in this or that race, when he was "about to be slaughtered" or victorious in the selective contests. His ambition focused on the Porcellian, the top club, of which both his father, James, and Theodore Roosevelt had been members. Franklin got into a couple of lesser societies but was not picked for the Porcellian. The rejection hit him hard. One of his relatives called it Franklin's "bitterest moment," and Eleanor Roosevelt said it gave him an "inferiority complex."[42] Years later, Franklin called it "the greatest disappointment of my life."[43] In the clubs he did get into, Franklin, the practiced collector, was assigned to librarianships. Cousin Theodore, always in his mind's eye, suddenly became President of the United States when McKinley was shot to death in September of Franklin's sophomore year. All in all, it is plausible to suppose that during this period the young man's psyche contained a strong compensatory need. The biographers are in basic agreement that that need came to focus on the *Harvard Crimson*, the student newspaper.[44]

Freshman Franklin tried out for the *Crimson* staff along with sixty-seven of his classmates. He was passed over in the first round, in February 1901. Two months later, his luck rescued him. He learned that his cousin Theodore was visiting Professor A. Lawrence Lowell. Franklin telephoned, and Theodore said they could get together right after he lectured to Lowell's class the following morning. That was news; the lecture had been kept secret to prevent overcrowding of the class. Franklin raced to the *Crimson* office and broke the story, which appeared in the paper next morning and resulted in some two thousand students gathering at the event. That scoop plus the fact that a good many original candidates had dropped out got FDR elected one of the five new editors.[45] He worked six hours a day on the paper. In the spring of his sophomore year he was elected secretary. In the fall of his junior year he was made one of the two managing editors in charge of getting out the *Crimson* two nights a week. In January of that academic year he was elected managing editor, which meant that the following year he would be "president"—the title of the editor-in-chief. He was scheduled to graduate that June (1903), thanks to his Groton credits, but he enrolled in graduate school in order to carry on his *Crimson* work.[46] That summer and the next year, Franklin concentrated almost entirely on the newspaper. "Every spare moment," he wrote his mother, was "taken up with the paper" so that he had "little time to think about courses."[47]

For at least two years, then, Franklin Delano Roosevelt devoted the major portion of his waking hours, day after day, month after month, to his newspaper work. What was that like? What did he derive from it? Given the compensatory context and the success he achieved, no wonder his *Crimson* endeavor emerges as "most important" among his college experiences.[48] "Nothing during his Harvard years meant as much to him as the newspaper and his role in it."[49] In those days "the *Crimson* came first for Franklin,"[50] as his biographers report, and Roosevelt himself later judged his work on the *Crimson* as "perhaps the most useful preparation I had in college for public service."[51] Yet here again, the gap problem unfolds in Roosevelt's biography. There are a few retrospective quotations, such as that as editor, "in his geniality there was a kind of frictionless command," especially in his relations with the two Scots printers, countered by another contemporary's view of him as "a snob," a person "ill at ease with people outside of his group."[52] There is the biographer's judgment that he did little to change the paper.[53] Years later FDR, apparently feeling the need to flesh out the story, described in dramatic detail how he got the scoop that Harvard President Eliot planned to vote for McKinley in 1900. In fact, another student did that.[54]

Lacking information on how Franklin Roosevelt actually spent all that time, how he developed over that considerable period, what the experience meant to him, and what he carried away from it into his political life, the biographers are left with the editorials in the *Crimson*, written by *Crimson* president Roosevelt. Accurately described as banal and unrevealing, they are nevertheless subjected to paragraph after paragraph of description and analysis, including speculation as to why he did not editorialize on various subjects. It is as if these writings must be dealt with because they are there, much as the products of "Editorial Writer Lyndon B. Johnson" of the San Marcos College *Star* subsequently were analyzed up, down, and sideways, before it was revealed that another student wrote them.[55]

VII

History leans on what is recorded. It is not that the historian necessarily believes what is written down, but that he or she depends on it.[56] The "Dark Ages" get their name not only from their tragedy but also from their obscurity—too little writing. In the present age of the copying machine, historians often face the opposite problem: too much writing. But in history and its subfield biography what exists "in black and white" is the stuff to work with. Politicians realize that fact, as when Theodore Roosevelt, coming to anticipate that he might one day be the subject of biography, began to write personal letters with that in mind, or when Franklin Roosevelt, wanting Louis Howe and perhaps others to think that he composed his own first inaugural address, copied out Raymond Moley's complete draft in his own hand.[57] Bess Truman tried to protect Harry Truman from historical embarrassment by burning his old love letters.[58] Nixon had reason to regret that he had not burned the Watergate tapes, and Reagan has been repeatedly caught lying on videotape. Politicians write their own memoirs and autobiographies—Jimmy Carter's appeared before his election—to help along their reputations.

Lacking records about obviously important events and/or periods, the biographer is in a bind. Barbara Tuchman illustrates the problem in *Practicing History*,[59] an unusually open and apparently candid account of how her histories get done. She is not of the mind that facts unknown do not exist; history is there, whether or not the historian perceives it. The tree falls in the forest even if listeners are absent: "If it left a space that let in the sun on a hitherto shade-grown species, or if it killed a dominant animal and shifted rule of the pack to one of different characteristics, or if it fell across a path of animals and caused some small change in their habitual course from which later changes followed, then the fall made history whether anyone heard it or not."[60] To the historical imagination, Tuchman believes, "Corroborative detail is the great corrective," checking the historian from "soaring off the ground into theories of his own invention."[61] As Tuchman's strongly documented works attest, she has been a diligent digger after facts. But she confesses that when she was unable to "find out enough to make it clear in my own mind" what happened at the battle for Alsace in August 1914, "I faked it, but nobody noticed."[62] And she found another way to fill in the blank in seeking corroborative detail concerning the Dreyfus case:

> When I was investigating General Mercier, the Minister of War who was responsible for the original condemnation of Dreyfus

and who in the course of the Affair became the hero of the Right, I discovered that at parties of the *haut monde* ladies rose to their feet when General Mercier entered the room. That is the kind of detail which to me is worth a week of research. It illustrates the society, the people, the state of feeling at the time more vividly than anything I could write and in shorter space, too, which is an additional advantage. It epitomizes, it crystalizes, it visualizes. The reader can see it; moreover, it sticks in his mind; it is memorable.[63]

But is it true? In this case, Tuchman writes, "The inspired bit about the ladies rising to their feet for General Mercier comes from Proust as do many other brilliant details"[64]—from a *novel* by Proust. She sees "no reason why a novelist should not supply as authentic material as a journalist or a general." She explains, "To determine what may justifiably be used from a novel, one applies the same criterion as for any nonfictional account: If a particular item fits with what one knows of the time, the place, the circumstances and the people, it is acceptable; otherwise not."[65] This despite her view that: "One must be wary in using [newspapers] for facts, because an event reported one day in a newspaper is usually modified or denied or turns out to be rumor on the next."[66]

Filling in a blank with a "corroborative detail" from a novel, accepted because it is consistent with other, factual details, is hard to justify as a solution to the gap problem. Such a detail becomes not corroborative but symbolic: it does not add to the factual evidence but is put in to represent it. And that is the province of the novelist, not of the historian. One can imagine Proust, groping for a way to symbolize Mercier's reputation, thinking up the scene of the ladies rising. Proust does not present his novel as fact, as a report of what he has observed, but as fiction, that is, a report of what he has visualized in his mind.

The temptation to exaggerate the significance and reality of what is recorded is subtler than the temptation to invent events and compose compositions in the manner of the fictionist. Especially in an age when "documents" no longer record only definite facts or even considered opinions, but all sorts of subjunctive hypotheticals and imagined possibilities, "documentation" takes on a different cast. That it can distort the reality of experience seems evident from the example of Roosevelt's work on the *Harvard Crimson*. On the one hand, there is the fact that he spent a great deal of time and effort, during a formative period, managing a newspaper. On the other hand, the few written references in letters, etc., are unrevealing and contradictory, forcing reliance of the graphophile on his editorials, which tell even less.

VIII

What, then, is the alternative? Again, as in the interpretation of his long times with his father, direct and simple speculation is preferable to specious fictions or warping quotations from the record. In substance, the matter is important. For politics at least, this is the media age, in which politicians spend countless hours and scads of dollars trying to bend the news to their purposes. Roosevelt was a master at this part of the role. Editors and publishers were largely against him, but he kept winning over the reporters. "Roosevelt's way with the press," Burns noted, "showed his mastery of the art of government. He made so much news and maintained such a friendly attitude toward the newspapermen covering the White House that he quickly and easily won their sympathy."[67] From time to time he let them know that he, too, had been a newspaperman.[68] More important to his rhetorical style as President, Roosevelt understood how to help reporters do their work by supplying them with stories. He understood that Hoover-type abstractions or Harding-type alliterative bloviations did nothing for the reporter responsible for coming up with an interesting story. He more or less listened to their questions, but emphatically supplied them with stories suiting his own purposes. The result was an amazing continuance of popular support won through media predominantly owned and managed by men who detested him.

Roosevelt's political style came to focus in his first independent political success: the seven years he served as Assistant Secretary of the Navy, out from under his mother's supervision.[69] But surely his tour of duty with the *Harvard Crimson* counts as a rehearsal. Whatever he wrote in his editorials, young Franklin could not have helped but learn—through extended daily experience—how to make a paper work. He must have learned how a reporter looks and listens in order to find a story. He could not have helped but get used to what it means to face a deadline after which your story does not exist. He inevitably got an education in wheedling quotations from the powerful, in the necessity for confirming observations of fact, in the posing of a contradiction or a paradox in the lead, in judging the right moment to go off the record, and so on. There is no indication that he himself became an expert journalist. But surely, in six hours a day putting out a newspaper, Roosevelt picked up an understanding of what a reporter is up against, far surpassing that of many another President-to-be. So when he encountered reporters in his later official roles, he knew the strongest possible way to bend a journalist: by lending him a hand.

IX

If Roosevelt's longtime relation with his father helped mold his pragmatic, empirical worldview, and his substantial experience with the *Harvard Crimson* trained his communications style, it is plausible to suppose that his trauma as a polio victim would have revealed and shaped the development of his character. Not yet forty years old, he was suddenly slammed down by that mysterious virus, suddenly reduced from a father to a baby, his legs cut out from under him. The pain was intense and continuous. The surface of his legs became so sensitive that even the weight of the bedclothes hurt them. A doctor mistakenly prescribed massage. Eleanor or Louis Howe would knead his legs as he desperately gritted his teeth, sweating in agony, and occasionally letting out a groan.[70] He could not control his bladder or rectal sphincter; he had to use a catheter.[71] He burned with fever. "Every shift of his body's position had to be made by others at the cost of excruciating pain to himself, for his tactile sensitivity increased at least in proportion to the failure of his motor nervous system."[72] He was utterly helpless. The odds were he was dying.

Following the long-drawn-out initial trauma came the increasingly evident prognosis: he would be a permanent cripple, never again able to walk or swim or sail in normal fashion. At first, Roosevelt dropped into a period of "black despair . . . utter despondency,"[73] "acute mental depression."[74] Years later he told his friend Frances Perkins that he had experienced complete despair, that he felt God had abandoned him.[75] Roosevelt hit bottom. Eleanor was with him night and day during the first month. "The jagged alternations between hope and despair; the necessity of giving blind trust to a physician even when the physician, cruelly pressed, could scarcely trust himself; the fearsome responsibility involved; above all the unpredictable oscillations of mood in the patient himself, which had to be ministered to with the utmost firmness, subtlety, and tenderness" burdened Eleanor.[76]

Characteristically, Franklin Roosevelt soon had his cheerful external persona back in place. He collapsed in mid-August, 1921; by September 21, he could joke that "I have renewed my youth in a rather unpleasant manner by contracting what was fortunately a rather mild case of infantile paralysis."[77] Eleanor, raised in the same Victorian mode he was, slammed the door on expressions of despair and reinforced his emerging hopefulness. Louis Howe, shrewdly recognizing the political importance of public optimism, got Roosevelt the brave and positive across to the newspapers.

Especially to his children, FDR was careful to convey good cheer. And weeks after the attack, when his old Navy boss, Josephus Daniels, came to call, Franklin reached out from the bed and smacked him hard with his fist. "You thought you were coming to see an invalid, but I can knock you out in any bout," he laughed.[78] His doctor told the New York Times that "He will not be crippled," that "No one need have any fear of permanent injury from the attack." FDR wrote the publisher Adolph Ochs that he had been skeptical when the doctors told him that. "But now that I have seen the same statements officially made in the New York Times I feel immensely relieved because I know of course it must be true."[79] Ordeal after ordeal was yet to come, but the old FDR seemed back on the stage.

What mark did this trauma leave upon the soul of Franklin Delano Roosevelt? While he communicated to some degree the level of his emotions—despair and then hope—their content remains obscure. What did he make of it? What did it do to him? He never said. Once Eleanor Roosevelt was asked a cruel question: "Mrs Roosevelt, do you think your husband's illness affected his mind?" and she answered, "Yes, I think it did. I think it made him more sensitive to the feelings of people."[80] Frances Perkins thought, decades later, that he had undergone "a spiritual transformation," that "the years of pain and suffering purged the slightly arrogant attitude he displayed on several occasions before he was stricken. The man emerged completely warmhearted, with humility of spirit and a deeper philosophy."[81] Eleanor herself came to think that his illness was a "turning point, and proved a blessing in disguise; for it gave him a strength and courage he had not had before." In the late 1940s she recalled that, "He had to think out the fundamentals of living and learn the greatest of all lessons—infinite patience and never-ending persistence."[82] Possibly—but apparently no quotation exists, no document is to be found in which Franklin Roosevelt himself, either then or later, revealed what polio did to his character.

Roosevelt's silence about his inner life was typical of him, not unique to the polio trauma. Even FDR's immediate family found him an enigma. His son James wrote that when he was a child, his busy father sometimes "inundated us with fun and activity—and with love, too—but in his special way, which was both detached and overpowering. Sometimes we felt we didn't have him at all." And later: "Father had very few 'soul-searching' conversations with any of us—Mother included—on matters other than public issues. . . . His great lack in life . . . was that, while he had lots of persons to whom he could talk, he had no real confidants. . . . Of what was inside him, of what really drove him, Father talked with no one." Eleanor Roosevelt said,

> I don't think I was his confidante either. He never would discuss an intimate family problem unless it was something that had reached the stage at which it just had to be discussed. . . . His was an innate kind of reticence that may have been developed by the fact that he had an older father and a very strong-willed mother, who constantly tried to exercise control over him in the early years. Consequently, he may have fallen into the habit of keeping his own counsel, and it became part of his nature not to talk to anyone of intimate matters.

His daughter, Anna, probably his closest family connection, explained his reticence: "Remember, this was a boy whose nearest friend lived about a mile and a half away. That was Edmund Rogers, who just happened to be there, the only one, I think. When Father went to Groton at fourteen he no more knew how to get along with boys his own age than the man in the moon."[83] Roosevelt the grown-up continued to keep his deeper feelings to himself. Which makes all the more intriguing what might be revealed by understanding what happened in his soul when his life fell apart.

X

To the biographer of pure Freudian persuasion, the ordinary accounts of what people said or did are nonsense. "Whoever undertakes to write a biography," wrote Freud, "binds himself to lying, to concealment, to flummery, and even to hiding his own lack of understanding, since biographical material is not to be had, and if it were it could not be used."[84] From this perspective the chatter of life, the rhetorical huffing and puffing, the sights and sounds humans report to one another constitute nothing but a smoke, released not to express the truth a person bears within but to prevent that expression, to protect the human reality from the danger of exposure. Seen in this light, even if FDR himself had gone on at length about what the polio trauma did to him, it would still be wrong.[85] Character is a secret, glimpsed through a glass darkly even by the person who carries it around. Character is shaped, not by gradual growth into a mode of adaptation but by critical events, real or imagined, particularly in early life. Character is revealed, if at all, not in the warp and woof of everyday self-awareness, but in moments of insight, such as Paul's conversion on the road to Damascus, Oedipus's sudden realization as to how he had related to his parents, or the modern patient's surprise when, all at once, his free associations clasp hands. Thus Freud's biographical study of Leonardo da Vinci focuses on one strange incident, real or imagined, in da Vinci's childhood, when a vulture opened his mouth with its tail and struck his lips repeatedly.[86] In the biographical segments of *Moses and Monotheism*, Freud concentrates on the single note that Moses was an Egyptian.[87] More recently, Erik Erikson's *Young Man Luther* places strong interpretative emphasis on one revealing outburst, Luther's "fit in the choir,"[88] and his biographical study of Gandhi brings analysis to bear on one event, a strike in which Gandhi shaped his leadership.[89] This approach renders trivial the image of the personality patching itself together a piece at a time as it steps along the trail of life.

Consider Caesar at the Rubicon. This is the classic moment of decision—should he cross over or not? The political implications were enormous. The effect of his decision turned out to be fateful for Western civilization. But no one knows what went on in his mind between the time he saw the river and the time he crossed over it. Given the decision's overwhelming significance on the one hand and its total obscurity on the other, subsequent writers felt impelled to fill in the blank. One author had Caesar recall the statue of Alexander the Great he had seen at Cadiz, the sight of which made him groan with envy. Another reported that the night before he crossed over he dreamed of committing incest with his mother, which meant "Mother Earth," which meant conquest.[90] The poet Lucan notes that the Rubicon would have been flooded with snow-melt on that January day and surmises that Caesar would have had to wait before crossing while his cavalry got their horses in to block the current while his infantry built a bridge. But Lucan then has Caesar encounter "a giant phantom of the Homeland in distress" and composes for Caesar a speech as he hit the far bank: "Here I bid farewell to peace and outraged justice. It is thee, O Fortune, whom I follow. Away with treaties! Let us surrender to destiny! Let War be our judge!"[91]

Subsequent biographical writers, unwilling to let the gap go unfilled, pictured it even more colorfully. Suetonius, for example:

> Well aware how crucial a decision confronted him, he turned to his staff, remarking: "We may still draw back but, once across that little bridge, we shall have to fight it out." As he stood, in two minds, an apparition of superhuman size and beauty was seen sitting on the river bank playing a reed pipe. A party of shepherds gathered around to listen and, when some of Caesar's men, including some of the trumpeters, broke ranks to do the same, the apparition snatched a trumpet from one of them, ran down to the river, blew a thunderous blast, and crossed over. Caesar exclaimed: "Let us accept this as a sign from the Gods,

and follow where they beckon, in vengeance on our double-dealing enemies. The die is cast."[92]

Plutarch moved the ghost from the riverbank into Caesar's mind:

When he came to the river Rubicon, which parts Gaul within the Alps from the rest of Italy, his thoughts began to work, now he was just entering upon the danger, and he wavered much in his mind, when he considered the greatness of the enterprise into which he was throwing himself. He checked his course, and ordered a halt, while he revolved with himself, and often changed his opinion one way or the other, without speaking a word. This was when his purposes fluctuated most; presently he also discussed the matter with his friends who were about him (of which number Asinius Pollio was one), computing how many calamities his passing that river would bring upon mankind, and what relation of it would be transmitted to posterity. At last, in a sort of passion, casting aside calculation, and abandoning himself to what might come, and using the proverb frequently in their mouths who enter upon dangerous and bold attempts, "The die is cast," with these words he took the river.[93]

"Without speaking a word"—yet Plutarch somehow is supposed to know what he was thinking, feeling, wondering.[94]

XI

The way of Suetonius—inventing events and dialogue—is out for the modern biographer who holds to the distinction between fact and fiction. But the way of Plutarch—supposing inner passions and calculations—is all the rage. One plucks a moment from a long history and turns it into a symbolic representation of the life itself. The interpretation overwhelms the known facts which, as the vivid speculation proceeds, become less and less significant in their own right. In the case of Franklin Roosevelt's terrible ordeal with polio, subsequent interpreters invested it with life-altering meaning. As Burns puts it, "A vast legend has grown up on this subject—namely, that his illness converted Roosevelt from a rather supercilious young socialite and amateur politico into a political leader of ambition and power and democratic convictions. . . . People jumped from the fact of physical change to the fiction of personality transformation."[95]

Burns's judgment makes sense. Roosevelt in the nearly forty years preceding this trauma had already developed patience and confidence. There is no evidence that his illness changed his political ideas in any fundamental way. "Was there ever a time during this period when Roosevelt's future as a politician trembled in the balance?" Burns asks, and answers no. The biographers who wanted to turn his polio into his Rubicon, a dramatic moment of decision whether to follow his mother, who wanted him to retire to Hyde Park, or his wife, who thought he should go on in an active political career, made too little of his previous history. "There was never the slightest chance of Roosevelt's retiring from politics," Burns concludes.[96]

Such quick gaps contrast with the long gaps in his history of life with father and with the *Harvard Crimson*. But they cry out to be filled because they come at crucial moments or in the form of character-changing traumas or rewards. As described, the work of filling them in fits nicely with the Freudian suppositions. But, in fact, it may well be that most political leaders-to-be, especially after they have reached adulthood, are unlikely to be changed very deeply very fast. In the case of FDR's polio, he may well have been so occupied with enduring pain that his imagination was, for the time being, put on hold. Like young Jack Kennedy, skidding across the deck of his PT boat as a Japanese destroyer cut it in half, suddenly thinking, "This is how it feels to be killed,"[97] Roosevelt most likely had his mind on preserving his life, not interpreting it.

On the other hand, it is quite clear that his character was *demonstrated* in his suffering and his recovery in a form many of his detractors in 1932 did not take into account. Those who saw him as a cream puff should have paid more attention to what he had been through, and how he came out of it. If his excruciating experience with polio did not create or transform his character, it certainly did reveal it in a significant dimension. As his Presidency would show, Franklin Roosevelt had a tough ego, a capacity to endure all sorts of attacks and failures and engineer a comeback. The simple message was there to read in his life history; many a President-watcher, mesmerized by the immediacy of his smiley campaign, let it pass.

XII

The gap problem will arise in every Presidential biography. The most important dimension of the problem is not literary but political, not retrospective but prospective. In politics, what his past has to say about his future is crucial in judging a candidate. The rational voter, taking into account the actualities of the political context as well as his or her own policy preferences, has only two things to go on in judging a contender: what he projects now and what he has been in the past. And to evaluate what the candidate says and shows the voter can only lean on the evidence of how his image now relates to his performance in the past.

Assessing a potential President's past goes beyond surface questions such as the consistency of his record; apparent inconsistency may well indicate a lively adaptive quality rather than a penchant for deceit. The voter has to make a judgment as to how the candidate is likely to deal with the challenges of the Presidency, challenges which can never be precisely defined in advance, but which, in their main shapes, tend to recur. At a minimum, such a judgment requires a strong focus on the Presidency itself, as practiced in the past, to provide criteria for assessment. It requires a direct application of those criteria to the particular candidates under consideration. And that requires finding out, as best one can, how their relevant beliefs, skills, and character have revealed themselves in the past.

In this context, journalism's appetite for novelty and immediacy fights against political rationality. The journalist must attract a generally sleepy audience to political thinking. To concentrate on the supposed attraction of news about what just happened, that is, the campaign, is one device, although as Presidential campaigns get longer and more routinized the spark of interest fades in that story. As the FDR case illustrates, campaign performance gives little clue to Presidential performance; indeed, that focus distorts and distracts attention from the core Presidential question. Fortunately some journalists have rediscovered what DeWitt Wallace found out years ago when he invented the *Reader's Digest:* that readers will savor stories from the past if they bear on the present and future. What entices interest is not what the candidate had for breakfast this morning but who this person really is, this applicant for the most powerful post in the world. That focus, in contrast to today's tidbit, opens the way for drawing on the candidate's past to illuminate his potential Presidential future. For example, how will he deal with the press? For example, will he stick to an ideology when facts refute it? For example, what will he do when he fails? And questions like that—explicitly relevant to the Presidency, as its history shows—may well turn attention to otherwise neglected periods and crises in the biography. For the question is not just what made this person tick, but how he will tick in the White House, a question very different from how he might do as a father, philosopher, or a general of the army.

What, then, is the responsible journalist to do when he discovers evidential gaps in probably significant periods? The worst solution is lying, that is, inventing events and conversations and reporting them as if they were true. The next worse is overtly shifting over into fiction, as in the "nonfiction novel," which supposes that invented details which are consistent with actual details somehow enhance the reality of the story. Perhaps as misleading is such a concentration on the surviving fragments of the record that the inference is shaped, not by the main things that happened back then, but by the available snippets of quotable writings. Finally, the exotic speculations of the psychoanalytic variety—stuffing into one narrow event or characteristic a truckload of theoretical meanings—has yet to produce a line of reasoning useful in the mundane political world.

Instead, the journalist working toward predicting performance in the White House can look straight at the gap and fill it in with the most obvious finding. The interpretations of the FDR gaps examined above are treated in that simple fashion, as distinct from the peregrinations of the novelistic mind. The journalist who dares to say the obvious when it is true, the awkward when it is real, and the old when it explains the new has a chance to lift the understanding of Presidential politics out of the wispy world of dreams and into the wide-awake world we have to live in.

II

Perception Shapes
Power

*"Spectators" among
the members of the
Connecticut General
Assembly illustrate
how politicians can
make a way of life
out of Sam Ray-
burn's advice, "To
get along, go along."*

7

Eye of the Beholder

CONNECTICUT'S CAPITOL build-
ing bears some resemblance to a rococo movie palace. In the Hall of
the House of Representatives, the bright blue rug, the ornate fixtures,
and the elaborate stained-glass windows create a certain theatrical
atmosphere. There were times during the session when the action
matched the setting. One thinks of the stately drama of the inaugura-

(1988: The research reported here is part of *The Lawmakers*, based on the following data: 1. Verbatim transcripts of tape-recorded interviews with twenty-
seven first-term members of the lower house of the Connecticut legislature. The
interviews were conducted during the 1959 session in a quiet study away from the
Capitol; they lasted from forty minutes to about two and a half hours, averaging
ninety minutes. 2. Questionnaire replies from eighty-three of the 150 first-term
members before the session, and ninety-six replies to a post-session questionnaire. The questionnaire could not be pretested. Comparison of early respondents,
late respondents, and nonrespondents indicates that the more active members, in
terms of legislative participation, are overrepresented in the returns. 3. Official
election returns, published biographical material, the records of legislative proceedings and committee hearings, newspaper accounts, statistics on constituency
characteristics, interviews with former legislators, and professional literature. For
the interview guides and questionnaire texts, see *The Lawmakers*, Appendix C.)

tion, the lighthearted Saint Patrick's Day celebration, and the sentimental, hatchet-burying ceremony with which the session closed. Occasionally, debate was dramatic (as in the struggle to reform the state's court system), or pathetic (as in the attempt to save a local hospital), or comic (as on questions of deer-hunting with bows and arrows and operation of barber shops on Washington's birthday). The original verse recited during the session would fill a small but entertaining volume. For the visiting legislative buff, the session had its moments.

But they were few and far between. Considered as pure entertainment, the day-to-day operations of the House—the long drawn-out committee hearings, the readings of the calendar, the perfunctory debates on minor bills and irrelevant resolutions—could not sustain for long the interest of an audience of outsiders. As one who watched a considerable number of House sessions (often alone in the gallery), the writer confesses that he often found his attention wandering to the pigeons conspiring on the windowsills. Most of the time, to the mere observer, the proceedings are dull.

The members of the House are not, of course, mere observers. Yet our first group of new legislators, the Spectators, appear to have reached a different conclusion. Like the other members, they have "competed" for nomination, "campaigned" for office, and "won" election, and are now empowered to take an active role in the making of the laws. But once in the legislature, they settle back into the role of members of the audience, attending regularly but participating little or not at all. Unlike other quiet legislators, they place a high value on the legislature as entertainment. "It's just fascinating to sit back and watch," says one; "what more can I say?—there's pageantry, there's entertainment. And you can watch the people—I mean, I like to watch the people. And I'm sitting where I have a pretty good view . . . I mean watching some of these discussions going on . . . and, ah . . . I watch all that. Every moment I'm in that House, I'm watching everything." Another confesses: "I just like being there. I like the idea of coming. I like the capitol building—quite impressive. And just to come in and sit at the desk. . . . It's an awfully good diversion. You hate to get in a rut."

Being a legislator, they find, is "a wonderful experience," "tremendously interesting," "an experience that can't be duplicated." "I'm enjoying every minute of it up here, and I wouldn't trade it for anything." In their replies to questionnaires Spectators are the members most likely to choose "listening to debate" as a favorite legislative activity.*

Who are the Spectators? What personal needs does their legislative experience serve? What problems do they encounter in adjusting to legislative life, and how do they try to solve them? How do their solutions of these problems affect the work of the legislature?

The Spectator Profiles:
Low-pressure Amateur

The Spectator category consists of the thirty new-member respondents who were low in activity and high in willingness to return. Three of these members were interviewed at length. All three claimed perfect attendance records at the time of the interview. Yet in the count of "comments in own committees" not one is noted as making any comments; in other committees, they averaged a bare 4.7 comments; and they spoke an average of only ten lines in the Assembly itself.

Looking first at the Spectator Legislative Activity Profile, we see a pattern of general passivity, in comparison with other members.

The Spectator Political Arbitions Profile indicates that while the Spectator is willing to return to the legislature for several more terms, he does not have a strong interest in seeking other political offices. The interviews confirm this pattern: none of the three subjects shows much interest in undertaking more extensive political roles. In his Political Background Profile the Spectator shows relatively few past political connections. The Spectator Personal Data Profile also indicates divergences from the other new legislators in directions that provide hints to factors underlying his political orientation.

The Spectator, then, stands out as a person of modest achievement, limited skills, and restricted ambitions, political and otherwise. He comes from a small town in which political competition is slight. He

---

* Spectators 37 percent, other new member respondents 21 percent. They are also most likely to answer that "the excitement involved in some issues" was "helpful, in that it stimulated my interest and attention." Spectators 87 percent $(N = 30)$, other new member respondents 65 percent $(N = 66)$.

Profile 1: Spectator Legislative Activity

	Spectators	Other new member respondents	Difference
Originated action to get nomination	17%	52%	−35
Attended many meetings in campaign	23	59	−36
Likes campaigning very much*	33	45	−12
Attributes election to own campaign efforts	7	15	− 8
Often introduced self to others at first of session	70	88	−18
Took an active part in major nego- tiations	47	71	−24
Was frequently sought for advice	33	52	−19
Achieved leadership or important committee post	12	27	−15
Considers self energetic rather than easygoing	50	67	−17
Considers self more influential than others	50	53	− 3
Self-rating as a legislator: superior or excellent	20	41	−21

* Indicates presession response and/or change during session: Spectator $N = 27$, Other $N = 56$. All other responses are from postsession questionnaire: Spectator $N = 30$, Other $N = 66$.

has lived there for a long time and intends to stay there. His energies have been less than fully engaged by his political activities.

But election to the legislature is one of the biggest things that ever happened to the Spectator. "It's an honor and a privilege," as one of them says.

Nominations: Available Volunteer

Working from these data and the interview records, we can begin to construct a picture of how the Spectators reached the legislature.

Profile 2: Spectator Political Ambitions

	Spectators	Other new member respondents	Difference
Identifies self as a "politician"	33%	44%	−11
Has considered seeking full-time elective office:			
Presession response*	26	52	−26
Postsession response*	30	46	−16
Change during session	+ 4	− 6	
Had considered full-time state appointive office*	23	36	−13
Was interested in district or state party office*	63	77	−14
Was interested in Assembly leadership position*	52	79	−27
Willingness to return for three or more future sessions:			
Presession response*	86	63	+23
Postsession response*	100	55	+45
Change during session	+ 14	− 8	
Ran again for nomination or election to Assembly:			
In 1960	83	79	+ 4
In 1962	57	38	+19
Ran for or served in some government office (including Assembly) after initial session	90	91	− 1

* See note for Profile 1.

In very many of the small towns of Connecticut the major problem for the local party committee is not resolving factional contests over nominations, but simply finding some minimally acceptable person to allow his name to be put on the ballot. The committee quickly exhausts the short lists of capable business executives, rising young lawyers, and civic leaders—most of whom are already loaded with community responsibilities for charity drives, club offices, church

Profile 3: Spectator Political Background

	Spectators	Other new member respondents	Difference
Parents interested in politics	54%	71%	−17
Relatives active in politics	57	67	−10
Occupation involves government contacts	30	59	−29
Had held party office*	56	48	+ 8
Had held elective office*	37	48	−11
Had held appointive office*	37	46	− 9
Had long considered running for Assembly	46	61	−15
Reports some competition for nomination*	56	80	−24
Saw election chances as 50–50*	22	25	− 3
Considers legislative activity most important he has engaged in	80	47	+33

* See note for Profile 1.

affairs, and the like. A host of part-time, unpaid town offices have to be filled—many towns are still ruled by a miscellaneous collection of boards, commissions, and committees—and these close-to-home offices take precedence over the more distant state representative post. The problem is one of "Who is available?" rather than "Which of these contestants should we favor?"

A considerable number of the first-term legislators were apparently swept into office on a tidal wave of votes for the governor, who carried the election by the largest majority in the state's history. Many of his party's candidates were surprised, to say the least, to find themselves election winners in towns where the party's nominees had been defeated with monotonous regularity. Ticket-filling sessions in these minority-party committees had degenerated, in some cases, to automatic rotation of the same nominees from year to year, or in at least one case, to a sort of political bingo game. Thus one Spectator reports his party's nominating practices as follows: "Came time to nominate

Profile 4: Spectator Personal Data

	Spectators	Other new member respondents	Difference
Sex: male	60%	86%	−26
Age: over 40	67	35	+32
Occupation: housewife	30	10	+20
Education: above high school*	34	66	−32
Income: over $8,000*	33	46	−13
Town population: over 5,000	40	71	−31
Resident in town: more than ten years	80	65	+15
Expects to remain in town	100	86	+14
Expects more income in ten years	33	71	−38

* See note for Profile 1.

candidates for local elections, we would put all the names of the town committee in the hat and draw them out and—'All right, you're going to run for mayor, or first selectman, and this and so forth.' Year after year, the same names running for different offices."

All too often, he says, nominating is a matter of asking, "Do you want it? Do you want it? Who's going to take it?" rather than a struggle for power. In another minority-party case the committee reached outside the party membership to find a candidate. The invitation "came as a complete surprise," says one legislator; "I think they asked me to run because they couldn't get anybody else."[1]

The situation in the majority party is different, but may involve equally severe recruitment problems. The majority committee has to find a candidate who will not only run but also serve. The committee cannot use the argument that accepting nomination means only a few weeks of minor publicity during a campaign. The five-month legislative session, becoming nearly a full-time job in the last two months at least, requires a candidate who can rearrange his schedule to spend the necessary time and effort away from his regular occupation. The busy executive or lawyer who wants to dabble in politics is likely to prefer some more convenient, more community-serving local board at which he can spend a few evenings a month with a familiar group of his neighbors. For those actively interested in gaining office the dominant party is the obvious channel, and we would expect more competition for office there than in the minority party. But when talents are in short supply the dominant party may have to sell the nomination even more vigorously than the minority does, because the nominee must be persuaded to take on two years, rather than two weeks, of politics.

The representative in office at the time nominations are made is normally in a strong position to gain renomination. The odds are about five to one against defeating an incumbent at an election for representative.[2] To the town committee of the majority party he is likely to be an attractive and hard-to-challenge choice. He has demonstrated his vote-getting power. He has experience. Few are familiar with his record at the distant capital, and in any case his votes were probably "right." His supporters on the committees are loath to desert him if he desires to run again.

When the incumbent decides he has served long enough, his voice is likely to be a powerful one in the selection of his successor. Open opponents of a retiring incumbent typically have an uphill fight in gaining the nomination, and the selection of a replacement whom he considers safe, friendly, and persuasible is a high probability. This was the situation in the selection of the third Spectator interviewed. At the town committee meeting, "They were discussing justices of the peace, for nomination, and the representative was coming up for election and our past representative was there. It never entered my mind that he wouldn't be running again. He's been in several terms so it's one of those habits you get into. And he's an Irish farmer and our town has a lot of Irish farmers. So he represents them—he's kind of a leader, y'know?"

The incumbent decided, however, that he had nothing to gain by staying on as representative and approached the candidate-to-be ("I thought maybe you'd be interested in it"). His approval was decisive in the choice. The Spectator reports: "I called the fellow the next day and he said, 'You'll run?' and I said, 'Yeah, I will.' And he said, 'Okay, I'll step down.'"

It is probably true that many a Spectator is chosen for nomination in circumstances like these. If he is short on competence for political leadership, he is long on availability and, as will be apparent below, on caution, tact, and loyalty. The Spectator—rooted in the community, generally apolitical and unambitious, flattered by the honor of the position—provides a quick, easy solution to a series of difficult problems. "Don't worry about it," one was told. "You don't need any background. You learn while you're there."

Reactions: The Search for Approval

In order to understand the personal needs that underlie the Spectator's political style, we must examine his reactions to his political experiences. What pleasures does he derive from political life? What causes him personal discomfort or pain? The Spectator "learns while he's there" in the legislature—learns how to be the kind of politician he eventually becomes. But his learning depends not on what lessons are directed to him but only on those he perceives and incorporates into his own behavior. This process in turn is shaped by the special sensitivities which he bears with him from the past. In the freedom of a long, exploratory interview, these sensitivities crop up repeatedly.

We have seen already in the general characterization of the Spectator a tendency to look to other people for reward; he is entertained, even fascinated, by others. But the interviews indicate that he wants more than a good show from his fellows: his main pleasures in politics seem to come from being appreciated, approved, loved, and respected by others. And his complaints center around situations in which he is left out, rejected, or abused. A closer look at the three Spectators interviewed illustrates this need for approval.

Sam Thompson: "A warm handshake"

The high point of Sam Thompson's day comes when someone appreciates him. Back in his home community, a small industrial town, he occasionally got the satisfaction of a friendly greeting: "And it makes you feel good when you walk through town and somebody comes up to you and says, 'Hiya, Sam, gee whiz, thanks for that favor.' It does make you feel good." But usually, back home, a legislator is "just an ordinary guy": "You get back home and a representative is not appreciated. A representative is just a person, well a $400-a-year man. I've noticed it on several occasions—not that I expect a heck of a lot. I don't."

As an example, Sam cites his experience at the Victory Picnic in honor of the winning candidates. He had to buy his own meal. His picture was left out of the paper. "There, again," he says, "that's a little blow to your ego." What he missed were not free food and pictures but the approval due a winner from his party: "There could have been an apology or something." Similarly, he feels that the salary of the legislators should be raised in order "to give the person that certain lift—not just in money matters, but in personal esteem." When he misses out on minor patronage, when the party in the legislature does not hold caucuses, the significant thing for Sam is, as he says, "I feel left out." Material rewards are important as signs of approval.

In contrast to his hometown experience, the legislature provides for Sam "a good feeling," "a warm feeling." "No matter how small it is," he says, "you are still a part" of it. He feels "the same as anybody else" there. "Everybody has a good morning—a friendly good morning, and people will go out of their way to be nice to you. At least that's the way I find it. I look forward to being here. It gives me that certain buildup." Perhaps the clearest example of Sam's reward from legislative service is found in his story of the Governor's Tea. A euphoric tone runs through his account of this event, only to be followed by a sort of ego-crash:

> We were very impressed. I mean you couldn't help but be impressed. It's a beautiful home. The Governor and his wife met us graciously and gave us the full roam of the house—"Go ahead, look at anything you want. Make yourself at home. We'll see you later on." And we wandered around. It's a beautiful home. Everything in it is beautiful. And, ah, then tea was served—so we had coffee (laughs). So we were sitting around, or standing there, and the Governor came by and he talked to everybody, and his wife talked with everybody. So—before that, we drove up in front of the house and a state trooper, there, he opened the car door. The passengers got out. I got out. The state trooper took the car, parked it for me. And, ah . . . so we

had tea, and the Governor talked with us. His wife talked with us. And when it came time to leave, we departed. And again, why—a warm handshake. None of this fishy handshake, but a warm handshake. And, ah, they thanked us for coming—whereas normally we should have thanked them for being invited. They thanked us for coming. And we got out there, the state trooper, he opened the car door. And off we go.

Well, as I say, we had a wonderful afternoon there. As I say, we were only there an hour, hour and a half. It was very impressive. You couldn't help but be impressed. And, ah, got back to town, tell different people about it and they got that—"Yeah? That was nice." No comment, you know? I mean your ego is built up so high, you're impressed here one moment. Then in the [time] it takes to get home, you're right back down on street level again.

This incident was apparently the high point of Sam's legislative experience. The doors opened for him, the gracious greetings and the carefully evaluated handshake, the unexpected "thanks for coming"—perfunctory as they may have been—all strike Sam as signs of approval. Others will go out of their way to show their affection. The callous indifference of his small-town neighbors stands in marked contrast to the warm social environment Sam finds in the legislature.

Sam's few complaints about his life in the legislature are heavily veiled behind the general aura of acceptance and warmth. Jokingly he says that back home, "If they want to call you a so-and-so, they'll call you that, whereas up here they can insult you and do it politely." And in the course of watching others—"how they react to different people"—he notices that "They'll be so friendly to them one time and then another time, maybe a day or so later, they'll walk by and ignore that person. Probably didn't make out too well."

Sam may have had such experiences himself. On the surface, though, he feels personally rewarded by even the most trivial of attentions: being spoken to, being allowed to watch. After the interview, he told the researcher, "What I want to know is your impression of me."

Tom Minora: "Everybody can be a gentleman"

Tom Minora is a quiet, tall, personable fellow from another small town. He is obviously somewhat less dependent on the approval of others than Sam is. In fact, he feels some sense of personal accomplishment as a legislator and takes some pride in having done a legislative job well. But several strands of the same seeking-for-approval pattern run through his conversation and receive special emphasis. Like Sam, he resents the slights he has received in his hometown, especially from leaders of the dominant party. "If you're not [an other-party member] there, you're *nothing*," Tom says. "While they're nice, they're not as friendly as they could be."

The legislature is a different world for Tom. In the assembly "everyone you meet is friendly, no matter who it is—whether it's the Governor or the Secretary of State or all the way down the line, through the legislators, senators and all of them. Very, very nice people." Simply by being a member of the legislature, Tom feels a warm fellowship with the other members. "Once you're a member there," he says, "you're just a part of everybody." On inauguration day he found the most impressive thing "being so close to the Governor, having the Governor speak to you—almost privately, you know?" He derives a glow of approval from such situations, despite the obvious fact that he was one of a vast audience for the governor's speech and one of a long line of handshakers.

In contrast to the disdainful attitude of the dominant party at home toward him and his party, the legislators treat him with respect. "I have yet to meet anybody that was other than a gentleman there," he says. "Very, very—I don't know if I should call it the best behavior, but . . . I think probably they're there with, and they know they're there with gentlemen and they behave as such. I think everybody can be a gentleman if they want to." Tom can thus feel accepted into a company that was, by and large, closed to him at home.

Personally, Tom is gentlemanly in the extreme—polite, considerate, cooperative. He seeks in the legislature the approval of other gentlemen, as a sort of confirmation of his status. In part this relates to his own estimate of his background, as revealed in the following passage describing his family's reactions to his nomination:

Tom: Well, they liked it very much—my family [he lists them]—they thought I should do it.

Interviewer: Well, why was that?

Tom (small laugh): Well, I don't know what their thinking was but they thought I—there was no one in our family that ever went into politics too much. Maybe . . . (long pause) . . . maybe it's because we have lived in the same town [for a long time] and . . . we weren't wealthy by any means. We had to work hard. . . . Well, ah . . . we never owed anybody any money. We weren't the best dressed in the world, and so on and so forth. We lived on what we made, in other words, you know? And didn't . . . and had come up it the hard way. And ah, maybe it's because we, ah, I thought that the family would be recognized more than we would have if we didn't have it. You know? There's a certain amount of prestige goes with the job anyway. And like I said, none of my family had ever been part or taken part in politics. Thought maybe this would be the break to get someone interested in it, you know?

To be accepted in the gentlemanly world of the legislature, where prestigeful persons treat him as a fellow gentleman, is a pleasant thing for Tom.

May Perkins: "We should speak to everybody"

May Perkins is a plump, well-dressed, highly voluble person, one of the many small-town lady legislators in the Connecticut House. During the interview it was hard to keep her on the subject. She chatted on and on, describing incident after incident in great detail. Almost all the tales have a common theme: they concern her adventures in conversation, her constant social round of speaking to others and being spoken to in return. It is in the course of this continual social interaction that May Perkins seeks the signs of approval that appear to mean so much to her.

Before she came to the legislature, May says, she had "always held it in awe, as something real nice, very—quite an honor to be in and all." But she quickly gets on to her main interest in the legislature:

"In fact, I've met a lot of people—I feel, when we're in there, we're all in there for the same reason, we're all in the House or the Senate or something, so we should speak to everybody." She was "real upset" when a member failed to greet her, even after repeated introductions. "He didn't even speak!" she exclaims. "What a snob. What's the matter with him?" Generally, however she finds the legislature a place where "I don't find any of them now that actually *will not speak*. I haven't noticed anybody that I wanted to speak to. In fact, some of them are more than friendly, you know, make a point of speaking and finding out your name and everything." In a situation she describes as "wonderful," "just so nice," she was spoken to from all directions: "One man called up to come up and talk to him and another man flagged me before I could leave—'Come over here and see me.' And there were a couple of others I spoke to. So it's real nice."

May is enthusiastic about the "many nice social affairs" connected with the legislature, especially the formal dinners ("fabulous!") and the regular get-togethers with the other female members. Before and after House sessions, she visits continually with those in neighboring seats, pausing to say hello and pass a few words with legislators as they find or leave their seats. May Perkins's happiness is increased when she is surrounded by acquaintances who reward her with attention, recognition, and approval.

May is little interested in the questions the interviewer asks. She has her own tales to tell, stories which almost always point out how others approve of her. When others "appreciate anything you do and they recognize—they know you"; when she is told she is "no detriment to society"; when another "listens very carefully now, because maybe my name will be mentioned" on television; when she is told that her group will be honored when others know she is a member— when these things happen, May feels a sense of well-being and, at the same time, demonstrates in the telling of the stories her need for the interviewer's approval.

These three Spectators thus appear to derive considerable personal satisfaction from the approval of others, and to feel hurt or at least uncomfortable when others reject them. This search for approval is perhaps best indicated by Sam's final plea to the interviewer: "What I want to know is your impression of me." The answer he wants is evident: that he is all right, that the other person feels positively toward him. In the legislature he finds, by and large, just the sort of warm, accepting social environment he is looking for.

The Spectator's rewards

The rewards the Spectator experiences are of three kinds, each stressed by one of our three Spectators.

In the first place, there is the reward of *admission*, of being allowed to become part of the group. All three Spectators show a positive reaction to this aspect of legislative life. They "become a part of everybody" simply by becoming members of the legislative body. For Sam especially, being admitted—having doors opened to him, being allowed the "roam" of the governor's mansion, being invited to attend the political show—are signs that he is valued by others. Thus the new member becomes an insider, with all the joys of belongingness at his disposal. He has passed through the electoral initiation ceremonies, and is now a full-fledged member of the fraternity. Simply being with others, close to them, seems to show that they value him. For otherwise, would they not send him away? His tendency is to blur over the fact that he holds his seat by right, that he cannot be excluded, and to feel his membership as a privilege accorded to him personally by his fellow members, thus proving that they like him and want him there.

In a second way, illustrated especially in Tom's case, the *prestige* of membership gives pleasure to the Spectator. The others who accept him are worthy as well as friendly. Tom grew up amid hard times in a community where people of his political persuasion were "nothing." Now he is in the company of gentlemen and feels that he can be a gentleman too, if he tries. To have the approval of one's peers is pleasant; to be accepted by one's betters is more so. The person who comes to the legislature from a generally lower status position may be particularly impressed by the fact that he is thrown together with governors and secretaries and chairmen.*

* In their questionnaires, Specators are the members most likely, after the session, to choose "Generally, the public looks up to a state legislator with respect" rather than "Generally, the public is overly critical of state legislators." Spectators 89 percent ($N = 27$), other new member respondents 71 percent ($N = 56$).

Prestige is, of course, a relative thing. The step into the legislature is upward, downward, or horizontal, depending on where one begins.[3] Certainly many a prosperous, highly educated legislator does not feel particularly flattered by his status as a representative. But neither does every lower-status person. Status-mindedness, here in the form of a desire to be approved by those one considers his betters, is in part a personal sensitivity, an inclination to perceive and attend to gradations in rank. The Spectator increases the quantity of affection he receives by thinking of himself as being liked by everybody, by all those other legislators. He increases the quality of the affection he receives by thinking of the others as worthy. To have the admiration of the admirable multiplies the joys of belonging.

Finally, the Spectator is rewarded by approval *expressed directly* to him. In his imagination Tom is able to feel that the governor's address is aimed at him personally, "almost privately." It would have been even more rewarding if the governor had paid his respects directly, face-to-face, so that there could be no doubt that they were meant for him. May Perkins, more than either of the other Spectators, is concerned with this problem. She must be spoken *to* in an approving way, and it is very important that her name be mentioned. In her continual participation in ceremonial greetings and small talk she gathers in tokens of affection that have a higher value for being paid in person. Sam's emotional apex ("your ego is built up so high") comes when the governor greets him personally, and with a "warm handshake" grants him approval from on high.

Expressed most abstractly, then, the Spectator's rewards of approval can be seen in three stages: first, he is allowed near the other; second, the other is worthy; and third, the other expresses approval to him.

Self: The Impoverished Ego

When we find members of the legislature continually turning to others for expressions of esteem and affection, showing marked sensitivity to the opinions and evaluations others express to them, we suspect the presence of some underlying need for this kind of behavior. Undeniably, all of us stand in need of affection from our fellow men. But the Spectator appears to demand this kind of reassurance from his social environment to an unusual degree. Why this continual reaching out for approval?

Apathy?

"Whenever we see glamour in the object of attention," writes David Riesman, "we must suspect a basic apathy in the spectator."[4] Our Spectators, as we have seen, place a good deal of emphasis on the glamorous aspects of the legislative show. And indeed, a close look at their interviews does reveal a basic apathy, a lack of deep feeling about themselves and their world. In a number of passages this emotional impoverishment shows through:

> I hadn't really any complete desire.
> I had no feelings one way or another.
> If I win, I win; if I lose, I lose.
> As far as any special plans or dreams, I have none. . . . And to me it didn't make a damn bit of difference whether I voted for or against it.
> I don't care if I get it or not.

Furthermore, the pleasures he does experience seem peculiarly superficial and temporary—

> I get a big charge out of that.
> It's such a nice new experience and we're all getting such a kick out of it.
> It gives a person that certain lift.

—or vague and clichéd: "wonderful," "interesting," "new," "nice." The Spectator as an individual, a person with his own special ideas, interests, and wants, does not emerge strongly in the interviews. Even in May Perkins' continual chatter there is a strain of the "weariness, anxiety and diffuse malaise" Riesman found among his "other-directed" subjects. Indeed, Tom Minora illustrates the other-directed type precisely, in this passage: "It's like the old story—when you're in Rome, do as the Romans do, you know? If you're a legislator, act as a legislator. And when you're outside, you act to . . . the environment, I guess." He appears to lack internal guidelines of his own, basing his behavior on a sensitive perception of the demands of the environment.

For such a person, the glamor and occasional excitement of legislative activities lend a much-needed spice to life. Lacking passion, he seeks amusement. So long as he can get a "charge," a "kick," a "lift" out of life, he can perhaps forgo the deeper satisfactions. And his own temporary excitement helps to reassure him that he is capable of feeling.

But in the light of psychological research, we must be suspicious of this characterization as well. Surface placidity or indifference may well conceal intense inner turmoil.[5] Riesman's formula can be extended as follows: "Whenever we see a basic apathy, we must suspect conflict within the personality."

Furthermore, "apathy" does not go very far to explain the Spectator's need for approval. Why should the person without feelings of his own ask affection of others? We need to take a careful look at the few occasions on which the Spectator talks about himself and describes the kind of person he is.

Self-doubt

Sam Thompson gives us an indication when he tries to answer the question, "How would you rate your own performance as a legislator so far?" Sam, hesitating, is encouraged with, "That's a hard question."

> No, not necessarily. I think I've done fairly well, to the extent that [long pause] well, gosh, that *is* a hard question. I think I've done fairly well to the extent that . . . I've a feeling of self-consciousness. And since I've come here to Hartford, I don't feel self-conscious any more. I feel as if I can mingle right in with them, and, ah—I first had a fear that, well, all that run for representatives are probably retired people, well-to-do people, people with financial means, so they could take the time off from their occupations and spend the day—and that all went through my mind between the time I was elected and the time I should go. But as the sessions went on, I feel I'm just as qualified to present myself to the Assembly as [another legislator]. Sounding a little like an egotist. [laughs] . . . And for that reason, I feel good. I mean I've overcome—yeah, over . . . came

some of this self-consciousness. Or whether it's self-consciousness, or, ah—doubt.

Sam classes himself with the "ordinary people" on a legislative committee, in contrast to the witnesses who come before it—people who,
with "their vocabulary, their wordage," are "educated—they know
what they're talking about." He feels he failed as a salesman: "Well,
I'm not aggressive enough."

Similarly, Tom Minora sees himself as "the type of person that's—
I, ah—self-conscious, shall we say?" He would have preferred another
committee than the one he is assigned to, "if I could have handled it."
He feels "like a plain dope" in conversation about politics. "If I'm
anything," Tom says, "I'm too much on the conservative side," by
which he means too unassertive, in contrast to people who "force
themselves on you." And May Perkins had doubts about accepting
the nomination: "I was a little bit scared at the idea of, maybe, what
if I couldn't do it satisfactorily?"

When he rates himself, the Spectator points to "self-consciousness,"
lack of aggressiveness, fear of performing unsatisfactorily. These self-
characterizations are consistent with the idea that the Spectator is
lacking in self-confidence. In fact, however, he seldom rates himself
directly. His main evaluations come in the course of watching others
watch him.

What others think

Sam makes a particularly revealing comment in this regard when he
is explaining why he finds the legislative experience "wonderful."
"You get back home, you're just an ordinary guy. You get up here,
it's 'Mister' and 'Sir'—*nobody knows who you are*, your bank account, the mortgage on your house. And so it's like a tonic to get up
here."

Later he repeats this thought: "You're treated with respect because
nobody knows who you are." The implication is clear: if the others
"knew who he was," they would not respect him. Who woould then
call him "Mister" and "Sir"? The real Sam Thmpson, he seems to
be saying, is not worthy of respect.

In Sam's search for approval a great deal depends on maintaining
a protective external facade, behind which his supposed inadequacies

can be safely hidden. When the front begins to break down, he expects disapproval: "I've seen different members of the committee—not that I'm knocking them personally, but this is just a broad statement—they got holes in their shoes. Their heels are run down. Their ties got spots on them."

When high-class witnesses appear, Sam says, "Sometimes I have my doubts. Sometimes I feel as if there might be some scorn in their eyes or something." His need to keep his inner nature hidden is evident: "I've countered some of my nervousness, so that a person looking at me might have some doubt that I'm nervous. I mean, I know myself that I'm nervous, but the person watching might have some doubts."

Sam can take care of his physical front by dressing neatly and guarding against the outward betrayal of his nervousness. It is when he has to speak to others that the danger of revealing his inadequacies is greatest. No wonder, then, that Sam feels threatened when he anticipates having to address the legislature: "Yeah, when you're in the session there and you have the mike in front of you and the button [for voting] there, that thing can scare you, you know? You have to pick it up and you have to speak into it and there is a tenseness."

Even in informal conversation, he feels a necessity for avoiding the revelation of his own personal preferences: "For myself, I like to play games with people. I like to confuse them. I get a little—I'll say one thing to them, and then in the course of conversation I'll twist my feelings around to the complete opposite. And, ah, I'll look at the people and they'll look at me and wonder what's going on. Words—it's only words."

The outlines of Sam's adaptation to the legislature become clearer in these passages. He judges himself harshly; he has doubts about his worth as a person. For this reason, he avidly seeks the approval of others, the reassurance of their affection. But sensing his own unlovableness, he fears that others will reject him if they find out what kind of person he is. Therefore he hides behind a conventional front, remains silent, and, when he must interact with others, avoids revealing his feelings to them. He thus cuts himself off from the deeper, more abiding affection that comes with mutual understanding. He must make do with the meager rewards of being called "Mister," of perfunctory handshakes and greetings. This is not much but is better than nothing at all. And the alternative—discovery and rejection—is considerably worse.

There is a similar theme in Tom Minora's makeup. One reason he would like to return to the House, he says, is that there he can remain "not too much in the limelight." He avoids political discussions in which he thinks he would perform badly. He tells of an innocent social mistake at the beginning of the session in which he wondered why he was "getting these kind of funny looks, you know?" and concludes, "That was stupid." Tom feels "a little bit squeamish" about speaking and was "very nervous" when he had to once. His retiring habits—"unaggressiveness"—very likely serve protective functions.[6]

In turning to others for self-evaluation, Tom finds a general reaction of friendliness in the House. But on several occasions he expresses doubt that others mean what they say when they praise him. When a town party official asked him to run, he said he thought Tom would be a good man. Reporting this, Tom immediately adds: "You know how they spread it on." His friends congratulated him—but, Tom says, "Of course there's no way of knowing whether they really mean it or not." He finds that witnesses before his committee are "very respectful," but implies that this is only because they are forced to act that way:

> Tom: Very respectful.
> Interviewer: They look up to the committee members?
> Tom: They know we're their judges—they've got to. If they don't know that then they shouldn't be there.

Thus Tom seems to feel it is implausible that others really respect and admire him, freely and willingly. When he is praised, he doubts the sincerity of the praise. Like Sam, Tom also seems to take a somewhat condemnatory view of himself, and to seek approval and reassurance in order to help assuage doubts about his worth. But he cannot quite bring himself to believe in the affection he receives. This suspicion hampers the confident acceptance of direct expressions of approval, and Tom settles for the lesser, indirect rewards of membership, vicarious participation, and withdrawal from the center of attention.

May Perkins appears in the interview as a lady who protests too much. She relates no fewer than eighteen incidents to show that others approve of her. If she were confident of her worth, would she go to such lengths to demonstrate it to the interviewer? Why the repeated effort to show that she really is appreciated, to prove in specific detail that others have responded favorably to her? It is a safe conclusion that she herself has doubts about her value and is trying to assuage these feelings by gathering compliments.

May, as we have seen, is excessively sensitive to the impressions that she gives to others and others give to her. Yet there is little in her interview to indicate insight into others' characters or individual variations at any level below the superficial outward aspect. She moves in a world of social surfaces. Her praise is reserved for those who put themselves over by the manipulation of their impressions.

Thus May is enthusiastic about a person who "is so *nice*" as a speaker. "He's got a nice face, to begin with," she says, and "he's so pleasant." "He always speaks and he always passes the time of day." "I guess I just like the Irish," May concludes. "There's something awfully nice—personable about them." The important thing is to give an impression of sincerity, not to be too "cocky" or "aloof," not too "stuck-up" to speak to people. "Did you hear Amos Walker speak?" she asks. "Wasn't he wonderful? He is so good, and he is so darn sincere. And everybody knows that he has nothing to gain by anything he talks on. . . . He's very sincere about it." "The only thing I've found in true experience," May continues, is that "everybody's sincere in his thinking." She then goes on to relate an experience when she was let down by someone who did not fit this rule—who tricked her into a situation in which *she* had to appear insincere. She felt considerable anxiety in this situation because her image was almost compromised.

In another context May evaluates a party leader: "I think he is trying sincerely to remember everybody. And he's very friendly—he just speaks every time he sees anybody. Maybe he doesn't know who we are from Adam, but at least he speaks, and he acts like he's seen you before." Here the importance of maintaining an impression is most fully revealed: the other is appreciated because he *acts* as though he knows her. A sincere front is the important thing. The reality may be too much to ask.

The differences between May and Sam and Tom in this respect are thus not as wide as casual observation might indicate. May is a talker; Sam and Tom are quieter types. But all three are excessively concerned with presenting a social exterior which they feel will bring them the rewards of approval and protect them from disapproval. The clear implication is that, from the Spectator's point of view, this protective exterior is necessary for approval, because the person behind the mask is unlovable.

The Spectator's need for approval from others, then, appears to spring from his doubts about his own worth. When he appraises himself, he reaches a discomfiting conclusion: he feels inadequate and inferior. Political participation offers opportunities to palliate these feelings, to gain a sense of personal worth by gaining from others signs of approval.[7]

But from the Spectator's own viewpoint, this dependence on others has a threatening aspect, too. The approval he receives is fundamentally spurious; others appreciate him only because they do not know him. His primary problem is a strategic one: he must manipulate his social environment in ways that maximize approval of him and minimize disapproval.

What techniques does the Spectator employ for these purposes?

Strategies: Followership and Its Alternatives

When a person confronts the gap between what he is and what he wishes he were, he experiences feelings of tension, feelings that may range from minor dissatisfaction to despair. Certain familiar social strategies are used to cope with such feelings. Without going into the genesis of these strategies,[8] we can summarize them briefly as follows. First, the person may react aggressively. He lashes out at others (either actually or within his own mind) and thereby displaces a good deal of the aggression he feels toward himself. This scapegoating behavior is familiar from studies of intergroup relations. Second, he may withdraw into himself. Especially if his inferiority feelings are based on a sense of failure to meet the norms of the groups he is in, he may fall back on internal norms of his own that he *can* satisfy. The superficially self-satisfied person who seems oblivious to his inadequacies is an example. A third technique for assuaging such feelings is achievement. The person recognizes his shortcomings and sets out to do something about them, to achieve self-respect by accomplishing valued ends. Finally, the self-doubting person may react by adopting a follower role. In effect, he seeks to satisfy and placate the demands of those who would reject him by giving in to them. He thus buys a certain amount of self-approval, at the cost of a certain amount of subservience.[9]

Over the course of a lifetime such strategies of adjustment tend to become habitual.[10] It is as if the person makes a decision, adopts one main method of adjustment, and then sticks to it. For each of these patterns pays off with some sort of reward: when the aggressive person finds that he feels better after having hurt someone else; when the withdrawn experiences a comfort in his own mind that he could not obtain from without; when the achiever knows the satisfaction of accomplishment; when the submissive person feels that others approve him for his service—these comforting feelings, if repeated often enough, tend to solidify into a fixed style of adjustment. The person has found a "solution" to his main adjustment problem.[11]

The more severe the internal problems an individual experiences, the more rigid this pattern becomes. At the extreme the psychotic person develops a fixed pattern, which ordinary experience simply cannot alter. Even when his behavior results in disastrous disruptions of his life, he still cleaves rigidly to a pattern that has brought him some reward or relief in the past. Reality no longer has any relevance to his happiness.

As we move from the psychotic extreme toward the "normal" person,[12] the interplay of internal problem and external environment alters. The individual is more and more in touch with reality, more and more able to alter his course according to the rewards and punishments he receives. The fixity of his pattern of adjustment depends, on the one hand, on the intensity of his need for a particular kind of reward, and on the other, on the availability of reward from the environment for the pattern he has adopted. If he feels only an occasional mild twinge of self-doubt, for example, he will probably be able to handle this problem with an occasional mild burst of aggression, withdrawal, achievement, or submission. He need not invest all his efforts in one reward-gaining pattern.

Even if his need for reward is great, however, the fixity of his pattern of adjustment will depend also on the availability in the environment of the particular kind of reward he seeks. The pattern will tend to break down under the impact of repeated punishments for attempts to maintain it—again, assuming that the individual is in touch with reality. The shy, withdrawn person, for example, who finds himself in a group where every member is required to perform publicly and receive criticism of the performance, tends either to leave the group or to change his pattern, perhaps by engaging in some tentative experiments in self-assertion. When the need is great and the environment offers reinforcing rewards, the pattern will tend toward rigidity and permanence. When the need is mild and the environment offers pattern-contradicting rewards and punishments, the pattern will tend toward flexibility and change.

We proceed now to examine the Spectator from this viewpoint. Which set of strategies does he tend to pursue? Given his particular needs, what is involved for him in changing this pattern? Given the legislative environment, what reinforcements does this pattern receive from without? And, therefore, how likely is it that the Spectator will continue to pursue this set of strategies?

Submitting

According to Sam Thompson, the proper role of the freshman legislator can be summed up in a simple formula: "The main function, far as I can see, in my position—I'm a freshman. The main functions of a legislator here are to keep your ears open, your mouth shut, and follow your party leaders." His main complaint against the leadership is that they have not taken a stronger hand:

> Sam: I feel left out. I feel that leadership is doing a poor job.
> Interviewer: How's that?
> Sam: Well, it's a known fact that—I believe there is about 100 new members of the legislature who have to be told what to do and what not to do. Otherwise, I—getting back into known fact—leave a [party group] alone and they'll fight. Right or wrong, they'll fight. And I think they have to be led, have to be steered. . . . The leadership has been too busy or they've taken the attitude that, well, the fellows can operate on their own. And I don't think that's right.

Similarly, Sam takes a "serving" stance toward his constituents. One of the things that has helped him as a legislator, he says, is

> the desire to show the townspeople that they didn't make a mistake, that I can get up there and work for them. Of course, in my campaign I told the people there that my—the limits with which I could work for them would be limited. Because I'm unfamiliar. I wouldn't know the patterns or the channels that certain things had to go through. Might be limited, but I'd certainly try. And for that reason I feel good.

These passages seem to indicate a searching for opportunities to submit to others, a searching for masters to serve.

Tom Minora agrees with Sam that "freshmen aren't supposed to open their mouths." He says that the party leaders should have done more by way of instruction at the first of the session, "so that you'd know which foot to step on first." "The senior legislators," he says, "don't take you by the hand—at least in my estimation—the way they should, and say, 'Now, look, this is the way you should do it.'" Tom resents the fact that his party has not held many caucuses to familiarize the new members with procedures and the leadership's wishes, "the party thinking." Personally, he does not like to bother the leadership with his problems, but he thinks they could have "done a much better job than they did" in instructing the membership. He seems to welcome the leaders' suggestions, particularly when he has no convictions of his own in regard to a bill.

May Perkins's attitude is somewhat different. She says that some feel her party has "passive leadership" in the House. On an important bill, she wondered "just how to go along" when pulled in one direction by a few of her constituents and in another by the party leadership. Finally she decided she "was safe in going along" with the people in her town. She explains that on "such big issues as that you just wonder if you're doing the right thing, but now I find that I did, because everybody in town has spoken since and they're very glad that I voted as I did. At least I feel that I'm not a party to it if it doesn't materialize properly."

May has a large collection of acquaintances to whom she turns for advice, especially among the older, experienced legislators. And although she says that "I still have to think for myself," her conception of the proper role of the legislator is strongly centered in the representative function: "The main thing is to be voting for the good of the people. We're supposed to be doing things for the people that they cannot do for themselves. We're representing the whole group of the people who couldn't come in here to do it. And we're supposed to think of them at all times, not ourselves personally." Others "know that I'm going to have to go along" with the views of the hometown party. May is in something of a dilemma about whom to go along with, but she, like Sam and Tom, is looking for guidance from others.

The taboo on personal aggression

Expressions of aggression in the Spectator interviews are extremely rare. May is friendly to everybody. "It's all hearts and roses for a while," she says. "You know how—throwing bouquets back and forth. And then we have our first big fight against the sides. He said, 'Well, the honeymoon is over.' [laughs] But on both sides, everyone's very congenial and, ah, nice. Nice harmony throughout." Sam realizes that he is "not the type to go in there and bang people over the head and say you've got to have this for your own good." He is careful to qualify his complaints about others: "not that I'm knocking them personally," "not that I expect a heck of a lot." Tom knows he is "a little reluctant to push myself on to someone—which isn't good, either."

Only two occasions appear in the interviews in which Spectators show fairly open hostility to others. The first is May's reaction to being snubbed. She "just got fed up" with being neglected by another member, and told him directly that she was "sick and tired" of his impoliteness. It is significant that this outburst resulted from a social snub. May can take a good deal from others, but being addressed is too important to her to be allowed to pass. In this case, repeated introductions had failed to gain friendly greetings from the other member. As a last resort, May strikes out at him. "So he doesn't forget me now," she says. The aggression has thus served to force the other to act as if he approved of her, whether he does or not. This behavior, then, is entirely consistent with May's approval-seeking behavior.

The second appearance of marked hostility in the interviews comes from Tom. He starts to report the "general opinion" that the lawyers in the House are resented. " 'They have another profession,' members say; 'they shouldn't even be in there.'" Tom then takes a personal stand: "And that is my point, too. I'm quoting myself and I'm thinking that those people that resent them concur with my feelings. I don't believe the lawyers should be allowed in the House." Tom feels the lawyers "tend to make laws to suit themselves," selfishly using the legislature for their own benefit. He seems unusually irritated on this point.

But he immediately pulls back from this aggressive stance. He amends his original statement: "Probably, I shouldn't say that there shouldn't be *any* of them there," he says. He explains that he does not express this feeling in public: "That's my own personal feeling—I haven't discussed this with anybody." And he concludes by reminding the interviewer that his irritation is shared by others: "I have heard several others make the remark about too damn many lawyers being up there." Thus Tom's attack is quickly blunted and hidden among his fellow legislators.

Such aggression as the Spectator feels is far more likely to be expressed indirectly, in the form of complaints about being abused by others. Sam complains that people back home do not appreciate him. Tom tells of a relative who was treated unfairly by opposition-party politicians. May feels she was taken advantage of by a constituent. But none of them goes on to say, "Therefore I am mad at that person," or to show any intention of taking aggressive action toward those who have abused them. The abused feeling remains.[13] The tension is not relieved by attack.

Avoiding loneliness

Nor do the Spectators appear to choose withdrawal as a pattern of adjustment. On the contrary, they place considerable emphasis on feeling related to others. It is important to Sam, for example, that he finds others in the legislature who are as lowly as he feels he is. At first, he says, "I supposed I might be faced with all these individuals who were financially responsible," but "since I've come up here I've found out I'm not alone." And, he explains, "That helped to build up my ego and helped me to like coming up here, to know that you're not alone in a certain group." May dislikes loneliness: "I couldn't just sit home and do nothing. It isn't my nature. I'm always either doing something for my relatives, baby-sitting, or for my neighbors, or doing something. I—I don't feel it's taxing me too much." Tom is more of a homebody than the other Spectators, but he, too, gains satisfaction from feeling "like any other businessman" and from knowing that he "fits into the middle group" on an issue.

Spectators are not much given to musing about themselves—adding up the past and planning for the future. Rather, they seem to avoid introspection, to restrict their attention to events in the passing environment. Part of the reason the legislature is a grand place is, as Sam says, that "everything is new. You come up here, you don't know what to expect. You don't know what to find on your desk." May sums up her legislative experience by calling it "such a nice, new venture." Her attention seems to be focused on the surfaces that surround her, perhaps *because* this is an alternative to introspection. In the midst of all the "nice social affairs" she has little time for thinking about herself. The "diversion" she finds in such affairs is evident in her description of a party for members of the House:

> May: On both sides of the ballroom—you know how long the ballroom is?
> Interviewer: Yes.
> May: They had tables set up the full length of both sides, loaded with food. And on one side was a great big backet of flowers—real flowers. A great big floral display. On the other side was an ice-basket, one of those molded ice-baskets? And that had real flowers in it, too. And they had a spotlight on it. Different colors? And it was just a beautiful sight. And then the food was arranged—the turkey and the ham were cut real pretty and laid on trays with pansies and parsley and all kinds of decorations on it. There were molded salads, potato salad and just everything imaginable to eat. And the place was just elegant—and French pastry for dessert—usually you don't get much for dessert at an affair like that.

None of the three Spectators thought long or deeply about accepting the nomination. None has given his political future a thorough personal assessment. Immersed in a world of other people, the Spectator seems to focus little of his concentrated attention on himself. In fact, he apparently needs interesting externalities as a distraction from introspection.

In a sense, the Spectator does withdraw from his environment: he keeps his social relationships superficial, avoids investing his emotions in others, builds a protective shield around his supposedly unlovable qualities. But he does not withdraw *into himself*. His retreat from others stops short of isolated, conscious self-examination. He pauses permanently at the self-other border, with his attention always turned outward.

The dangers of success

The fourth pattern of adjustive strategies, personal achievement, is also largely missing in the Spectator's behavior. There are scattered references to legislative success in the Spectator interviews. Sam feels that he "controlled" one executive session of his committee—although his control seems to have consisted of making the first motion to approve a series of bills he knew the committee majority favored. Still, this experience gave him "a shot in the arm." Tom is pleased that he and another member got one bill through—although he feels it was an "insignificant" bill. May says she is "satisfied with what I have done" and that she has "voted very fairly on everything." She, too, has joined in sponsoring a bill, but she says "I don't think it will do any good" because the bill is bound to be defeated. Thus the Spectators see their achievements as minor. They tend to rationalize their lack of participation by claiming that it results from their high standards: "I'm the type of person that I'd never want to speak unless I'm fairly positive about what I'm talking about. And being unfamiliar, I'll keep quiet and listen." Or from the impossibly difficult nature of legislative work: "By being a freshman there and being unfamiliar with all these bills—God, there's over three thousand bills—and I don't think that any individual should be expected to remember all those bills." Nevertheless, the satisfactions of personal achievement are not entirely missing.

When we look at other incidents in which the Spectator might be expected to take pleasure in personal achievement, however, we see what appears to be a strong tendency in the other direction—toward feelings of discomfort and anxiety at personal success. This is especially marked in his report of the election night. For the approval-seeking person, we might suppose that an election victory would bring a glow of satisfaction. He might feel that hundreds or thousands of people had thought enough of him to go to the polls and cast a ballot in his favor. Here is approval on a massive scale.

The Spectator does not react that way. Sam says that while being a candidate "didn't bother me that much," the "big shock" came when he was told, "You're elected." He had worried about arranging the time off from his job: "All the while there was uncertainty—How would I work? My job? Coming up here?" "Oh, well," he thought, "you probably won't get elected anyhow," and "you keep throwing it out of your mind, you know? Back and forth." His feeling when the results were in was one of "responsibility":

> I've got beaten in other elections so it doesn't bother me. And the actual feeling of winning the election—I don't think that would have been such a surprise. Just the feeling of responsibility. Of course, I may have been subconsciously evading the issue beforehand, but the results were in—you can't evade it any longer. That's it.

Sam gives no indication here of personal pleasure at his success. Rather, he feels anxious about the responsibility he has attained almost inadvertently. He has won a victory, but his mind is occupied with thoughts of burdens he can no longer escape. Why does he pass up this chance to pat himself on the back? One gets the impression that he would have felt more comfortable as a loser.

Furthermore, Sam appears to want to excuse himself for any success he might attain. He explains that his nomination was almost accidental: "I'm inclined to believe that it was on the spur of the moment." The town chairman "just happened to see me" at the nominating meeting. If Sam had not attended, someone else would probably have been chosen. Similarly, his election was due not to his efforts or his popularity but to the pulling strength of others on the ballot. "Sam Thompson didn't win the election" in his town; the governor won the election, and "Sam Thompson was on his ticket."

Sam may be giving a fairly objective report of circumstances in these passages. That he chooses, however, to dwell on the self-deprecating aspects of the situation and neglects to express any self-satisfaction at his election is inconsistent with the pattern of pleasure in personal achievement.

Tom Minora's reaction to his election victory was extreme tension accompanied by sudden illness. "I was very happy I won," he says, "but unfortunately . . . I was deadly sick that night," so sick that he felt he would "rather be dead than alive." He attributes this trouble to "the pressure that apparently had built up inside of me, nervous tension and so on." Asked how he accounts for this tension, Tom says, "Well, you couldn't prove it by me that I was nervous. I didn't know that I was nervous myself. It was just subconsciously, you know?" We cannot, of course, be sure that the election victory brought on this illness, but Tom tells us directly of the extreme pressure, the nervous tension, he felt on that occasion. He does not indicate that the tension was assuaged by news of victory. Whatever the psychosomatic connection, Tom's reaction does not fit the picture of the happy winner.

May Perkins reports that she felt no gratification over her election. "In fact," she says, "I went home that night after election and I wasn't elated one little bit. I felt kind of bad because I didn't win by a terrific margin. . . . I was a little disappointed." May was chagrined that some others thought she had not worked hard enough. "So I just went home after we tallied the votes and that was it, that was the end of my celebration." No pride in success, no glow of approval, no self-congratulation. May, too, conveys a mood of dejection when she talks about her election victory.

Spectators show a consistent tendency to assert themselves or to seek success only in conjunction with others. Sam says that, in his campaigning, "I honestly don't think I've been talking for myself so much as talking for victory. And I consider myself not what you call a real candidate, but talking for the party's victory in the town." Party success, success which can be shared, is legitimate; personal success is questionable as a goal. Tom Minora feels that his success in the legislature "is not earned by myself . . . only in my efforts. The success of us being up here is dependent on so many other people up here who are willing to cooperate." Tom thinks that ambition for any political position above that of representative "would probably be selfish interest," "seeking for prestige." He doesn't have "the desire to be a big politician." May Perkins feels "it would be nice sometime" to hold a higher political office, but she appears to have no well-developed plans on this score. Her actions regarding legislation consist mainly of trying to figure out which side she is "safe in going along with."

Descriptions of political issues in the Spectator interviews tend to be in "we" rather than "I" terms. Furthermore, the Spectators expect initiative to come from others. All three, for example, want to take a receptive stance toward their constituents. Sam dislikes house-to-house campaigning because he sees it as "pleading, begging the people for their vote." He should not have to do that—the others should come to him: "If these people don't have the civic pride or the desire to get out to a town meeting or a caucus or any of these speaking occasions we have, then their interest is pretty small." "I'm sure that there's a lot of legislation that would benefit my town in particular," Tom says, "but yet we are never requested to do this, to put a bill in for it, you know? And I don't feel that we should go in on our own and introduce a bill. As representatives of the people it's okay for us to do it, but they should come to us and ask us to do it." May has let her constituents know that she welcomes their phone calls, so that she can "get their general ideas." And the Spectators take a similar attitude toward the party leaders: they should undertake to advise the newcomers.

The Spectator's inability to take pleasure in personal success, his tendency to submerge his achievements in those of the group, and his turning to others for initiatives indicate that the achievement pattern does not play an important role in his legislative adjustment.

The dynamics of followership

We are now in a position to attempt an explanation of the Spectator's choice of the follower pattern and his rejection of the other three patterns. We begin with the fundamental psychological problem he experiences: the nagging doubts about his worth as a person. In order to assuage these doubts he seeks signs of approval from others. But this turning to others involves the risk of rejection as well. If the others were to discover what he suspects about himself—that he is unworthy—they would disapprove of him. Therefore, he develops a pattern of adjustment that maximizes his chances of gaining approval and minimizes the risk of exposure and rejection. Part of his pattern consists of a set of perceptual habits by which he can interpret events in his environment as indicating approval with minimal risk of exposure: he makes of his *membership* in a prestigious body a sign of approval. He overinterprets perfunctory greetings as signs of approval. He participates vicariously in the course of watching others perform. He is able to reap these rewards without taking any legislative action whatever except the effort necessary to attend the session.

Beyond this passive reception of impressions, the Spectator attempts to convey impressions to others that will bring approving signs from them. He maintains a front of pleasant, moderate, polite conventionality, to which others are likely to respond with similarly superficial pleasantries. At the same time the formalism of this front prevents others from penetrating below the surface, leaving his secret self-doubts undisclosed. Conversation is kept on the plane of conventional pleasantries.

On occasions when the Spectator is expected to take some positive position—as, for example, when he must vote on a bill—he seeks to gain approval by submitting to the appropriate authority. His own preferences are generally weak, diffuse, and not very interesting to him. Submitting to the preferences of others (for example, the party leaders, experienced legislators, constituents, general opinions of the legislature, etc.) fulfills the requirement that he take a position, frees him from lone responsibility (being "in the limelight") for that position, and gives him a sense of belonging with others.[14]

The Spectator's adaptive strategy, then, consists primarily of three techniques: vicarious participation, superficial socializing, and submission to others.*

---

* Some Spectator questionnaire replies reflect these themes. They are most likely to answer that "social affairs connected with the legislature were very enjoyable" (Spectators 37 percent, others 15 percent). They "made a special effort to memorize the names and faces of other members" at the start of the session (Spectators 80 percent, others 65 percent). With a stranger, the Spectator would "reserve my trust until I know him better" rather than "trust him until he lets me down" (Spectators 63 percent, others 36 percent). $Ns = 30, 66$. Before the session Spectators answered "the new legislator will very frequently have to rely on the advice of others with more experience or ability" rather than "the new legislator ought to figure most things out for himself, to the best of his ability" (Spectators, 74 percent, others 57 percent). $Ns = 27, 56$.

The Persisting Pattern

The personal costs of change

The costs to the Spectator of switching his behavior to one of the other patterns may be considerable. It is perhaps easiest to see why he does not utilize the aggressive pattern. Aggression directly expressed to someone else would put an end to expressions of approval from that person. The Spectator is already predisposed to anticipate being abused by others—he never quite trusts them; he suspects that aggressive feelings toward him lurk behind *their* fronts. He has staked his self-approval on the approval of others. Even one person who feels hostile toward him confirms his self-doubt. He cannot afford the risk involved in aggressive behavior.

Furthermore, aggressive feelings, even though not expressed, are likely to make him feel uncomfortable: they contradict the "nice" impression he wishes to convey; they make him feel insincere. His pattern of adjustment requires the constant repression of aggressive feelings. They come to the surface, if at all, in the form of complaints at being abused, taken advantage of, or neglected in some way. In this form, such feelings do not challenge his front: he sees himself still as a nice person who suffers at the hands of others.

The withdrawn pattern is threatening to the Spectator because it turns him back into himself—the very court of judgment from which he habitually seeks escape. Introspection is painful because it reminds him of his inadequacies. Furthermore, being left alone cuts the Spectator off from his most important source of reward—approving signs from other people—and at the same time demonstrates to him that he is not worth the attention of others. He depends on others for guidance; left alone, he feels at sea. He depends on others for stimulation; left alone, he feels bored and dull. Left alone, he might gain a certain respite from anxiety about how others see him, but the risks of despondency are too great.

To a minor degree, the Spectator does utilize the achievement pattern. But there are strong inhibitions operating within him to hamper his productive efforts. Striving for personal success involves for him a direct attack on his feelings of inadequacy. In order to attempt achievement he must at least temporarily convince himself that he is capable of action, that he is really not so inadequate as he had thought. Since he has based his reward-seeking activities on opposite assumptions this change requires a violent wrenching away from a whole set of adjustive habits. Personal achievement attracts attention to him as an individual. Such individual prominence invites inquiry from others as to who he is, why he wants to gain these goals, or how he has managed to attain them. His strategy of concealment is thus in danger of compromise. He wishes to avoid seeming presumptuous and insincere; others might mistake his honest satisfaction in a task well done for personal conceit.

Two other factors block achievement for the Spectator. In the first place, achievement involves aggression against the external environment. Political achievements—winning an election, getting a favorable committee report on a bill, building a majority for or against a measure—require efforts at persuasion which always include a certain amount of "pushing." Here all the Spectator's taboos against interpersonal aggression come into play, making him hesitate to force himself onto others.

Similar obstructions seem to operate when the Spectator considers asserting himself in ways that involve little interpersonal aggression, such as in drafting legislation, studying bills, and the like. As Horney has pointed out, the very language we use to discuss the mastery of intellectual tasks is saturated with aggressive imagery: we speak of "taking hold" of ideas, "tackling them, grappling with them, wrestling with them, checking them, shaping them, organizing them."[15] The Spectator's inhibition against aggression toward others seems to be reflected in similar inhibitions against these more private forms of self-assertion.

In the second place, personal achievement involves personal initiative, offering proposals to others. But the Spectator's stance toward his social environment is receptive. Others should come to him; he should not have to "beg and plead" for approval. It is as if the Spectator were saying, "Approve me for myself alone, not for what I have done." His preference is for *unearned* affection and support from his environment; praise which has a reason behind it, even if that reason is respect for some achievement, is sullied. One finds many instances in the interviews of expectations of approval as a reward for *being* a kindly, likeable, helpful person. Expectations of approval for *doing* worthwhile things are considerably rarer.

This analysis of the inner dynamics by which Spectators adopt and reject patterns of adjustment is necessarily hypothetical. But such tangential evidence as we have supports a view of the Spectator as a person with strong doubts about himself and strong attachments to certain ways of ameliorating those doubts. The intensity of his inner problem tends to rigidify his pattern of adjustment. Viewed from the inside, then, the Spectator pattern does not seem likely to change with time.

Environmental support

In estimating the rigidity of the Spectator pattern it is necessary to view it also from the outside. To what extent is the political environment supportive or destructive of this pattern? We will consider the three main elements of the pattern, in order: vicarious participation, superficial socializing, and submission.

At no stage of the processes of nomination, campaigning, election, and membership in the legislature is there a formal requirement of verbal participation. One can be nominated by another, remain silent during the campaign period, and sit quietly through committee hearings and floor debates. No member is required to vote on any issue, in committee or on the floor. It is perfectly possible for a legislator to serve an extended series of terms without opening his mouth. Thus at the outer limits, legislative life has a place for the Spectator. The formal environment includes this alternative.

But what of the informal, normative expectations present in the environment? On the one hand, there may be a set of expectations that press the Spectator toward participation. The town committee may require some evidence that he is a bona fide candidate as demonstrated by his active, verbal pursuit of the nomination. His constituents may expect him to speak on their behalf in the legislature. And his fellow committee members and legislators may look to him for an occasional contribution.

On the other hand, other expectations frequently prevail. In some town committees the norm is for the office to seek the man. Candidates are expected to accept only after a decent courtship. In many a small town, audiences for campaign speeches by candidates for the state legislature are simply not available; and where nomination is tantamount to election, community traditions may work against active campaigning.* Once in the legislature, the member often receives little attention from his constituents. In fact, he may conceive of his chief business as watching out for bills that may harm his home community, rather than pushing for beneficial measures.

As we have seen, Spectators subscribe to the general opinion within the legislature that freshman members should avoid speaking, should sit back and listen until they have at least one term of experience behind them. As the session wears on through committee hearings and floor debates, many members find more and more of their time taken up with legislative work. They want to get home or back to work at their regular occupations. Every comment, question, and speech lengthens the working day. There are strong taboos against "wasting the committee's time," or "becoming an orator" in floor debate.[16] The Spectator thus can find considerable support in the legislative environment for his stance of interested, though silent, observer.

Furthermore, legislative norms frequently penalize the speaker who is badly prepared. In two passages from the Spectator interviews, members tell how they learned to be cautious about taking an active role. May was persuaded to introduce a bill that "I didn't know very much about." Opposition to the bill in committee led to an unfavorable report. May concludes, "So that was the end of that. And I thought, 'From hereafter, I will know better when I present a bill— I'll study it out first, or put By Request on it.'" Sam has learned the same lesson vicariously.

> Now, ah, I heard several examples of that—where one person gets up and makes a favorable statement on a bill and another person gets up and he makes a fairly good speech against the bill—a spontaneous speech. He just thought of it from a certain angle, and it was a good answer. Then the third person got up and spoke in rebuttal to the second party, even though both were on the same side. The third viewpoint made me stop and think: now, that second guy didn't know what he was talking about. It

---

* See Tom Minora's remark: "Down our way there's no campaigning. They just put it on the ballot, or you're nominated and it's publicized through the papers, so on and so forth. You're either elected or you're not elected. You state in the paper what you're going to try to do when you come up here, and that's about it."

was just a good idea at the moment. But it certainly didn't carry its weight. And if I'd have been in that position, I'd have been embarrassed. Because I don't like to speak for the sake of hearing my voice. . . . And had he sat back a little longer, that would have been explained. So I'm in the same position, being a freshman there, I'm—afraid to stick my neck out because I know that what might be a good idea at one moment might be knocked down the very next moment.

As time goes on, the Spectator may find more and more environmental pressure to "sit back a little longer."

Political life offers considerable support for the second Spectator-adjustive technique: his superficial socializing. There is a strain of surface camaraderie running through almost all social relationships in politics. People find themselves together in occasional meetings held for temporary purposes. Deep friendships may develop out of such encounters, but often the acquaintanceship remains fixed at the level of small talk. The constant handshaking, first-name-calling, and exchange of gossip in politics are perhaps more substitutes for friendship than evidences of it.[17] Canvassing for votes, "making the rounds," the candidate moves from house to house, visiting lightly with people he will not meet again until the next election. Such experiences encourage one to develop a sort of genial but noncommittal, pleasant but somewhat formal, demeanor.

The legislature is also a mannered place, where, as Sam says, "they can insult you and do it politely." By tradition, legislators refer to one another in debate in the third person, and committee members are supposed to be considerate of witnesses and of one another. The whole affair has a ceremonial aspect, a deferential restraint and formality that fit the Spectator pattern closely. From the viewpoint of his adjustment, the contrast between the back-slapping atmosphere of campaigning and the formality of the legislature is less significant than their similarity: in different ways, both environments offer opportunities for the maintenance of superficial relations with others.

The legislator who has no bills of his own, no political demands to press on the legislature, owes little to his fellow members. His place depends upon the voters back home, not on his legislative colleagues. Thus the politically instrumental value of deep friendships is slight for the member who is not oriented toward personal achievement. Since Spectators present few political demands, this aspect of the environment largely passes them by. They have less reason to cultivate other members than has the ambitious or achievement-oriented member.

Opportunities for superficial socializing are manifold in and around the legislature. The cafeteria, the lobby, the women's lounge, some administrative offices, and numerous neighboring restaurants and bars are available for informal get-togethers. The spectacular Inauguration Ball, committee trips and dinners, and interest-group parties help to fill the social calendar. Members find the House chamber itself a convenient place for socializing before and after the daily session.

At the more formal "outside" social affairs there seems to be a rather mildly enforced stricture against talking shop. Tom refers to this when he says that at committee luncheons and dinners, "I don't think they discuss too much politics there. Just a friendly gathering. You have a couple of drinks and, ah—the topic of the day. And one thing leads to another, you know—it's not strictly politics and that. . . . Everybody has a good time. Let themselves loose." This norm helps the Spectator avoid serious conversation. His superficial socializing pattern is reinforced.

The Spectator finds no shortage of opportunities for submission in his legislative life. Others with clearly defined political aims press him for favorable votes. In the small-town political party such pressures are intensified by the face-to-face character of deliberations. Decisions may be made unanimously by tradition, so that deviance is unexpected and is penalized when it occurs. Loyalty to the party or faction may be highly valued and may become a criterion for membership. In the legislature similar pressures tend to develop in the committee phase. The group shares responsibility for a committee report: maverick behavior violates group unity toward the legislature as a whole. The party in the legislature constitutes another group with demands for conformity, as does the total membership on unanimous or near-unanimous decisions. The Spectator is thus surrounded by environmental pressures, which urge him to cooperate, to go along with group demands.

Furthermore, expectations that a member will conform to group demands are widely held. The member wears a party label. He is addressed in formal debate as "the gentleman from, . . ." His name, occupation, age, and place of birth are listed in the legislative manual. These labels identify him to other members as belonging to various groups with which he is expected to agree. The Democrat who votes with the Republicans, the rural representative who votes for urban renewal, the retired person who votes against old age pensions—all are looked at askance.

The dilemmas of submission

The Spectator's submissive tendencies may get him into painful situations if he is exposed to conflicting demands for submission. For example, submitting to the party leadership might involve risks of irritating his constituents. In such situations we would expect to find the Spectator trying to avoid commitment or, when avoidance is difficult or impossible, expressing himself cautiously and moderately.[18] Both these reactions, as we have seen, typify the Spectator's behavior.

But if his submissive pattern is to be maintained it must not bring down upon him too much tension and grief. If the environment subjected him to continual, severe stress over which group or leader to submit to, the Spectator's general appreciation for and optimism about the legislature would fade. In fact, a number of factors work to reduce the severity of this form of punishment.

In the first place, constituency pressures for legislative action may be nonexistent or mild and diffuse. Legislators frequently comment on their constituents' lack of interest in state affairs. The representative puts an ad in the paper inviting them to let him know their wishes. But no one calls. The town party committeemen, especially in the small town, are primarily interested in local affairs and in the election process. They may lose interest once the party slate is elected. Thus important issues on which the legislator receives demands from constituents and the legislative party may be rare.

This type of conflict is further reduced by the political norm that no legislator should be required to vote against strong demands from his constituents, especially if in response to such demands he has committed himself publicly to a position on the issue. There is a mutual recognition of the requirements of election survival, which tends to legitimate deviation from the party in such circumstances.

But the chances are high that the demands of the member's legislative party and those of his home town supporters will *not* conflict, but will overlap and reinforce one another. Simply because demands reach the legislator from different sources, we cannot assume that they are in conflict. The rural community in Connecticut is likely to send a Republican to the legislature. Demands from his legislative party and those from his rural constituency are far more likely to be mutually supporting than contradictory. The process of nominations and elections tends to select members with complementary group memberships. At the extremes, for example, the elderly, wealthy, Yankee, Protestant, rural Republican and the youthful, poor, Irish, Catholic, urban Democrat may each receive a multitude of demands from his groups. But for the individual, on most issues, all these demands are likely to push him in the same direction.

Even when demands from the member's groups conflict, they are not likely to balance precisely. Yet it is the balance that concerns him. Legislative issues are two-sided: whether to vote yes or no on particular issues. It is highly probable that the demands pressing the member toward one of these alternatives will be predominant. The legislator does not have to decide whether his constituents are wholly right or his party is wholly right. He does not have to resolve all their philosophical differences. He does not have to calculate how their preferences on all legislative issues, taken collectively, can be arranged in a transitive schedule maximizing rewards for both sides. He is faced with a particular bill to vote for or against. Whatever conflicts exist among his groups at the level of justification for a particular vote, he will feel little concern as long as all or most of them fall on one side of the yes–no line. The multiplicity of demands reaching the Spectator from different groups may simply multiply his opportunities for submission. He can "go along" with several of them at the same time.

The sequential nature of the legislative experience also works to reduce conflicts among the demands for submission reaching the Spectator. He moves from one scene to another, in this order: meetings with the town committee, encounters with the voters, the inauguration and initial legislative session, committee hearings, committee deliberations on bills, and floor debate. At any one time he receives face-to-face pressures for conformity primarily from only one of these groups. Particularly because he is a person who attends sensitively to his immediate environment, the Spectator weighs such face-to-face demands heavily. Thus he may well find that the demands from his immediate colleagues acquire a predominance that overwhelms considerations of past commitments and future confrontations. He can always change his mind, on the ground that he has gained new evidence. That face-to-face group pressures tend to reach him one at a time makes it easier to decide which demands to conform to.

Finally, the hierarchical organization in the legislature helps to ease the pressure of such conflicts. The structure of authority is not entirely clear—does the county whip outrank the committee chairman?—but the Spectator can distinguish among those who present demands at least partly on the basis of the formal positions they hold. Direct pressure from the state party chairman is likely to carry more weight than pressure from a fellow freshman. The majority and minority leaders, whips, chairmen, the speaker, and the governor and his assistants all bear official authority superior to that of the ordinary member. Similarly at the local level, official positions within and outside the party can be used as reference points in resolving conflicting demands.

These elements of the legislative environment can be thrown into relief if we consider hypothetically the maximum conflict situation. The Spectator's problem of choosing among demands for submission is most severe when he perceives (a) equally intense demands, (b) from persons of equal status, (c) who share group memberships with him, (d) who express these demands in the presence of him and of one another, and (e) the demands are equally divided on an important, specific yes or no question. Actual departures from this situation indicate the extent to which the environment offers escapes from the discomfort involved in submitting to others. As we have seen, many such escapes are available. Demands from his face-to-face and reference groups are unlikely to meet in such direct and contradictory fashion.[19] Usually departures from this model situation will reinforce one another, pushing the legislator in the same direction. Only occasionally will the Spectator experience severe punishment from his legislative environment for his submissive behavior.

The probabilities of pattern change

We cannot estimate with any great accuracy the probabilities of change in the Spectator pattern. Events may arise that press him toward new and different styles of behavior. But there are powerful forces working in the other direction, serving to maintain his pattern. Looked at from within, his techniques of adjustment have their roots in a personal history built up over a lifetime. To expect him to make drastic alterations in these techniques at this late stage in life, simply because he finds himself in a somewhat new situation, is unrealistic. There is a continuity about personality that is not easily altered when, in adulthood, one must adapt to new roles. The Spectator has been making similar adaptations for many years—in the family, on the job, in his friendship groups. Such learned processes of adaptation tend to become habitual, altered only at the expense of considerable stress and strain within the personality. Environmental pressures on the Spectator to behave "like a legislator" thus must compete with entrenched pressures to continue behaving like Sam or May or Tom.

Looking at the Spectator pattern from outside, we have seen that the legislature provides significant environmental support for the pattern. Punishments for taking an innocuous, passive role are few and are blunted by the Spectator's perceptual screening: he is seldom faced with pattern-threatening forces that he cannot shunt aside by ignoring or reinterpreting them.

The Spectator and the Work of the Legislature

What are the effects of the Spectator's pattern of adjustment on the substantive work of the legislature, the process of considering bills and deciding on them? Our prediction must be that the Spectators will make few direct contributions to these tasks. They attach their interest, feelings, and energies not to the specifics of issues but to matters peripheral to the main business before the legislature: the social round, the entertaining speeches, the fellowship of the legislature. They are unlikely to develop specialized competence in particular subject-matter areas, in part because they do not derive personal rewards from the kinds of achievement specialization brings. They are thwarted from developing and communicating reasoned opinions about legislative issues by a host of inhibitions.

Nor are they likely to be accurate evaluators of the opinions of others: they listen and watch, but what they attend to are signs of the speakers' manner and status rather than the substance of what is said. Just as in their minds they fail to link their own needs and desires with legislative issues, so they are little able to gauge these connections in other people. Spectators are unlikely to perform effectively as negotiators, who must develop special sensitivities for reading in what others say what they will do, how far they will go, how deeply and intensely they feel about the subject. Furthermore, their inhibitions against aggressiveness and their continual hesitation make it unlikely that they will press others to make prompt decisions. The main business of the legislature, then, is not usually the main business of the Spectators. They occupy positions on the outer edges of the substantive legislative process.[20]

Thus they are unlikely to cause much trouble for those who *are* primarily concerned with action on bills. Their quiet habits and reluctance to "interfere" keep them from making many demands on the leaders, and their submissiveness makes them easy to persuade. Despite their tendency to be swayed emotionally by the rhetoric and audience reactions of the legislature, Spectators are unlikely to vote these emotions. Rather they will choose the safe path, voting with their parties with great regularity.

This throws burdens of responsibility on party leaders that would be more widely shared if Spectators were replaced with more task-oriented types. The leaders and active legislators find themselves saddled with an immense volume of work, relieved only in part by division of labor among a few members of each committee. To cope with these demands, legislatures have developed advisory councils on bill drafting, research, and the like rather than mobilizing the full resources of the membership. These efforts have been partially successful, but largely in the area of technicalities. Insofar as the legislators themselves cannot perform the essential decision-making functions—perceiving and balancing demands, mediating conflicts through compromise, deciding among alternative courses of action—these responsibilities tend to leak away to administrators, constitutional conventions, lobbyists, and other outside forces. Or the legislature may adjourn in a flurry of last-minute bill-passing, leaving behind a legacy of unresolved problems and ill-conceived measures. The Spectator, by filling a seat that might have been occupied by a more capable and energetic member, thus contributes indirectly to legislative irrationality. He does not interfere much; but neither does he help share the main legislative tasks.

Looked at strictly from the point of view of the major tasks of the legislature, the Spectator makes little direct contribution. However, his pattern of adjustment to legislative life has other effects, which support and further the substantive work. In fact, it may be that the policy accomplishments of the legislature depend to a significant degree on the Spectator's presence there.

Role in reducing legislative tensions

The legislator is subjected to considerable strain in attempting to perform his official tasks. The sheer volume and complexity of decisions to be made force him to act continually on the basis of incomplete information. He must live with the feeling that he may be making important mistakes, which could be avoided if he had more time and higher competence. If he is to perform effectively he must find ways to overcome or control this anxiety, to continue to apply his powers of observation and judgment as best he can. If his nerve fails, the legislative process suffers.

But the legislator has more to contend with than the intellectual difficulties of mastering complex subject matter. His tensions are aggravated by the multitude of external pressures to which he is exposed. His tenure is uncertain, dependent on his ability to satisfy constituents who are unfamiliar with the difficulties of his task and generally disdainful and suspicious of "politicians." His powers are limited; he can almost never be completely satisfied with the results of his work. His efforts at achieving substantive goals risk conflict with others, thus adding to the strains of rational calculation the strains of interpersonal antagonism.

As we have seen, the legislator may react to these tensions by adopting defensive strategies which, in effect, place him outside the mainstream of the legislative process. Only insofar as at least some members are able to cope with these problems of strain and at the same time channel their attention, abilities, and energies into the main policy-making tasks will the legislature operate effectively. Thus the problems of reducing tension and the problems of policymaking are closely related. The pressure for deciding on bills introduces a disturbing element into the legislative community.[21] Successful decision-making depends in no small part on the success of the legislature in resolving these tensions so that active members are freed to concern themselves with major substantive problems.

It is in this tension-reducing task that the Spectators make their main contribution to the work of the legislature. Their orientation as applauding members of the legislative audience helps to maintain an atmosphere of affection, esteem, and respect which is encouraging to those who carry on the main tasks. Their optimism, mild humor, and politeness help to smooth over the interpersonal hostilities introduced by conflicting opinions on bills. And their feelings about the prestige of legislative office, spread among their constituents, work to counteract the more extreme negative attitudes toward politics and politicians.[22]

A legislature composed entirely of Spectators would be a disaster—the work would grind to a halt. But it is perhaps equally true that a legislature without any Spectators would degenerate into an ill-tempered, bickering collection of prima donnas.

The Spectator's political future

It is difficult to predict how long the Spectator will last as a legislator. One suspects that despite his present willingness to return, the place would eventually begin to pall on him. The probability is low that he would be diverted to an appointive position, because he neither demands rewards of this kind nor possesses unique talents. Probably the more important determinants of his legislative longevity will be the recruiting practices of the local town committee. If they want to—and can—attract a more capable candidate, the Spectator will be quickly replaced. But if they prefer his pliancy and easy availability he may be in the capital, watching, for many years to come.

Is "pluralism" an objective community characteristic? Research with eighty-five government officials in twelve Connecticut towns shows they differed markedly in their perceptions of power and that perceptions of self help explain the variations.

8

Motivated Sociology

POLITICAL POWER is a *cultural* phenomenon: power is shaped and distributed and concentrated by participants in accordance with certain shared values and perceptions. What is an obstacle to one is an opportunity to another. The motives people bring to politics, and the perceptual habits they have constructed to advance those motives, account for a very large proportion of their action.

An alternative viewpoint hypothesizes power as an objective structure, either in legal-constitutional terms or behaviorally as a given pattern of interaction largely independent of the psychology of any particular actor.

Testing these alternatives formed part of a research project on decision-making in local boards of finance (budget committees) in Connecticut, beginning with extensive field work, visiting their actual meetings, and then concentrating on twelve boards as they met to simulate their regular work in the small groups laboratory at Yale. Interviews and questionnaires supplemented the systematic observations in the lab, based on applications selected from the enormous "small-groups" literature.

Dissensus on Community Power Structure

In the questionnaires administered immediately after the discussion on the board of education problem, each member was asked to choose "which of the following two statements comes closer to describing decision-making in the town" (Q 29). The alternative statements were:

A	B
Almost all important community decisions are made by a small group of people. These few leaders usually take the initiative in starting projects: they almost always stop any project they oppose. Members of this group frequently get together informally to discuss their plans. Their influence is dominant over nearly all community affairs, regardless of the subject. They seldom find it necessary to concern themselves much with the opinions of other groups or individuals. In short, the town is pretty much run by a small group of persons with a great deal of influence.	Almost all important community decisions are made by a process of give and take among a large number of groups and individuals. On one issue, one combination of interested people will develop; on another issue, an almost entirely different combination is formed. Many different persons bring up important issues for consideration; there is no one group which can stop nearly every project. Leaders find it necessary to pay close attention to what most people are thinking in the community. In short, the town is pretty much run by constantly changing alliances in which many individuals and groups play significant parts.

Six answer categories allowed the respondent to indicate whether he saw the town as "much more," "somewhat more," or "slightly more" like one or the other alternative. The shades of preference were subsequently combined to distinguish simply between those who chose A, the elitist alternative, and those who chose B, the pluralist alternative. All but one of the eighty-five members answered this question.

Table 1 shows the distribution of responses for each of the twelve boards. The first thing we notice is that there is considerable disagreement among members of the same board regarding the general out-

Table 1 Perceived Power Structure and Community Population

Population category	Elitist	Pluralist
Small towns (1,200 to 2,900)		
Board 1	3	4
Board 2	3	3
Board 3	3	3
Board 4	3	4
Middle towns (7,300 to 19,500)		
Board 5	2	2
Board 6	6	3
Board 7	5	2
Board 8	2	6
Larger towns (30,000 to 46,200)		
Board 9	8	0
Board 10	6	3
Board 11	1	3
Board 12	3	6
Total	45	39

lines of power in the community. In only one board, Board 9, are the members unanimous in their choice. Nor is there any clear trend in either the elitist or the pluralist direction as we move from the small to the larger towns. Each of the small towns divides on the question as closely as possible. In the middle towns, one is split, two lean in the elitist direction, and one leans toward pluralism. Two of the larger towns have majorities for the elitist view and two for the pluralist view.

The picture is not particularly clarified when we look only at the seven boards which deviate from the closest possible split (Boards 6 through 12). For example, we might expect that towns characterized as elitist would display a lower level of political conflict than those viewed as pluralist. But statistics on political conflict show no consistent pattern: competition between the two political parties was just about as close in the elitist towns as in the pluralist towns. The four elitist towns were 64, 39, 51, and 54 percent Republican in party registration in 1960; the three pluralist towns had Republican registrations of 57, 67, and 25 percent. The average winning margins in percentage of votes for the local chief executive in the three most recent elections were 4, 21, and 3 percentage points for the pluralist towns and 2, 12, 1, and 13 percentage points for the elitist towns. Perhaps other data would show a more definite pattern, but at least in terms of partisan divisions there is no clear difference between towns which the board members tend to see as dominated by a power elite and those seen as pluralistic.

In previous work we have shown how, in the course of making practical decisions, members of boards of finance tend to accept a pluralistic view of power in their communities. They refer again and again to the necessity for bargaining, the desirability of cooperation among equals. We infer from this that there is a shared, positive orientation toward pluralism which tends to shape actual decisions on specific policy proposals. But when the question is posed at a higher level of abstraction, as in the paragraphs above, the members show much more mixed preferences. The reason for this apparent contradiction probably lies in disparities between highly generalized opinions and opinions invoked in particular contexts.[1] A person may adhere to a general belief in freedom of speech—and yet bring other values to bear when he is considering whether or not to allow an atheist to teach in the public schools. In much the same way a public official embroiled in a highly pluralistic situation, and continually invoking pluralistic premises as he makes day-to-day decisions, may nevertheless agree, when asked, that a small coterie of influentials runs his town. As evidence in specifying the objective realities of decision-making, broad generalizations by participants are obviously suspect.

As need-fulfilling opportunities, however, such generalizations are of interest. The links between very abstract beliefs and practical action are weak; this means that, to a large degree, a person can believe what he wants or needs to without this interfering much with his behavior. Viewed from this perspective, the choice between alternative models of community decision-making as posed in the elitist-pluralist question probably indicates more about the person answering than about the realities of power in his community. Some of our data illustrate how it is that the kind of general report on power in his community that a board of finance member might convey to the researcher can represent personal needs more than political realities.

Perceptions of Self and Perceptions of Power

The data concern relationships between self-images and images of community power.[2] The hypothesis is that a person will tend to perceive a community power structure which is consistent with his perception of himself. Or, to put it the other way around, he will tend to choose that description of community power which is less dissonant with his self-image than other descriptions are. The self-image is a fundamental feature of personality; the image of community power is a derivative, relatively peripheral perception, one with only tenuous behavioral implications. Consequently, the person is relatively constrained in altering his self-image, but relatively free to shape his image of power. Before attempting a more thorough explanation, let us see how some responses by the board of finance members fit this interpretation.

A primary dimension of a person's self-image is evaluation—one perceives himself as doing relatively well or relatively poorly in important activities. Two items in the questionnaires provide evidence on self-evaluation. Members were asked, "How would you rate your own performance so far on the board of finance?" (Q 13). Answer categories were Superior, Excellent, Fair, Poor, and Very Poor. No one selected the last of these ratings, so the responses could logically be divided between high (superior or excellent) and low (fair or poor) self-evaluations.

Another question, placed elsewhere in the questionnaire, asked the respondent to complete the sentence, "When I am a leader I am usually . . . ," with Excellent, Very good, Fair, or Not so good (F5C). Again the first two answers were scored as high and the second two as low.

In tables 2 and 3, the relationship between these self-evaluations and images of community power is indicated. The data suggest that there is some tendency for those who rate themselves high as members and as leaders to see the community as elitist; those who are more critical of their own performance tend to perceive a pluralist power structure.

A second dimension of the self-image concerns dominance. A person may see himself as one who typically plays a directive, authoritative role with others, or he may stress mutuality and cooperation

Table 2 Perceived Power Structure and Self-Rating of
Performance as a Board of Finance Member

Self-rating of performance	Elitist	Pluralist	Total	N
High	68%	32%	100%	28
Low	41	59	100	46

Table 3 Perceived Power Structure and Evaluation
of Self as Leader

Self-evaluation	Elitist	Pluralist	Total	N
High	59%	41%	100%	49
Low	44	56	100	34

in his interpersonal relationships. A question from William Schutz's
FIRO-B series provided data on these tendencies (F 2). The respondents were asked to choose between the following descriptions of
their own behavior, one (on the right) emphasizing directiveness, and
the other (on the left) emphasizing sharing:

When I am responsible for
organizing and carrying out a
task, the most important thing to
me is to try to include those who
are working with me in the
decisions and the responsibility
I have. I consult them before I
make a decision, and we discuss
it and try to come to agreement
about what should be done. After
the discussion I try to divide up
the task and have everyone take
responsibility for his own part.
Then if anyone fails to do what
he should, it's up to him to
correct it. When someone does

When I am responsible for
organizing and carrying out a
task, the most important things
I try to do are make sure
everyone knows exactly what is
expected of him and make sure I
know my job thoroughly. Then I
try to see to it that the task is
carried out according to the rule
laid down. If I let anyone violate
the rules we're following without
being disciplined, I lose the
respect of those under me, my
authority and effectiveness are
endangered, and it is not fair to
those who are doing their job.

fail to do his job I usually don't
exert my authority but let the
group work it out themselves.

Sometimes it is necessary to
make an example of someone by
disciplining him publicly so that
the others know the rules are
being enforced.

Table 4 shows the distribution of responses to this question and
to the elitist-pluralist descriptions of community power. It appears
that individuals who see themselves as playing a rather directive role
are more likely to see their communities as elitist, while those who
stress mutuality and cooperation in their interpersonal relationships
are prone to see these qualities in their community too. The tendencies toward congruence between one's self-image and his perception
of community power are evident.

A third dimension of the self-image is affectional, the degree to
which a person sees himself as engaged in warm, close relationships
with others or as more withdrawn and impersonal. Another question
from Schutz's FIRO-B series (F 1) taps this aspect of the self-image.
The alternative statements were:

I try to keep my relations with
people on a fairly impersonal
basis. I really don't enjoy getting
too involved with people, partly
because it interferes with my
desire to be by myself. I don't
especially appreciate people
coming to visit me at any hour,
though I do recognize they're just
trying to be friendly. There are
many times I don't feel like

I try to make friends as quickly
as possible with virtually
everyone I meet. To me, being
liked is the most important thing.
I try to have my relationships
with people informal and very
close. I like to discuss personal
problems with close friends. I
like people to drop in on me at
almost any hour of the day or
night, and practically always I

Table 4   Perceived Power Structure and Self-Rating of
Directiveness as Leader

Self-rating of directiveness	Elitist	Pluralist	Total	N
High	67%	33%	100%	30
Low	45	55	100	53

seeing people—I'm content with what I'm doing. I feel that I can handle my personal problems better by myself. If I want to talk about them with anyone I would rather it be someone I don't know well than a close friend. In a group I don't get involved with personalities but prefer to stick to what we're supposed to be doing.

will go out somewhere with them if they ask me to. I will go out of my way to make people like me and do a great deal to avoid being disliked by them. Sharing experiences and being partly responsible to others is very important. In a group I almost always try to get to know the other members well, because I enjoy the group more then.

Table 5 shows the distribution of responses on the dimension of personalism. Those who choose the alternative stressing warm, close relationships with others are also likely to see their community as dominated by an elite. The socially cooler members tend to see a more pluralistic power structure.

One additional set of answers shows how elitists and pluralists tend to differ in the needs they seek to satisfy through participation in group activities. Members were asked to complete the sentence, "When I am in a group, the thing I like most is to be . . . ," by ranking three possibilities: Very well liked, A leader, and Prominent in the activities (F5D). In table 6 these responses are scored high (first or second choice) or low (third choice) and related to the perceived power structure. The results show a slight tendency for those who value being liked and leading to select the elitist description, while those who want to be prominent in the activities of the group are far more apt to choose the pluralist one.

These marginal tendencies can be summarized as follows. Elitists— those who perceive their communities as dominated by a power elite—

Table 5   Perceived Power Structure and Self-Rating of Personalism in Social Relations

Self-rating of personalism	Elitist	Pluralist	Total	N
High	61%	39%	100%	44
Low	42	58	100	38

Table 6 Perceived Power Structure and Self-Estimation
of Desired Rewards from Participation
in Group Activities

Self-estimation of desired rewards	Elitist	Pluralist	Total	N
Being liked				
High (first or second choice)	56%	44%	100%	50
Low (third choice)	36	64	100	28
Being a leader				
High	55	45	100	40
Low	41	59	100	34
Being prominent				
High	44	56	100	68
Low	92	8	100	13

are more likely to be those who perceive themselves as excellent performers as members and leaders, exercising dominance when in a leadership role, and striving for close, affectional relationships with others. Pluralists—those who see their communities as run by bargaining among a wide variety of power centers—are more likely to be those who perceive themselves as performing less capably as members or leaders, using a cooperative leadership style, and seeking independence and individual prominence in their social relationships.

How are these findings to be explained? It seems evident that the broad and simple characterizations of community power offered in the elitist-pluralist alternatives have little direct connection with the kinds of operative assumptions upon which the members base their actions. It is probably true that public officials, like other people, seldom act on the basis of deduction from general principles; that is, the usual mode of decision-making does not proceed from the abstract to the concrete, but the other way around.[3] Typically the decision-maker finds himself confronted with a practical situation involving choice. Most of his attention is taken up with the factual details of this situation. But in part to guide his decision and in part to justify his intuitive preference, he refers to a collection of generalities, rarely formulated in any systematic way, and selects certain of them as relevant to the particular choice he has to make. These moral and behavioral premises are invoked to fit a specific set of circumstances and are expressed when and if they appear to have persuasive possibilities in the group deliberations. The resulting collection of expressed (shared) premises constitutes the operative political culture of the group. If these common premises depart very far from reality the group will fail in its attempts to adapt to the environment in which it operates. The penalties for groups and for individual members of groups who do not adhere to realistic principles in their everyday operations can be severe.

But there are few penalties for idiosyncratic beliefs held by individuals so long as these are not invoked or expressed in some context of action. As isolated items in a person's storehouse of generalities, they are available for other purposes, for meeting needs other than the need for rationalizing decisions.

The self-image, on the other hand, is a central feature of personality. Although dependent to some extent on immediate external circumstances, and subject to some change over time, the self-image tends toward stability and persistence. Consequently, when there is a conflict between one's image of himself and some highly abstract perceptual formulation regarding the world around him, it is the latter which is likely to be distorted to fit the former. In the case of our elitist-pluralist dichotomy, this explanation appears to fit the evidence.

Clearly, members of a board of finance are in a position to think of themselves as part of any power elite in their town. As formulated in the questionnaire, the elitist alternative stresses at least three features of the elite: exclusiveness, directiveness, and cohesiveness. Each of these features tends to resonate with an element of the self-image. The exclusive aspect is emphasized in the characterization of the elite as a "small group," a "few leaders," who "seldom find it necessary to concern themselves with the opinions of other groups or individuals." A boundary is drawn, a distinction perceived, between the select few and the excluded many. This distinction is much more blurred in the pluralist alternative, in which "a large number of groups and individuals," "many different persons," "constantly changing alliances," are described as involved in important decisions. Here the consonance between the elitist viewpoint and a high self-evaluation is clear. The person who thinks he is an excellent performer has a psychological stake in a view of the community which stresses the distinctiveness of the ruling group. Such a perception supports and enhances his sense of being a bit better, a cut above the others in terms of ability and effectiveness. An equalitarian community, on the other hand, renders less relevant the possession of higher talents. Free to select an elitist or a pluralist general description of community power—because the choice need not make much difference in practice—the man who thinks of himself as exceptional is apt to find the elitist view the more comfortable one. Pluralists tend to be more self-critical (although not necessarily self-denigrating) and, thus, to feel more at home with a community power description which puts less emphasis on distinctions in personal qualifications.

The elitist alternative also stresses directiveness: the elite is "dominant over nearly all community affairs," and "the town is pretty much run by a small group of persons with a great deal of influence," who "almost always stop any project they oppose." Leadership, as described in the pluralist alternative, is much more cooperative: there is a "process of give and take," initiative and veto power are widespread, and leaders cannot afford to neglect public opinion. The self-perception, "I am dominant," is obviously more consonant with the elitist characterization than with the pluralist one. The person who sees himself as directive, authoritative, and disciplinary feels at home in a system organized for the exercise of direction, authority, and discipline. Similarly one who conceives of himself as a negotiator finds his place more readily in a pluralistic system. In both cases the temptation is to warp perceptions in these need-fulfilling ways.

Finally, the elitist position stresses the cohesiveness, the intimacy, of relationships among the elite. They form an in-group; they "frequently get together informally to discuss their plans." The person who values warm relationships with others, who wants to be liked even more than he wants to lead or take a prominent part, tends to be attracted by this aspect of elitism. The more distant individualist, or the man who actively resists social intimacy, feels more comfortable in a less cozy political environment, one in which the commitment to others is looser and more tentative. Again, the psychologically peripheral perception of community power tends to be altered to fit the psychologically central self-image.

These pieces of evidence suggest tendencies rather than laws, marginal shadings rather than blacks and whites. But they are, perhaps, distinct enough to indicate the necessity, in the investigation of political power cultures, to ask the right questions about the right data. If the purpose is to understand linkages between images and actions, the analysis calls for concentration on the ways in which these elements are connected in practice.[4] To suppose that adherence to some general position implies some particular set of choices about specific policies is to suggest a hypothesis rather than to announce an obvious truth. Conversely, it is dangerous to leap from data about the premises invoked in the course of decision-making to predictions about the participant's reactions to abstract statements. As Justice Holmes put it, "General propositions do not decide concrete cases." Nor did the concrete cases necessarily determine the general propositions, in the minds of our respondents.

Stunned by the Kennedy assassination, citizens of New Haven (such as cooks, nurses, firemen) recovered by sharing with their friends certain hopeful formulations.

9

Sharing Constructs

WELL, WHEN I first heard, my husband ran back in and he said, "You know, Mary,"—he was on his way to work—he says, "You know, the President has been shot." I said, "Oh, turn the television on, quick, quick." We turned the television on and . . . I felt terrible, just awful, so I said to myself, "Well, he'll be all right, he'll be all right. I know he'll be all right." And then a few minutes later here it came, he's dead. Well, then I just went all to pieces and said, "Well, he will not die in vain," and I cried. That's how I felt.

It is all there: the sense of shock and horror, the immediate turning to television, the hope against hope, and the tears. Mary expresses in these sentences thoughts and feelings that were shared by the whole national community as the news of the President's murder spread. Over the following weekend the nation engaged in concerted mourning, spending hour after hour watching and listening to television. The rapid recovery, the sense of continuity and confidence that promptly reasserted itself, can be largely attributed to the networks' decision to broadcast nothing but programs related to the President's death. This provided the public with a sustained opportunity to participate, vicariously but intensely, in the experience and expression of grief. The contrast with the slow and incomplete recovery following Lincoln's assassination is clear.[1]

The communal character of this experience went beyond membership in a national audience. Many people were at work when the news came; they learned of the assassination from fellow workers, and their immediate reactions were expressed in group settings.[2] Many felt the need to be with relatives or friends, or at least to telephone them. A nurse who was at home when the news came told me, "I saw my neighbor from across the street and she came over and we kind of sat and talked. It seemed good to have someone to talk it over with." People watched television in small and large groups, and talked to one another about their reactions as the story unfolded.[3] And in the days following, families, neighbors, and friends sought explanations and meanings in informal conversations.

The content of these conversations is important for understanding the public's reaction. Survey data on individual responses can tell us which of the many themes from the media were retained by the public. But communication in natural groups provides significant, additional information. Group members consciously or unconsciously select certain themes to tell those with whom they have continuing, close relationships. These themes encounter reinforcement or resistance in the group setting. Interpersonal influence processes come into play, shaping a collective interpretation that fits the particular needs of the group. Over time, these group-formulated and group-supported interpretations tend to override or replace idiosyncratic individual ones. They become part of the group myth, the collection of common opinions to which the members generally conform.[4]

In an attempt to get at the dynamics of this process, I tape-recorded conversations among eight groups at their places of work or recreation. These sessions, averaging about thirty minutes each, took place on Monday after the funeral and on Tuesday morning. With one exception, the people in the groups were of equal job and social status; a fire chief was the only superior present (although not participating) in any group. The groups were: four male cooks, six female kichen helpers, four truck drivers, eight female laundry workers (but two had to leave during the session), four firemen, six nurses in a Catholic hospital, four members of a service club, shortly before their weekly meeting, and four young men, between about nineteen and twenty-one years old, in a pool hall. All but the last two groups were recorded at their places of work.

I posed four broad questions:

> Now that you have had a chance to think about this whole set of events, what do you think its meaning will be? What is the significance of it?
>
> How did you learn about it and what was your immediate reaction?
>
> Who or what do you feel is really responsible for this?
>
> What is it going to mean for relations among various groups in this country such as Negroes and whites, Catholics and Protestants, Republicans and Democrats?

The respondents were encouraged to develop their answers in their own way; additional questions were posed when necessary to keep the conversation going. The group members appeared to be responding to one another at least as much as to me, developing side conversations and reacting to themes others introduced.

Analysis of these data suggested a focus on the social recovery from the shock of the assassination. The transcripts show the intensity and character of identifications with the President that were shared by the group, and also the ways in which a variety of socially pathological interpretations of his murder were corrected or modified in the course of the group discussion. The severity of psychological disturbance can be traced to the strength of the links these persons had developed, perhaps largely latently, with President Kennedy. In turn, the shock set the stage for the emergence of personal fears and anxieties in the form of certain new political perspectives, which, if they had been allowed to spread and deepen, might well have resulted in considerable damage to the stability and rationality of the political system. That such themes were expressed and that groups could draw on resources of confidence and reason to check them are significant facts for the maintenance of central democratic values.

Shared Links to the President

Examination of the transcripts reveals a number of sources for the common feeling that the loss was personal, linked in a variety of ways with the respondents' own lives and fortunes. The most frequently mentioned type of linkage was familial. Here two dimensions stand out: an awareness of the President in a family role like that of the respondent, and a sense that he was a model performer in that role, one to be imitated by all Americans. A nurse said, "I think he was a good father. . . . I think many of us identified ourselves as being a family like that." A woman laundry worker said, "He really cared for his family. He was a husband to all his family as well as . . . President of the United States." The "father image" inherited from the Eisenhower presidency appears to be only one aspect of the response to Kennedy. In his middle forties, he could be perceived from several angles. Thus a cook with a young family said, "It's really a big loss. And my youngest boy, whose name is John too, says, 'I wonder who is going to take care of little John.' . . . It's still going to be tough to get used to the idea, because I know, I have a couple of kids myself and it kind of makes me wonder, well, suppose the same thing happened to me?" A college boy in the pool hall saw the President as "a typical American, like a family man. You think of your family, if your father got killed, it would be just as important to you as it was to Kennedy's family."

The many family roles in which Kennedy was known—son, husband, father, and brother—permitted a wide range of familial identifications. In this sense many respondents appear to have felt that they were like Kennedy or a member of his immediate family. They felt they knew how those near him must have thought and felt and acted, by extrapolation from their own similar family experiences.

Other comments stressed the President's family life as an example to be imitated. For instance, in the following passage an elderly kitchen helper invoked this ideal:

> If a man and woman stick together like those two people, I think it's not necessary to live like this—one hate the other. Just example from them—the people got to realize we got a man and

a wife in the White House. They're supposed to follow that too. They'll be no argument, they'll be no this nor nothin'—just pleasant life for everybody. But nobody think about that. They think to be mean to one another. But if they watch that family, wherever they went or wherever they go to trip, to pleasure—everybody likes them.

Here the link to the President's family does not depend directly on a consciousness of similarity, but on an ego ideal, one that may have been brought into many a family argument. Thus identification, both in the sense of likeness and in the sense of a model is evident as a personal linkage.

Identification with President Kennedy as a Catholic and as a religiously devoted person was evident in several responses, but presented a special problem. One pool-hall boy, asked if he had had similar feelings before, said, "The nearest I came to it was when Pope John died." A nurse in a Catholic hospital stressed the President's religious devotion, and introduced the difficulty others had to deal with: "I felt that he stood up for his religious rights as well. He went to mass and behaved as he should, and yet I don't feel that he let it interfere at all with his state duties." Two respondents, one Catholic and the other probably a Protestant, illustrate clearly the conflict some felt regarding Kennedy's religious image. The Catholic, an Italian kitchen helper said, "On the Catholic part—was not interfere with his duty at the White House. Catholic, you know—it was first with him the Catholic religion, but he was keepin' aside to the duty of the White House. Religion come after, for the family and the kids." The Protestant, a young Negro woman working in a laundry, said:

At first, people were against President Kennedy because he were a Catholic. But he was so good and so everyone has shown a feeling and expressed their feeling toward [him]. Everyone, mostly, I've talked with about how they feel about Kennedy, you don't hear them say, "Well, he was a Catholic and I don't like him because he was a Catholic." They are very upset just about the shock of his death, that he was such a wonderful man. But his religion, regardless, if he is a good man, what type of religion that he like . . . it's just only one God.

It appears that Kennedy's expressed position on his religious convictions and their relation to his official duties got through to these two people. Both are able to maintain a relatively elaborate identification with the President as a Catholic and, more generally, as a religious man, while agreeing with his church-state position. For the first respondent, the dissonance is resolved by compartmentalization: Kennedy's religion was for Sunday and his family, and was kept separate from his White House work. The second respondent manages the problem by referring it to a higher unity: the President's belief in the one God of all. The fact that a religious identification can be maintained in the face of considerable complexity testifies to its strength and significance.

A third set of personal linkages can be classified as characterological. Some of the respondents commented on specific virtues of the President that were of particular significance to their groups. For example, one of the Negro laundry workers explained, "He's not a man that, when you talk, he look in the other direction. He look right toward you just as though you were in the audience, like you to me." A young man in the pool hall mentioned Kennedy's youthful look, and a nurse, on duty Monday night after the funeral, pointed to his hard work: "He worked way into the late hours of the night on government matters and things like that, and he was always a diligent worker. . . . It seems everybody made him their ideal." And the service club members, several of whom disagreed with the President's policies, seemed to admire him for courageous adherence to principle:

> R_1: Well, if courage makes a man great and if understanding makes men great, he'll be great if he's measured in those terms. He certainly had courage, there's no question of that.
>
> R_2: He certainly had the courage of his convictions.

These comments suggest that people tended to evaluate the President's character in terms of values most salient for their particular groups. Underlying the generally favorable reaction to Kennedy as a good man, selected characteristics were stressed in special ways.

Respondents identified with President Kennedy partly because they liked his policies. Of special significance were what they perceived as actions that benefited them and as his steadfast control of threatening forces. Both the laundry workers and the kitchen ladies, for whom the matter was of direct import, commented enthusiastically that the President raised the minimum wage, that he was "trying to do something for the working people," and that he "fixed it so that unemployed people have jobs." Here the rewards seem direct and personal; they are perceived as flowing from the President's own efforts. The laundry workers developed similar themes about care for the needy:

> R_1: I think President Kennedy was more for the colored people than any other president.
> R_2: Yeah, yeah, that's right. Because he wanted the two of them to be alike—am I right or wrong?
> R_1: He wanted us to have equal rights.
> R_3: That's right, he did.
> R_1: He tried to have them integrated.
> R_3: Together, to get along.

The image of the President as a "benevolent leader" who mediated practical and emotional help is evident in these comments.[5] Respondents also stressed Kennedy's steadfast pursuit of international stability, holding Castro and Khrushchev in line without risking war. A fireman who was critical of Kennedy nevertheless called his stand on Cuba "probably the greatest thing that he did during his three years in office." A cook explained, "Well, one thing . . . I liked about him, he didn't mix his words. He didn't say one thing and do another. . . . take like this Castro deal—I mean, he really stood up and he didn't back down for nothin'. Very strong character." A kitchen helper emphasized Kennedy's maintenance of the balance of power:

> He keep Khrushchev level: "I'll level with you and you level with me," he says. "Don't go any further step because I'll catch you. I don't go any further step because you going to catch me, so let's stay level." When you don't talk, you shoot the gun and that's bad.

These responses appear to delineate the two major dimensions of Presidential policy, dimensions against which the public measures other Presidents. He is appreciated for making life easier at home and safer abroad. These policies are seen as springing from his personal characteristics: he is at once kind and strong.

Reviewing these responses, one is impressed first by the variety of identifications that can be developed; there is nothing here reflecting a uniform public response imprinted by exposure to a single source of information. Rather, the identifications people have with the President are those that fit their own particular life situations and that are strengthened by being shared with friends and coworkers. Furthermore, the main ones appear to be related to some of the deepest dimensions of human experience: the family, religion, character, and basic needs for sustenance and protection. Had the President been perceived as just another distant public official, it is doubtful that so many would have reacted so intensely to his death. The evidence suggests that the profound sense of bewilderment and grief was one result of the sudden shattering of personal bonds with an important ego ideal.

The Need for an Interpretation

In the aftermath of the asssassination, people sought to "make sense" of what might have been considered an absurd accident. Once the reality could no longer be escaped, it had to be worked into some acceptable interpretation. The respondents were concerned with three primary problems of interpretation. First, they wanted an explanation, an understanding of the causes of the President's murder. A laundry worker struggled with this problem as follows:

> The only thing you heard about is, why did this guy kill him? Why were they not for him to be the President of the United States as long as he could be or until the Lord has taken his life away? Why would a man have to take his life away? I mean, I think that what everyone are really concerned about. At least me, myself, I like to be knowin' why. And now that they have killed him, he can't say why.

Second, they wanted meaning, some positive, significant implication for the good. Like Mary, the kitchen worker whose reactions I quoted at the beginning, a truck driver "would like to think his death was not in vain—I hope, certainly I hope it wasn't." Third, people wanted reassurance, a prediction that somehow or other the nation would come through without severe harm. One of the pool-hall boys showed this concern when he said:

> I think if it has any political affiliations or anything like that, that's the thing most people are afraid to even think about. If it is true, then we are in for an awful shock very soon, because they got to the point where it came out in the open that a President was shot for political reasons—then something's going to happen very soon.

Six of the eight groups carried on this search for interpretations. The two deviant groups—the service club members and the laundry workers—illustrate blocks in the group recovery process.

Perhaps the least healthy response to the assassination would have been no response. People needed to grieve, to share their grief with others, and to work out some acceptable set of feelings about the situation.[6] In the service club group there was very little emotional expression. They discussed the details of the two murders and the television coverage. Only near the end, and then tentatively, did any positive feeling toward the President emerge. Their tendency to avoid emotional expression may have left them with unresolved tensions. For such groups, recovery was likely to be slower.[7]

The laundry workers let their feelings flow freely, but there was very little thematic development in their discussion. The pattern was assertion and agreement; almost any interpretation want unchallenged. The killer should be cremated; a gang, possibly the Mafia, was responsible; Ruby was Oswald's confederate, etc. What seemed to be accomplished here was catharsis but no correction. The group atmosphere encouraged unfettered expression of whatever came to mind. No one opposed or criticized another's idea. Interpretations spilled out one after another. There was no attempt to develop a coherent group position.[8]

In the other groups, one finds both expression and constraint, the development of some relatively consistent and reasoned interpretations. These more common conversations show how several somewhat dangerous themes met corrective responses.

Dangerous Tendencies

When the news came, "I felt like I'd been struck by a thunderbolt," said one man; "I felt sick at my stomach," said another. Close on the heels of shock and disbelief came fundamental emotions that had to be managed in some way by individuals and groups. The ways they managed them, the interpretations they developed, in many cases had implications which could have led to widespread demands for political policy changes detrimental to democratic order.

In the first place the violent surprise of the assassination, which was so quickly followed by another murder, engendered fear that something had gone fundamentally wrong and that the normal restraints on violence had broken down.[9] A nurse expressed this fear of contagious violence when she said, "I think it shows the emotional state of mind of people of this day. They go into a frenzy and a state of frustration. It just seems that anything could happen really, the way they react." The "killing and frenzy," she felt, "could go on until it's all the way back up here." A pool-hall boy thought that "something's going to happen very soon," and explained:

> Well, I think something else will come out in the open like that . . . couldn't say mass assassination, but some sort of mass demonstration where the same thing will happen in key positions all over the United States. That's what I'm worried about. If someone could master-plan something like that where high people in positions of authority all over the United States could be assassinated at the same time or captured at the same time . . . it could be just as easy to overthrow this government as any other government.

A cook expressed similar concerns: "I mean, it puts a lot in your mind to think, because they have someone like that can actually get at a President. I mean, it's hard to tell just what is what in times coming. 'Cause anything can happen." The dangerous implications of such feelings are hinted at by a truck driver's comment that "something has to be done so a thing like this should never, ever happen again." Fears of violence, a breakdown of confidence in the safety and stability of the system, might have resulted in demands for extraordinary preventative measures, demands, for example, that the President be confined behind armed guards or that mass demonstrations be outlawed. At a somewhat deeper level, fear of this kind probably works to inhibit public acceptance of innovation and experimentation in politics. There is a sense that only the tried and true are safe. And since fear often causes withdrawal from the threatening situation, it might lead people to turn away from active political participation, to escape from an arena of action that had become dangerous.

Another frequently expressed emotion, derived in part from those fears, was hostility, especially toward Oswald and others thought to share the responsibility. A truck driver suggested a classic punishment: "They should let him loose in the country and don't let anyone do anything to him. Just let him walk around with that guilt. That's my feeling. Just let him walk around knowing that he shot the President." The pool-hall boys reported their immediate desire was to "string him up," or subject him to "medieval torture or something along that line." A kitchen helper felt that "it's too good to give him the electric chair . . . too quick to die like that. They have to make him suffer, royal." One is reminded here of the interviews shortly after Oswald's murder with some Dallas citizens, who were mainly glad about the revenge. The threat to democratic order in such sentiments is obvious: a breakdown in standards of justice, a willingness to make the kind of exception that can weaken and eventually destroy the rule.

But some responses indicated hostility reaching beyond the individual murderer. Some revealed a suspicion that a gang of some sort was really responsible. A truck driver saw a tangle of conspiracy surrounding Oswald and Ruby:

> I think the man that shot Oswald . . . was hired by someone . . . because I don't think he'd give his life that freely, just run up and shoot him in front of everyone. . . . He couldn't possibly get away so he was either forced to do it or he was threatened. They'd probably kill his family if he didn't.

The next comment reluctantly attributed blame to Southern segregationists: "I don't like to make a statement like that, but there was a lot of ill feeling in the South due to the fact that Kennedy's civil

rights program was something they didn't care for." In the cooks'
conversation several groups were mentioned:

> R_1: We have a lot of Communists in this country. We have it
> in all walks of life.
>
> R_2: These people who are against civil rights. . . . There could
> be a lot of groups that would just say, well, "He stepped on our
> toes."
>
> R_1: You have right-wingers. You have left-wingers. You have
> everything in this country. I mean, you have them in all walks
> of life. . . . You have Communism. I mean, it's been in the pa-
> pers for years and years. There are doctors, lawyers—you even
> have professors . . .

The variety of available targets for blame, and uncertainty about
which of them might be really responsible, dampened the force of
these responses. The political harm inherent in such sentiments is,
however, evident: the threat of breakdown in the sense of political
community, an unwillingness to tolerate dissent or to enter into nego-
tiations with the supposedly guilty ones. The destructive crosscurrents
of group blame and guilt that followed Lincoln's assassination are
reflected in these comments, albeit in considerably milder form.

A third strong response, already illustrated in quotations above, was
the wave of adulation for President Kennedy. Paradoxically, these
feelings might well have disrupted the people's ability to judge their
political leaders rationally. Some of those who were most enthusiastic
about Kennedy as President and person found it difficult to accept the
idea that Lyndon Johnson could carry on effectively. One kitchen lady
said, "Mr. Johnson will never be the man Mr. Kennedy was . . . he
isn't capable enough in any way." "The greatest President," "another
Lincoln," "a hero who died for his people," would be extremely difficult to follow on the national stage until other, calmer standards were
brought to bear.

Thus imbedded in the healthy expressions of feeling after the assassination were certain themes that, had they not been brought out into
the open and dealt with effectively, might have spread and interfered
significantly with the maintenance of national confidence, devotion to
fair procedures, and adherence to rational standards of political evalu-

ation. How were these problems resolved in the conversations of ordinary citizens?

Group Response

Perhaps one of the healthiest responses in the group discuissions was willingness to withhold judgment until the social recovery process had run its course.[10] Although the respondents were ready to express their feelings and opinions, they did not fasten irrevocably onto interpretations in the immediate aftermath. A cook wanted to wait "until the smoke clears" before he decided what the impact would be; a nurse was glad there will be "a full investigation" because "the case is not closed" regarding Oswald; a fireman said, "We'll have to wait and see just how well we can bring about the transition of power." These groups kept their thoughts tentative, exploring possible implications without committing themselves to any. The conspiracy theories, the predictions of more violence, the doubts about Johnson's abilities, most often met a wait-and-see attitude that left the door open for later correction.

The most frequent type of response to fears that violence would spread throughout the country or lead to the overthrow of the government was to isolate the threat by concentrating on detailed events.[11] This is clear, for example, in the reactions to a nurse who repeatedly generalized the dangers, predicting outbreaks of "emotional frenzy." The comment that immediately followed her first suggestion that "anything could happen" moved at once from the general to the particulars of Oswald's murder: "The police had arrested the suspected murderer. . . ." The fearful nurse picked this up in her next comment: "I studied the television picture of Ruby, the man who shot Oswald. Well, if you notice the expression on Oswald's face. . . ." After some group discussion of the Dallas Police, she reiterated her concern that "there could have been a lot more killing and frenzy," but receiving no encouragement for this theme, she joined in the discussion of details: "I think the greatest reaction was people saying there was no top there on the car." Some minutes later, she tried again, referring to a general "emotional crisis," but the response she got discussed Oswald as "emotionally unstable." At last she dropped the contagious violence theme and ended the discussion on a positive note: "I think of the good Kennedy will leave with the people rather than anything else." Tendencies to exaggerate the scope and intensity of danger were averted by a continual returning to the scene of the crime. The implications were isolated and restricted to the particular situation.

A second response to fear was to perceive the threat as normal, as a risk that is necessary and has been borne before without disrupting the whole society. The pool-hall boy who feared that "hate has traveled into politics and it's traveled into everything, every field of life" met this reaction from the next commentator:

> Well, as far as it happening, I don't think it has that much to do with this country. I mean that's been around since Caesar was assassinated. . . . It's still the same basic thing that goes on in every country, but is just happened to strike us with the President getting killed. . . . people are getting killed every day, people are getting beat up, skulls bashed in, but its shock was really because it's someone who was at the pinnacle of the highest office you could get in the country—it happened to him.

The cooks developed this theme as follows:

> R_1: All I can say is it's a crying shame that you can't control something like that . . . but you can't overprotect anybody, and you can't let the President go out for a walk and turn out an entire regiment to protect the man. . . . There's always a person like this in the world that will try something like that.
>
> R_2: There's always someone trying to gain recognition through one way or the other.
>
> R_3: There's not a President we've had who hasn't had it tried after him.

The invocation of the historical context and of similar crimes was a reminder that nothing fundamentally new has happened, that the danger was to be expected and therefore should be taken in stride. As one cook put it: "I don't think there will be any drastic changes. There may be some changes, because it's an ever-changing world to begin with, let's face it. We don't know what's goin' to happen next week. I don't think they'll be any big changes, though."

Many respondents felt that, far from generating more conflict, the assassination would either soon be forgotten or teach people tolerance. The latter theme was especially prevalent, and was typified by a fireman's remark that "it will make people more patriotic and give them a better approach to the problems of the country. There won't be so much hate spoken and things like that. It will draw the country closer. Maybe . . . it could be a good lesson." Less frequently expressed was the idea that attention to the assassination would be short-lived, as when a truck driver said that within a few weeks "they'll be watching the Giants play on Sunday and I think they'll have forgotten—not entirely yet and maybe not in two weeks, but certainly in several months, I think it will be all over."

The result of these responses to expressions of fear was to leave them without much social support and to turn attention elsewhere. Of the severel themes taken up in the discussions, the contagious violence theme was the one most rapidly interpreted away.

As we have seen, the impulse to punish the President's killer was strong and was shared by many respondents. But in almost every case it immediately encountered assertions that the law should take its course. For example, in the truck driver's discussion, the respondent (R_1) who thought that Oswald should have been left to wander the earth like Cain met this immediate response:

> R_2: The law should take justice, that's all. Justice should be dealt out to him by the law and nobody else, and if the law is death, he should get death. Whatever the law of the country is, he should get.
>
> R_1: In my feeling, death's too quick.
>
> R_2: It shouldn't be taken into the hands of any individual or anything. Whatever the laws of the country are, that's what we have to abide by.
>
> R_3: I agree. He's right. He should get a fair trial, and that's it.

The pool-hall boys worked this out in similar fashion, differentiating more clearly between their feelings and their recommendations:

> R_1: Just a regular punishment is enough and sufficient unless you're a sadist and want to see the man—well most of the peo-

ple *want* to see the man tortured and pay for this deed he has done. But the same punishment as anybody else should pay; just because [Kennedy was] a high official doesn't mean he should be rendered any worse punishment than a regular person that has killed a man, which is the same thing—a man is a man, no matter what position he holds and no matter how he dies.

R_2: He should get just the regular justice, because actually he just committed an act of murder. As he just said, this is not a federal offense; he should just have been given a regular trial.

R_1: That's the *right* thing to do, but that's not the reaction I had.

More succinctly, a kitchen lady replied to the suggestion that Oswald be made to "suffer, royal," "This is America. We don't do that here."

Attempts to blame the assassination on groups or forces beyond Oswald got responses that maintained the right to dissent. Few felt any sympathy for the Communists, hoodlums, or segregationists seen dimly in the background, but most felt that their rights to exist and to have their say should be protected. The cooks, for example, after elaborating on various possibly guilty parties, proceeded in this way:

R_1: Let's face it—everybody's an individual in their own rights. That's why you have all these different groups. Ah, in this country . . . it is a free country where you could have them.

R_2: There are always going to be some, what do you say, hullabaloo or name-calling or mud-slinging between the different masses. It has to be, because otherwise it wouldn't be a democracy if it wasn't. We each have our own rights to say what we want, and what I think about him or what he thinks about me.

Or, as a fireman explained,

Well, I think Oswald represents the lunatic left—definite left-wing as opposed to representing the right-wing. There will be, I think, certain pressures and probably some proposed legislation on curbing the activities of these groups, such as Fair Play for Cuba. But I personally don't think that there should be any curbs on it. This is a nation that is based on people being able to express their opinions whatever they are.

To these invocations of democratic ideology, most groups added another dimension: the assassin as mentally ill. Oswald was pictured, not as a moral leper to be scourged, but as "emotionally disturbed" (by a nurse), "an unstable individual" (by a fireman), "mentally sick" (by a truck driver), "a deranged person" (by a pool-hall boy). In several cases there were long discussions of Oswald's background, full of details picked up from television, offered as explanations for his crime. The emphasis here was on understanding the killer's motives rather than on stereotyping him as essentially evil and thus more readily available as a target for aggression. Explanation substitutes for blame. As the discussions moved past reports of initial reactions, Oswald began to emerge as a person more deserving of psychotherapy than of torture.[12]

In the early phases of these discussions, when the respondents' whole attention was devoted to the slain President, Kennedy was described in extremely positive terms, as a man of exceptional character and a President of heroic proportions. These feelings were not amended in the conversations; the affection was as strong at the end as at the beginning. But as these people turned their thoughts to the future, they slowly shifted their frame of reference from the man to his policies, and the latter were evaluated in a more balanced way. The truck drivers supply an example. Two of them expressed strong feelings of appreciation for President Kennedy as one who "loved the people of the world, because after all his job, that he took upon himself, he really didn't need"; he was "for the poor as well as the rich . . . a second Lincoln." The next respondent said, with some hesitation, that he was not "a supporter of Kennedy or Roosevelt and I . . . still haven't changed my views on Roosevelt or would I change them, I doubt very much, on Kennedy. I don't think he accomplished much in his short period of time in office." A third member then picked up the argument and developed a synthesis:

> I think he tried to do a good job where he could. I think he was partial in some ways. In some ways I think he was . . . a good man for trying to bring a better understanding among the colored and white in this country. I still uphold him for his admiration of President Eisenhower, and I like to say this, . . .

at which point he began a discussion of Kennedy's efforts to close the missile gap, his fostering of science, and so on. Similarly the firemen got into a long conversation about Medicare, federal aid to education, civil rights, and tax reduction; in this area there was little hesitation about criticizing particular details of the Kennedy program. The transition was made from an emotional reaction of respect and affection for the President as a person to reasoning about his policy recommendations. The hero was still there, but he could be wrong.

Initial feelings that Lyndon Johnson could not possibly match President Kennedy's stature give way to the idea that Johnson is different but adequate to the role. A cook who felt that President Kennedy was "dynamic" and that Johnson "will never get reelected . . . I don't think he has the energy, to begin with," was answered as follows:

> I think President Kennedy was a very great man. His whole life, his background, and everything showed it. But, now you take Johnson, from what I've read about him . . . in the newsreel when he traveled around and has been close to the President . . . that man has . . . been second to nobody in all his climb to political power. And he has always been a man to stand on his own two feet in a more definite way, where President Kennedy was more energetic and . . . commanded respect because of his dignity and the way he was, while Johnson, in his way of coming up to it . . . he had a bull-like way of forcin' it on 'em. And, in a way [laugh] it almost amounted to the same thing in how he used pressure. And, like I say, as far as political, I don't think too many people would push Mr. Johnson around either. I think he'd be a pretty firm man too. . . . In political procedures his tactics might be a little different but if they achieve the same end, it's the same end. . . . It's what you think a man can do.

When one of the kitchen helpers said that Johnson "will never be the man Mr. Kennedy was," that "he isn't capable in any way," her Negro friend replied:

> R_1: Well, he's an intelligent man too, been in politics for years.
> R_2: I guess he knows. He knows a lot, too.

R_3: He can't be fooled. He can't be fooled by anybody in the United States because he knows the government situation from the foot up. He knows it. He knows the crisis we're in. Some young President like President Kennedy, coming in from the North, ah, he studied wide in Europe, he knows about European countries and things, but to know the bitter hatred in the South, he did not know it.

And an Italian added that Johnson has traveled "all over the world to see what's going on" and "he know the same as much as President Kennedy know."

Finally, there was a focus on continuities in government. A truck driver thought that Johnson or whoever else would be elected in 1964 would "reap the benefits of what's been done in the Kennedy administration." He felt that "it's the science that's behind this government that makes a President able to talk strong or not be able to talk strong." A fireman stressed the fact that "we're committed to a foreign policy that's supposedly the ideas of several people and Johnson [cannot] really deviate radically from our policy as it is now." Another mentioned that the Presidency is still in the hands of the same party. Others referred to the carryover of the Cabinet.

Turning from admiration to calm evaluation was difficult for these people. But they did recover their balance. A cook summed up their feelings, "History is going to keep going on, whether we like it or not. The government's going to keep going on. . . . Things will have to fall into place as they have in the past."

The main outlines of the group recovery process that emerges from these data can be summarized as follows:

1. Certain personal links to the President, particularly familial, religious, characterological, and political, were expressed in ways salient to the group and were reinforced by social support from peers.

2. When these strong links were broken, respondents felt the need for interpretations, particularly explanation, meaning, and prediction, that would palliate the disturbance. They sought these interpretations in group conversations.

3. Strong emotional reactions to the assassination, particularly fear, hostility, and adulation, were expressed to others. This was a healthy

catharsis in the group setting, but it also had potentially pathological implications of breakdowns in important political orientations.

4. These dangerous tendencies were corrected by the process of group discussion. Of particular interest are the specific mechanisms by which socially healthier interpretations counteracted and replaced the less healthy ones.

By the time these conversations were completed the day after the funeral, processes of social recovery were already well advanced. People had expressed their feelings and reestablished their political equilibrium. They concluded that the country would go on, that no radical changes were called for, and that the basics of democracy still held true. Their ability to roll with the punch of the assassination had revealed for the moment some strong, shared resources that support democracy in the face of crisis.

How a brilliant politician, John Bailey, played on Connecticut legislators' perceptions of past, present, and future to create unprecedented party conformity.

10

Gathering Influence

No one doubts that leadership is important in producing legislative party cohesion, but there is little in the literature of political science about how leaders build cohesion. More than a decade ago, Duane Lockard showed that party cohesion in the Connecticut General Assembly was remarkably strong; he posited centralized organization, interparty competition, ideological similarities, and discipline as the major bases of party control.[1] The topic of this article is the political strategies party leaders use to transform these bases into party votes, and why these strategies succeed. It draws on data from a session of the Connecticut House of Representatives during which both cohesion and leadership activity were in full display.

Despite the emergence, in recent research, of the legislator as an active, sentient being (rather than a passive register of pressures),[2] not much is known about legislators' party orientations. For example, in their four-state study of *The Legislative System*, based on interviews with almost all the members of both houses in each state, John C. Wahlke, Heinz Eulau, William Buchanan, and Leroy C. Ferguson find that "the party man may act independently and the independent may yet be more or less of a party man," "The role of 'party man' is a highly ambiguous one," and "The line between a 'party man' and an 'independent' or a 'maverick' is a tenuous one."[3] New Jersey legislators were nearly unanimous in rating party conflicts important, while only half of the Ohio legislators did so.[4] Frank J. Sorauf's research on the Pennsylvania legislature finds a "virtually unanimous unwillingness to admit the guidance of party" combined with "an impressive overall degree of party cohesion."[5] These uncertainties suggest that the links between the member and his party are subtler than has been supposed and that the role of leadership, varying from state to state, may be an important intervening variable between constituency characteristics and party votes. Cohesion is undoubtedly in part a product of background factors such as the degree of competition in the campaign, but such factors, in order to produce party votes on particular bills, have to be translated from the general to the specific, aroused and brought to bear in a different environment.

In the 1959 session of the Connecticut House of Representatives, certain conditions brought forth maximum leadership efforts for party cohesion. Democratic Governor Ribicoff, elected by a massive landslide, began the session with a Democratic margin of three seats in a House of 279 members. The Democrats had been in the minority for eighty-two years. As a result of a death and special election half-way through the session, the Democrats ended with a one-seat margin. Only a quarter of the Democrats had any prior experience in the legislature, as opposed to 62 percent of the Republicans. Under the leadership of Democratic State Chairman John M. Bailey, a "spectacular feature" of the session, according to press comment, was the cohesion of the Democratic contingent which held together in a "united action never before witnessed in the party." The Governor's program, including a series of basic and far-reaching reforms, was enacted practically without exception. As one reporter wrote, "Throughout the entire session, the Administration lost none of its favorite bills."

How was it possible for the party leadership to make of this slender majority a cohesive, disciplined force capable of passing, over the opposition of their more experienced opponents, all of the governor's major program proposals? In part to explore this topic, I conducted long interviews during the session and gathered pre- and postsession questionnaires.[6] Material from this study illustrates certain congruencies between the goals the party leadership pursued and the cohesion-building strategies they used to attain these goals.

The leader's major goal is to control the legislature's policy production,[7] which means that he is motivated to maximize party cohesion only to the extent that he can establish and maintain control over his party. Cohesion at the price of loss of control defeats his purpose. In a very real sense, the leader may be a prisoner of his own party, so it is a mistake to count every high-cohesion vote as an indicator of leader effectiveness. Thus what a legislative party leader wants to establish is a type of conformity, of which three degrees or varieties are significant. First, he may be able to establish in the minds of some members a highly generalized decision to conform automatically, to go along with the party as represented by the leadership on nearly all significant issues. The "party hack" who responds to patronage and pressure comes most quickly to mind as the exemplar of this comprehensive conformity. No new decisions on his part are required as new issues arise; no new action (beyond timely notice of his preference) is required of the leader. More nearly typical of members is a second degree of compliance with leadership that might be called normal conformity: a disposition to support the party and its leadership "by and large," "in general," "other things being equal." The leader's problem with legislators of this persuasion is to arouse party loyalty and to interpret that loyalty as implying compliance with the leader's preferences. Finally, the leader's minimal goal is a kind of conformity—adherence to his position on a particular piece of legislation. Even members who lack strong general tendencies to conform may be brought around by techniques for structuring particular decisions.

The effective leader spends his limited resources of time and effort economically. The more members he can recruit to the comprehensive, automatic type of conformity, the more he can conserve such resources. For the large middle group of normal conformers he may be able to rely on relatively simple propaganda techniques. For the remaining minority requiring persuasion on specifics, he may have to call on his most sophisticated and detailed efforts. What conditions and strategies contribute to these types of conformity? Obviously all strategies are aimed at party votes, but there are marked differences in the main strategies emphasized as one moves from optimal to minimal varieties of conformity.

Patronage and Pressure; Establishing Comprehensive Conformity

If the party leadership had to depend entirely upon quid pro quo exchanges of jobs or nominations for votes, party cohesion would soon be disrupted. At any one time there are far too few desirable positions available to be dispensed in comparison with the number of votes needed. Given this restricted supply, the direct offer of a job to one legislator may alienate numerous disappointed applicants, along with their political associates. For these and other reasons, as Sorauf says, "The implication that party loyalties and activity rest on so slender a reed as the promise of political spoils is at least open to question."[8]

However, the fact that few members receive direct offers of jobs in return for specific votes does not mean that patronage is unimportant. For most members, and especially for the new ones, *political possibilities in the future are extremely ill-defined*. Party allegiance is motivated in part by vague hopes that sometime in the future, should the member want help of some unspecified kind—a job, an administrative decision, a local bill passed—the leadership would remember his yeoman service in the party ranks. As one legislator said, "It isn't what you've been promised, it's what you hope for that helps, that will swing a person into line." Frequently lawyers advanced the opinion that "every lawyer wants to be a judge someday," but as one explained,

> It doesn't occupy all my waking hours. And in fact it doesn't have any immediacy for me. I say that in all honesty, I don't even know if I want to be a judge. I assume, I understand, that as your career progresses a judgeship becomes more and more interesting, you know. Looks much better . . . I wouldn't do it today—accept a judgeship. That doesn't mean I wouldn't do it in the future . . . I certainly don't have any specific goal in mind in terms of a specific elective or appointive position.

Another member, not a lawyer, says that his political future is "up to fate," and asks:

> Who knows? I may not be here. But I would like to run for higher office. There's no question about it. But that's something I can't answer, now anyway, until I see how the picture is.

These themes appear repeatedly in the interviews, indicating not a sharp focusing of ambition on some particular office, but an amorphous anticipation that certain opportunities might eventually develop and that one should be ready for them. On the other hand, many members express no interest whatsoever in running for or being appointed to any office; many even lack interest in getting favorable action on bills they have introduced (often at the behest of some insistent constituent). Such legislators are beyond the reach of patronage, although one suspects they may have momentary or private flashes of ambition. But for a considerable number, the relevant patronage is not that which can be offered here and now, but, in effect, *all the patronage which the leaders are expected to control in the future.* For these members the important thing is to build a favorable record of party service, so that when and if some opportunity is presented, perhaps years hence, they will be among the eligibles.

A similar picture emerges regarding negative sanctions. Of the legislators who returned postsession questionnaires, 70 percent agreed with the statement, "Many legislators experienced a great deal of pressure from their party leaders during the session." Seventy-two percent agreed that "Far too many legislators blindly follow their party leaders." But only 21 percent assented to the statement "I personally was pressured by the party leadership." As Lewis A. Dexter has written of Congress, "Pressure is how you see it."[9] Generally, it is something that happens to other people, especially people in the other party. Very few of those I interviewed confessed that they had received "pressure" from the party. One who did defined it as "just mental pressure," apparently referring to his own difficulty in making up his mind on an issue. A lady legislator who said she had been "pressured to death" explained that she was "teased" for entertaining maverick ideas. Like the carrot of patronage, the stick of pressure is perceived in a variety of configurations.

Typically, *pressure is not experienced, it is anticipated.* The anticipation substitutes for the reality. "Pressure" enters the folklore of the legislature, not entirely as a myth (for there are occasional well-publicized incidents) but as a widespread belief and expectation that sanctions will be applied to those who deviate.

Few legislators were able to describe in any detail just how pressure was exercised. But they *knew* it was:

> I am not so naive as to think that it doesn't go on.
> I assume the reporters know what they're talking about.
> No documentary proof—it's just what you hear.
> Just reading between the lines.

Once established, these assumptions can be mobilized rather easily to produce party conformity. As one member said,

> The pressures—the threats and promises—are unspoken. They're there. They're not always visible, but—they're unspoken. They're not expressed. They don't have to be expressed, see. Of course, in this session the way it's put is that we wouldn't be here, you know, except for the tremendous victory of the governor. That isn't a threat or promise—it's merely a statement of fact, which nobody can deny, certainly. It evokes a feeling of humility in a person. And also attached to it is the possibility that there might be some reprisal for, you know, for defection. . . . Because it's well known that, you know, the professional politician has a long memory.

Another legislator generalizes about the process as follows:

> They would not *threaten* you, I mean—which has happened with the parties, I mean, come up and say, "Now look: either you do this or else that's it." They wouldn't do it that way there. I think they handled it very diplomatically. I mean, you got the feeling that—get in line and they would go all the way. They would go to lengths to take care of you, so to speak. So you got what they meant, the way they talk to you, when you spoke with them. They didn't have to threaten you. It would be phrased diplomatically, but you knew what it meant: "Get in line or else."

The legislator who approaches his encounters with the party leadership anticipating pressure is likely to interpret even the vaguest sort

of appeal as a warning and a promise. For such members, it is unnecessary to specify exactly what will happen if they do not follow
along, just what the "or else" might be. A Delphic pronouncement—
for example, "The governor needs this bill"—will do in most cases.
Here, as in the case of patronage, a resource the leaders possess is
magnified in significance many times over precisely *because* it need
be used infrequently to have an impact on many members.[10]

A large part of the successful party leader's manipulation of patronage and pressure is essentially manipulation of expectations. He works
to convince members (a) that he has unquestioned control over the
distribution of political rewards and punishments, and (b) that he is
sure to distribute these rewards and punishments in such a way as to
maximize party voting. But members are left uncertain as to precisely
how and especially *when* such "pressure" will be applied. This means
that the member who fears reprisals or hopes for favors will have to
estimate for himself the risks involved in any single deviation. The
only datum offered him in the immediate situation is the degree of
emphasis the leaders appear to be placing on party loyalty in the particular case at hand. As illustrated above, the member should "get
what they mean" from the significance they place on a certain vote,
without any definite political contract being concluded.[11]

Success in the game of pressure and patronage conserves the leader's political resources, which would soon be exhausted if it were
necessary to barter them for individual votes. The situation is defined
as a series of credit-building operations in which the member perceives his party votes as accumulating a store of credit upon which
he may someday want to draw, and the leader communicates his
acceptance of this interpretation but avoids specifying the exact conditions of repayment.[12] Rapid turnover of legislative personnel means
that relatively few members are in a position at any one time to demand, on the basis of loyalty demonstrated over a number years, a
specific quid pro quo.

From the member's viewpoint, automatic conformity to the leader
is stressful in that it requires a surrender of independence in order to
gain safety or preferment. Some justification, plausible to himself and
to others, is needed. Two themes which appeared in a number of
interviews serve this purpose. The member can perceive himself as a

pupil, temporarily taking instruction as preparation for independent action later. Thus one defines his situation as follows:

> You're coming in green off the street and you're put in the position of a legislator. Now to me that doesn't seem right. You can't be, say, a salesman one day and a lawmaker the next. . . . The only way you'll learn is following your party leaders.

He concludes that "the main functions of a legislator here are to keep your ears open, your mouth shut, and follow your party leaders." The demeaning aspects of conformity are obscured by concentration on its supposed training value.[13]

A second common justification is that the patronage and pressure game is inescapable and therefore legitimate. As another member explains,

> Some of these deals are dirty, are—certainly, probably shouldn't be done. But they're done every day by everybody else, and you get to thinking, "Gee, why don't we try and do it too?" . . . If you're going to let everybody else do it—you can't stop it. You're fighting something that's bigger than all of us. The human mind, I guess.

Here the diffusion of questionable motives among the entire political population serve to ameliorate feelings of guilt.

Loyalty: Conditions and Strategies for Normal Conformity

While comprehensive conformity appears primarily as a prospective or anticipatory phenomenon focused on considerations of what to do next, normal conformity has a retrospective focus, an emphasis on continuity with the past. Almost all legislators bring to the legislature a set of party-favoring predispositions, learned over the years, which incline them toward supporting the party leaders as a general rule. These loyalties, intensified during the campaign period, are continually stimulated and reiterated by the party leadership. Fully 60 percent of those members responding to questionnaires had "very strong" feelings of support for their party, and another 32 percent reported "fairly strong" party loyalties. The meanings and sources of these loyalties vary considerably from member to member, however. For example, only 19 percent found the two parties "very different" in their principles. Many who reported strong feelings of party support did not see this as implying down-the-line party voting. In other words, general loyalties must be mobilized by the party leadership, brought to bear in particular cases.

Party loyalties appear to be strongest when they are linked with other, more fundamental identifications the individual has with his family, ethnic group, religion, social class, or (rarely) political ideology.[14] The legislator whose father took him to "all the rallies" instead of "ball games and circuses and things like that," and then set him to work driving voters to the polls when he reached sixteen, says that "Naturally, I just moved right into" party candidacy upon coming of age. An elderly member explains that his family has had the same party identification for generations, that he grew up among the old settlers in a small town where there was overwhelmingly party consensus, and thus his preference was "born and bred in me, you might say." Another relates his party to "the working people who came over on a later banana boat" as opposed to the other party which "came over on an earlier banana boat with all the convicts." These strong and early family connections, familiar from studies of political socialization, make of the party more than a convenient organization for accomplishing certain tasks. The party for many is an extension of the clan.

These loyalties are strengthened when marked contrasts with the other party are perceived. Interviews in both parties show a remarkable consensus on the nature of these contrasts, although the evaluative implications are of course different. Republicans see themselves as serious, cautious, capable, and responsible; Democrats translate these characteristics into snobbishness, coldness, lack of "heart." Conversely, the Democrats stress their free and easy ways, which the Republicans tend to see as childish and lazy.[15] These themes are evident in the remarks of two legislators, the first a Democrat, the second a Republican. The Democrat explains that "the worst snobs" are

Republicans. And I hate to say it, but I've found it more and more and more as I go along, and if I'm prejudiced to the hilt then that's what it is, I don't know. But I just have such a different feeling amongst a group of Democrats as amongst a group of Republicans. And not, you understand, because I'm outside or anything, but they just seem to *think* differently. They seem to *act* differently. They seem to be more free—the Democrats—and easygoing and they don't take themselves quite so seriously. . . . Generally speaking, I think there's a predominance of Republicans who do take themselves very, very seriously, as compared to a same group of Democrats, who do not.

The Republican says that "practically the only section that runs Democrats" in his town is "the slum," inhabited by

The floaters, the men, the workers, like that. They expect people to hand them things on a platter. Now, I'm not going.to say that that's the difference between a Republican and a Democrat—it isn't certainly. But nevertheless, to me it's an indication that you've got a group that's looking for something, and which your Democrats have been looking for for some time. Ever since Roosevelt. Give them something. Don't make them work for it. Hand it to them. That's what we've got there. If it wasn't for that group in there, we could get rid of half our police force.

These themes appear to reflect long-standing and widely shared stereotypes which enhance the appeal of party loyalty. When these feelings are the result of years of struggle and effort in local party affairs, they can be potent bonds indeed. The jocular atmosphere of the Democratic caucus performs the same function here as the rather heavy sincerity of their caucus performs for the Republicans—arousing and reinforcing memories of similar hometown party gatherings.[16]

Another predisposing factor is the way the member perceives interaction between the parties. The legislator who says:

I enjoy politics—why?—the *competition,* in a word. The reason in one word. I think the competition is wonderful. It's a great thing for any fellow.

is predisposed to fight with his team against the enemy. The sportive team spirit is introduced in a mixture of metaphors by another member:

> It's a fascinating game—it's a dirty game. And it's a hard game. And to say what I like about it, I don't know, it's like playing a game of ping pong or basketball or football—it's a game. You like to get into a contest and you like to make friends and try to build up your own fences, and sometimes see them topple over and then rebuild them. And try to go and if you're stopped, you try to get up and go again. It's a game.

This theme, the party as a group engaged in a contest with an opposing group, adds to the contrasting party perceptions an element of countervailing action, a heightened awareness of the "side" one is on.

These party-favoring perceptions—strong in some cases, weak in others—are the raw materials the party leader has to work with. He does not have to create anew the sense of loyalty, the community feeling, or the combative team spirit within the party. What he must do, however, is to translate party feeling into willingness to take *his* instructions. This process is facilitated if the member identifies the leader with the party as an organization. The ideal way of thinking, from the leadership's viewpoint, is expressed by the member who says, "I believe in organization, party organization, and if you commit yourself to any one party you should try to go along with the *administration*." Or, as another member put it, "Leave a group of Democrats alone and they'll fight. Right or wrong, they'll fight. And I think they have to be led, have to be steered." The legislator who "shudders to think what would happen to the party" if the chairman resigned expresses this theme. The leader is perceived as personifying the organization, performing an essential function in maintaining group unity. The implication is: no leader, no unity, no party.

The legislator is reminded that he ran as a member of a party which stated its purposes repeatedly during the campaign, that he was elected by voters who were made aware of these purposes, and that he is therefore mandated and, indeed, obligated to help carry out platform promises. Furthermore, he is asked to recall that he occupied a relatively minor place on the party ticket, and that in all likelihood he owes his election to the drawing power of those above him. As a member explained:

> Now take this last election. I didn't win the election in Localville. The Governor won the election and I was on his ticket. His platform—I had a small idea of what it was about, but I had no idea of the major issues. Like on Court Reform. Court Reform was Court Reform—whatever that meant I didn't know. Personally, I didn't care. But as you go along, we learn what it really covers.

This learning takes place in the already established context of appreciation for the governor, who is perceived as the champion of the platform—"his platform." In handling the court reform bill, the leaders reminded members that "it was in the party platform," as one legislator reports, "and they certainly couldn't go against their word now." It appears that for many new members the detailed implications of the platform are understood only long after the election. The member who feels he should have known then what the platform meant is open to the argument that he in fact committed himself to it by accepting nomination. The translation process proceeds by the retrospective elaboration of obligations which were far from fully appreciated at the time they were undertaken.[17]

Party leaders can build personal loyalties by helping to alleviate the tensions members experience in adapting to a new legislative environment. Here the manipulation of prestige, respect, and affection is a potent technique. Like everyone else, legislator need is to maintain a favorable self-image, a sense of self-esteem which strengthens one to endure uncertainty and occasional failure. Leaders who act to bolster the member's self-esteem establish a feeling of personal gratitude which heightens his sense of obligation and lays the basis for appeals to loyalty.

The stories some legislators relate show this clearly. One says of the Governor's Tea:

> We were very impressed. I mean you couldn't help but be impressed. It's a beautiful home. The governor and his wife met us graciously and gave us the full roam of the house—"Go ahead, look at anything you want. Make yourself at home. We'll see you

later on." And we wandered around. It's a beautiful home. Everything in it is beautiful. And ah, tea was served—so we had coffee (laughs). So we were setting around, or standing there, and the governor came by and talked to everybody, and his wife talked with everybody. So—before that, we drove up in front of the house and a state trooper, there, he opened the car door. The passengers got out. I got out. The state trooper took the car, parked it for me. And, . . . so we had tea, and the governor talked with us. His wife talked with us. And when it came time to leave, we departed. And again, why—a warm handshake. None of this fishy handshake, but a warm handshake. And, ah, they thanked us for coming—whereas normally we should have thanked them for being invited. They thanked us for coming. And we got out there, the state trooper, he opened the car door. And off we go.

Well, as I say, we had a wonderful afternoon there. As I say, we were only there an hour, hour-and-a-half. It was very impressive. You couldn't help but be impressed.

Another reports an occasion on which a high party official, "in a very jovial mood," accosted him in the hallway and said, in the presence of half a dozen other members, "Sammy, look: I want to tell you one thing. Don't forget this. I know what's going on up here at all times, and to my way of thinking you're one of the better freshmen legislators." The recipient of this compliment says, "I enjoyed this very much, as I say, because of course I'm in politics." He will not speculate on the motive behind this ploy, but draws the appropriate conclusion:

> Don't ask me what his reason was, because I couldn't tell you what's going on in his mind. Well, I think his record speaks for itself. There are times I think I will disagree, but there haven't been up to today.

Asked if he has felt "pressured" in the legislature, this member answers "Not at all."

On the other hand, the member who fails to follow along may find himself deprived of such favors. Despite his disclaimers, one member interviewed seems to have felt the effects of this form of "pressure."

> Because of my stand on two or three (platform) planks, I have been more or less ostracized by the brass—little things, that big men, or grown men should not do. And it's hurt me in this way, that I didn't believe they would do it. I'm not hurt otherwise. If I am ignored, that's all right with me. But it's disappointing in my faith in grown-up people. I know that among children that they'll do things to each other sometimes, they'll ignore one person to make that person feel bad. But to find it among grown-ups is very much of a surprise to me.

The sanctions here are negative ones: not being spoken to, invited to report bills, or given committee responsibilities. Furthermore, they appear to be invoked only *after* some act of deviation, and do not seem, at least in this case, to have been effective in bringing the member into line. The impact of this type of discipline is probably indirect: others learn from this example how uncomfortable it can be to be cast outside the circle of prestige, respect, and affection which surrounds the party leaders.[18]

Polling: Strategies for Specific Conformity

The payoff for the party leader's cohesion-building effort is a majority vote on an important bill. For three reasons the leader may find it necessary to manage carefully the deliberations on individual measures. First, many members are unwilling to surrender their independent judgment, despite patronage, pressure, and the perplexities of the legislative task. Second, members inclined to support the party on most issues may see the specific issue at hand as an exception to the rule. Third, and probably most significant, the leader himself is uncertain at any given time of the degree to which his efforts to create comprehensive or normal conformity have been successful. Rational strategy thus requires him to *ensure* a safe margin of votes by special arrangements for special bills.

Emphasis on legislative decision-making as a process focuses attention on what is so often forgotten: that few members have fixed preferences at the beginning of the process, that many seek guidance and information in the course of making up their minds, and that the *sequence* and timing of events in this process can be of considerable significance to the outcome. The roll call vote is the end point of a series of decisional phases through which the legislator passes as he narrows down a multiplicity of possibilities to a single yes or no decision. Party leaders can and do make the most of the member's informational needs and uncertainties as he moves toward the vote.

Members are often asked to indicate a position long before they have enough information to make a reasoned decision on the alternatives. In the early stages leaders poll their members, individually or in caucuses, to determine the extent of their support. This polling has the effect of pushing the member in the direction he knows the pollster prefers. For example, on an important bill the leader would express his own clear preference, ask the member for his, and at the same time request, as one reports, "that if you had no convictions of your own, they (the leadership) would like you to vote with them." At an early stage, then, when the member lacks information upon which to base resistance, he is confronted by a polite request that he say, in the presence of his chief, where he stands.

If he attempts to avoid an early commitment—usually with the excuse that he is uncertain as yet—he may be subjected to a barrage of persuasion. As one leader explained, the way to get compliance from the undecided is to:

> Talk to them. And talk. And pressure them—by pressure I mean not holding anything over their head. Just the pressure of continual talking and argumentative pressure, which was done for this Court Reform bill. A lot of pressure was put on and by "pressure" I mean a continual hounding of a person, until you either break him down or he breaks you down, argumentatively— not any other way.

All of this occurs, typically, before debate, before the appropriate committee's decision and the reasons for it are known. At that particular time, only a few members can draw on enough facts to put up against the tide of argument they receive from the leaders. But having given even a tentative commitment at this time, the member has difficulty justifying a later change of mind.[19] He knows the leaders have made extensive, careful calculations based on these early indications of preference. The tentative nature of the commitment fades every day it is left standing, every time the leadership is thought to have used it in some computation. The convenient, consistent course is to say yes and stick to it.[20]

This polling is often done in a county or plenary caucus, where the pressures of majority opinion can be very strong. The atmosphere of a caucus meeting is much less formal than that of a regular session. "Only yesterday in our caucus," a member relates, "when I again spoke, you know, in opposition, those around me said, 'You've had it!' And I got very angry at that." Catcalls and applause are frequent. Not many members who oppose the leadership are willing, as one member put it, "to get down to brass tacks and stand up and be counted in the caucus." The polling is done by or for the party leadership, who can decide whether to conduct their inquiry with legislators one at a time or in larger groups. Experienced leaders can usually determine, or sense, just which technique will work best in given situations. Certainly the impact on undecided legislators of a large majority of pro-leadership caucus votes can be considerable.

A more complex strategy involves maneuvers on the "middle ground" between two alternative courses of action—usually between a vote for or against a bill. In a large group of uncertain legislators faced with a highly controversial decision, there is a tendency toward compromise, toward some moderate, middle-of-the-road position. One such alternative, for example, is simply to absent oneself from the chamber so as to avoid pressures to vote at all. Party leaders encourage this among their adamant opponents, but send "truant officers" (whips) after those who are faltering but probably safe. Another type of middle ground alternative is to vote for amendments or substitute or compromise bills which modify the main bill to make it more "moderate." Here again the strategy varies with the leader's purpose. If he is interested in getting the bill passed he may well operate in the following way, as reported by a legislator who attended a caucus on a critically significant bill:

> All he [a party leader] wanted to know at that time was how we felt, either for or against it. And so there were three or four people who were undecided. And the rest of them came out in favor of it. And then we met again later with [the main party leader]

and he explained the bill to us, what was going on. . . . He said, "Regardless of how you vote on the final issue, don't vote for the compromise bill." He said, "If you're going to vote against the party bill, all right. If you do, if you have to, okay. But please don't vote for the compromise bill." Everybody agreed that they wouldn't vote for the compromise bill. Then he asked, "When we caucused before there were some people in doubt. Is there anybody in doubt now?" And everybody apparently had their doubts settled.

Here the leader effectively invokes majority pressures to remove from consideration the middle ground alternatives and then asks for a definite decision. The three or four undecided members, forced to decide, choose to support the leadership. Similar pleas were offered regarding voting for amendments on the floor; members were asked to vote with the party against all amendments, but then, if they so desired, to vote with the opposition on the main bill. The effectiveness of this technique was substantial. In a tense and crowded chamber, members voted eleven times to defeat amendment after amendment. Cheers and boos followed every vote as the decision on the main bill approached. It would have taken a courageous member indeed to desert to the other side on the final issue. Yet no party leader had *demanded* a final pro-party vote.[21]

Control over the formulation, timing, and group processes of decision thus strengthen the hands of the party chiefs.

The Limits of Technique

Needless to say, these techniques do not always work, although the record in the particular session examined does show a remarkable degree of leadership success in maintaining party cohesion. There are members who arrive at the legislature having already committed themselves in the campaign to a public position opposed to that of the party and who feel that they cannot renege on this commitment. Some members from constituencies atypical of their party may in fact owe their election to their party-deviant stands.[22] Still others resist simply out of plain conviction or stubbornness, or because they are unwilling to accept a hierarchical rather than a collegial view of the party.

There are also limits to the manipulability of the many legislators who do not have such fixed commitments. A primary limitation is that the member expects his leaders to provide him with reasons for voting with the party. At least an appearance of persuasion must characterize the relations between leaders and members. As one legislator said, "They've got to lead me in such a way that I have to believe in what they're leading me to, see?" Persuasion legitimizes pressure. As long as the leader-follower relationship can be perceived as a situation in which the leader furnishes information, seasoned judgment, and technical guidance, members are inclined to accept instruction.

An incident reported in the press and emphasized in many interviews illustrates the delicacy of this relationship. At a general party caucus early in the session, a member asked, "How do we know how to vote?" The leader's answer was to the effect that, "If I am going to be the guide, watch how I vote." This was widely interpreted as an attempt to encourage blind obedience, although there is evidence that the leader's intention was simply to show how leadership preferences could be rapidly communicated on minor bills. A frequent reaction was that of the member who said, "That didn't set well with me at all. I didn't look up to see how he was voting. I'm going to vote the way I want to vote." Another reported that this "follow me" incident "destroyed the party caucus," so that thereafter only county caucuses were held. In the other party, later in the session, many members reacted negatively to a sudden switch in the position of the leaders shortly before a major piece of legislation came to a vote. A compromise had been worked out between the leaders of both parties; time did not permit lengthy explanations. Members who had been convinced to vote against the bill were now asked to vote for it. "I think it is a lot of nonsense," one said.

> These decisions where people all rush into one little office and beat each other over the head and come up with an answer— especially when it's been thrashed out properly pretty well beforehand, and people have agreed on issues and taken a stand, then to be stampeded.

These events show clearly what a legislator meant by his view of the leadership: "They're not to push—they're to lead." On a great many minor bills and on major ones when developments must move rapidly, there is a temptation to bypass the normal practices of persuasion, of offering *some* reason, however inadequate, for following the leadership on a particular bill. When the leadership commands without explaining, they risk the plausibility of their image as functional specialists, responsible for providing a certain expertise, and appear as bosses. The reality of being bossed can be borne by many legislators who find the appearance of it unendurable.

Conclusion

Hypotheses derived from data on a single legislative session obviously need verification elsewhere. What broader dimensions for the analysis of legislative party cohesion do these examples of successful leadership suggest? First, they point to the key significance of time dimensions in the legislator's party orientation, particularly anticipations, memories, and short-term sequences of events. Leaders can parlay a severely limited supply of immediately available patronage into a much larger store by keeping members uncertain about their futures. By making it quite clear that he has control over future political rewards and deprivations, that these will be distributed on the basis of party support, but that the time for settling accounts is indefinite, the leader can bring a substantial number of members into line without much effort. By invoking memories of the campaign and of the older, deeper roots of party loyalties in ethnicity, religion, class, and family, the leader encourages the transfer of general party sentiments to the legislative party. A member's past "commitment" to the party platform—usually undertaken casually—is retrospectively reinterpreted as a definite, inclusive moral obligation. To hopes and fears for the future is added an indebtedness from the past. In addition, timing in the short-run development of decisions during the legislative session can be manipulated to maximize party voting. The first step is to establish, early in the game, the right to poll the party membership on particular issues whenever necessary. This opens up a range of tactics, from approaching uncertain members individually before they know much about an issue, to holding caucuses once a clear majority of the party is persuaded. In all these respects, the fact that the legislator's time perspective includes a loyal past, a hopeful future, and an uncertain present is of crucial importance to effective leadership.

A second major dimension is the member's problem of adapting to the legislative environment. Leadership promises order, a value important for the member trying to make sense of a complex and rapidly changing series of events and to find a useful role to play in them. But beyond this service to the intellect, the leader can provide important indulgences of needs for prestige, respect, and affection. To the outsider, members' stories about being flattered or complimented may have a somewhat maudlin ring to them, but for the person actually immersed in a tension-ridden, uncertain social environment such personal rewards can be powerfully persuasive. Nor are these effects confined to state legislatures: one thinks of the apparent impact on Congressmen of an invitation to the White House. Conversely, the member who is cast into the outer darkness, ostracized by his party colleagues, inevitably feels anxious and is tempted to return to the fold. A focus on the legislator as a human being encountering a difficult situation provides clues to the nature of conformity that are likely to be lost on the analyst who views him as a statistic.

A third dimension of legislative party leadership is rationalization. That is, the effective leader meets the member's need for justifying conformity with a variety of ego-saving appearances which may or may not reflect reality. The basic requirement is for some substantive argument, however brief, for going along with the leadership. For many the mere assertion that a bill is part of the governor's program will do. Others require more extended persuasion. Perhaps the strongest position for the party leader is established when he can get general acceptance for legislative norms supporting conformity, such as that new members should serve an extended apprenticeship under his tutelage, that party voting is expected except under very special conditions, and that the arcane arts of "politics" should be left to the expert. The member's ego is safe as long as he can perceive the leader as a functional specialist whose job it is to collect, order, evaluate, and communicate information relevant to important decisions. In general, the most effective way to convey this image is actually to perform these tasks.

Seventeen hypotheses on the operation of the process of pluralization in government, a critically significant, self-reinforcing development, illustrating the linkage of culture and system.

11

Culture and System

WHAT ARE THE likely consequences for policymaking in the future of the fact that governments are "fragmented," "pluralistic," "multicentered," and becoming more so? At all levels of American government, in all major public and private institutions, we see the proliferation of new organizational units at a faster rate than old ones disappear. If this trend continues—to 1984, to the year 2000, to 2068—what will be the main dimensions of a political system originally designed for discord and subsequently patched together by a series of ad hoc adaptations? Answers for the long run depend in part on a close look at the immediate effects of small-scale increments in pluralization. What happens today and tomorrow as new units are added? The empirical propositions below, none of which is proved, are steps toward formulating bigger pictures of the years beyond the now emerging future, pictures we might be able to improve upon if we could perceive their shapes.

By pluralization I mean the creation of new, distinct, but interdependent organizational units. This approach focuses attention on marginal transitions from a system with fewer distinct units to one with more such units. It contrasts with categorical approaches in which a system characterized as pluralistic in some overall sense is compared with a generally hierarchical or generally anarchistic system. Is Congress pluralistic or hierarchical? I shall not try to answer that. But the creation of a new congressional committee is clearly a step in the pluralistic direction. Similarly the devolution of important responsibilities to field offices in administration or to lower courts in the judiciary constitute pluralistic moves. The proliferation of task forces, coordinating committees, new boards, councils, departments, and offices at any level of government increases the number of separated but functionally interdependent centers of decision. For simplicity's sake I refer to all such bodies as *units* and to the process of their creation as *pluralization*.[1]

1. *Pluralization is self-reinforcing.* That is, the process tends to acquire a momentum of its own, stimulating the creation of separate but interdependent decision centers at an increasing rate. In the first place, pluralization becomes a precedent: the establishment of a new unit serves as an example for all others in the system, especially for those operating in the same general problem area. Pluralization enters the list of political strategies as a legitimate gambit for pursuing the stakes of government. (For example, creating a new unit helps focus attention on a new problem.) Arguments against using this strategy are weakened every time a new example appears. Put another way, pluralization progressively becomes the norm, both in the sense of something expected to happen and something reasonable to do.[2]

Second, creation of a single new unit sets in motion interactions with numerous other units. Each such event thus multiplies the number of relationships which must be coordinated to produce action. In time the "load" on coordination channels tends to increase and to reach a point at which it becomes useful to regularize them. Committees or individuals are assigned to pull together the efforts of several units on specific tasks. Participants come to expect interunit relations to be handled by certain formally or informally designated persons. In time, these persons tend to acquire the status of functional specialists in coordination and to gain more and more control over the content of decisions. The opportunities for the proliferation of coordination units increase in an exponential way as the number of new substantive units increases.

A third factor reinforcing pluralist trends is the tendency for old units to react to the challenge of new units by seeking to expand and/or intensify their own activities. The appearance of a new unit in a task area threatens the prerogatives of all old units in that area.[3] Fears of being replaced or reduced in significance stimulate the old unit to demonstrate its vitality and importance by undertaking new functions. In many cases it will demand additional functions as the price of its consent to the creation of a new unit. Thus new relationships and activities are multiplied, spreading out in waves from the splash made by any single act of pluralization.

Finally, processes of proliferation are reinforced by new divisions of labor, especially at the lowest levels of decision-making. As social change produces new configurations of problems for government, strains appear in the existing organizational fabric. New units are created to fit current conditions more closely. The result is a more detailed and interdependent set of relationships, a finer tuning, between governmental organization and pressing contemporary problems. But the more elaborately an organization is articulated and tied in with the present, the more rapidly it is outdated by the march of events. Specialization thus has built into it a tendency to speed up the frequency of demands for further and/or new specializations, as social change renders existing arrangements obsolete. Meanwhile, institutional loyalties, habits, and interests militate against the elimination of old units as new ones are instituted.[4]

2. *Pluralization increases the incidence of conflicts in the system.*

3. *Pluralization decreases the intensity of conflicts in the system.*

By proliferating new relationships among separate but interdependent decision centers, pluralization provides an increasing number of occasions for conflict. There are at least two reasons for this, one interpersonal and one jurisdictional. Each new pluralistic relationship involves communication at a distance, enhancing opportunities for misreading messages. Interunit disparities in timing and emphasis, special languages, and different definitions of the problem increase the probability that mistakes will be made in attributing motives, expectations, plans, and resources to one another. Erroneous interpretations are more difficult to correct quickly by communications in writing or through third parties than in the give and take of face-to-face communication. Thus pluralization increases the likelihood of "misunderstandings" developing among decision-makers, even if they are determined to cooperate.[5] In addition, however, the disjunction involved in pluralization depersonalizes and thus legitimizes conflict. In the more intimate intraunit environment, aggressions are repressed and mollified. (If not, intraunit bickering produces its own paralysis.) It is difficult and risky to express (perhaps even to feel) hostility toward those with whom one is in daily personal contact. Aggressions are more readily channeled toward the new external targets—other units.

Conflict incidence is also increased by the inevitable overlapping of jurisdictions, which accompanies unit proliferation. The event of formalizing a new unit obscures the fact that transfers of function occur gradually. Typically, an old unit has been performing at least some of the tasks allotted to the new one: in practice these responsibilities are not suddenly torn away from the old and handed to the new, but are defined and redefined as particular issues arise. Thus jurisdictional conflicts are strung out over the early history of the new unit. Furthermore, new formal jurisdictional boundaries are elaborated, representing new ways of analyzing artificially problems which are in fact highly integrated. In the course of attacking "its" problem the new unit finds itself more and more involved with connected problems, finds it more and more difficult to avoid trespassing on the jurisdictions of others. Thus the gradual and artificial character of jurisdictional innovations furnishes additional chances for interunit combat.[6]

However, the proliferation of decision centers also tends to reduce the intensity of conflicts. This is in part due to the need for economizing energies: involved in a growing number of conflicts, a unit can spend only so much time and trouble on each. To concentrate on any one conflict is to neglect others and risk defeat. The more units active in a field, the more any one of them will be concerned to ward off threats from many directions.

Viewed in the aggregate, the system as it pluralizes is less apt to polarize. That is, the situation in which two large, internally united, and persistent alliances face one another in conflict become less likely. As issues change, organizational fragments will cluster differently. The kind of conflict escalation which takes place when two powers of approximately equal strength confront each other is unlikely to go far in a system engaged in dispersing power pluralistically.

4. *Pluralization channels energies into problems of interunit rela-*

tions and away from problems of substantive program evaluation.
The more units there are involved in a policy process, the more necessary and difficult it is to predict and manipulate their reactions to proposals. Questions are thus increasingly posed in the form, "How will
units X, Y, and Z receive this proposal?" and, "How can we best in-
sure a favorable response?" rather than, "What would this program
do if put into operation in the field?" These questions are not entirely
distinct—one evaluates in part by getting opinions from others. But a
new relationship of interdependence means that, to some degree, consent as well as advice must be sought. Therefore increasing attention
is devoted to exchanges of information on the current status, predilections, and intentions of other units—in short, on "inside dope" about
"what will go" with them. In cybernetic terms, feedback from within
the system itself tends to overload the communications network, reducing its capacity to handle feedback from outside the system.[7]

5. *Pluralization increases the number of proposals initiated.*[8]

6. *Pluralization reduces the number of proposals adopted.*

The newly created unit is in a sense an experiment. It is expected
to prove the necessity for its very existence within a limited time period, unlike old units whose continuance is assumed. At first its substantive purposes are much clearer than its internal organization and
procedures. And external restraints on action are not yet clearly defined. Members of the new unit, all selected at the same time, share
attitudes of commitment to the program for which they are responsible; shared attitudes in old units are more likely to center on commitment to the organization as a going concern.[9] The political resources
mobilized to bring the new unit into existence are available to support
initial proposals for action. The fluidity of the situation both within
and without the unit stimulates individuals and the agency as a whole
to capture attention by suggesting innovations. For all these reasons a
flow of proposals is likely to spring from newborn units.

Old units of government are apt to respond to these initiatives with
a mixture of skepticism and jealousy. In order to maintain and advance their bargaining positions (and to demonstrate that they can be
active too), old units are motivated to produce counterproposals. Thus
the number of suggestions fed into the machinery of government from
existing units increases as pluralization proceeds.

But as units proliferate, the number of proposals adopted—that is, actually put into operation—declines, due to changes in the aggregate character of the system. Intially there is an increase in communication, not only between new and old units but also among old units about what the new one is doing. Gradually, these communications lines are transformed into "clearance" channels: officials learn to or are compelled to gather reactions to their proposals from other units. In time, clearance procedures tend to develop into approval-disapproval procedures. That is, pieces of paper are in effect annotated "Okay" or "No" in addition to conveying technical or advisory comments. Especially because pluralization exacerbates jurisdictional conflicts, more and more units are motivated to demand veto power over proposals originating in other units. As a matter of course, the "defensive advantage"[10] is strengthened and the probability that any proposal will survive declines. Organizational majority rule—that is, that the *balance* of positive and negative reactions will determine outcomes—gives way to an organizational minorities veto rule—that is, that a minority with intense objections anywhere in the system can stop action. What began as a kind of simultaneous voting system is transformed into a sequential voting system. The number of actual adoptions comes more and more to depend, not on the number of proposals advanced, but on the number of approvals required from separated, differentiated, and interdependent units.[11]

7. *Pluralization raises the probability that proposals will be adopted, when they are adopted, in bunches.* By increasing the opportunities for vetoing and delaying broad government action, pluralization tends to allow social problems to build up to crisis proportions. A point is reached at which failure to act threatens to bring about relatively marked social or political upheavals, demands for redistributing power in the system, agitation for changing the rules of the game. Frustrated in their programmatic efforts, interests turn on the structural characteristics of the system, thus challenging established habits and prerogatives. At this point many units may suddenly suppress their differences and agree to cooperate.

Once started, cooperation may spread rapidly, in a variety of bandwagon phenomena. First, the more severe any social problem is allowed to become, the more closely it is linked with other social problems. For example, mild and localized juvenile delinquency may be defined as a "youth recreation" problem; chronic and widespread delinquency may be defined as involving unemployment, education, welfare, housing, and health problems. Thus a collection of programs by a wide range of agencies is called for on substantive grounds. Second, in a crisis atmosphere, normal restraints on innovation are temporarily weakened or suspended. Exceptions allowed for particular purposes sap the forcefulness of generalized rules; the agencies may take this opportunity to press for other innovations related only indirectly (or not at all) to the current crisis. The "time is ripe" for "something to be done."

A third reason for the bunching of adoptions in crisis periods is that the price of rapid action is compromise, which may take the form of a "package deal"[12]—lumping together a rather miscellaneous collection of proposals in order to gain consent to the crisis-oriented ones. The more urgent the pressure for action in a hurry, the less stringently criteria of relevance and consistency will be applied.

As the process of pluralization continues, this bunching tendency will result in longer time periods between spurts of increasingly intense and variegated government action.

8. *In the short run, pluralization increases the radicalness of proposals initiated.*

9. *In the long run, pluralization increases the conservatism of proposals initiated and adopted.* The same factors operate here as in the case of the number of proposals initiated and adopted (see above, numbers 5 and 6). But additional cognitive and strategic elements contribute to these trends. Pluralization, by generating specialized units, simultaneously brings some units into more intimate contact with substantive social problems and removes these problems from the immediate concern of other units. The widening of this intimacy-remoteness gap makes it more and more likely that innovative proposals on any particular topic will spring mainly from the specialized unit most immediately concerned. Compared with all other units in the system, the initiator is apt to be the one most aware, knowledgeable, certain, and confident of its judgment about the special difficulties with which it must deal. Its focus of attention is on the needs and wants of its clientele; its orientation is toward solutions of problems. In the initial formulations of proposals, therefore, the new specialized unit asks, "What should the government do to take care of this situation?" The odds are that proposals conceived in the midst of a hot

struggle with stubborn social realities will stress the necessity for more action on more fronts as soon as possible.[13]

With ideas of what needs to be done, the new unit turns to strategic considerations: "How can we get consent for an adequate program from the other units in the system?" Looking ahead to the obstacle course that a proposal will have to run, the initiator is tempted to inflate his estimates, on the surmise that other units will discount them. The more approvals required, the greater the temptation. The tendency, then, is for pluralization to stimulate relatively radical proposals from new units. But over time, feedback processes work to modify this tendency. Reviewing units learn that their discounting practices have been anticipated, and come to distrust the sincerity of radical innovators. Initiators learn that inflated requests are hard to defend and that such exaggerations detract from a reputation for integrity. Thus, as organizational units mature, proposals become more and more conservative, representing only marginal departures from the last set of adopted proposals.[14]

The conservative tendencies of reviewing and evaluating units stem in part from their cognitive orientation. Their focus of attention is on proposals, not problems. At least one step removed from the needs and demands of the social situation, they concentrate instead on the information at hand—namely, the new proposal considered in the light of the last one advanced and adopted on this subject. By focusing on departures from precedent, they conserve their intellectual energies and simplify their decision process. The magnitude of each departure looms large in their minds partly because it is the one item of information about which they are sure. The burden of proof is placed on those who want, in effect, to repudiate or at least amend the last decision made. Successive reviews of proposals tend to whittle them down closer and closer to the standing decision left over from the past.[15]

The increasing overlap of clearance procedures in a pluralizing system contributes to this conservative tendency. Decision-makers are confronted with a growing number of proposals from many different sources. This in itself makes examination of substantive issues more difficult and increases the tendency to stress comparisons with precedent. It also introduces another basis for decision: comparison with the demands of other units. Lacking substantive reasons for preferring one proposal over the others, the reviewing unit may adopt an equality criterion. That is, approximately equal departures from precedent will be allowed for each proposal. If unit X is granted a 10 percent increase, units Y and Z, on ground of "fairness," also deserve a 10 percent raise. The entry of new units into this picture has at least two effects. It may be necessary to reduce the "fair share" increment in order to accommodate a new proposal within the framework of action on other requests (or, in budget terms, to "hold the line" of total resources allocated). Second, the clearing unit is under pressure to treat proposals from new units on the basis of the same rule they have established for old ones. Yet it is the new units which are most likely to propose relatively radical departures, to provide the cutting edge of innovation and progressivism in the system. The larger the overlap in clearance procedures, then, the greater the drag of the old on the new.

10. *Pluralization increases the cost of government.*

The long-run effects of pluralization are conservative with respect to the character and program costs of individual units. But the costs of operating the aggregate system rise radically as pluralization proceeds. Part of this is simply the incremental cost of creating new units without eliminating or curtailing old ones. Another effect tends to become multiplicative, in the following fashion. Functional interdependence among units makes each of them capable of disrupting the system by striking. The strike is the ultimate weapon; milder forms or threats of noncooperation are also available. Strikes aimed at gaining nonmonetary program goals, such as new legislation, or a reorientation of other units, are unlikely to be successful because the system's sequential veto pattern makes approval unlikely, and because the striking unit finds it difficult to maintain mobilization of its forces in a risky enterprise for programmatic ends (unless members are willing to endure severe and continuing deprivations for the cause). But strikes for money succeed because the threat can be met, by emergency increases in the total budget, without wide (parallel) clearance, and because the striking unit is strongly motivated and thus more able to maintain mobilization. No single unit will be able to use the strike (or semi-strike) mechanism often, but increasing numbers of units will try it once in a while, and increasing interdependence among units will increase the effectiveness of strikes in extracting money. This pattern will be imitated; in a pluralizing system there will be even more imitators. Thus costs escalate.

Finally, pluralization increases the claimants for money anticipated in any new program. Each will be after its "share." Thus the size of each share gets smaller, as do the odds that any individual share will be "adequate" to achieve the program's stated purposes for that unit. The consequence is an expansion of demands for refunding at higher and longer-term levels.[16]

11. *Pluralization increases the number and complexity of formal rules.*

12. *Pluralization increases the incidence of behavioral departures from formal rules.*

There is a built-in tendency for rules to expand in proportion to the distance and the degree of interdependence among agencies. By simultaneously increasing uncertainty (because it is more difficult to predict what the other units will do) and increasing the probability of conflict (for reasons already described), pluralization stimulates a search for certainty and stability. Formal rules are thus likely to be proposed; they are likely to be adopted for a number of reasons. Most generally, it is difficult to find legitimate, publicly arguable reasons for opposing formal recognition of an existing situation. If, in fact, a new relationship has been established between units A and B, why should anyone object to recognizing and writing down rules to govern this new set of interactions? Of course, there are many practical reasons; the point is that they are hard to defend to broader publics.

Second, the rules have important power implications. Old units will attempt to tie down the new ones with jurisdictional and other restrictions, perhaps as the price of consent for the creation of the new units. Those currently in an advantageous position will strive to stabilize the situation by pressing for rules, recognizing that the odds are rising that their authority will be challenged. Finally, changes in organizational structures and functions are likely to conflict with old rules. The incidence of "violations" of increasingly complex formal rules will mount, and there will be demands that the old rules be amended or strengthened to handle this problem. But since repeal and relegislation are much more difficult to accomplish than amendment or accretion, the rules will tend to pile up.

However, this process tends to proceed at a slower rate than the proliferation of ad hoc, informal linkages among units. Only after a new relationship has been established for some time can it be argued that procedures have become regular, standard, normal, and thus amenable to formalization. Those currently disadvantaged will resist freezing the situation. Furthermore, a special problem arises in formalizing the role of coordinators. As long as this role is left indefinite, the coordinator can appear as a servant or equal of the units coordinated. Formalization tends to elevate him to a higher status and authority, and so may be resisted by the other parties. Finally, as the rules become more complex and detailed, relatively minor shifts in issues loosen the fit between rule and problem; officials increasingly find it necessary to bypass the formalities in order to get anything done. Thus, in a paradoxical way, the more rules there are the less revealing they are to the student of political decision-making. As new units proliferate—whether vertically (creating new hierarchical relationships) or horizontally (creating new coordinate relationships)—the rules will grow more numerous, complex, and irrelevant.[17]

13. *Pluralization enhances the relative power of large, permanent, and highly organized interests in the society.*

Weakly organized interests may be almost as potent as strongly organized ones in stopping government action. In a veto system, control over only one unit is necessary. But as pluralization progresses, in order to get significant proposals adopted interests must exert pressure at an increasing number of points. In normal periods, the proliferation of units increases the time lag between initiation and adoption of proposals. Temporary bursts of activity decline in effectiveness. The interest which can sustain its attack over months or years, from the first suggestions to program implementation in the field, has an immense advantage over its momentarily active opponents. In crisis situations the prizes go to the groups capable of taking vigorous action on many fronts simultaneously. These tendencies are accelerated by pluralization, so that the interests possessing many political resources—members, money, time, skills, and so on—are progressively advantaged.

Government officials are increasingly motivated to seek powerful allies outside the government, as the incidence of conflict in the system increases. And especially in new programs being implemented by new units, there are good reasons for seeking cooperation from powerful interests. The new unit needs some quick proof of success, some striking demonstration that it deserves to survive and expand. If it can find already in existence an organized interest with expert information, lines of access, and other resources which can be added to its own resources (even with certain conditions attached), the chances for showing some positive result rapidly are better. In deciding which problems to attack first, the new unit is under some pressure to take up arms against problems already nearly solved, and to postpone consideration of those which require much groundwork before any result can be anticipated. Thus, for example, policies formulated to help the disadvantaged in the society are very likely to be transformed in execution into policies regarding the advantaged. The history of farm policies in the United States is perhaps a good illustration (as are many other programs in which the progressive's idealism and energy confront the resentment, apathy, and suspicion of the most needful).

Powerful interests are also likely to be rewarded disproportionately in the initial stages of pluralization. Large, permanent, and highly organized interests are best able to gain a voice in the selection of new unit personnel, the definition of purposes, the magnitude and type of resources allocated, and so forth. The new unit is indebted to and to some degree dependent on the interests which gave it its start.

Large, permanent, and highly organized interests are powerful in any political system. The proposition here advanced is that marginal increases in the number of interdependent but distinct units—in the complexity of government organization—decrease the probability that interests lacking any one of these resources can get the government to take action on a significant scale to meet their needs. Again it should be emphasized that the basis for comparison is not hierarchy versus pluralism, but organizational unity versus marginal diversification.[18]

14. *Pluralization increases the multifunctional character of units.*

Tasks may be distributed among governmental units on the basis of geographical area, subject matter (such as agriculture), or function (such as rule-making). But functional divisions of labor will be difficult to maintain over the long run in a pluralizing system. Interests in the society are almost always organized either by area or subject matter rather than by function. We have national labor and business organizations, not separate private organizations for legislating, executing, and judging policies in either field. In an increasingly fragmented government the probability that any organized interest will succeed in gaining access to *some* unit increases. There are many such entry points; what fails with one may succeed with another. If the purpose is simply to obstruct government action, strong access to one or a few units in a clearance system may be sufficient. If the aim is to get comprehensive programs adopted, other strategies, noted in number 13 above, are indicated. But many interests pursue goals falling between vetoing and broad policy innovation; they seek restricted but positive action by government. Such groups will encourage the functional growth of friendly units, will press them to deal with "the problem as a whole." Since the officials themselves are also likely to desire expanded functions, the interest finds allies on the inside.

Thus the "independence" of regulatory agencies gets stressed; a functionally constructed unit like the House Rules Committee undertakes to review the substance of legislation; the Supreme Court takes initiatives in setting national civil rights policies; and national party platform committees are involved in candidate selection maneuvers.[19] The pluralistic bases for these developments lie in (a) the increasing ease of acquiring access somewhere in the system and (b) the increasing difficulty of acquiring access to many separated units performing different functions on interest-salient problems.

15. *Pluralization increases the demand for and rate of circulation of elites.*

As a system pluralizes, more units will find it necessary to devote more time and effort to recruitment of new personnel and to counteracting offers by other units for present personnel. Specialization of the "personnel" function is likely and will handle most of the problem for staff below the upper levels, but staffing at and near the top cannot easily be delegated in this way; the main decision-makers in the organization will then have added to their other duties a good deal of work in identifying, selecting, and recruiting new and replacement staff and in finding ways to retain the talent they have.

The basic reasons for this are fairly simple. A new unit needs a top man (perhaps a "big name"); an executive director; a group of top-level generalists capable of participating in organizationwide decisions; and others. The net increment of demand results from the fact that old units are not eliminated as fast as new ones are created.

The identification of top leadership potential is difficult; most units will seek to reduce uncertainty by focusing on persons who have already demonstrated leadership ability—that is, on leaders in other units. This competition will lead to more rapid circulation of elites. From the "recruitee's" standpoint, there is an increasing number of plausible alternative opportunities to his present place. The more such opportunities, the greater the probability that one or more of them will be more attractive than his present position. Careers involving many switches are thus more likely.[20]

16. *Pluralization enhances the roles of lawyers and budget-makers.* As coordination becomes more difficult, the significance of common elements increases. Two ubiquitous elements in interunit coordination are laws and money. Laws, because relationships among units are defined and linked by laws to more inclusive sets of relations. As laws proliferate and gain importance as manipulable elements, successful action comes to depend more and more on the legal technician and on the lawyer as "omnicompetent amateur" (David Riesman's concept). Money, on the other hand, provides the main basis for comparison among activities by substantively different units, with the consequence that the requesting-budgeting-appropriating-accounting institutions are in an extremely and progressively significant strategic position. Yet neither lawyers nor budgeters, once they have been included in the process, can be excluded effectively from any part of it. While these actors may think of their roles as narrowly technical, they in fact make decisions involving the whole range of substantive decisions. The size and status of legal staffs in government agencies and the kinds of questions raised in appropriations committees would seem to confirm this development.[21]

17. *Pluralization increases the demand for, dependence on, and power of those with extraordinary political talents.* The lawyers and the budgeters gain power because they deal with commensurable commodities. The politicians' speciality is making the incommensurable commensurable. Successful negotiation among proliferating organizations is an extremely difficult art. It requires the ability to anticipate a wide and inconstant range of reactions, to manipulate representations of units to one another without sacrificing plausibility, to parlay limited resources which one only partly controls into effective power, and many other things. Such talents are extraordinarily scarce, yet with-

out them a fragmented government tends to degenerate into unproductive bickering and stalemate. Robert Moses of New York, Mayor Lee of New Haven, and Lyndon B. Johnson as Senate Majority Leader illustrate the significance of political skills in holding a pluralistic system together.[22]

Only the most sketchy account of these tendencies, illustrated with a few examples, is presented above. Let us suppose for the moment that they are all confirmed by appropriate empirical evidence. What broader, longer-range implications do they suggest for a pluralizing system? At least three basically different kinds of outcomes seem possible.

Meliorative politics. Over the long run, it might be argued, pluralization produces an impressive variety of ideas, proposals, plans, and projects. The system in operation is under constant criticism; it tends to correct itself. Marginal improvements remove at least some frictions and dampen the intensity of conflicts. The system is relatively stable and peaceful, pursuing a moderate course by requiring widespread consensus on any basic policy change. The system is an open one in which a great many interests are linked, through their organizations, to their government. (The joys of participation are widely available.) At a minimum, a pluralistic government is unlikely to be a tyrannical one in any positive sense.

Crisis politics. Others would argue that pluralism's tendencies toward stalemate are extremely dangerous to the long-run peace and stability of the system. The widening gap between, on the one hand, rapid social change and increasing rates of proposal innovation, and on the other hand the growing difficulty of producing effective government action breeds disappointment and disillusionment.[23] The longer social problems go unsolved, the more unlikely it becomes that they can be solved by some modest, limited program. Unorganized, isolated, and impoverished segments of the society are progressively disadvantaged in comparison with the rich rewards heaped on the already better-off. There is, in the long run, always the possibility that, with skillful leadership, the disadvantaged, who have grown suspicious of behind-the-scenes government and cynical from continual disappointment, will take the occasion of some crisis to alter the system in a fundamental way. In any case, ill-considered, irrational policies will characterize government by crisis.

Feudal politics. A third possibility is that units will succeed in reducing their dependence on one another. Each may stake off some segment of government as its special, separate bailiwick. Interest groups may establish connections with particular units and manage to convert them into independent domains, each ruling over its clientele with a minimum of interference from without. The practice of delegating great authority to "czars" for various problem areas might continue and grow, resulting in a system not unlike medieval feudalism. Areal decentralization (for example, in the name of "states' rights" or "community control") might proceed in a similar fashion. The result would be a society governed in relatively distinct groups, each governmental unit being responsible for protecting and caring for many of the needs of its special clientele.

Of these three conceivable outcomes, most political scientists probably would prefer meliorative politics to feudal politics, and feudal politics to a politics of crisis. Yet such evaluations are heavily dependent on the often unexpressed premises of one's political philosophy.[24] Pluralization is a technique of governing, a means toward ends which need to be specified more clearly than they have been. Its existence as a common activity in a surviving system demonstrates neither its inevitability nor its desirability.[25] Careful testing of hypotheses such as those advanced above might contribute to a more useful evaluative scheme than the polemical posing of grand alternatives can offer.

Until that happens, we are guessing. An entirely plausible guess, of an order different from those above, is that government—that is, those institutions we now call governments—will be largely irrelevant to the major social concerns of the year 2000. The continual raising of hopes which cannot be fulfilled, the domestic "wars" which peter out into bickerings, the transfer of attention from exchanges within the society to exchanges within a government community busily ruling, financing, manning, and coordinating itself—may bring on, not revolution, but simply a turning away from government in favor of other mechanisms for social action. We might then view the activities of formal governmental institutions as expensive entertainment, a series of fake but amusing posturings and rituals spiced up with an occasional foreign escapade, taken seriously only for an irreducible set of domestic and international peacekeeping functions. Even if pluralistic trends continue apace, they may take longer—say to the year 2100, to reach this point. One might look to developments in the wanings of Rome and of medieval society for analogues.

An alternative extension of American experience would suggest that pragmatism will forestall pluralism. Negative feedback will stimulate corrective invention. What might some of these correctives look like? At least the following are imaginable at this point:

Population Control

At some time between now and the year 2000 a "war for simplification," much more comprehensive and thoroughgoing than those in the past, might decimate the population of separate but interdependent units. Large numbers of units would be abolished and their functions either destroyed or captured by the remaining units. Such conflagrations would have to be repeated periodically in order to sustain the effect. A less disruptive invention would be the collapsible unit purposefully created with a congenital defect: a pre-set anticipated life span at the end of which it automatically ceases to exist. Another would be the practice of requiring the elimination of a comparable unit as a precondition for creating each new one, or of allocating funds so as to permit only such proliferation as could be accommodated within a fixed supply of sustenance.

Pledges of abstinence—for example, a President's campaign oath against pluralization—might be attempted. Alternatively, the creation of new agencies might be restricted to a sharply defined period each year or decade, which would facilitate comparative evaluations of such proposals. Difficult, high-level review procedures might be institutionalized to rule on acts of proliferation, perhaps requiring long, drawn-out preparations. Permission would be granted only with reference to individual cases, setting no precedents. Units which added new functions without creating new organizations would be rewarded financially. Permission to form a new unit might be made contingent upon the approval of the old unit most threatened by the proposal.

Short-circuiting

Given the strong pressures for pluralization inherent in an ideologically activist society, measures for unit "population control" are going to be difficult to establish and sustain. More probable is a series of indirect techniques for bypassing or short-circuiting stymied subsystems and achieving other policy purposes at the same time. Leapover policies such as the negative income tax or guaranteed annual wage might, if established, render much less significant the complexities of welfare structure. In an analogous way, PPBS and other social monitoring and accounting systems might provide objective grounds for eliminating units or reallocating functions among existing units, steps very difficult to accomplish as long as program evaluation is neglected, methodologically primitive, and propagandistic.

New political alliances between national leaders and deprived populations may develop through the political parties. Instead of virtually disbanding between national elections, the parties might develop and sustain continuing relationships, much more direct than those of the government, between leaderships and citizens. These continuous parties could furnish a base for making comprehensive demands on the government, mobilizing citizens across government-clientele boundaries, and maintaining the pressure beyond policy formation to policy achievement.

Collegiate Policymaking

Within the government, collegial bodies of policymakers might be constructed and/or strengthened. These would be gatherings of equal generalists responsible for decisions across very wide segments of the policy spectrum. No divisions of labor among colleagues would be permitted; rather the members would be served collectively by extensive specialized staffs in command of technical expertise (particularly information processes) and by specialized groups of wise men as advisers. Conflict among both types of experts would be designed into the system. But the body of colleagues would consider issues only as a plenary consortium, never as complementary specialists. Decision-making would be simultaneous; that is, all the members would consider an issue at the same time and would decide it by the majority process. Members would hold no officially defined responsibilities other than their collegiate status.

The supply of such generalists would be increased by carefully designed programs of university training, in which the ability to identify and define key issues, pinpoint the critical evidence required, and resolve the conflicting advice would be fostered, through combinations of learning and action. The selection of members would be democratically controlled, but continuing special relations with constituencies would be handled by an ombudsman system (a series of officials selected simultaneously and in parallel with the collegial members.)

Such collegial or conjugate[26] bodies would manage even their internal business, such as agenda-setting, by common action through majority votes, thus forcing a scheduling consistent with widely shared priorities. Action on comprehensive budgets would probably form the core of their activities in normal times; budgets would in all cases be expressed programmatically, and questions of funding would be considered in conjunction with questions of program content. But the body as a whole would be prohibited from delegating responsibility for decisions to any staff or to any subgroup of members.

Not everything can be accomplished by rearranging decision-making structures. But steps as these might contribute, nevertheless, to eliminate stymies and lessen lags, attract appropriate talents, focus conflict, rationalize program packages, and direct attention to major decisions. The number of such collegiate bodies would not be large.[27]

Reorganization of Persons

Organizations are congeries of persons. In most of the propositions above, pluralization derives its dynamic from human responses to organizational situations. Such responses very often have a strong component of defensiveness. Distrust, aggression, overcontrol, stereotyping, fear, envy, pride, and a disposition to cloud the truth all contribute to the ineffectiveness of institutional arrangements. In many cases pluralization appears to exacerbate this defensiveness, in part by increasing uncertainties but also by channeling energies and ambitions in ways destructive of productive cooperation. Steps might be taken to counteract this defensiveness more directly than is possible through structural simplification.

In a wide variety of settings, techniques for reducing interpersonal defensiveness have been successfully applied. The training group and other methods for exploring, directly and explicitly, how officials in interaction perceive and respond to one another, and for developing interpersonal trust could contribute to this purpose in the political system. Recent applications of such techniques at policymaking levels of the Department of State illustrate their practicality.[28]

Obviously, the baseline for these diagnoses and treatments is a value scheme which emphasizes government as an active force for human welfare, a productive government responding effectively to the social needs of a problematic age. Clearly, productiveness is not worth buying at the cost of democracy; an entire range of related questions, regarding especially the system of parties and elections, needs attention if we are to have a political order that is both fruitful and free.

The answers to such questions, suggested by speculation from unsystematic observation, require both the development of theories which will get at the underlying flow of activity in the political system and the careful testing of induced and deduced hypotheses. Far from being esoteric "academic" exercises, these efforts will speak directly to the state of the political order in the year 2000. But at present we are not far beyond guessing how to guess.

III

Mediated
Leadership

Democracy depends on political rationality—which has to be motivated. Therefore, the literary excitement of political journalism is crucial. Need that mean the end of factuality?

12

Characters in the Campaign

OURS IS THE post-Hitler generation: we know that "advanced" civilization is no safe protection against tyranny, that modern technological rationality stands ready to enlist in dreadful causes. Ours is the post-Vietnam and (one continues to hope) the post-Nixon generation: we know that the marriage of high technique and low purpose is no peculiarly German phenomenon. We have got past the more naive versions of the myth of progress, past the habit of relegating intense political evil to the olden times. We know that attention must be paid to *now* and *here* lest yet another Pied Piper lure away our children. Eternal vigilance, alas, really does turn out to be the price of liberty.

Yet for all our generation's weary sophistication we still get mesmerized by political magic. Meg Greenfield in "What Is Merit?" (*Newsweek*, March 13, 1978) says that:

The great holy grail of American political reform is an idealized, unattainable—and frankly weird—state in which there is no dis-

cretion, no judgment, no flesh and blood, no better and worse—
in short, no human politics. We have a couple of broad, if
doomed, techniques by which we are continually seeking to
achieve this elusive and beatific condition. One is to put the thing
on automatic, to opt for wheel-of-fortune choices, as distinct
from deliberate political choices for which someone has to take
responsibility. I have in mind, for instance, the lottery reform
of the draft, or the seniority principle of selection of Congressional chairmen, procedures that may end up working great in-
justices, but which we nevertheless believe have the enormous
advantage of *not being anybody's fault.*

The quest for that holy grail, the search for some systemic Automatic
Pilot to relieve us of reliance on flawed discretion, got going in 1787
when a generation of squire-politicians, fumbling quickly through
their intellectual baggage, found Montesquieu and Locke and Newton
and the idea of the well-balanced machine. Some opposite instinct
reacted to insist on a Bill of Rights—however plausible that the
machine might work, several motions must be explicitly denied it.
From then to now, as Orwell's year approaches, we Americans have
been revering our Constitution as we bend it to serve new purposes,
banging at its gears and flywheels, attaching auxiliary wires and
pipes and safety valves. The chant of the mechanics echoes down
through the years, like Dean Rusk's toot-toot litany on Vietnam,
whistling through the graveyards of 600,000 dead in a *civil* war, another 600,000 in one battle in the mud of the Somme, and a few
children in a ditch at My Lai, not to mention the milder ways we
have continued to wound one another here at home.

In recent years the search for no-fault politics has focused on elections—the key democratic choices—and particularly on the choice of
the President—the fatefulest choice of all. The result (and there were
other causes) is a system in which the voices of the traditional recom-
menders—political party leaders, public officials, and other elites—
fade out. The concept of nomination, some leaders naming other leaders as worthy of election (the original *idea* of the electoral college),
has given way to "name-familiarity" as the touchstone of notability.
The parties are shattered. No one seems to care who Father Hesburgh
prefers. Announcement of Tip O'Neill's allegiance fails to electrify.

Neither Max Palevsky nor Derek Bok can deliver much of their worldly and spiritual treasures; not even Bruce Springsteen can make the lightning strike. Just who was it, for example, who nominated Jimmy Carter?

There are those who think that Jimmy Carter was nominated by Mr. R. W. Apple, Jr., of the *New York Times* in a front page story on an Iowa poll, headlined, one envious candidate staffer thought he remembered, in type as large as that announcing the fall of Saigon. The line of thought that attributes the fault or glory of serving up Jimmy Carter to Apple—or the press or "the media"—leads into a vast quagmire of speculation about power that has been drowning intellectual talent since Aristotle sketched out the forms of causality. It is a topic which fits smoothly into the mechanistic approach because it suggests rearranging power relationships as the cure for whatever seems problematical: reshape the FCC, break up the networks, license reporters, subsidize competing newspapers, et cetera ad infinitum. Much political science writing on power winds up shaking a finger at various hypothesized dummies who supposedly do not realize how complex it all is. What gets lost in such enervating debates is the common sense observation that what the press in this country does or does not do is a very important factor in the process by which we pick a President. Reporters do not invent the world they see, nor do they take note of every stimulus-bit that invades their sensory equipment. What the press says is not universally noticed or believed, but nearly all the public's political information and wisdom comes through the press. Re: power, full stop.

What is the alternative to the mechanistic, Tinkertoy approach? One might try to find out how, within the more or less structured constraints, journalists grapple with politicians. One might suppose that both sets of grapplers have minds (and thus memories and anticipations) and that they come at their encounters with different desires. One might make the normative assumption that decisions on both sides have consequences—for instance, that it makes a difference who the particular President is and how he is evaluated. In other words, one might focus on the personal and cultural blood of the situation, on what makes the machine of human politics stop and go. My thesis is that the mode and manner of the journalistic enterprise have significant effects on reporting about potential presidential characters, and that significant improvements may be possible if journalists want to make them, leaving the machinery roughly as it is.

I will concentrate on the problem of news reporting as a literary endeavor. As writers, journalists are artists whose vocation calls them to the muse of truth. As news reporters, they are responsible for carrying back to their readers a representation of reality. How do old and new news genres depict political characters? Does "objectivity" mean reducing politicans to objects? Does "subjectivity" (as in the honest admission that the reporter is *there*, reflecting) means unleashing the fictive imagination? What of the new mixtures, such as "faction" and "docudrama"? In the rough and tumble of the quotidian contest, how can the reporter tell the truth he knows while reporting the facts he sees?

Examples are taken from 1975–76, but in a way that I hope will draw on the past and throw light ahead. That season was, I think, a propitious one for understanding character reporting. No large, clear issue happened to coincide with our rigidly quadrennial election schedule. No obvious winner dominated the scene; the incumbent had not been through a national election, and new rules had ruined the old calculations. The standard ideological left-right cadence was lost in a bewildering cacophony of scattered themes. And strong attention was focused on character because experience with Johnson and Nixon had brought home a hard lesson: we the people, for all our savvy and data, could still err mightily, could freely choose the tragic course. For these reasons 1975–76 is probably as nearly pure a case for character as history is likely to hand us.

I hope I may be forgiven for saying obvious things, as strangers are wont to do.

What Reporters Are After

The reporter sets out not to find facts, but to find a story (preferably a story that happened today or that can first be told today or that says a new thing about tomorrow). Indeed, to remain a reporter he must find a story. The luxury of silence is denied him. Perhaps if he does not write today, he is thinking. If he does not write tomorrow, perhaps he is composing. But if he carries on that way, he is not a reporter anymore. Like Scheherazade, he will die (professionally speaking) when his story can no longer be continued. His story-seeking is not merely for his private amusement or instruction. The story becomes real and professionally sustaining only if it is put forth for others to share. When he was dispatched on his mission, his editor may well have told him why the trip might result in a tellable tale, and when he returns he may well have to argue that he found it and that it is worth telling—especially compared to competing stories. He has to work quickly lest all his effort be garroted by a deadline. Tomorrow he has to do it again. And he may never produce just the same story twice or repeat it just as told by another. Thus the first fact of journalistic life is not that the reporter is skeptical or naive or biased, but that *he will tend to notice those aspects of the situation that lend themselves to storymaking.* He looks in order to show. He listens in order to tell. At peak form, his whole perceptual apparatus is attuned to pick up, in the cackling confusion which surrounds him, the elements of a new communicable composition. He grows a "nose for news."

The first whiff of a story is a lead and a lead is like a joke. It gets its punch from the juxtaposition of incongruities, much as a comedian's one-liner is a crisp combination of elements ordinarily apart. Dog bites man will not do. Thus *a story begins when one notices contrasts coinciding.* The reporter's raw material is differences—between what was and what is, expectations and events, reputations and realities, normal and exotic—and his artful eye is set to see the moment when the flow of history knocks two differences together. The simplest spark of a story is figure-against-ground—the appearance, for example, of yet another candidate through the political fog. Better yet is a previously unremarked contradiction between, say, liberal Bayh and liberal Udall, and best of all is when those two have at one another.

Watching candidates, the political reporter is struck by their *distinctive* qualities—their contrasting and identifying idiosyncrasies and (better) eccentricities. Fresh as we are from 1976, there is no need to supply the names for these fellows we met, one at a time, decked in their assigned personae:

". . . a tall and witty former professional basketball player . . ."
". . . gentlemanly President of Duke University . . . ."
". . . Earthy, barrel-chested new radical with a folksy populist pitch and a quick mind . . . ."
". . . low-key former cable-television executive with the look of a persecuted nebbish . . . ."
". . . shrewd and ambitious politician with strong labor support and a deceptive veneer of country-boyish looks and backslapping cordiality . . . ."
". . . husband of Eunice Kennedy Shriver, brother-in-law of Ted Kennedy . . . ."
". . . stocky, boyish-looking foreign policy specialist . . . ."
". . . the freshest of new faces, preaching the politics of skepticism and diminished expectations . . . ."
". . . veteran of thirty-five years in Congress and recognized expert . . . ."
". . . rich and antiseptically handsome . . . ."
". . . soft-talking, evangelist-sounding peanut farmer . . . ."
". . . crippled, confined to a wheelchair, hard of hearing . . . ."
(from Jules Witcover's *Marathon*)

Then the contrasts could be seen to coincide. Each noticeable candidate acquired a question to be asked about him—a surface contradiction upon which many a lead could be based. A clear series of examples in the titles of the impressive *New York Times Magazine* series in 1975 and 1976:

"Puritan for President" (Jackson, November 23, 1975)
"Peanut Farmer for President" (Carter, December 14, 1975)
"Wallace's Last Hurrah?" (January 11, 1976)
"Liberal from Goldwater Country" (Udall, February 1, 1976)
"Peach-pit Conservative or Closet Moderate?" (Reagan, February 22, 1976)
"What Makes Hubert Not Run?" (Humphrey, April 4, 1976)
"The Rockefeller Campaign. Campaign?" (June 27, 1976)

New questions and thus new stories proliferated from these.

The story form is exceedingly old, perhaps the very oldest form of human discourse, compared to which even prayer and argument may be late-life novelties in the biography of mankind. The reporter's requirement of novelty bars him from that strange appeal the repetition of already known stories has for people but connects his writing with the nearly hypnotic effect one notices when a child settles down to "once upon a time," an adult sighs and eases as the lights go down in the theater. This appeal is mysterious, but an obvious part of the lure of, in Sir Philip Sidney's words, "a tale which holdeth children from play, and old men from the chimney corner" is the promise of action. But it is action of a special kind—interior action—that entices. Descriptions of scenes, personae, and motions are beside the point unless they intimate (explicitly or not) what is going on in the minds and hearts of the characters.

This point deserves pausing over, I think, because many journalists would question it. Action is to be distinguished from passion, event from meaning, happenings from "soul stuff." Yet I would contend that for journalists, too, the story—even if it depicts only physical actions (e.g., a fire)—takes off only if it displays or implies inner action. Journalism as literature shares a reversal contrary to the common sense that motive precedes and thus explains action; rather actions are used to educe motives, and actions which fail to meet this criterion are "irrelevant." In a story, what seems concrete is really symbolic. Somehow, the lead must lead inside.

That is evident in the oldest stories, long before Proust and Joyce, as in Aesop's tales—crackling with action, but only action which lights up character. Similarly, reports of Odysseus's travels, the chronicles of the Crusades, and Ernie Pyle's war reporting. Even peoples we would suppose to be utterly dominated by the physical facts of life and death make inner stories of outward events, as in the tales Eskimo hunters tell.

If it is true that reportage and literature both pulse with inner meaning, it is also true that neither can get along with *merely* motivational peregrinations. One can imagine long and even interesting passages of interior dialogue—say, Birch Bayh in the style of Penrod, Fred Harris as Molly Bloom, Milton Shapp as Herzog. But even such would be full of metaphorical *action*. Wendy Robineau surveyed a thirty-five hour sample of videotaped network news campaign stories broadcast between December 1975 and May 1976, and reports in an unpublished research paper that nearly all newscasters (with the notable exception of the female ones) in nearly all their stories drew on action metaphors from sports ("kick-off," "race," "sparring," "cross the goal line," "winning streak," "trading punches," "decisive knockout," etc.) or war ("political battle," "friendly territory," "survivors," "media blitz," "left flank," "campaign wounds," etc.). Journalism insists also on at least some element of real-world action to peg down the story in actual life. It shares with literature an initial concentration on the act as primary datum. In the process of creation, plot comes first.

In journalism, then, *the story consists of actions selected to reveal character.*

Almost all the actions journalists observe politicians doing are verbal actions, physicalized into "stands," "postures," "positions" perhaps, but consisting in fact of verbal pronouncements. That the system now requires the candidates (they think) to travel endlessly helps with physical story material, but the main facts are words—quotations—and thus the main literary link is to the drama. Jules Witcover, in an interview, said a good campaign on issues goes "he said—I said—he said," a running dialogue in which the stuff of action is the verbal duello.

A story is a drama in another sense: it develops. At a given moment in its progress, it points forward, its "rising action" piques expectation. This is true for any single story-within-the-drama, which cannot be just one damned thing after another, bumping down the inverted pyramid; ideally the plot thickens piece by piece. Thus *the reporter is prepared to notice patterns of causal linkage*—threads potentially available for dramatic sequencing. The simplest form is action-reaction, but there are also unfolding, unmasking, confirming, and a thousand other patterns. Not that the reporter necessarily explicates these patterns (or any others), but he will avoid, if he can, tossing around in the random salad his senses serve him—a candidate's ploy, the shape of a teacup, tomorrow's strategy, the reek of Ramada Inn rugs, his headache.

Like Suzanne K. Langer's definition of dramatic action, a good news story is "a semblance of action so constructed that a whole, indivisible piece of virtual history is implicit in it, as a yet unrealized form, long before the presentation is completed." As Erving Goffman points out in *Frame Analysis,* even "when the lead neatly encapsulates the story line, giving the show away, as it were, the story can still be written in the gradual disclosure form, as though the reader could be counted on to dissociate his capacity for suspenseful involvement from disclosive information he had been given a moment ago." The reporter watches for action pressing forward, for a causally *connected* narrative linking past to future.

Writing the Future

In political reporting, the drama continues beyond any one news gig. Indeed, one reason the campaign is so heavily reported is that it is a natural, structured, long-lasting dramatic sequence, with changing scenes, pauses and spurts of action, heroes and villains, winners and losers, and a measure of suspense. The reporter may aspire to move from story to saga; news magazine writing stretches the perspective to a week, the monthlies and quarterlies beyond, and "book journalism" has emerged as a new genre. Straining against the perpetual demand for novelty, the reporter hopes for the luck of a "running story" he can board and ride for awhile. An analogous lure for the literatus may go vignette-anecdote-short story-novel-trilogy. Thus, *a reporter is on the lookout for stories that will lead to other stories.*

The clearest example from campaign reporting is the "scenario," a term picked up, I think, from movie-making, and developing as a journalistic form out of the "violin" at the first of the news magazine (to sing like a gypsy violin and thus entice the reader onward) and then the cover story and "situationer." But everyone in the news business commits scenarios—any business must, to plan, and every human does anyway—and many get published. Explicitly, the scenario story is a summarization and prediction, an ordering and projecting. The ground is chaos, the figure is order. But an evident secondary function is to define a new ground against which new figures can appear. *Time*'s Stan Cloud sees that "by doing such a story you create a situation that creates further stories off of it"; *Newsweek*'s Ed Kosner smiles as he says "whatever we think now is going to be wrong." Mel Elfin notes that "deviations from a straight line make life exciting and adventurous." Similarly "investigative reporting" turns over little rocks to find big dragons, and the assignment of reporter to candidate commits the reporter to discover dramatic development in the quest of middle-aged man.

One could argue that news is not essentially about what happened, but about what is about to happen. If its zest is partly attributable to its artful portrayal, through action, of inner life, part of what it links to there is a fascination with the future. George Steiner in *After Babel: Aspects of Language and Translation* notes that the metaphysician and historian Ernest Bloch thinks man's essence is his "forward dreaming," a bending into the future without which "our posture would be static and we would choke on disappointed dreams. . . . Natural selection, as it were, favored the subjunctive."

Ace reporters are of mixed mind about the virtues of "forward dreaming" in journalism, though they have no doubt it happens continually. Thus in a feisty and relaxed interview, Martin Nolan and Anthony Lewis (in their tennis togs on the way to the Duke courts, March 1976) resolved a mild disagreement about scenarios in their common disdain for one mode thereof:

> Nolan: I will try to kill scenarios with one stone. The metaphor in political writing has shifted in the last few decades from that of the race track to that of the theater. Nobody really writes about front runners and dark horses and grooming candidates for sweepstakes—if they do they ought to be thrown out on their ass. Rather we go with something more sophisticated. We have candidates projecting their image and how the charisma works, et cetera. But scenarios are what we used to call hedging bets and ought to be treated as such. It is just a wonderful way to say, "Well, on the one hand, and on the other hand," but to do it by using these fairly novelistic dramatic techniques. And it's utter bullshit to sit down—anyone that really sits down and says, "Here's what's going to happen"—and then Ted Kennedy gets a phone call in Hyannis and Hubert does this and that— they're crazy to do it.
>
> Lewis: Well, if it involved that sort of thing I would agree, but I don't see how you can avoid looking ahead to an extent. . . . For example, we were discussing the impact of Jerry Brown. You can have, I think, a useful speculation in a political column about whether, when you finally get to California, Carter and Jackson

will be so clearly the serious candidates and that Jerry Brown will merely look like a stiff and the voters will not transfer to him as a Presidential candidate, so-called, the awe they show for him in the opinion polls in California. That's a thing that one can use for speculation. . . .

But Lewis and Nolan agreed that magazine scenarios were "too wearying to read," "frivolous and futuristic," "so hyped and frantic and frenzied." Yet it would be fair to say that these newspapermen, in their own styles and modes, have also been known to peep over the wall to the future, looking for a story that might spawn publishable progeny.

Romance and Irony

Literature has its styles, and writers of an age tend to share them. The available repertoire is wide, the typical selection therefrom much narrower. Political reporters write pastoral pieces (New Hampshire), mythic tone poems (the South), ritual exercises (election night), and any number of other generic effusions. But these days (post-everything, pre- we are not sure what) *two genres, the romantic and the ironic, predominate* in political journalism and perhaps even feed on one another.

The empathetic journalist can hear, in this outline of medieval romance, themes more than rarely encountered in stories on the quest for the Presidency:

> The protagonist, first of all, moves forward through successive stages involving "miracles and dangers" towards a crucial test. Magical numbers are important, and so is ritual. The landscape is "enchanted," full of "secret murmurings and whispers." The setting in which "perilous encounters" and testing take place is "fixed and isolated," distinct from the settings of the normal world, the hero and those he confronts are adept at "antithetical reasonings." There are only two social strata: one is privileged and aloof, while the other, more numerous, is colorful but "more usually comic and grotesque." Social arrangements are designed to culminate in "pompous ceremonies." Training is all-

important: when not engaged in confrontations with the enemy, whether men, giants, ogres, or dragons, the hero devotes himself to "constant and tireless practice and proving." Finally, those engaged in these hazardous, stylized pursuits become "a circle of solidarity," "a community of the elect." (Erich Auerbach, quoted by Paul Fussell in *The Great War and Modern Memory*)

Obviously this type of quest romance—in fiction or in politics—need not be naive nor even sentimental. Bunyan's *Pilgrim's Progress* is no tea party; Christian is jolted again and again. But the drama's force derives from encounters, of uncertain outcome, between our hero and external obstacles to his progress, in which his *virtue* is tested. The question is whether or not he will prove strong and good and true enough to win. And romance is hopeful in the sense that the process of testing culminates in a just decision, that justice inheres in and is produced by the process itself, as in medieval trial by combat or John Stuart Mill's wrestling match between truth and falsehood.

Irony makes no such assumptions. Odds are, the process and the outcome are farcical—just, if at all, only by accident. The forceful scenes are not fighting encounters but discoveries of erroneous calculation, of Don Quixote mired down in misplaced intentions. The devil refuses to wear his uniform. The question is not one of virtue but of insight: whether the protagonist, brave and true as he may be, will realize in time that he is playing the fool. Romance arouses indignation as our hero is temporarily bested by the beasties. Irony sees him win and then fall off his horse, and smiles knowingly.

Northrop Frye has thought his way down analogous transitions in modern literature and Paul Fussell gives a succinct summary:

> "Fictions," says Frye, "may be classified . . . by the hero's power of action, which may be greater than ours, less, or roughly the same." . . . [T]he modes in which the hero's power of action is greater than ours are myth, romance, and the "high mimetic," of epic and tragedy; the mode in which the hero's power is like ours is the "low mimetic," say, or the eighteenth- and nineteenth-century novel; and the mode in which the hero's power of action is less than ours is the "ironic," where "we have the sense of looking down on a scene of bondage, frustra-

tion, or absurdity . . . "In literature a complete historical "cycle" . . . [goes] . . . myth and romance in the early stages; high and low mimetic in the middle stages; ironic in the last stage.

One can make too much of cycles. In political journalism, though, there may be a similar rough drift toward the ironic and beyond. In television, from Walter Cronkite (the romance of space shots) to John Chancellor ("low-mimetic" Dickensian realism) to David Brinkley (Old Irony Asides) to Tom Snyder ("sacrificial ritual and dying gods"). In newspaper work the drift may go from James Reston (America) to Tom Wicker (Dickens again) to George Will and Garry Wills (the willful ironists) to Hunter Thompson (the Kierkegaard of the causeways). From a larger perspective, the news magazines are generally romantic, as witness their bicentennial celebrations; the newspapers ironic; and television flickers gently in between. In specifically political campaign reporting, I think one could inoffensively consider Jules Witcover tending to the romantic—as witness his indignation at candidates who wouldn't talk issues and his subsequent book, *Marathon*, chronicling "a marathon obstacle course that consumes time, money, and humans like some insatiable furnace," a race in which "nearly all stick it out as long as money, physical endurance, and emotional stability last, and the dream of success is not overwhelmed by the reality of failure." And Richard Reeves might agree to serve as ironic exemplar since his book *Convention* starts with an anecdote in which Clare Smith, youngest delegate, arrives in New York and goes in a couple of hours from feeling "sort of flattered" to "Oh, screw you!" The book ends with Robert Strauss being served the wrong sandwich.

Romance and irony are symbiotic opposites. In order for irony to work there must be hopes abroad. Thus F. Scott Fitzgerald feeds on the ghost of Rudyard Kipling. In order for romance to work the threat of defeat must be real. Thus *Gone With the Wind* is nourished by *The Red Badge of Courage*.

The ironists and the romantics need one another, lest either lose their distinctiveness. It is an open question whether anybody needs Tom Snyder and Hunter Thompson; perhaps they will do for journalism what Kurt Vonnegut and Donald Barthelme are doing for literature. But if Frye is right, yet another mythic era may loom ahead. The acids of irony may bubble away, as the audience tires of the tales of error. Maybe Jimmy Carter's success signaled that.

What Gets Left Out

At this point it is no longer possible (if it ever was) to continue characterizing political journalism as a whole, or even that part of it concentrated on the candidate's character. Already the romantics and ironists are distinguished. What may be useful is to pause to reflect that each of the regularities I have hypothesized—as emphases—implies the tendency to neglect its opposite. Thus journalists tend, I think, to pass over aspects of the situation which do not lend themselves to narration, which lack story potential. They tend to ignore commonalities among the candidates, in favor of the distinctive. They tend to slight contrasting elements which remain, in the flow of observable history, apart from one another; which is why, for example, Catherine Mackin's famous 1972 juxtaposing of what-Nixon-said-McGovern-was-saying with what-McGovern-was-saying got yanked off the air as shockingly unprofessional. Reporters are generally loath to speculate directly about the inner life of the humans (candidates, voters, etc.). They observe, preferring revelatory actions (statements, polls, etc.). But in selecting actions to report, they tend to disprefer those which do not in some significant way represent or affect the actor's inner life. The reportorial focus on the story as a minidrama directs the reporter away from causally isolated items; if a noticed action appears to be causally isolated (take Ford's slip, in the 1976 debates, that the Soviets did not dominate Eastern Europe), the reporter will tend to seek out plausible linkage (as, say, to Ford's intentions or memories or rigidity or intelligence)— to "make something of it," something developable. Similarly, in the larger dramatic framework, the reporter is likely to be unstruck by dead end, one-shot, used-up stories, unresurrectable in the future he strains to foresee; perhaps Hubert Humphrey's passion for extended argument should be an example from last season, or, more significantly, Nixon's compulsiveness from the season before that. And journalists covering politicians tend to craft along the main highroads of contemporary literary culture, turning aside from old timey byways and dangerous new trails.

The Sentient Reporter as His Own Man

Departing from the general to the individual, we encounter in modern political journalism the reporter on the way out of the closet of objectivity. He is not alone; for centuries the literati have been tensing over the issue of the relation of the artist to his art—art as extant or expressive, the artist's self as enhancer of or detractor from the aesthetic experience. Aristotle sounds like an avuncular editor wising up a cub when he advises in the *Poetics:* "He who feels the emotions to be described will be the most convincing: distress and anger, for instance, are portrayed most truthfully by one who is feeling them at the moment." Probably good reporters do the same thing: as a technique for discerning more clearly the candidate's subjectivity, one gets vicariously into his shoes, feels as he must feel, notes the other in himself. But does he *publish* these notes? Increasingly, I think, reporters feel ambivalent about this. Walter Mears, the former wire service ace, says proudly, "I don't give my impression of him; I collect material on what he *did*, how he performed." A lead Mears would disdain is Norman Mailer's opener, "Plains was different from what one expected." The *Washington Post*'s Howard Simons worries about "that creeping little feeling in the back of your head, when a reporter comes back with an interpretative piece—are we sucking our thumb?" But television's Jack Perkins says, "You make your own judgment first, because over four or five days you can find film to support any kind of piece you'd like to do." Certainly one can find, in the journalistic fraternity, pledges of allegiance to every conceivable flag of "objectivity."

One need not pause long over the image of the reporter as a mere mirror, reflecting a world he randomly discovers. Not even Mears would buy that. What Charles Beard, in *The Discussion of Human Affairs*, wrote of "the broad and general field of history, sociology, and interpretation" is true of journalism:

> [E]ven the person who claims to proceed on no assumptions is
> in reality employing some hypothesis in the selection of facts
> real and alleged from areas of apparent order and areas of ap-
> parent chaos. If no hypothesis is consciously adopted, then sub-
> conscious interests and predilections will affect the selection, for
> such interests and predilections exist in every human mind. If
> anything is known, that is known.

But even the most icy-eyed newshawk, his mind a tabula scrubbed
rasa for each new assignment, totally devoid of sentient selectivity,
blankly inquiring "what happened?"—even if such exists—his analogue among the readers does not exist: the story will be turned into
evidence for or against a supposition.

Nor are the important questions exhausted in the continuing debates about "bias" and "balance" and "fairness." There is no objec-
tively definable Golden Mean. One man's middle-of-the-road runs
through another's left field. Today gets canted askew when one tries
to balance it against yesterday. Of course one should try to be fair.
But the reporter in his persona as writer—as a literary man—has a
deeper problem: where, if anywhere, is there a place for *him* in the
story, for his own "special gifts" or "touch of madness"?

In practical terms, objectivity seems to mean not letting your emotions get mixed up with your reporting and sticking to the facts.

In the first meaning the reporter stands apart, noticing and even
fostering his apartness. The *Post*'s William Greider, his sensitivities
undulled by years of close professional work, told me he thought a
hard look at the reporter in action would reveal the romantic-ironic
tension in the reporter's emotional involvement: "I just bet if you go
out on the campaign and see people covering stories and how they
react, you will see that the cynicism in the humor and the hard-boiled
stuff is very shallow and that basically, when you get past that, they
take it very seriously." But even more seriously, the reporter can come
to love his independence, "the purity of the calling," his sense of himself as "the outsider, working for an organization, yes, but really out
there alone, slogging along doing something clean that the organization doesn't have anything to do with. And you know, this is very
powerful." Greider thinks he "could think of two dozen reporters of

similar class and background and education" who had similar feelings
when they went into journalism:

> We all read Riesman and William H. White and we looked
> around us at our college classmates and we thought, "My God,
> that's right—that is the way the world is and I don't want any
> part of it." . . . You looked for a safe harbor where one could
> keep his ideals, where you didn't have to wear a hat to work and
> carry a briefcase, and they might even tolerate some eccentric
> habits. . . . And in terms of the real world where real things
> happen and people get killed and buildings get built and trains
> run on time, you don't really have much responsibility . . . I
> mean, sure, in a very narrow limited sense, if I go out on a story,
> I have a responsibility to do a good job and come back with all
> the information and write it clearly and so forth. . . . But I am
> not *doing* anything. I am an observer. And in my sort of blind-
> ered perception, I'm not hurting anybody. . . . I know that can
> be horribly wrong but that's the way reporters look at it. . . .

Russell Baker sees the reporter as Willie Loman,

> on the road, laden down with a typewriter in one hand and a
> suitcase in the other and a trench coat, trudging his way through
> the mob, living a rather dreary life with the reality of it roman-
> ticized with good booze, sitting up nights and telling old tales.
> Basically, he's a guy who is riding out there with a shoestring
> and a smile, and he's easily shot down. (from Lou Cannon's *Re-
> porting: An Inside View*)

Holden Caulfield or Willie Loman, these visions share an image of
the reporter as a loner, a man free—or abandoned—to see and say
the truth. Those who pay him haven't bought him. He flits or slogs
his way, loyal to his muse, not his masters. That is a large item in his
covenant of objectivity. He is unbeholden to those above and he
stands to one side of the history he observes. Greider's theme implies,
I think, that the reporter would lose his essential definition were he
himself to step into the action.

Other Objectifiers

Richard Salant of CBS News says, "Our reporters do not cover stories from their point of view. They are presenting them from nobody's point of view." Other newsfolk adopt, if not nobody's point of view, at least the interest of those off-the-scene "nobodies," the readers. The journalist's profession warns him not to lust after mere popularity and not to lapse into the didactic and exhortatory modes. But in a subtler way, the reporter can use his sense of "the reader" as a check on his own subjectivity. David Broder, in a 1975 interview, explained:

> At the early stages, most readers don't give a damn and those readers who do rarely find it convenient to be where the candidates are. So you are eyes and ears for particular readers. And you do have a responsibility there. I think in any situation in which you are asking questions, you ought to ask yourself whether the question you are pursuing is simply a matter of personal interest or whether you have some reason to believe it's the area that needs to be brought to an audience. I am going through that exercise right now, because I'm on a "Meet the Press" panel with Ford this Sunday. Now there are 300 things I would like to ask Ford about personally. Assume you've got perhaps ten questions—what ten are really most important to push him on? There you really do have to think for the public, in your role as a proxy or surrogate for people who are not going to have that chance to ask those questions themselves.

Broder and his colleague Haynes Johnson (who agrees with the above perspective) spent many an hour in 1975 searching out and listening to *voters*, as such; no doubt some were also readers, but that was not the focus of the research. Reporters in general, like professors, are remarkably incurious about how their audiences are receiving them. Editors used to tell *New York Times* reporters to write for a twelve-year-old girl, a category with which not many reporters were known to hang around. Broder facing "Meet the Press" is thinking, I think, not how Suzy Jones would question President Ford, but what he should ask in her interest. His own "personal interest"—his subjectivity—is subjected to that discipline.

Like creative artists in other fields, journalists may guard objectivity by avoiding introspection, lest the caterpillar tangle to a halt.

Broder's boss, Howard Simons (who would not so describe himself), says, "You just automatically *do* it, because if you ever stopped, you would never get started again." Simons's boss, Benjamin Bradlee, brasses on by the question how the press chooses candidates to cover—"We decide by fiat who a serious candidate is." Behind a physical and mystical barricade at the other end of the floor, Philip Geyelin—"I report to the publisher, and we're totally distinct from the news side"—maintains his editorial writers in the purity of their anonymity—"it's kind of a monkish life." Such separations, though never complete, protect the writer from drowning in external and internal chaos, free him to get on with his work. Little time is taken in thinking through how his separatenesses shape that work.

Sticking to the Facts

It is in the work itself, many reporters would say, that objectivity or the lack thereof inheres. The work is a *Ding an sich*, whatever the worker's intestinal condition. The work "stands on its own feet"; even an obviously autobiographically based novel like *Memoirs of a Fox-Hunting Man* can be wrenched away from the life of Siegfried Sassoon, objectified, and evaluated for what *it* is. Which brings us to the second facet of objectivity: the journalist's injunction to stick to facts. Admitting they are his facts (see above), how does he handle their recounting?

A few brief passages highlight the beginnings of the reporter's passage—in his work—from Invisible Man to Man in the Scene.

Theodore White has been our age's most influential artist of pointillistic journalism: microscopic fact-dots blended by the mind's eye to compose a meaningful conglomerate. (White's other major contribution, incorporating demographic analysis into popular political writing, is less often remarked.) White got into the candidate's hotel room and took it all down. His books are chockablock with facts. "It would be good," White writes in *The Making of the President 1964*,

> if the private lives of public figures could be sealed off from their political records, and their leadership discussed as an ab-

stract art in the use of men by other men. The politics of an open democracy, however, dictates otherwise. Men and women both vote, and they choose a leader by what they catch of his personality in the distortion of quick headlines. Yet the private lives of public figures are as three-dimensional, as complicated, as unyielding to interpretation by snap judgment as the lives of ordinary people.

This is the philosophic prologue to White's exploration of Nelson Rockefeller's divorce and remarriage, the facts of which, he thinks, merit attention "as much to show how greatly public report distorts, as for their shattering impact on the politics of the Republican party in the seeking of a candidate for 1964." And now the scene:

> It is the estate at Pocantico Hills that gives the clearest impres-
> of the isolation and separation so characteristic of all the Rocke-
> fellers—as well as the near-paralyzing effect the Rockefeller
> fortune has on those who approach too casually its field of force.
> Only forty minutes from Manhattan, off a winding road in West-
> chester County, surrounded by a low fieldstone wall, the estate
> stretches away to the Hudson, so hidden from the public eye that
> the hurrying motorist will miss the gate unless forewarned. Be-
> hind the wall stretches some of the greenest and loveliest land
> anywhere in America—low, rolling hills, perfectly planted yet
> not manicured, that come to a crest in a Renaissance mansion
> built by the original John D. Rockefeller shortly after he trans-
> planted his family here from Ohio in 1884. It is a beautiful man-
> sion, yellowing now with mellow age, with grottoes for children,
> a loggia, a terrace, a swimming pool. From the terrace on the far
> side one looks out over the Hudson River as it winds majestically
> down from the north, with all its freight of the American past,
> before it is squeezed into the angry present by the Palisades.
> Both sides of the valley are equally green with grass and forest,
> and as one gazes down in enchantment on the broad-flowing
> river, it is difficult to imagine sorrow or anger or any ordinary
> human concern penetrating this paradise.

Here White is not merely rambling around the outdoor inside of a country place, like a Junior League guide on a house tour. His mind commands his eye and the facts he sees evoke the sense he seeks to convey: isolation and the "near-paralyzing" oceanic feeling a city boy can get in too wide-open spaces. More subtly, the finished lineaments of God's and man's architecture—"equally green with grass and forest," "grottoes for children"—and the flow of history from "freighted" past to "angry present" get us ready to feel along with Nelson Rockefeller when, it turns out later in the narrative, he feels imprisoned there.

Ward Just thinks "Teddy White did for political journalism what *Madame Bovary* did for the novel"—but Just also thinks the trend has gone too far. "To Teddy White" has become a verb form roughly translatable as "to write the scenery." Part of White's objectivity is the primacy of ineluctable fact in his reporting. The adjectival material may verge poetical, but the material stands out, reinforcing the reader's sense that he would sense it as White does. Another part of his objectivity is White's literary economy. His imagination is disciplined, prevented from ranging beyond the boundaries set by his thematic purpose. A third part of his objectivity is the unobtrusiveness of his person. Obviously he is there—the "hurrying motorist," the "one" gazing, the surveyor of his own feelings finding it "difficult to imagine sorrow or anger"—but not very obviously, not as an object of *primary* interest in the account.

Compare the following. From the December 1, 1975, *New Yorker*, here is Elizabeth Drew on the campaign trail with Mo Udall:

> Monday, October 20th: Buffalo. Mercifully, Udall's plane did not arrive in Boston until eight, after which it had to be serviced, so we were not awakened until seven-forty-five. The pilots had not wanted to fly the plane to Boston during the night. Some of Udall's staff members were up most of the night talking to people in New York and Washington, rearranging plans several times. One staff member says that a hairdressers' convention beginning today in Buffalo made it impossible to arrange for a commercial flight there. On his way out of the hotel this morning, Udall was interviewed for a Worcester television station. After driving to Boston, we boarded the candidate's chartered plane, and are now arriving in Buffalo at twelve-fifty, over four hours late. Normally, Udall's plane—called Tiger, after the can-

didate's nickname for his wife—makes it easier for him to get around. The plane, an F-27 twin-engine turboprop, seats sixteen and is comfortably appointed. It costs fifteen thousand dollars a month to lease. Udall can afford the plane now, because when he travels he is accompanied by anywhere from six to ten Secret Service agents, whose way is paid by the government. The Secret Service agents are also helpful in making it easier to get to and from airports, on and off planes, and through traffic, and in various other ways.

From the February 20, 1976, *New Times*, here is Marshall Frady watching Sargent Shriver:

> [Shriver] is by far the most zestfully urbane of the whole company, carbonated with champagne urbanity, an ebullient insouciance for all his unlikelihood. A certain tautness in his movements, a starchiness in his neck and arms, in his crisp speech, with heavy eyebrows like stripes drawn by charcoal, and a heavy cap of hair like a toupee over his rosy chicken hawk's face, he had at Jackson with a gleeful, flurrying combativeness unmistakably Kennedyesque, that same spry and spiffy incisiveness of licks in exactly the same kind of creaky, crinkly voice like cellophane crackling, like a speeded-up tape recorder.

From the September 26, 1976, *New York Times Magazine*, here is Norman Mailer reporting his interview with Jimmy Carter:

> Having failed with the solemnity of this exposition, but his voice nonetheless going on, beginning to wonder what his question might be—did he really have one, did he really enter this dialogue with the clean journalistic belief that ultimate questions were to be answered by Presidential candidates?—he now began to shift about for some political phrasing he could offer Carter as a way out of these extensive hypotheses. The sexual revolution, Mailer said hopefully, the sexual revolution might be a case in point. And he now gave the lecture he had prepared the night before—that the family, the very nuclear family whose security Carter would look to restore, was seen as the enemy by a large fraction of Americans. "For instance," said Mailer, clutching at

inspiration, "there are a lot of people in New York who don't trust you. The joke making the rounds among some of my friends is 'How can you put confidence in a man who's been faithful to the same woman for 30 years?'"

Carter's smile showed real amusement. . . .

Each quotation illustrates a departure from White, at once sharing and shedding different aspects of his literary objectivity. Drew is reporting what happened, facts the accuracy of which could be directly, immediately verified by any other reporter, whatever his mind-set. Hers is the authority of the industrious person on the scene, like the war correspondent who has smelled the cordite, touched the chilly mud, hefted the sack of grenades. She herself barely appears, as one of "we." But the point of her observations is obscure, her principles of economical selection less than self-evident, so the reader is significantly more dependent on her personal authority than he is on White's. In another passage Drew takes nearly two *New Yorker* columns listing the cities the candidates visited in October 1975. As far as I know, she tells no lies. But what is the truth of the piece?

Frady's claim to credibility is parallel to Drew's—his data also consist of candidate observations—but his heavy foot is on the adjectival accelerator, racing out beyond the independently testable facts. He risks the accusation of idiosyncracy in order to gain the authority of sensibility. Unlike Drew, who presents none, he presents too many interpretative themes, like a stage drama composed of nothing but asides. Shriver himself is shattered in a kaleidoscopic visual cacophony. For that to work, we the readers must, to a significant degree, enter the world of Frady's imagination, suspend disbelief, take his words for it, and try, as the art appreciation teacher would say, to "get inside the artist."

The Mailer passage is a sample; there is much more to the same effect. One must read well down into the paragraph before who's who is clear. The object—Jimmy Carter—is virtually absent, exists only as a foil for the Mailer drama. The language is straightforward enough—even the joke is flat—and the thematic topic perfectly evident: Mailer wrestling with Mailer. It is an interesting match. Mailer is like a city (he contains multitudes), so that Mailer quoting Mailer quoting a joke Mailer heard barely ripples the narrative flow. But it has nothing in particular to do with What's-his-name, the politician. Insofar as it is factual, the facts are about Mailer.

I do not mean to pedestalize White as a guru of objectivity. He was wackily wrong about Nixon, that genius at ambushing journalists. White's drama is operatic in part because it is restrospective; knowledge of the outcome always reinforces the tendency to see fate at work in the gambles of the past. But he did, it seems to me, stimulate in political literature a fresh sense of seriousness and sensibility and artistic discipline—a standard against which the work of the Drews and Fradys and Mailers can be measured—as he sought to see through the facts to the truth.

Across the Line to Fiction

For all his admiration of Theodore White, Ward Just thinks Teddy-Whiting "has gone too damn far." Journalists "are promising more than they can deliver, not really living up to what they can do best, playing to their weakness rather than their strength. And it is going to get worse before it gets better." Just's admiration for working newsmen is also intense; his is the criticism of a caring colleague, who spent his life in the craft and nearly gave it his life when he was severely wounded by a grenade in Vietnam. Now he writes novels in Vermont because, he feels, he could not tell his truth as a journalist. When we talked in January 1976 he was working on understanding that decision.

For too long now—what with Watergate, the war, the Pentagon papers, impeachment—reporters have been "living on adrenalin," Just says.

> And since in the United States it seems to be unacceptable to revert back to anything—you always have to step forward in this country—there is a desperate search for this new form, for a way to tell the story all at once. And it means that everybody is jumpy. There isn't any sense of reflection or relaxation or going out and simply writing a story, whether it is dramatic or isn't dramatic. There is a sense now that some metaphor must be

imposed on every public event, a kind of national metaphor illustrative of something deep in the American psyche or a vision of the future or mirror of the past—you know, whatever. Each public event must be invested with mythic significance.

In the search for novel metaphors, Just thinks Richard Reeves "has had a terrific effect" as has Martin Nolan—"a Nolan phrase will enter the air and will stay around for awhile." *Post* editor Harry Rosenfeld's question: "New cliches are being made—shouldn't we be making them?" A prime example is Morley Safer's story.

> He was the guy who got them flicking the cigarette lighter and burning down the village—which had an enormous effect on everybody. It was one of those leaps of the imagination. All of a sudden one story changed the context in which the war was reported. All of a sudden, all those things that guys had seen and hadn't reported—it wasn't that they were trying to downplay it or anything like that, it was that they didn't see the context in which to put it. Morley Safer gave them a context. And after that the stories just came like drum fire.

Just's own path in Vietnam took him away from his professional home:

> I ceased to believe that facts could lead me to the truth. And when that happens, when you really lose a certain essential respect for fact, you are useless as a journalist. Useless. You are not worth a good goddamn. And when I came back from the war, I did this sort of Nixon thing and then started to write editorials. But I am not by nature either a preacher or a teacher. I mean, I was okay at it, but I knew I didn't want to do that for the rest of my life. I had always wanted to write fiction and I knew damn well that if I didn't do it then—I was thirty-five years old then—I would never do it.

I asked Just to explain how facts no longer lead to truth.

> If you assemble for yourself fact A, fact B, fact C, fact D, and fact E, all you essentially have are those five facts. Because of my particular view of the unknowability of human motive, I don't think you can go beyond that to anything larger that's very

damned helpful in trying to convey the essence of the situation, the terrain of the human heart—not to get too elaborate about it. But that's really what I mean. I find no way in journalism to do that, because there isn't a way nor should there be. That isn't the journalist's terrain: it is the terrain of the novelist. Once you become fascinated by motives and the connections of people one to the other, journalism doesn't take you very far. Say you become fascinated with Haldeman and Nixon, just as a relationship. You can poke around the edges. You can find out how many times Haldeman sees Nixon in a day. You can go back into Haldeman's background and back into Nixon's background and you can make a couple of pretty good educated guesses. But by Jesus you never really know what that *was*. If you were lucky you would see them talking together twice, but that would be all askew because you are there watching it. Okay, so the tapes come out and you know a little bit more, and if you can listen to the tapes to hear the tone of voice, you are a little bit farther. Even with all that evidence, you can't do it as well as a fellow can do it in a novel. I am not talking about a *roman à clef*, such as "I am going to take Nixon and I am going to take Haldeman and I am going to imagine what they might have been like and I am going to write my novel about this." That's silly. I am talking about creating two people—make them a university president and his aide or a police chief and his sergeant—two types of men and what draws the one to the other. If that's the sort of thing you are interested in, journalism won't take you very far down that road. There isn't much of a form to work it into print. It is very difficult. I mean, the form is very hard, but well, it won't work anyway.

Then what *would* work? Just is not sanguine, given the recent journalistic history he has shared in:

As Nixon would say, let's look at the record. What do we have for the last twelve years? We've got Nixon, Lyndon Johnson who got us into the worst war in history, and John F. Kennedy, who, now in retrospect—there is going to be no hide left on that poor bastard in about five or six years. . . . With Kennedy we voted to move the country ahead and we got the goddamned

Bay of Pigs and a whole passel of other difficulties. With Johnson it was "no wider war"; we got the widest war in history. With Nixon it was "bring us together" and we have never been more divided. In each the reverse has turned out to be true, so you do have to wonder at the ability of journalists to fulfill the contract.

But still, what is the alternative? Should everybody quit journalism and go write novels?

Oh, hell no. But in my heart of hearts I am not sure that in the real world we live in—not Plato's *Republic*—journalism can be done much better than it is being done. On Watergate, everybody goes back now and says, "Oh, we should have done it a year before, two years before." Oh, bullshit. To me it was just an extraordinary demonstration of old-fashioned, hardworking tenacity. Look at the people who are in journalism now. They are really a collection of the most able, by and large intelligent, by and large decent people. No, my question is a little darker than yours: if those guys can't do it, given the form—hell, I was about to say maybe the form is wrong. I think the form is okay. I can see no alternative to the form. I mean, I am up a blind alley. We shouldn't expect anybody to peer into the future. If a fellow simply reports on what he sees and hears and what his best judgment tells him appears to be the situation—Christ, that's all you can ask of him. And if it turns out wrong, you shrug your shoulders, because events aren't always satisfactory and the future doesn't always fall into place, as it ought to, like a row of dominoes.

Just's insights clarify strikingly several dimensions of objectivity in political journalism. He sees how reporters, seeking stories, are pressed to impose novel orders on the flux of reality—to find, in progressive American fashion, new metaphors, new cliches, new leads, new juxtapositions of incongruity, and that that professional demand makes necessary the intrusion of the reporter himself, his own creative artistic imagination. He recognizes the power of new metaphors to redirect radically the vision of the journalistic fraternity, not just that of the creating individual: Safer's soldier's lighter burns down the current perceptual structure as it ignites a grass fire of new sensitivities. That process moves well within the standard journalistic *form*, anchored in external objects and actions.

Hunter Thompson slips that anchor, but not all the way. The danger is induplicatability: unleashing Thompsonian gesticulation from the discipline of potential replication. The further danger is a fundamental corruption, a muddy mixing of forms, each of which has its own purity. It is not that Thompson is a poet, but that he pretends to be a journalist. Formwise, he is a moderate masked as a radical.

Case in Point: *Roots*

Just has concluded that facts—however many facts—cannot add up to truth. He used to think journalism "could deliver *anything*," he says. Now he thinks the gap between fact-based journalism and the most significant kind of truth—truth about motive—is unbridgeable. It is not a matter of the journalist trying hard and doing better. Essence, not accident, separates the disciplines. Not only does the inner truth perpetually elude the journalist; factuality ruins fiction, renders it "silly."

An example Just might nod yes to happened in the translation of *Roots* from book to television film, as described in *The Inside Story of* TV's *"Roots."* The book was already a mixture of novelism and journalism; the novelism enabled Alex Haley to tell what his characters were feeling. But the screenwriter, William Blinn, had to represent feelings by actions: "I had to find ways for Kunta Kinte and other characters to visualize or verbalize things that were inside their heads." Thus the Wrestler was brought forward as "someone for Kinta to *talk* to," to make Kunta's thoughts dramatically extant. Blinn then confronted a second formal problem, telejournalism versus telefiction:

> In the original concept, Alex Haley was to have played a considerable role. The film would have begun in the present, with Alex Haley tracking down leads about his ancestors. Then there would have been a flashback to the day Kunta Kinte left his village to go look for a tree to make a drum for his father. Then

we would have flashed forward to Haley again, and back and forth, until the whole story was told.

It took four or five months for Blinn and the producer, Stan Margulies, to see that "the plan was dull" and decide to drop Haley. "Suddenly the story became stronger and clearer." Margulies explains:

The minute we dropped Alex . . . the thing took off. Bill and I have talked about how two experienced people like us got into that terrible spot. The answer is that we were simply seduced by Haley. I felt at first that we could best tell the story through a sophisticated citizen of the United States of America in 1977. We'd understand him in a minute because he is obviously one of us, and if we liked him—and most people love Alex Haley—we could then get into his story.

Margulies faced Haley, the narrating journalist, with Kunta, the fictional character, and told Haley, "You can't stand up to Kunta Kinte. Kinte is bigger than you are. Any time we take away from Kunta Kinte is lost time." Haley grasped the point immediately. His attitude was "I know the story and I know what it takes to write a book about it, but I don't know anything about movie-making. . . . Is it really much better without me in it?" Margulies said, "Alex there is no contest," and the decision was made.

The forms work when kept apart, fail when folded together.

Case in Point: Broder's Hope

From the other side of the barricade between fact and truth—or is it truth and fiction?—David Broder has fought for a way, within journalism, to get at the inner life. Back in 1966 when he left the *New York Times*, Broder wrote his editor an explanation of his departure. Good political coverage, he thought, should include

the portrait of men under pressure, their gaffes, their gropings and their occasional moments of greatness as they strive for power in the Republic. This is the dimension of politics that you described to me at one of our early meetings as "gossip and maneuver." I believe that one has the right to expect in a paper like the *New York Times* that the major actors in the political drama will emerge as live human beings. But that is not the case today. . . . (quoted in Bernard Roshco's *Newsmaking*)

Unlike Just, Broder thought that *could* be the case: "Any good paper can get live human beings on its pages if it just lets its reporters know it wants them there, and then gives the reporters space and freedom to sketch them." Instead, the message came through loud and clear: "Stick to the spot news, buster, and those nice safe formula leads. . . ."

Nine years later, Broder was still chafing against the lead rope. He tried hard to get the *Washington Post* off the campaign racetrack—all those set pieces about "front-runners" and "home stretches"—with at least some delaying success. "The real work of political journalism," he wrote with only a blip of humorousness, "is not to provide advance insights into coming events; that is clearly beyond us. Our true skill lies in inventing imaginative rationalizations after the fact for any implausible thing that occurs." Broder knew what it felt like to guess wrong about the future: his *Post* series on the constituencies of *ten* presidential candidates in 1975 did not take him to Georgia. But more important than what's ahead was what's within: reporters should ask:

> Where do the candidates come from? What motivates them to want to be President? What kinds of records do they have? Were the governors and former governors good leaders of their states? How do they get along with others they work with? How do they treat their underlings? Are they aggressive or weak? When they have to make a decision do they pull in a big group of people or go with whatever seems the consensus or do they go off by themselves and meditate on what they should do? Do they have a sense of humor? Are they really open for questioning, or do they go into a debate or press conference to defend their own views? (*Washington Post*, November 2, 1975)

Broder thinks there is room in reporting for these characters. Still, he is glad there are Ward Justs around. For example, he told me,

There is a limit to how much of Fred Harris you can get into the neat corners of a typical *Washington Post* news story about a campaign and a candidate. There are wonderful and terribly important dimensions of him of which you really have to say, "I am dealing with a character out of a novel here" and write him in those terms.

Hadn't there been some pretty poetical Fred Harris stories in the *Post*—the campfire, Ladonna, the Winnebago van? Yes, but that is "the tip of the iceberg," said Broder, and asked me to turn off the tape recorder so he could delve deeper. The important thing, Broder thought (and I think Just would agree), is that "the reader ought to be able to tell, fairly early on in an article, whether it is fiction or non-fiction he is reading."

Mixing the Forms

And that is the point. What rattles objectivity out of the brain are the mixed forms. On the one hand, fiction, however clearly labeled, has enormous power to fix the imagination. Who can hold tight to objectivity with respect to, say, Richard III, Huey Long, and Martin Luther, undistracted by their depictions by Shakespeare, Warren, and Osborne? Who can hold steadily in mind that *Roots* expresses a particular vision of eighteenth-century African village life, or that the screenplay for the television series *King* shuffles a few historical sequences in order to convey a more striking truth? We get public Nixon, then the doctored tapes, then the transcripts read theatrically by first newsmen and then actors, then Ehrlichman's lightly disguised "President Monckton," then the television dramatization *Washington Behind Closed Doors* starring Jason Robards, then Robert Coover's *The Public Burning*—"real historical people and events, mixed with made-up people and events, mixed with made-up events happening to real people," says Arthur Levine in the March 1978 *Washington Monthly*. The ragged confusion of the Cuban missile crisis is crisply tailored for television. It is rumored that one of the networks contemplates a Carter drama spliced together from film of real and fancied performances. Scenarios zip out past subjunctivity to plausibility ("Robert Strauss screamed, 'Stop this goddamned thing, we're losing control.' Albert: 'But a roll call is in progress.' ") to wowsville ("Carter dueled Wallace first, both men playing plectrum banjos, taking off on *Foggy Mountain Breakdown.* It was thrilling! We were at the apex of the entire American political process! . . . Hombre!"). And at the factual base, Anonymous Source slips into They Say and on into Apparently. The footprints of Capote's *In Cold Blood* and Doctorow's *Ragtime* are all over this no-man's-land.

On the other hand, when real history blazes forward scattering sparks of fact, standard journalism seems to shine. The "whirl of experience" can blow a reporter's mind, reduce him to a twitching telegraph, juice up all the old *Front Page* excitement. War is in the long run dangerous for journalism, not only because some professionals get killed or hurt, but also because thousands of amateurs can check what they read against what they see. But when it is happening, war is very short run. In covering Vietnam, Charles Mohr said, "You see these things, these terrible things, but in an odd way they're good stories." Julian Pettifer of the BBC said, "There is simply no point in arguing whether the war is right or wrong. You're always left with the fact that it is there and it's your job to cover it." The professional passions are fully engaged in getting it right, now. Even there, even then, the fictive imagination intrudes. Phillip Knightley in *The First Casualty* gives two examples:

> Michael Herr, making a dash, with David Greenway of *Time,* from one position at Hue to another, caught himself saying to a Marine a line from a hundred Hollywood war films: "We're going to cut out now. Will you cover us?" One should not be surprised, therefore, to find that GIs sometimes behaved, in the presence of television cameras, as if they were making *Dispatch from Da Nang.* Herr describes soldiers running about during a fight because they knew there was a television crew nearby. "They were actually making war movies in their heads, doing little guts and glory Leatherneck tap dances under fire, getting their pimples shot off for the networks."

Later, David Halberstam saw what had gone wrong and why:

The problem was trying to cover something every day as news when in fact the real key was that it was all derivative of the French Indo-China war, which is history. So you really should have had a third paragraph in each story which would have said, "All this is shit and none of it means anything because we are in the same footsteps as the French and we are prisoners of their experience." But given the rules of newspaper reporting you can't really do that. Events have to be judged by themselves, as if the past did not really exist. This is not usually such a problem for a reporter, but to an incredible degree in Vietnam I think we were haunted by and indeed imprisoned by the past.

Michael Herr concluded that "conventional journalism could no more reveal this war than conventional firepower could win it." Gavin Young closes the circle: "The Vietnamese War awaits its novelist."

Political campaigns in their climactic phases are not all that different from battle campaigns: events harden, speed up, hurl causatively into one another. Not even Broder could stem the tide of horse race stories; indeed he wrote a few. To see how the press for facts can turn aside the quest for truth, consider Edmund Muskie, leading Democratic contender for the Presidency, as the 1972 season opened.

Case in Point: Muskie Mad

Campaigning in 1968, Muskie had impressed reporters with his cool handling of an antiwar heckler, conveniently decked out in long hair and dirty jeans. Muskie invited him to the microphone and gave him ten uninterrupted minutes to discover the difference between passion and eloquence. Then Muskie quietly told the story of his father's coming to America and, before he died, seeing his son elected governor. "Now that may not justify the American system to you," he said, "but it sure did to him." Even the students applauded. The incident appeared on all three network news shows.

Then in November 1970, Muskie came on television right after a speech by Nixon at his worst, raging defensively at a partisan rally. John Mitchell called it Nixon running for sheriff. The scene shifted to Muskie sitting quietly in a Maine kitchen. He spoke of the need to be fair to your opponents. From then at least until he was thought to have wept in public in New Hampshire (Muskie denies it) in 1972, the image he had with the great American public was "Lincolnesque."

A goodly number of reporters knew otherwise. In a postelection book, *Us and Them,* James M. Perry said he knew that

> Muskie is not quick and, God knows, he is not cool. He is a very special breed—a plodder with a roaring temper. It takes him weeks, sometimes years, to make up his mind about things like equal rights and the war in Vietnam, and then it takes him seconds to unleash lightning and thunder on those who wonder why it took him so long.

The *Boston Globe's* Richard Stewart knew and wrote—back in June 1970—that "when Muskie is frustrated and bored, his irritability threshold is down around his ankles. The public appearance of calm and control belies the monumental temper he can display in private." In February 1972, Muskie, the odds-on front-runner and poll leader, took to blowing up at questions from students as he toured New Hampshire high schools. One night, playing poker with reporters, Muskie failed to draw to an inside straight and, swearing, threw down his cards.

In *The Making of the President 1972,* Theodore White recounted, again after the election, that beneath Muskie's

> image of the grave moderate were, however, two essential qualities not yet recognized by the public but more than casually troublesome to Muskie's staff. He had a tendency to emotional outburst; and an even graver disability—a lawyer-like, ponderous way of dealing with all issues and even the most trivial decisions.

Hunter Thompson in *Fear and Loathing on the Campaign Trail* put it more pungently:

> It was not until his campaign collapsed and his ex-staffers felt free to talk that I learned that working for Big Ed was something like being locked in a rolling boxcar with a vicious 200-pound

water rat. Some of his top staff people considered him dangerously unstable. He had several identities, they said, and there
was no way to be sure on any given day whether they would
have to deal with Abe Lincoln, Hamlet, Captain Queeg, or Bozo
the Simpleminded.

The *Post*'s Lou Cannon made up his mind at the poker throw-in
that Senator Muskie "seemed a little temperamental to be President
of the United States." Cannon's candid reflections in *Reporting: An
Inside View* highlight the problem: "What does a political reporter do
with this kind of insight? Frankly, I don't know. Muskie was known
to have a temper, but I had yet to read a story saying that he was
showing it all over New Hampshire in response to questions asked
him by high school students. I didn't write the story, either." He did
check out the facts in one student's complaint, found them correct,
and ended his column with this passage: " 'Sen. Muskie doesn't suffer
fools gladly,' says [press secretary] Dick Stewart. The best guess of
the New Hampshire primary is that the 'fools' category includes anyone with the temerity to question the plans or policies of Edmund S.
Muskie."

Cannon wishes he had a second chance:

> If I had it to do over again, and could get away with it, I might
> lead with the poker game. In my crowd, a poker player's blowup
> when he fails to draw the statistically unlikely inside straight on
> five cards is considered more significant than the bawling out of
> a high school student. Whatever the lead should have been, I
> wish I had brought the independent perspective of that campaign
> trip (where I knew few of the reporters) and that column to more
> of my political reporting. Usually we find it difficult to write that
> most important of all stories: "The emperor has no clothes." If
> we took that approach we would have written several stories
> about key political figures at various head tables falling fast
> asleep, literally, during speeches by Gerald Ford. We might have
> written also, as Tom Wicker once suggested, that "Hubert
> Humphrey opened his 1972 campaign today by misrepresenting
> his 1968 campaign." And we certainly would have written dif-
> ferently than we did about Nixon in the same campaign.

Here Cannon is saying what the philosopher Michael Polanyi in *The Tacit Dimension* put this way: "We know more than we can tell." That is in the large sense true of all knowing-telling relations— it would be true if Cannon had all the space, time, and freedom his heart could desire. The answer is not simply more facts, getting it all down and out. Polanyi notes that "an unbridled lucidity can destroy our understanding of complex matters." Nor is the answer in some new mechanical form: "the process of formalizing all knowledge to the exclusion of any tacit knowing is self-defeating," makes it impossible to decide what to call a thing before one knows it, what questions to bring to bear. It was Cannon's hunch, germinated by the fall of a card, jelling into an "independent perspective," growing into definition as a journalistic problem that let him see Muskie in a new light. There he follows in the path, not only of all the great creative artists, but of all great creative scientists. Polanyi explains:

> It is a commonplace that all research must start from a problem. Research can be successful only if the problem is good; it can be original only if the problem is original. But how can one see a problem, any problem, let alone a good and original problem? For to see a problem is to see something that is hidden. It is to have an intimation of the coherence of hitherto not comprehended particulars.

But Cannon, like Halberstam, having glimpsed a new problem, a different kind of story, bumped smack into journalism's literary tradition—not only in the instructions of their editors (one supposes) but also in their own professionally reinforced habits of mind. The reporter listens in order to tell. Especially when standard journalism is working well, in the sense of throwing up plenty of storiable event-clashes, he may feel that, "like a beaver whose teeth grow constantly, he must chew incessantly, not to eat, not to build dams, but simply to keep his jaws from being locked shut." (Wallace Stegner, "The Writer and the Concept of Adulthood," in *Adulthood*, Erik H. Erickson, ed., p. 233).

Would Muskie's slow deciding and fast exploding, transposed to the White House, have radically endangered his country? Picture President Muskie drawing to an inside straight in the Cuban missile crisis. The question was barely raised in 1972. Indeed, the opposite

("Lincolnesque") image prevailed. Ward Just's worry about the track record seems justified as does the plaintive appeal Stan Cloud imagines a reader addressing to him: "You are able to see what this guy is really like. *Tell* us for God's sake."

Case in Point: The Wallace Problem

George Wallace would make a terrible President. If on nothing else, the nation's press agreed on that. The editors of *Time*, for example, "judge George Wallace not fit to be President," says one of their Washington reporters. And the *Washington Post* came out squarely against him editorially, in the only exception since 1952 of their nonendorsement rule, says Phil Geyelin. Yet coverage of Wallace in 1975–76 illustrates, I think, how reportorial tradition can get in the way of objectivity, of the reporter trying to tell that reader what he knows or, most especially, what he remembers.

Even now it is hard to remember how seriously threatening Wallace was reckoned in 1975. *Time*'s William Shannon wrote in July:

> The persistence of Mr. Wallace's political strength despite his lack of seriousness, the emptiness of his "program," and the fraudulence of his posing as a Democrat—is a sinister phenomenon. His appeal derives its motive power from racial hatreds and fears and from the popular fantasy that there can be simple answers to complex problems such as crime, poverty, and economic injustice.

Wallace was guilty of "nasty innuendoes" and "false bravado." Herblock took out after him with his powerful pen. Tom Wicker's January 18, 1976, *New York Times* column titled "Back in the Gutter," led this way:

> George Wallace has lapsed for the first time in years into his true gutter style. At a news conference in Montgomery the other day, he cast off the respectable robes in which too many politicians and too much of the national press have tried to drape him and came out snarling and kicking like the alley fighter he is.

Television commentaries, while taking note of apparent changes in Wallace's "message," did recall his old cry for "Segregation Forever!" Journalism's *editorial* voice was clear enough.

What made Wallace suddenly newsworthy was that this time he might really have a chance—if not to be President, at least to wreck what remained of the Democratic party. In March 1975, Gallup gave him 22 percent of the Democrats, compared to Humphrey's 16, Jackson's 13. He was rolling in money and it kept rolling in, thanks to a highly professionalized direct mail operation. The new finance and delegate selection rules played into his hands. While it can be argued in retrospect—and was argued by Jules Witcover and a few others at the time—that it was awfully early to take the poll results so seriously (and to neglect the fact of massive *anti*-Wallace sentiment), the press had cause to fear Wallace. Clearly a major element in early stories on Jimmy Carter and Terry Sanford was their potential as Wallace-killers.

Wallace sought the Democratic party nomination, but leading Democrats were loath to take him on. Senator Eagleton had commented on his sincerity; Senator Kennedy had blessed him with a Fourth of July visit in 1973, noting mildly that he and Wallace "have different opinions on some important issues" but share other values, such as Wallace's devotion to "the right of every American to speak and be heard." Wary of offending Wallace's followers, the active candidates avoided direct reference to his racist history. Birch Bayh was on record that he could "see circumstances where there might be a balancing effect: I would support him for Vice President," though Bayh was now edging away from that. Even the Republicans cozied with Wallace: Nelson Rockefeller said casually, "George and I didn't always agree, but we always respected each other, and were the two who stood up for what we believed." President Ford noted that on domestic issues he and Wallace "have many similarities." With fine impartiality, the official Democratic party gave him a hand: "We're helping all of the candidates," said the party's national chairman. "We're giving all of them lists and information and advice on delegate selection and everything else. But the truth is we're giving Wallace more help than any of them" (quoted in Arthur T. Hadley's *The Invisible Primary*). The scenario going around the top journalistic circles in the spring of 1975 was that Wallace might well come into the national convention with 30 or even 40 percent of the delegates; that and other chaos-generators might well capsize the creaking party hulk. In an April 1975 interview Broder worried:

> The presidential selection process is in such bad shape now, in terms of mechanisms, procedures and values, that it is likely to be perceived by the end of 1976 that we really do have a national crisis in the way in which we choose our presidential leadership . . . . There is going to be a great hue and cry to say we've got to rationalize this process. At which point if Congress takes it on, there is a substantial danger their answer will be to nationalize the process—some form of national primary, an open primary . . . . And at that point, any hope of party cohesion or identifiable party positions is essentially down the drain.

If the Democracy was incapable of inoculating the public against the Wallace Yellow Peril, who could? With his usual precision, Jules Witcover in *Marathon* describes how journalism went about it:

> In early 1975, at a dinner meeting with a group of Washington-based reporters . . . Udall's plight as a liberal *and* a pragmatic politician became painfully obvious. Settling his long and wiry frame into an armchair, he nursed a scotch and water and fielded repeated questions about Wallace. Was Wallace a demagogue? Well . . . . If he thought so, why not say so? Well . . . . Would he have Wallace on his ticket? If not, why not say so? Udall tried patiently to explain, then and through dinner, that he saw no need to go out of his way to antagonize any segment of the electorate. He would run his campaign and let Wallace run his. The voters would decide. Muskie had seriously erred, Udall said, in calling Wallace "a demagogue of the worst kind" after Wallace trounced him and the rest of the field in the 1972 Florida primary. That statement was an unnecessary dig at Wallace's constituency and he was not going to make that mistake. But still the questions came. Was Wallace a racist? If so, why not say so? In the end, the harried candidate reluctantly acknowledged that he couldn't run on the same ticket with Wallace, but he wasn't going to throw rocks at him either.
>
> The interrogation by a group of political reporters who had been

out around the country and had some feel for what was going on made a strong impression on Udall. He began to worry more about "the Wallace problem," his aides later acknowledged, or more exactly about how the press and liberal circles viewed his handling of it. At breakfast with another group of reporters several weeks later, Udall was still playing it cozy, but not confidently.

Eventually, Udall attacked Wallace openly, said he would have no part of him.

To get into the news columns of the newspaper, Wallace had to make news—or it had to be made for him. In the summer of 1975 the trouble was that Wallace would not *do* anything. "I'm just sitting here not saying a thing, and not straining," he said, "and it seems I'm the one all the others are talking about." In September he led all other Democrats in a New Hampshire NBC poll. In October it came out that in the previous two years, Wallace had raised over $4 million, more than all the other candidates combined, including Ford.

The subsequent coverage of George Wallace, far too extensive for detailed review here, came to focus on events, including revelations by enterprising reporters. Factual material about Wallace's health was reported—that unlike FDR he was paralyzed from the waist down, that he suffered from deafness, that it took him some three hours of preparation to begin his daily work, and that on the other hand he could easily lift a fifty-pound barbell. Television and news photography rarely left out his wheelchair, and when his leg was broken, one saw the doctors in the hospital hallway. He would not let reporters go with him to Europe, but his gaffes and goucheries were headlined along with such nonevents as his failure to see the Pope or German leaders; his inability to think of anything to say in Berlin but "I am a Berliner"; his reflection, on returning, that he had seen nothing much he couldn't have seen on television. He was quoted in the September 11, 1975, *Washington Post* as saying he hoped to "see some electrocutions in this state," as he signed a bill restoring the death penalty. The February 1, 1976, *New York Times* noted: "Wallace Isolated by Tight Security." Wallace's record as Governor was raked and piled—from welfare to liquor permits, from the number of hospitals constructed to Alabama's cellar standing in almost any comparison among the states.

His media campaign was skeptically dissected; CBS let the camera's eye rest on him as, filming a commercial, he fumbled with a telephone and his hearing aid and his thick glasses.

These stories were to the point. But reporters struggling to get across the truth—the Brechtian absurdity of "George Wallace for President"—were up against hard obstacles. They knew—everyone knew, didn't they?—that this was the George Wallace who, well into his grown-up political life, boiled with the rage of a frustrated hit man:

> Nigguhs start a riot down here, first one of 'em to pick up a brick gets a bullet in the brain, that's all. Let 'em see you shoot a few of 'em, and you got it stopped. Any truck driver, steelworker would know how to deal with that. You elect one of these steelworkers guvnuh, you talk about a revolution—damn, there'd be shootin' and tearin' down and burnin' and killin' and bloodlettin' sho *nuff*. Hell, all we'd have to do right now is march on the federal courthouse in Montgomery, lock up a few of those judges, and by sunset there'd be a revolution from one corner of this nation to the other. (quoted by Marshall Frady, *New York Review of Books*, October 30, 1975)

He talked that way; his men had done that way, as any number of veterans, black and white, of the struggle for justice—never mind mercy—in Alabama could testify. Could one count on those voices echoing between the lines of stories about, say, Wallace's chances in the Florida primary? Some blacks in Alabama had had to learn to live with George Wallace, even to work with him politically. But as Roger M. Williams of the Southern Regional Council was given space in the *Washington Post* on November 16, 1975, to recall,

> Wallace rode to political success on the backs of black people. Playing masterfully on white prejudice and fear, he defied the federal government and the courts, and he helped create the climate in which civil rights workers were murdered, a Birmingham church was bombed and a twisted allegiance to "states rights" was elevated to the highest rank of public virtues.

Out in the American countryside, one had to strain to hear Old Wallace behind New Wallace. From the start of October 1975 to the end of April 1976, the *Houston Post*, for example, had forty-four news stories featuring Wallace; one two-incher on November 11 quoted his memory that the South "never did have any segregation except in the schools." Another (by Eleanor Randolph) mentioned a bit of his racist history. Otherwise, it was health, polls, money, travel, issues, and the rest.

If the echoes were soft at home, they were weak indeed abroad. The *London Daily Mail* found him smashing: Wallace "is emerging that most beloved of U. S. figures, the folk hero." And the *London Times* found it "impossible not to admire the shrewdness, good humor, courage and sheer willpower of a man paralyzed by the bullet of a would-be assassin in 1972, but determined to fight on."

Poetic Marshall Frady in the *New York Review of Books* saw literary connections in the continuing Wallace story: "George Wallace's life by now has taken on symmetries of irony that would be almost too pat even for hack melodrama. It's as if he has passed out of reality altogether, and become a character in an Allen Drury novel." Frady spotted

> a constant gap in vision between pleasant assumption and the gutteral actualities . . . [a] polite disparity magnified to a continental popular dimension that [Wallace's] campaigns have always operated on. They have, in a sense, proceeded on that most ominous of all disruptions and divisions in American society, beyond even race—the increasing disconnection between language and meaning in the conduct of the nation's life.

I think it could be argued, as Ward Just would, that it was precisely journalism's restricted vision that let Wallace climb onward. Journalists who tried to let him show through the news hole were continually distracted by optical illusions. Wallace could shut out the press, as he did on his Europe trip, or just shut up in their presence. But reporters given access could find, almost every time, good copy. He had only to be courteous to suggest he had changed. He could be outrageously funny. You could count on him to attack. His language was full of dialectical action. You couldn't be sure what he was going to come up with from one day to the next. He was dangerous—a real scenario-buster. He was a walking bundle of contradictions. Whenever the great saga started to sag, Wallace was there to jack it up—from Birmingham to Boston to Bonn—or to enliven his shallow tragedy with new hamartia. He came from America's storyland, down South; James T. Wooten's excellent profile in the January 11, 1976, *New York Times Magazine* starts out like Aesop or Uncle Remus:

> One fine afternoon last spring, at just about the time of day when the scarlet-and-white colors of the Old Confederacy were being reverently lowered over the chalky dome of the Alabama Capitol, a middle-aged black man timidly poked his head around the corner of a door to the Governor's office and asked permission to enter.

The escalating crash of momenta in the spring of 1976 did not leave much room for accounts of Wallace's past, or anybody else's. Every time he appeared—in a list, a vote, a scene—the legitimacy he had been lusting for so long got another lick of gilt because of what was *not* said. The early historical profiles, largely published back when, as Broder put it, "most readers don't give a damn," were often curiously balanced—Wallace *had* built some hospitals—and murkily contextual, as in the wispy debates about whether or not he was a "Populist." What was needed, I think, was not more history as much as some way for the reporter, writing news, to evoke a certain memory.

The *New York Times* on October 26, 1975, reported that George Wallace, touring Scotland, told a reporter, "It's not your background so much as what you stand for in public affairs that counts at election time."

What Might Have Been and Might Yet Be

If it is an objective fact that journalists, as literary men and women, inevitably convey a *particular* vision of reality, how might it be possible, within their system, to write news stories communicating the truths most needed by the choosing voter? Suggestions from outside the craft have been notoriously utopian, notoriously blind to the real world constraints of space and time that no mechanical reformist magic is likely to charm away. But inside those constraints, there are, I think, significant freedoms. Confinements of the mind can be escaped. Experiments in new traditions are triable. Literary assumptions need not be carved in stone. The common culture, strengthened by sharing, is not beyond the reach of imaginative invention.

Much "media criticism" is at once too pessimistic and too optimistic. The indignant mode prevails—righteous wrath directed at journalism's moral turpitude, often accompanied by a demand for return to mythic good old ways. That happens in every age of transition, which every age is. It supposes that nothing but moral revival will work— and that that *will* work. On the contrary, accusation arouses defense, the past is forever gone, and worn-out visions give way only to fresh ones.

Recognizing the possibilities might begin with an expansion of the dramatic horizon. Agreed that news reporting must hook into today, what questions should guide selections from among the nearly infinite array of phenomena? Clearly events cannot define themselves as newsworthy. The questions bound the answers. More often than is necessary, I think, concentration on immediate consequences of today's actions restricts the scope of operations. Scenarios projecting into the middle-range future are not entirely useless to the voter, because he does not want to waste his precious attention on hopeless cases. But in practice, scenario-writing, while it pretends to concern itself with the future, is in fact unrealistically reifying the present, weighting down a current configuration of chancy changes with more responsibility than it will be able to bear. Once published, the scenario itself becomes an event and very shortly drops like a wet diaper into the can of the past. It seems no one ever reviews scenarios to see not just whether they guessed right or wrong, but why.

The larger trouble with scenarios is that they do not reach far enough ahead. The campaign's basic dramatic force is there because the race is for the Presidency. Yet campaign drama and Presidency drama are curiously disjunct. It is not that the Presidency is neglected: "Ford," for example, appeared in front page headlines of the *New York Times* late city edition 239 times in 1975 and there were eighty-eight front page pictures of him in the same period. What is mostly missing is a perspective on the candidates as potential Presidents. To get at that a reporter must shift his stance toward the subjunctive, tune his imagination out of New Hampshire's Wayfarer Inn and into the White House, sniff out the Presidential qualities in the campaign smoke. Certain practices—such as assigning the same reporters to cover the Presidency and the campaign, providing more opportunities for professional intercourse between reporters with these different tasks, holding editorial sessions on which qualities it is essential to notice—recommend themselves. Far from detracting from the drama, such sensitizations could lend the story a new liveliness, against the grayer background of yet another primary.

For Just and Broder are right—Just, that the track record in choosing Presidents does not inspire confidence; Broder, that the official and empowered nominators do not perform effectively. Journalism cannot fix all that, but the opportunity for an expanded contribution is there.

Journalism's "forward dreaming," then, might be encouraged to dream on past the upcoming primary to the Presidency itself.

Once stories on that theme were encouraged, it would follow that the candidate's past, and with it the journalist's memory, would gain relevance. That need not be a loophole for idiosyncratic reportage. In Wallace's case, for example, the truth about him was very largely agreed on; it was not some individual reporter's flight of fancy. Here again, the dramatic horizon can be broadened and can enrich coverage of the day-to-day. One focuses on the person as embodying his historical development, playing out a character born and bred in another place, connecting an old identity with a new persona—the stuff of intriguing drama from Joseph in Egypt on down. That can be done explicitly in biographical stories. Jimmy Carter must have recognized the appeal a "life" can have when he wrote and published his own campaign biography. But it can also be done inexplicitly: the reporter adjusts his vision of today's whirl of experience to glimpse therein those facts typifying and contradicting the historical who behind the what. Or the reporter asks him to explain what he thought he was doing, back then, when he was moving and shaking a different banana tree. How much more interesting—and useful to voters—such stories are, compared with, say, his "stand" on alternative baby-prevention techniques!

But it is perhaps in an expanded literary space, rather than time (backward, forward), that the promise of political journalism could best go exploring. Journalists who understand that they are sharers in their age's literary conversation, with all its false starts and stutters, might seek through that connection a deeper discipline than reliance on the facts alone can impose. Particularly in news reporting, the discipline of fact is indispensable. The drift to docudrama and faction is threatening because, as these forms pretend to speak the journalistic language, they impose a false sense of order—invented, not discovered—on events. An artificial neatness results and can have extraordinary aesthetic power, adding to the enticements of historical curiosity the overwhelming propensity of the human mind to believe a really good story. If the discipline of fact did nothing else, its contribution in demonstrating that life is not neat would justify it.

But one can stick to the facts without getting stuck in them. The literary imagination has its diciplines, too—economy, for example. News stories which jam together in a few paragraphs "everything" that happened in the campaign today break that rule. Antifloridity is another—the Christmas tree should show through the adjectival tinsel. Concentrating on the artistic product, not the artist, is a third. There is nothing wrong with Mailer writing about Mailer, but if the object is to unravel Jimmy Carter, Mailer should focus his mind on that. There is nothing wrong with writing "I asked" or "I said" when that is a true part of the story—but only then.

Novelists have often done poorly as reporters. Hemingway's dispatches were notoriously dull and inaccurate. Yet reporters might, if they would and could, draw on their own insight and creativity much as a novelist does. At a minimum, they might insist on getting across those facts which, from time to time, impel them to a major conviction. At a maximum, they might consider whether the only live alternative to the predominant ironic and romantic modes is a descent into the genre of sacrificial ritual and dying gods. For their thoughts will mother deeds.

The baseline political conflict story and its resonance with newspaper reporting is illustrated in the history of Theodore Roosevelt's emergence, to the good fortune of Hearst and Pulitzer.

13

Fighting Story

THEODORE ROOSEVELT *scared* politicians. Woodrow Wilson thought him "the most dangerous man of the age." Mark Hanna, the great Republican boss, called him a "madman." Even Mark Twain saw him as "clearly insane . . . and insanest upon war and its supreme glories." But there were those who loved him. Chief among them were reporters.

Mad as he sometimes seemed, Roosevelt was no radical. On the issues he was a reformer, a fixer-up-er, an advocate of change within the system. He sounded radical because he roared and pounded and thrashed about. He started off the Presidential politics of the twentieth century with a bang—the election of 1900—and he dominated American politics for a dozen years, even when he was off in Africa hunting lions. A war hero with enormous energy and a genius for publicity, Roosevelt fit the battle story perfectly. He was also lucky. Continually opposed by his party's chieftains, he could not have climbed to the Presidency without an alternative channel to power. For TR the channel was the new mass-circulation newspaper, exploding on the scene in New York City just as he was gearing up his career. Newspaper journalism had found a new focus and produced a

lasting image, the image of the active, combative, crusading, irrever-
ent, emotive, and endlessly surprising journal of the day.

TR and the newspapers were lucky that history handed them the
chance to start a real war, one he could fight in and they could report.
And in the larger perspective, Roosevelt was lucky in the election that
paved the way for his emergence: 1896, when a frightened nation
chose comforting William McKinley and began to ease back into prosperity and, in time, to lust for fresh adventures. Peaceable McKinley
was as unsuited for the combat of 1900 as Roosevelt was for the gen-
tleness of 1896. Thus candidates come and go, their characters sometimes fitting, sometimes at odds with the pulse of politics.

1896: A Sigh of Relief

By 1896 fear and violence had been wracking the national nerves for
a decade, from the Chicago Haymarket riot in 1886 (four protesters
hung), to the Homestead uprising in Pennsylvania in 1892 (ten killed,
seventy wounded), to the Panic of 1893 (layoffs, breadlines), to the
Pullman strike and Debs's arrest and Coxey's "Army of the Common-
wealth of Christ" marching to Washington to demand jobs in 1894.
That year alone there were some fourteen hundred strikes; more than
660,000 men were thrown out of work. Farmers by the thousands gave
up and sold out. There were rumors of "anarchy"—even "revolution"—especially among the wealthy. The unwealthy did not want
revolution. They wanted money. The campaign was about how to get
more of it without losing what you had, how to achieve and maintain
an easier, safer, more comfortable existence and bring to a close the
too long and too wearing years of turmoil and distress.

For all its economic complications, the Democratic panacea, free
silver, came on as a magic cure for a real disease. Its prescriber was
Bryan, the Democratic nominee, who at age thirty-six (barely old
enough to be President) had already mastered the grand old American
oratorical art of sounding profound while committing nothing. Bryan
was nominated because the many other contenders could not sort
themselves out and because he wowed the national convention with
his high ambiguities sonorously delivered. The delegates amened again

and again as he warned of those who would "crucify mankind on a cross of gold."

What Bryan was saying was part of what millions of anxious Americans wanted and needed to hear: compassion for their plight, castigation of a ruling class that had forgotten the meaning of the stewardship of power, a prophetic reminder that the pursuit of happiness is a human right above and before allegiance to any particular economic arrangement. He spoke to their concerns, to great and little crowds of them. "The fountains in the hearts of men were stirred," wrote Jonathan Daniels. Bryan himself set out with the feeling that "this is going to be a campaign of sentiment."

Nearly all the heavy thinkers in the universities and the great corporations stood against free silver. Their man was McKinley, then governor of Ohio. He had no magical solution; he *was* a magical solution. His curative powers were, they thought, in his personality more than in his policy—which was not entirely clear, though he was basically against fooling around with the money. "Good money never made times hard" was his campaign slogan and his campaign song was "The Honest Little Dollar's Here to Stay." In contrast to Bryan, whom Roosevelt called "a mere boy," McKinley exuded solid maturity. He looked prematurely embalmed, with that little smile funeral directors learn to put on to assure the bereaved of the departed's heavenly destination. Up close he was a sweet man, kind and patient and sturdily humble; he left the hardball politics largely to his manager, Mark Hanna, though he called the main shots.

McKinley was constitutionally against aggressive campaigning. "I cannot get the consent of my mind to do anything that places me in the position of seeming to seek an office and anything I might say or do would at once be interpreted as an effort in that direction," he wrote a friend. "Everything looks very comfortable and anything like seeking to promote my personal interests is very distasteful to me." He would not make or respond to attacks and he would not give out interviews. Instead, he set up a marvelous, continuing media event at his homestead in Canton, Ohio. Personally "averse to anything like an effort to bring crowds here," he cooperated with the drummery of the Republican National Committee. The railroads cooperated by setting excursion rates so low that the trip was "cheaper than staying at home," one newspaper said. Nothing was left to chance. The leader of each visiting delegation came to Canton in advance and submitted his statement in writing; anything embarrassing was edited out and sometimes new sections added. Pilgrim bands of veterans, farmers, merchants, church people, and every other kind of group journeyed to his front porch.

It was wonderfully appealing. For that and other reasons the editorial press was overwhelmingly pro-McKinley. In New York, only William Randolph Hearst's *New York Journal* backed Bryan (Hearst held a fortune in silver) and cartooned McKinley as the puppet of a grotesque Hanna dressed in a suit of dollar signs. The newspapers were full of vituperative exchanges by lesser candidates and campaigners and the editors themselves. True to his character, Roosevelt lit out after the Democrats, such as the delegates to the Illinois convention in June—"murderers, horsethieves, burglars, libertines, crooks of all kinds—men who have been convicted of crimes ranging from pickpocketing to arson." By October he was lumping together "Messrs. Bryan, Altgeld, Tillman, Debs, Coxey and the rest" as "strikingly like the leaders of the Terror in France in mental and moral attitudes." But the two Presidential candidates floated above it all, Bryan scarcely mentioning his opponent or his party, gently reproving such hecklers as the Yale boys who threw eggs at him. McKinley simply smiled.

That fall, as if in benediction, the weather brought in a bumper wheat crop in America and a wheat shortage abroad; prices shot upward before the election. McKinley won by more than a million votes. Late on election night his brother James discovered the winner kneeling in prayer with his mother's arm around him, she whispering, "Oh, God, keep him humble." The *World* editorialized, "The pall is lifted. The paralysis is removed. Apprehension will give way to confidence." Of the inauguration another New York newspaper headlined, "Republicans Take the Helm. Under Bright Skies and with Fair Winds, the Ship of State Sails for the Haven of Prosperity." The Republicans would hold that helm for sixteen years. In the fall of 1897 New Yorkers returned safe old Tammany to power by overwhelming majorities, setting off wild celebrations in the streets. "To Hell with Reform," read the banners.

The election of 1896 ended in a sigh of relief and relaxation. In the course of it the American electorate reshuffled their partisan loyalties more fundamentally than would happen again until 1936. At the time, though, 1896 felt more like an end of the miseries than the start of an electoral realignment. Four years later it could be seen as background music for one of the hardest-fought shoot-outs in American political history.

The Battle with Bryan

By 1900 Bryan had been pummeled out of his silver obsession by the Democratic bosses, who at last succeeded in persuading him to resist "the allurements of so-called consistency," as one of them put it. Times had changed, drastically. Prosperity was abroad in the land. Silver moved down the list in a program stressing antiimperialism and antimonopoly—and there was Bryan, buying it all, ardently pressing his blessings on the Tammany bosses. Roosevelt strode into the Republican convention and was whooped into the Vice-Presidential nomination by the exuberant delegates. McKinley would stay home again. Hanna told Roosevelt that virtually the whole burden of the campaign would be his. TR was up for it: he said, "I am as strong as a bull moose and you can use me up to the limit."

The issues that year were exceedingly complex, as both parties, sniffing victory, edged toward the muddled middle of the political spectrum. The Democrats were against imperialism but for landed expansion. The Republicans kept bringing up free silver, which the Democrats now wanted forgotten; Roosevelt's party, like Bryan's, was against trusts but found the Democrats' solutions unworkable. They agreed, however, on one enemy: public indifference. Mark Hanna saw "General Apathy" as McKinley's main enemy, and Bryan's manager worried about that having "failed to awaken the lethargic American conscience." It looked like a close fight. Democratic fortunes had picked up in the state elections of 1899; Bryan had lost in 1896 but he polled more votes than any previous Presidential candidate. Arousal could make the difference, and so both candidates hit the trail running hard.

The campaign made up in steam what it lacked in substance. In that railroad age Bryan roared around the country, 16,000 miles of it in seventeen states, making 600-odd speeches in five and a half weeks, thirteen to sixteen hours a day. Roosevelt surpassed that, traveling 21,000 miles through twenty-four states in eight weeks. Aflame with fight, Roosevelt soon got over his early fear that, as second man on the ticket, he would appear "like a second-class Bryan," and left behind his sense of accepting the nomination as "a man absolutely and entirely in the second place whom it is grossly absurd and unjust to speak of in any other capacity." Bryan became "my opponent"—so strikingly so that when Mrs. Bryan came to write the Bryan memoirs she referred to her husband's defeat "by Mr. Roosevelt." Mr. Dooley, the comic sage of the newspapers, had it right: " 'Tis Teddy alone that's runnin' and he ain't runnin', he's gallopin'."

He boomed "my beloved Republicans"—and their gallant leader William McKinley when he thought of it—but mainly he assailed the Democrats. Anticipating another fighting candidate sixty years hence, his main theme was this: "It rests with us now to decide whether . . . we shall march forward to fresh triumphs or whether at the outset we shall cripple ourselves for the contest." His book, *The Strenuous Life*, was republished and given wide circulation.

Out in the field Roosevelt let loose his vituperative vocabulary:

> Our opponents have not any more even the poor excuse of honesty for their folly. They have raved against trusts, they have foamed at the mouth in prating of impossible remedies. . . .
>
> Mr. Bryan himself is sufficiently strident when he talks about those figments of disordered brains, militarism and imperialism; yet he coos as mildly as a sucking dove when he whispers his unchanged devotion to free silver. . . . If they came into power, their mere possession of power would throw this country into convulsions of disaster.
>
> The policy of the free coinage of silver at a ratio of sixteen to one is a policy fraught with destruction to every home in the land. It means untold misery to be head of every household, and, above all, to the women and children of every home.
>
> Mr. Bryan seeks to sow seeds of malice and envy among Americans. Jefferson and Jackson he quotes. His political school has nothing in common with theirs. He is a pupil in that most

dangerous political school, the school in which Marat and Robes-
pierre were the teachers.

Militarism! Here in this building a week ago Mr. Bryan repeated what he either knows, or ought to know, to be an absolute slander, when he said that our little army had been created
with the purpose of putting it into forts to overawe the working
men of our great cities.[1]

The vituperative mode did not come as naturally to Bryan as it
did to TR, but he got his licks in. It was "a contest between democracy on one hand and plutocracy on the other"; it was a fight against
a "Republican party . . . dominated by those influences which constantly tend to substitute the worship of mammon for the protection
of the rights of man." In one supersentence Bryan laid out the devious hypocrisy of his enemy:

Republicans who used to advocate bimetallism now try to convince themselves that the gold standard is good; Republicans
who were formerly attached to the greenback are now seeking an excuse for giving national banks control of the nation's
paper money; Republicans who used to boast that the Republican party was paying off the national debt are now looking for
reasons to support a perpetual and increasing debt; Republicans
who formerly abhorred a trust now beguile themselves with the
delusion that there are good trusts and bad trusts, while, in
their minds, the line between the two is becoming more and
more obscure; Republicans who, in times past, congratulated the
country upon the small expense of our standing army, are now
making light of the objections which are urged against a large
increase in the permanent military establishment; Republicans
who gloried in our independence when the nation was less powerful now look with favor upon a foreign alliance; Republicans
who three years ago condemned "forcible annexation" as immoral and even criminal are now sure that it is both immoral
and criminal to oppose forcible annexation.[2]

Republicans, said Bryan, justified imperialism as the American "destiny"—but "destiny is the subterfuge of the invertebrate, who, lack-

ing the courage to oppose error, seeks some plausible excuse for supporting it."

The *New York World* saw the Manhattan throngs for Bryan as "A Whirlwind of Fire," but Roosevelt gave them newspaper drama: "Elmira Toughs Threw Turnips at Roosevelt," "Governor's Carriage Mobbed in the Street by Crowd Who Called Him 'Scab' and 'Fakir' and Hurled Missiles," "Many Men Hurt in a Political Riot," and the next day, "Roosevelt Declares That Coker Incites to Riot and Mob Violence at the Polls." Roosevelt had responded to a *World* reporter with a conversation-stopper: "I will not give any statement of any kind to the *New York World* of any sort or shape"—which the *World* printed on page one. In a mocking editorial titled "A Lack of Strenuosity," the *World* drew on news of another Rooseveltian riposte:

> Asked an impolite question at one point the terrible Teddy only yelled, "That's a lie!" If it was a lie, the man who asked it was a liar; and yet the idol of the cowboys neither shot his ear off nor jumped down and "cut" him nor offered to lick him after the meeting. . . . It is not difficult to fancy the astonishment and disgust with which One-Eyed Ike, Dead Injun Bill and other really strenuous chums of Roosevelt out West will read of this incident.
>
> To a cry of "Down with the trusts!" from a man in the crowd who had evidently taken seriously the condemnation of these monopolies in the Republican platform, the candidate for Vice-President shouted: "You look like one of those men who work exclusively with their mouths. You interrupt this meeting because you are a hoodlum and nothing else. Now, then, go back to your fellow-hoboes." . . . And yet, as we have said, there is a disappointing lack of strenuosity in Roosevelt's campaigning. If a soft answer turns away wrath, a hard answer fails to "knock-out" anybody. Until Teddy shall actually shoot, stab or lick some of his interrupters it is inevitable that his reputation will shrivel among his kindred spirits.[3]

When that same month Bryan again visited New Haven, souvenir-seeking Yale men "grabbed him from all sides, knocked his hat down over his eyes, pulled his necktie awry." The Great Orator was rescued from this desecration by William Randolph Hearst, who shoved the attackers aside and led Bryan to safety.

McKinley and Roosevelt won, by fewer than a million votes in a low-turnout election. Before another year had gone by, an assassin killed McKinley and Roosevelt was President, the youngest ever at forty-two.

TR Rising Like a Rocket

Roosevelt reached this apex of attention by a most circuitous route. By the time he achieved notice his political character had its basic shape. Had he been merely mad, as Hanna thought, he would not have been nearly so interesting. But behind all his clamorous strenuosity was a remarkable personality, a man who had shaped from his triumphs and tragedies an extraordinary approach to life as adventure that found an outlet in voracious reading and wild-game hunting, in remarkable literary productions and in frontline combat, in righteous indignation and an unmatched talent for friendship. He liked the rough and tumble of politics; bellicose he was, but he was also the first American to win the Nobel Peace Prize. He was terrific copy. Writing in 1950, historian Frank Luther Mott said Theodore Roosevelt was "probably more constantly page-one news than any other President the country has had."

Roosevelt had begun to catch the reportorial eye and ear as a young state legislator in Albany in the 1880s. It was his idiosyncracies reporters noticed, the features and manners that set him off from the other typical dude aristocrats who would occasionally drift in and out of that body without disturbing its equilibrium. He looked and sounded different. "Young Roosevelt of New York"—he was just twenty-four—appeared as "a blond young man with eye-glasses, English side-whiskers and a Dundreary drawl in his speech," said one report. His voice was high and his speech halting, but he could easily be heard calling out shrilly for recognition, "Mr. Speak-ah! Mr. Speak-ah!" He broke into the news by demanding an investigation of a stock-jobbing scandal, drawing heavily on evidence fed him by the city editor of the *New York Times*. This outrageous proposal "was like the bursting of a bombshell," a member remembered, at which "a great silence fell over the whole Assembly for a while. It was a thunderbolt to them." Jay Gould, then owner of the *New York World*, ordered this whippersnapper treated with the contempt he deserved. On the substance Roosevelt won and lost: there was an investigation, but its result was a finding of no wrongdoing. But as he saw it, "I rose like a rocket." He got a reputation. The following year he was reelected by a wide margin, though his party suffered large losses.

Roosevelt's fireworks were the natural stuff of the newspaper story. His journalist friend Mark Sullivan saw that "Roosevelt's fighting was so much a part of the life of the period, was so tied up to the newspapers . . . as to constitute almost the whole of the passing show." Even his critics had to watch him; one said, "Roosevelt has the knack of doing things, and doing them noisily, clamorously; while he is in the neighborhood the public can no more look the other way than the small boy can turn his head away from a circus parade followed by a steam calliope." Publisher Joseph Pulitzer, who came to detest him, found him nevertheless "wonderfully interesting." Publisher Hearst eventually saw Roosevelt as an "unspeakable blackguard," but he could not keep his eyes off him. His devotion to "the strenuous life" was contagious in this age of Kipling.

Roosevelt the newsmaking legislator emerged as "the most successful young politician of the day," said the *New York Evening Post*. He mixed into Presidential politics in the Republican convention of 1884 as a vigorously conniving and orating delegate. After two years of ranching and hunting in the Dakotas (to recover from the tragic deaths of his mother and his wife on the same day), he came back to run for mayor of New York as a vigorous reformer still only twenty-eight years old. "If I find a public servant who is dishonest," he promised, "I will chop his head off if he is the highest Republican in this municipality!"—but he lost in a three-way race. In 1889 Henry Cabot Lodge got President Harrison to appoint him to the U.S. Civil Service Commission in Washington, where he stomped around demanding reform until 1895, when he came back to New York to take over the police commission. On the morning of May 6, 1895, he gathered up reporters Jacob Riis and Lincoln Steffens and marched into headquarters—"Where are our offices? Where is the Board Room? What do we do first?"

New York was awash with corruption. Payoffs to police from brothels, saloons, and gambling houses surpassed $10 million a year. TR, to the delight of the press, swung into action. The *New York World* (May 17, 1895) wrote up his trial of errant policemen in a front-page story copiously illustrated with drawings of his gesturing hands, teeth, ears, and "eyes, nose and glasses." The lead set the tone:

> Sing, heavenly muse, the sad dejection of our poor policemen.
> We have a real Police Commissioner. His name is Theodore Roosevelt. His teeth are big and white, his eyes are small and piercing, his voice is rasping. He makes our policemen feel as the little froggies did when the stork came to rule them. His heart is full of reform, and a policeman in full uniform, with helmet, revolver and night club, is no more to him than a plain everyday human being. He is at work now teaching the force that it is paid to work, not to boss.

Within two weeks of the policemen's trial, he hit the papers again, as "Haroun-Al-Roosevelt," prowling the midnight streets in search of patrolmen to be accosted and corrected. Riis and Richard Harding Davis went with him; "The *World*'s all night and ever-present reporter" Davis saw through his disguise—"a turned-up coat collar and a soft hat"—and brought back the story. " 'This is devilish police work!' exclaimed Mr. Roosevelt, wiping the night dew from his glasses, while he examined the gutters, dark recesses, and open doorways for the missing policemen."

Roosevelt's flair for "publicity, publicity, publicity," as a *World* subhead stressed, owed much to his natural friendship with the men who brought in the news. He knew how to help them with their own job. He lived his adventure in action, not fantasy; he went places and did things—physical things—in a time when most fateful decisions were being made behind desks. And he talked their language, the language of lead and hype and sensation reporters needed to get their stuff onto the front page.

Roosevelt's boyish behavior and aggressive idealism endeared him to reporters as friends, not just as feeders on his exploits. Throughout his career he had terrible fights with newspaper publishers—eventually he sued one for $10,000 for calling him a drunk (the award was six cents). When his son Ted was harassed by newshounds at Harvard, Roosevelt wrote him advice he himself could never take: "The thing to do is to go on just as you have evidently been doing, attract as little attention as possible, do not make a fuss about the newspaper men, camera creatures, and idiots generally, letting it be seen that you do not like them and avoid them, but not letting them betray you into any excessive irritation. I believe they will soon drop you, and it is just an unpleasant thing that you will have to live down." But reporters found TR irresistible. One who traveled with him said, "I don't think any sane man could be with him two weeks without getting to like him." Jacob Riis, who revealed *How the Other Half Lives*, became his constant companion in New York City: "For two years we were together all the day, and quite often most of the night, in the environment in which I had spent twenty years of my life. And these two years were the happiest by far of them all. Then life was really worth living, and I have a pretty robust enjoyment of it at all times." Richard Harding Davis became his lifelong friend; when Davis died, Roosevelt called him "as good an American as ever lived," one whose "heart flamed against cruelty and injustice." The great sportswriter turned political reporter, Frank Cobb, caught "the Roosevelt obsession." Roosevelt would yell out his office window to his friend Lincoln Steffens: "Hey, there, come up here. . . . I just want you to see the kind of people that are coming here to intercede for proven crooks. Come on. . . ."

Roosevelt always realized how fragile his popularity was, how much in need of perpetual propping up. Some turned against him when he hired a female secretary ("young, small and comely, with raven black hair, and wore a dark closefitting gown," leered the *World*). The German community turned against him for closing beer halls on Sunday—but he joined their protest parade and when an irate guzzler loudly demanded, "Wo ist der Roosevelt?" the commissioner flashed his teeth in a grin and shouted back, "Hier bin ich!" When he closed down soda-water fountains and delicatessens on Sunday, opposition spread. The *World* fabricated and printed a story of a mother taken to court for buying ice on Sunday for her sick child, coming home too late, finding her child dead. He favored a law allowing liquor on Sunday in hotels, defining "hotel" as ten bedrooms and meals. Imaginative saloon keepers set out ham sandwiches and knocked together ten tiny rooms for prostitution: a furniture company offered to furnish all ten rooms for $81.20; nine months later there were two thousand such new establishments in New York. The unity of the Police Board collapsed. The *World* hit Roosevelt for hypocritical self-advertisement. The *Journal* concluded: "He has a very poor opinion of the majority. But there is one compensation: The majority has a very poor opinion of Mr. Roosevelt." Perhaps most damaging, the cartoonists turned his distinctive features against him, picturing him as a toothy juvenile in a tantrum. But for every editor who decided Roosevelt had fallen from grace there was a reporter who found him fun and fascinating. And he kept moving. On April 17, 1897, he resigned as police commissioner, leaving behind a solid record of reform, to become Assistant Secretary of the Navy. War, real war, brought together his extraordinary dramatic sense and the newspapers' need for conflict, and set him on course for the Presidency.

The Paper War in Cuba and at Home

All in all, the Spanish-American War was the ideal war. It took longer to start than to win. The victory was sharp and clean and total. In no time at all, it seemed, the memory of that other War—of grinding attrition over weary year after year to a still wounded peace between Blue and Gray—was wiped away and an easier road cleared toward a Great War, a road to Verdun and the Somme.

For more than a decade Roosevelt had been itching for a war— with Mexico, Chile, Venezuela, Canada, England, whomever. He glorified "the rugged fighting qualities" a nation needed to "achieve real greatness." Two days after Christmas in 1895 he said, "This country needs a war," although the "bankers, brokers and anglomaniacs generally" were for "peace at any price," and the likes of Harvard's President Eliot (who saw Roosevelt as one of the "degenerated sons" of that institution) were infecting America with "a flabby, timid type of character, which eats away the great fighting qualities of our race." Over the years his belliphilia deepened. A nation "slothful, timid or unwieldy, is an easy prey for any people which still retain the most valuable of all qualities, the soldierly virtues. . . . Peace is a goddess only when she comes with sword girt on thigh. . . . No triumph of peace is quite so great as the supreme triumphs of war. . . . A war with Spain . . . [would bring] the benefit done to our people by giving them something to think of which isn't material gain, and especially the benefit done our military forces by trying both the Army and Navy in actual practice." "It will be awful if we miss the fun," he worried as the event approached, though he vehemently denied that he himself would "expect to win any military glory" or go to battle "in a mere spirit of recklessness or levity."

Roosevelt's saber-rattling could not have suited better the purposes of his hometown newspapers, then passionately engaged in their own "war"—the war for circulation between Joseph Pulitzer's *World* and William Randolph Hearst's *Journal*. Absent the newspaper fight, the real war might never have happened and Roosevelt might well have been shunted aside as a maverick out of phase with the age of McKinley. Day by day these two titans of journalism had been brawling and braying their way to unheard-of popular appeal in New York; their battle shaped history, in and out of journalism.

Joseph Pulitzer—tall, gaunt, with black hair and a pointed red beard, looking like a cross between Mephistopheles and Rasputin—got there first, in 1884. An impoverished Hungarian immigrant, Pulitzer had worked his way to ownership of the *St. Louis Post-Dispatch*. With fierce energy and a wild journalistic imagination, he revolutionized the paper. "I want to talk to a nation," he said, "not a select committee." The prose had to be stark. Not "Quadruplets Born"— "Four Babies at a Time." Politics was his passion and battle its metaphor; politicians at conventions charged and fell—"Grant's Column Dies Heroically in the Last Ditch." Pulitzer the foreigner knew he could never be President: "But some day I am going to elect a President," he said.

The *World* took Gotham by storm. Within two weeks after first publication circulation leaped up by 35 percent. When it reached 100,000, Pulitzer had a hundred cannons fired off and bought every employee a tall silk hat. At the height of the Spanish War Crisis, nearly 1.5 million daily copies were sold. Pulitzer exulted. His paper proclaimed itself "forever unsatisfied with merely printing news" and "forever fighting every form of wrong." In a celebratory issue in 1895 appeared a large drawing of the *World* as a draped Brunhild, brandishing a huge quill at her quailing enemies. By 1896 the circulation of the competing *New York Times* ("It Does Not Soil the Breakfast Cloth") was down to a mere 9,000 copies.

Hearst came to town in 1895 and set out to beat the *World*. He looked like a chronically dyspeptic version of Franklin D. Roosevelt, particularly when boredom descended on him. Journalism to Hearst was "an enchanted playground in which giants and dragons were to be slain simply for the fun of the thing," said a friend. But his *Journal* was no fairy tale. With Napoleonic vision he warred against Pulitzer with stunts, crusades, fireworks, revelations, and "crime and underwear" stories. As reporter Davis and artist Frederick Remington fed him material from Cuba, he demanded more and more sensation, eventually sending a muscular reporter undercover to Havana to rescue from prison the pretty daughter of an insurrectionist, a story that ran on over the weeks to 230,000 words, and culminated in a tremendous parade through Manhattan and a rousing national tour. At the top of the war coverage the *Journal* and the *World* were neck and neck in circulation.

The summer of 1897 was frustratingly quiet, a happy time for peaceable President McKinley. In Spain the government fell and the new regime offered Cuba self-government within the empire. The new atmosphere of conciliation prompted McKinley to approve a friendly gesture, a visit to Havana by an American battleship, the *Maine*. When the great gleaming white ship eased into Havana harbor on January 25, 1898, courteous Spaniards welcomed her with a case of Jerez sherry and much polite palaver. The next evening, at his first diplomatic dinner in the White House, the President sat the Spanish minister next to him, though nine other envoys had protocol precedence. Meanwhile, Hearst and Pulitzer competed in wild vituperation. *Journal* headlines, sometimes in red, sometimes printed from carved wood blocks because no metal type was large enough, blazed away at Spanish imperfections. Equally heinous crimes, Hearst seemed to be saying, were "Spaniards Butcher Hundreds of Helpless Starving Cubans" and "Americans Taunted in Havana Streets." What could be wrong with President McKinley, pictured in the *Journal* as an enormous snail, refusing to act? Roosevelt said privately that McKinley "has no more backbone than a chocolate eclair." Hearst thundered publicly, "There are little Cuban babies crawling about in the dirt without a rag on their brown bodies, without a crust in their poor little hollow stomachs, that have more natural courage than Mc-Kinley. . . ."

The *World* had begun to imitate the *Journal* in earnest as early as the spring of 1896. A new Spanish general, Valeriano Weyler, had been sent from Madrid to suppress the rebelling peasants, and Hearst quickly had him nominated "the prince of all cruel generals this century has seen," a "fiendish despot." The *World* traced "The Hideous History of Old Spain" up to current scenes of women clubbed in the streets, massacres, and garrotings. The *World*'s own feature writer, Nellie Bly (who had earned her spurs as a reporter by racing around the world in less than eighty days), volunteered to lead a regiment with all women officers against the tyrant. Somehow a dispatch describing Weyler as a decent and capable man sneaked into the *World*, but soon a new man on the scene got the tone right: "Blood on the roadsides, blood in the fields, blood on the doorsteps, blood, blood, blood! The old, the young, the weak, the crippled, all are butchered without mercy. . . . Not a word from Washington! Not a sign from the President!" But it was hard to beat the *Journal* headline, "Feeding Prisoners to Sharks," and the *Journal* story of Spaniards "roasting twenty-five Catholic priests alive."

On the night of February 15, 1898, the *Maine* blew up in Havana harbor; 260 of her 350 officers and men were killed. The government in Madrid and the Queen Regent sent their regrets and sympathy and official Havana went into mourning. The dead were honored, the wounded cared for.

Returning home from the theater, Hearst got a message to call his office.

> "Hello," he said. "What is the important news?"
>
> "The battleship *Maine* has been blown up in Havana Harbor," the editor replied.
>
> "Good heavens, what have you done with the story?"
>
> "We have put it on the first page, of course."
>
> "Have you put anything else on the front page?"
>
> "Only the other big news," said the editor.
>
> "There is not any other big news," Hearst said. "Please spread the story all over the page. This means war."[4]

The newspaper business went wild. Over at the *World* that week one exhausted editor, existing on crackers and milk, broke under the strain, dashing madly about the offices crying "War! War!" until restrained and sent home.

Roosevelt raged. Now in Washington as assistant navy secretary, he quickly leaped to the conclusion that "the *Maine* was sunk by an act of dirty treachery on the part of the Spaniards." But McKinley said, "I don't propose to be swept off my feet by the catastrophe." "I have been through one war," he said, "I have seen the dead piled up, and I do not want to see another." He called for an investigation—which dragged on and on. In fact, the *Maine* had been a floating bomb, its forecastle packed with gunpowder and its magazines laced with shortable wires. But Hearst would not wait—the *Journal* printed diagrams of just how a Spanish "Infernal Machine" had hit the hull. Roosevelt took advantage of his superior's momentary absence one afternoon to order the Pacific squadron to sea, put the European and South Atlantic stations on alert, order immense supplies of guns and ammunition, and demand that Congress authorize the unlimited recruitment of seamen. When at last McKinley's investigation reported the cause of the sinking as an "external explosion," the die was cast. Even the *New York Times* saw no alternative to war. McKinley suffered on, offering delay and silence, sleepless, dosing himself with narcotics, breaking into tears at a White House musicale. It was no use; he finally had to come around.

The *Journal*'s front-page slogan asked, "How Do You Like the *Journal*'s War?" The paper printed an interview with Theodore Roosevelt congratulating Hearst and company. Roosevelt promptly demurred: "I never in public or private commended the *New York Journal*"— which the *World* printed on its front page, adding the comment that *Journal* war news was being "written by fools for fools." But not long after, TR told a reporter friend, "I have done all I could to bring on the war, because it is a just war, and the sooner we meet it the better. Now that it has come, I have no business to ask others to do the fighting and stay home myself."

Roosevelt, his dramatic instincts intact, took off for Cuba with his Rough Riders—western cowboys and New York swells. Hearst himself appeared one day on the deck of a steam launch off Cuba. Spot-

ting the enemy on the beach, he pulled off his pants and leapt over-
board into the surf, waving his revolver. He rushed up to twenty-nine
quivering Spaniards and, with his comrades, took them into custody.
A burial party was detailed to dispose of a few washed-up corpses,
then Hearst hustled the prisoners onto his ship, put his pants back
on, and ordered the signals raised to announce, "We have prisoners
for the fleet," as his ship steamed victoriously down the line of American battleships. It was the Fourth of July. Photographic equipment
was set up on the deck to picture the hapless Spaniards as, quickly
persuaded, they huzzahed three cheers for George Washington and
President McKinley. Hearst ordered a full meal for the lot before
delivering them, while sailors cheered, to the American warship *St.
Louis*. He got a receipt: "Received of W. R. Hearst twenty-nine
Spanish prisoners." The news was quickly dispatched to the *Journal*.

Another day, a *Journal* reporter, wounded in battle, suddenly had
a familiar comforter:

> Some one knelt in the grass beside me and put his hand on
> my fevered head. Opening my eyes, I saw Mr. Hearst, the pro-
> prietor of the New York *Journal*, a straw hat with a bright rib-
> bon on his head, a revolver at his belt, and a pencil and note-
> book in his hand. The man who had provoked the war had come
> to see the result with his own eyes and, finding one of his own
> correspondents prostrate, was doing the work himself. Slowly
> he took down my story of the fight. Again and again the tinging
> of Mauser bullets interrupted. But he seemed unmoved. The bat-
> tle had to be reported somehow.
>
> "I'm sorry you're hurt, but"—and his face was radiant with
> enthusiasm—"wasn't it a splendid fight? We must beat every
> paper in the world."[5]

Richard Harding Davis, handsome model for the famous "Gibson
Girl's" escort, arrived in Cuba—with eighty-eight other journalists—
dashingly attired with a scarf around his hat, high plastic collar, blue
coat, trousers tucked into field boots, and field glasses slung at his
side. He tried to talk his way into an early landing because unlike
the "ordinary reporters" he was really a "descriptive writer." The
general who refused him got short shrift in his stories. Davis wrote
home to tell his family how Cuba was treating him:

Dear Family: Santiago, July 1898

This is just to reassure you that I am all right. I and Marshall were the only correspondents with Roosevelt. We were caught in a clear case of ambush. Every precaution had been taken, but the natives knew the ground and our men did not. It was the hottest, nastiest fight I ever imagined. We never saw the enemy except glimpses. Our men fell all over the place, shouting to the others not to mind them, but to go on. I got excited and took a carbine and charged the sugar house, which is what is called the key to the position. If the men had been regulars I would have sat in the rear as B——— did, but I knew every other one of them, had played football, and all that sort of thing, with them, so I thought as an American I ought to help. The officers were falling all over the shop, and after it was all over Roosevelt made me a long speech before some of the men, and offered me a captaincy in the regiment any time I wanted it. He told the Associated Press man that there was no officer in his regiment who had "been of more help or shown more courage" than your humble servant, so that's all right. After this I keep quiet. I promise I keep quiet. Love to you all.

Richard[6]

Davis was with Theodore Roosevelt on what TR called "the great day of my life," July 1, 1898, when he and his irregular forces charged up a hill adjacent to the San Juan fortifications, under withering enemy fire. Watching the battle get under way, Davis thought "someone had made an awful and terrible mistake." But there came the intrepid colonel, upright in his saddle, a blue polka-dotted scarf fluttering from his sombrero "like a guidon," urging on the reluctant—"Are you afraid to stand up when I am on horseback?"—and pushing aside the careful regulars—"Let my men through, sir!"—and then waving his hat as he whooped his meager band to the crest. Roosevelt stalked about the trenches, "reveling in victory and gore," a friend reported; "Look at those damned Spanish dead," he crowed.

The New York press went wild with enthusiasm. Davis would never forget that on that day he "had the luck to be with Roosevelt." The feeling was mutual: TR gave Davis his picture, inscribed "To my fellow on the firing line." Back home, Mr. Dooley had Roosevelt laud "me brave an' fluent body guard, Richard Harding Davis."

Roosevelt came home to a hero's welcome, featured in the papers coast to coast. In that November of 1898 his famous exploits got him elected governor of New York. Campaigning in October, Roosevelt would step out into the rear platform of his train as a bugler sounded the cavalry charge. Seven uniformed Rough Riders grouped around him. "You have heard the trumpet that sounded to bring you here," he began. "I have heard it tear the tropic dawn when it summoned us to fight at Santiago." After his speech, Sergeant Buck Taylor came front and center: "I want to talk to you about mah Colonel. He kept ev'y promise he made to us and he will to you." No one seems to have taken the sergeant too literally when he concluded: "He told us we might meet wounds and death and we done it, but he was thar in the midst of us, and when it came to the great day he led us up San Juan Hill like sheep to the slaughter and so he will lead you."

The day after the election a reporter told Roosevelt that "a clear trail" ran from Albany to Washington. TR blew up at him for suggesting that ambition. But the next spring he went out to New Mexico to a Rough Rider reunion and came back talking about the wild greeting he got—"exactly as if I had been a Presidential candidate." The *New York Times* so speculated. Roosevelt issued a denial. But the worm was working. Henry Cabot Lodge carefully outlined for Roosevelt a strategy to get him elected President in 1904. Assessing each conceivable interim alternative, Lodge concluded he had to go for the Vice Presidency in 1900. At first TR balked. "I do not like to be a figurehead," he wrote Lodge, "I should be in a cold shiver of rage at inability to answer hounds like" some of the senators. Up to that time no Vice President had ever been elected President. Roosevelt told New York's boss Thomas Platt that he "would greatly rather be anything, say a Professor of History." But Platt and company dearly desired to get Roosevelt out of New York; they intimated that he might not be renominated for governor.

Roosevelt wavered. At first, McKinley's Washingtonians found it funny that he kept refusing an invitation that had not been tendered. "He came down here," Secretary of State John Hay wrote a friend, "with a somber resolution throned in his strenuous brow, to let McKinley and Hanna know, once for all, that he would not be Vice-

President, and found to his stupefaction that nobody in Washington, except Platt, had ever dreamed of such a thing." Face to face with the agitated Roosevelt, Hay said, "I think you are unduly alarmed. There is no instance of an election of a Vice President by violence." Secretary of War Elihu Root smiled through Roosevelt's denials and said, "Of course not, Theodore, you're not fit for it." McKinley himself chuckled softly "about some of T.R.'s characteristics." He decided to leave the choice to the convention.

Roosevelt did go to the convention—"I would be looked on as a coward if I did not go." He stalked in slightly late wearing his big black Rough Rider hat, to the profound excitement of the assemblage. That night western delegates stormed up and down outside Hanna's hotel suite shouting, "We want Teddy!" An anxious national party official telephoned Washington to report: "The Roosevelt boom is let loose and it has swept everything. . . . The thing is going pellmell like a tidal wave." He sought instruction, referring to a base law of the politician's power: "We cannot afford to have it said that something was done in spite of ourselves." The word came back: "The President has no choice. . . . The choice of the convention will be his choice; he has no advice to give." Hanna was furious: "Don't any of you realize that there's only one life between that madman and the Presidency?"

The midnight scrambles that typify national convention politics (generating the nervous exhaustion that has led to many a bizarre choice) rattled on. Roosevelt was nominated in a rafter-packed session to the music of tumultuous demonstrations. It was announced that he had received every vote but one—his own. Then he lit out after Bryan.

The Press's President

The following March, Roosevelt, the newly inaugurated Vice President, presided over the Senate for only four days before that body adjourned until December; TR went off to vacation at Oyster Bay. On September 6, 1901, President McKinley, receiving citizens in Buffalo's Temple of Music, reached out to shake hands with a man who suddenly shot him twice in the body. As the assassin was wrestled to the ground, McKinley managed to say, "Don't let them hurt him." The President died on September 14. The new President led the nation into a period of intense and prolonged mourning.

As ever, Roosevelt recovered. Not given to humble hesitation, he behaved as if he had been elected President by a landslide. Action after action zipped out of the White House—on conservation, the tariff, trusts, and banking, on the Philippines and Panama. "This country cannot afford to sit supine on the plea that . . . we are helpless in the presence of the new conditions," he said. His cousin Franklin remembered TR roaring around in exasperation—"Oh, if I only could be President and Congress too for just ten minutes." He managed to move against the big corporations without totally alienating them. "The criminal rich and the fool rich," he said, "will do all they can to beat me," and indeed they did carp against his as a "political adventurer." But he moved away from trust-busting to regulation, which the capitalists learned to live with and even to exploit. And when Mark Hanna threatened to run for the Presidency himself in 1904, Roosevelt went around him, maintaining connections with alternative bosses, exercising his patronage power to good effect.

His words—millions of them—poured forth in equal volume. He got on famously with his friends the reporters, providing office space for them in the White House and an endless stream of exciting news. He took fancy-pants ambassadors hiking through the wilds of Rock Creek Park, and when he went hunting he took the press along, hyping his image all the way. "The first bear must fall to my rifle," he said. "This sounds selfish but you know the kind of talk there will be in the newspapers about such a hunt, and if I go it must be a success, and the success must come to me." Famous and popular, Roosevelt enjoyed the endorsement of such papers as the *New York Sun*, six weeks before the convention in 1904: "RESOLVED: That we emphatically endorse and affirm Theodore Roosevelt. Whatever Theodore Roosevelt thinks, says, does, or wants is right. Roosevelt and Stir 'Em Up. Now and Forever; One and Inseparable!" With no trouble at all he got the nomination. But, sensing the movement of the pulse of politics into its moral phase, he stood Presidentially above the hustlings. The Democrats nominated clean but dull Alton B. Parker, an obscure New York judge, whose major political virtue was his personal virtue. Roosevelt was finally smoked out on a morals charge—that he had accepted large campaign contributions from businessmen who expected to be repaid in nonprosecutions. Privately Roosevelt fumed. "What infernal liars the independent press does contain," he wrote a friend. The "professionally virtuous creatures like the *Times, Evening Post,* etc." were "venomously attacking" his upright friends; the "mugwump's scoundrelly yell" was "designed to divert attention" from "eminent purists" in their own camp—underhanded bosses and millionaires. Only near the end of the campaign did TR, demonstrating his rhetorical flexibility, take to the stump with righteous indignation and self-defense. He won in a walk and moved into his first elected term.

After the election of 1904, Democrat Parker announced he would not run again, opening a way for Bryan to cap that year's appeal to what he called "the moral sense" of the nation. But Roosevelt, despite all his love of the Presidency as a "bully pulpit," once elected revealed again his old appetite for a fight. His inaugural address called for "the vigor and effort without which the manlier and hardier virtues wither away," and the term that followed sparkled with fighting action as Roosevelt championed more and more progressive reforms. The ripsnorting battle of 1900 was his kind of politics.

Roosevelt's successful rise to the Presidency, confirmed in his election in 1904, was fueled by his remarkable relationship with the reporters of his day. Had the Yellow Press not found the style to tell his story, Roosevelt's determined political opponents might well have succeeded in muscling him off the national stage. Instead, he brought to popular journalism just the vigor and flash it needed. In the course of that adventure Roosevelt put the story of politics as war on the front page. There it would *stay.* Its vivid imagery and dramatic form would shape political realities long after Roosevelt was dead.

*Television news is
the major teacher
of mass America
concerning politics.
Monumental but not
insuperable difficul-
ties confront that
task.*

14

Civic Education

ONE CAN PICTURE Thomas Jefferson seated at his desk in Monticello, his collar loose and the glassed doors open to catch a bit of the evening breeze at the end of a hot August day. The candlelight flickers gently on the old wood, on his lined, attentive face, on the sunbrowned hand that moves his pen across the page. He pauses, looks out into the gathering darkness. His mind's eye sees the pen and hand moving across another page, nineteen years ago, inking into the second paragraph of the Declaration, ". . . governments are instituted among men, deriving their just powers from the consent of the governed . . . ." Jefferson sighs and returns to the letter he is writing. We hear his mind composing as he writes:

> I do most anxiously wish to see the highest degrees of education given to the highest degrees of genius, and to all degrees of it, so much as may enable them to read and understand what is going on in the world, and to keep their part of it going on right: for nothing can keep it right but their own vigilant and distrustful superintendence. I do not believe with the Rochefoucaulds

and Montaignes, that fourteen out of fifteen men are rogues: I believe a great abatement from that proportion may be made in favor of general honesty. But I have always found that rogues would be uppermost, and I do not know that the proportion is too strong for the higher orders, and for those who, rising above the swinish multitude, always contrive to nestle themselves into the places of power and profit. These rogues set out with stealing the people's good opinion, and then steal from them the right of withdrawing it, by contriving laws and associations against the power of the people themselves. Our part of the country is in considerable fermentation, on what they suspect to be a recent roguery of this kind. They say that while all hands were below deck mending sails, splicing ropes, and every one at his own business, and the captain in his cabin attending to his log book and chart, a rogue of a pilot has run them into an enemy's port. . . .

For my part, I consider myself now but as a passenger, leaving the world and its government to those who are likely to live longer in it. That you may be among the longest of these, is my sincere prayer . . . .

What would Jefferson, transplanted to our time, think of the American multitude and of the prospects for our civic education? Could his sanguine intelligence comprehend the masses of the propertyless, the blacks, the immigrants, the women, and the young people who have come crowding into the electorate? In the United States today there are more than a thousand "functional illiterates" for every soul alive in Boston the day Jefferson worried over the degrees of genius and the proportion of rogues. The minimasses of his day—that "swinish multitude"—were largely unfranchised; our contemporary hordes can vote if they want to.

That is the central fact confronting civic education today. No reasonable writing from the Federalist Papers on down has supposed that the great public can be educated into expertise or persuaded to devote most of its time and attention to public affairs. Indeed, there are reasonable reasons for hoping it never will; Hitler had his people pretty well involved. Rather, the problem is one of learning readiness. When the time comes for the people to judge, will they bring to the judging such knowledge and values and interest to choose, if not the best, at least leaders good enough to keep the ship afloat? If we cannot make Everyman a Solon, can we at least equip him for the "vigilant and distrustful superintendence" Jefferson thought essential?

Who Are Those People?

It is a tribute to American teacherdom that they have tried as hard as they have to find out who their students are—though it is a bit disconcerting that all those researchers have yet to tell us definitively how to teach reading to grade school kids. But compared to journalists and college professors, "educators" are hell-bent to understand the audience. In Ron Powers's *The Newscasters*, Richard Salant sounds very much like a professor irritated at being asked to pass out course evaluation forms: "I really don't know and I'm not interested. . . . I take a very flat elitist position. Our job is to give people not what they want, but what we decide they ought to have. That depends on our accumulated news judgment of what they need." Newspapers sometimes do surveys asking people what they like and would like more of (people know how they are supposed to answer that), and the circulation department has a rough idea of market demographics, but when print journalists are asked to imagine what their own readers are like, they go blank. The ready rationale is professionalism: the surgeon does not inquire of the patient where to cut; the lawyer does not ask his client when to move for a mistrial; the minister does not poll his congregation on what sort of gospel they would like today. Even a little knowledge of the audience could be a dangerous thing if it warped the journalist's professional judgment away from truth-telling to popularity pandering. Better to craft the best possible product and let who wants it take it.

The great exception is television market research, and television news is the great medium for reaching the politically unwashed. Polls in 1975–76 indicated that three out of four Americans say they get most of their news from television and half say they get *all* their news there. Sizable majorities also say they "trust" television news more than other sources. People untouched by higher (i.e., later) education are far more likely to say they rely on television than are the cognoscenti. Compared with the circulation of any newspaper or magazine, the number of sets turned on to television news is enormous—tens of millions. Even more significant for potential civic education are the vast masses who, fully equipped for television reception, do not yet tune in the news. For the 23 million "functional illiterates," it is reasonable to suppose that television and radio are the only now available links to national politics. What all this adds up to is the machinery, the broad public predisposition, and the resource to revolutionize popular civic education in the United States. What makes it all the more curious is that the television industry knows so little about how people relate to the news. Even those who are unwilling merely to humph away the topic with a professional shrug have to fall back on conventional wisdom, typically agreeing that the public is (a) dumb—the proverbial Kansas City milkman who moves his lips as he reads—and (b) shrewd—the proverbial old Yankee crinkleface who can tell a silk purse from a sow's ear. Typically, these clashing images pop up when the quality of television news is questioned, the first to imply that the message suits the messagee and the second to imply that he can make sense of whatever he gets. The dumb public theme reinforces the prescription, "Give them what they want"; the shrewd public theme reinforces the caution, "The viewers won't stand for that."

Television market research churns out data on the number of sets tuned into a given channel at a given time, electrically recorded. There are numerous technical difficulties—high proportions of busted meters; rapid turnover; underrepresentation of poor, rich, away from home, and foreign language viewers. Neil Hickey in the May 8, 1976, *TV Guide* describes the fall of 1975 when the machinery seemed to show an unprecedented 6 percent drop in household viewing, "the news hit like a thunderbolt hurled down from Parnassus to wreak confusion on the innocents below." Just as the critics were gearing up their indignant explanations, centering on the supposedly abysmal quality of the programs, the Nielsen company explained that a handful of aberrant zero-viewing households had temporarily botched the findings; soon the sets-on figures were back to normal. Even more error-prone is the diary technique: viewers are asked to write down what programs they watch, a family novelty which soon wears off, tempting the diarists to put off the task till the end of the week or month, when, perhaps with the help of *TV Guide*, they struggle to remember what was flickering forth when. But even if these numbers were perfectly accurate (and they are, of course, taken very seriously by those who buy and sell the advertising), they give no help at all to program makers trying to understand what kind of connection, if any, they are establishing with the people at the other end of the tube. Like figures on enrollment in college courses, the numbers stand mute on the crucial question—the question of educational effect.

An implausible substitute for science in this research is casual acquaintance. Like other Americans, reporters and broadcasters tend strongly to party with their own class and race and neighborhood. Earnest forays across these boundaries can perhaps give the journalist some sense of how he is being received, but as a regular event Harry Reasoner is not to be found incognito in a waterfront bar taking surreptitious notes as he watches himself with the dockworkers. In the scale from mass to elite the journalist's attention is focused upward, where the newsmakers are. On the campaign trail the boys are isolated in the bus or outside experiencing the people as the candidate himself does, in crowds and momentary encounters. Even more restrictive are the peculiar schedules of the journalist's life which cut him off from the popular flow. Typically, the *Washington Post* reporter is hard at it in the office with his typewriter as America settles down to watch the evening news—and the evening newscasters are at the studio. More bizarre yet is the life of the morning television journalists. Rising in the dead of night, whisked in their limousines to the studio, they labor away toward dawn—every weekday dawn— to compose and present a refreshing version of the news. According to Robert Metz in *The Today Show*, the performers "knew that theirs was a world apart. Working in the predawn hours and sleeping during the day meant that, except for the people they knew on the show, almost everyone else in their lives, including family, existed on a different planet." By 1976 Barbara Walters had been at that for almost sixteen years. This weird existence presses the sufferers together like combat soldiers. In *We're Going to Make You a Star*, Sally Quinn reports that she and Hughes Rudd, fellow fighters for the "CBS Morning News," meeting to ride to the studio, had a standard greeting: "Every day the first thing one of us asked the other was if he had gotten enough sleep. Sleep was everything. It was our major preoccupation. If I wasn't sleeping I was trying to sleep or worrying about whether or not I would be able to sleep." If they were lucky, sleep came in the afternoon light and deepened through America's dinner hour.

The professor's "eat-with-the-students" routine is rarely an option for the journalist. R. W. Apple gets his sanity bolstered by eating from time to time with a cellist friend, and *Newsweek's* Hal Bruno grabs at chances to pick bluegrass with his musical pals. But the normal rhythm of their lives is abnormal. And when the journalist does manage to get together with a civilian friend, odds are the conversation centers on topics other than how they affect one another professionally.

There is a little shaky evidence that newsmen who imagine a friendly reader report good news more accurately than bad and that those who imagine a critical reader do bad news better. But former *New York Times* reporter Robert Darnton probably has it about right when he argues in the spring 1975 *Daedalus* that "whatever their subliminal 'images' and 'fantasies,' newspapermen have little contact with the general public and receive almost no feedback from it. . . . All too often, 'publishing a story can be like dropping a stone in a bottomless pit: you wait and wait, but you never hear the splash.'"

As always when information is lacking on a salient matter, supposition slips in. For instance, take the question of "media power." Early critics of television raised the Spectre Enormous—mass hypnotism by manipulative Svengalis at the controls. Dan Schorr in *Clearing the Air* worries about that today:

> By forging a magic electronic circle, coast to coast, television has created a national séance. Millions sit figuratively holding hands as they are exposed together to a stream of images and suggestions, mixed-up facts and fancies, playing more on their senses than their intellects. Television may be on its way to doing in America what religious mysticism has done in Asia—dulling the sense of the objective and tangible and making the perceived more important than the fact. There is at least a superficial similarity in the trancelike state that accompanies both experiences.

Schorr's speculation could be right, but the standard reasons for thinking so leap over some deep logical gaps. Exposure does not equal influence: if anything is known about human communication, that is known. Effort does not equal power: the fact that millions of dollars, millions of hours, millions of gallons of sweat and tears go pouring into the persuasive enterprise tells us nothing reliable about impact. One could raise the same questions about the nation's vast higher education business. In his darker moments Robert Hutchins used to wonder whether it was not all just babysitting—keeping the adolescents safely off the streets while their limbs lengthened and their neurons synapsed.

What is known—and what we professors find hard to hold in mind— is that the audience for news is a *volunteer* audience. To cut me off, a student has to walk out in the middle of class, which can be kind of embarrassing for him and for me. The news reader has but to let his eye slide a little; the viewer has but to touch the switch. His particular teacher will never know that he was the particular one who tuned out. No examination looms ahead at the end of the term. He will not need a letter of recommendation from Walter Cronkite. If he attends, absorbs, believes, remembers, and acts on what he has learned, it is because he wants to. Like voting, political news is something the citizen can take or leave. Professors who approach television with what Anthony Smith in the winter 1978 *Daedalus* calls a "combination of disdain and social grief" might pause and remember that it is not for them as it is for us: rows of ready perceptors with nothing else to do.

There is evidence that the voluntary quality of television viewing is becoming more significant. Television sets are nearly universally available now, not only in homes but increasingly in motels, bars, airports, offices, schoolrooms, dormitories, hospitals, prisons, and even cars. Ninety-eight percent of homes wired for electricity have at least one television set, and the statistics on multitelevisioned homes are galloping upward. New technologies—UHF, cable, videodisc and cassettes, videorecorder—increasingly make it possible for the viewer to get at many more broadcasting channels and to see what he wants when he wants it. The growth of public broadcasting and the adaptation of movies for television increase the range of *kinds* of programming. Radio, with an average of *four* sets per home plus 74 million in cars as early as 1969, broadens the range even further.

What do the volunteers do with all this opportunity? That, too, appears to be in rapid change, though the evidence is shaky. Back in the early years of television it seemed plausible to believe with Marshall McLuhan that television, in contrast to radio, was a highly involving, "participatory" medium. McLuhan in *Understanding Media* thought that "radio will serve as background-sound or as noise-level control, as when the ingenious teenager employs it as a means of privacy. TV will not work as background. It engages you. You have to be *with* it." But in the 1930s radio had been an engaging, with-it medium: one remembers the family gathered around the cathedral-style receiver, listening intently to the Mercury Theater of the Air or William L. Shirer, entranced, staring through the furniture. Early television was like that: the set was small, black and white, and the picture jiggly—you had to watch closely to see what those little people were doing. The family stared together over their warmed aluminum plates—a household communion, a séance of sorts. Now radio is everywhere, from the elevator to the sidewalk to the trees in Forest Lawn Cemetery; it is fed into the telephone to keep you calm while on hold. Increasingly, the same thing is happening to television. Today's "ingenious teenager" does his homework while "watching" television. In England televiewing is becoming "a *secondary* activity"; in the United States, according to Michael Robinson in the summer 1977 *The Public Interest*, the audience for television news "is an *inadvertent* one—which, in large proportion, does not come purposely to television for news, but arrives almost accidentally, watching the news because it is 'on' or because it leads into or out of something else." Michael Arlen in *The View from Highway 1* catches the contemporary mode in a morning scene:

> On the television screen, soldiers were now walking slowly down a country road. "Patrols fan out from the city, looking for insurgents," said a voice.
> Mother said, "Joey, you finish the toast."
> Joey said, "How come I have to do the toast when I don't eat toast?"
> "Do you think it might be in the laundry?" Father said. "It might have fallen to the floor of the closet, and somebody might have put it in the laundry." Father passed by Clarice on his way out of the kitchen. "Don't talk all day on the phone, Clarice," he said. Clarice rolled her eyes at the ceiling.

Frank Blair said, "Armored cars and Russian-made tanks broke up the disorder. A curfew and a state of national emergency have been proclaimed."

There was the sound of a crash from the back of the house.

"Eggs are ready, everyone!" Mother said. On the television screen, two tanks were firing into a brick wall. "Fix the set. That's too loud, Joey," she said. "Everyone! The eggs are getting cold . . . ."

Father and children left for work and school.

Outside the window, two robins padded on the snow. The rumble of the dishwasher filled the room. Mother sprayed the skillet with a jet of hot water. Charles Colson said, "There was certain information of that nature which was passed to us in the White House in 1972." The refrigerator clicked on. The dishwasher churned. The telephone began to ring. "Hi, Beth," Mother said. "Wait a minute while I turn the TV down. We were just listening to the morning news."

New and striking research by Robert L. Stevenson and Kathryn P. White is consistent with Arlen's impression. The standard question asking people "where you get most of your news about what's going on in the world today" (64 percent said television in 1976) is knockable on a number of counts, but the main knock is that most of nothing is still nothing. Stevenson and White cite a careful study by the Surgeon General's Scientific Advisory Committee on Television and Social Behavior—a national sample of six thousand adults kept viewing diaries for two weeks. About half reported they did not watch one network evening news program in those fourteen days. About a fifth said they watched six or more times. By contrast, 90 percent said they had read yesterday's newspaper. But another ingenious study casts strong doubt not only on the meaningfulness of the Nielsen ratings but also on these diary and self-report estimates. Twenty Kansas City families let cameras be set up in their homes to videotape the watchers and what they watched for six days. On questionnaires asking how much viewing they did, yesterday and over the six days, the families inflated the actuality by 40 to 50 percent. And Nielsenites would be shocked to learn that almost half the time the evening news shows were blazing forth into these living rooms, no human eye at all was focused thereupon. Stevenson and White's own careful national research gives the same rough picture: half of America does not watch the evening news, one in four watch it occasionally (one to four times in two weeks), one in fifty watch it every night (thirteen or more times), one in a hundred confess to every-night viewing at "full attention."

In this light it is not too surprising that many a message misses. Thomas E. Patterson and Robert D. McClure in *The Unseeing Eye* note that a *majority* of viewers cannot remember two minutes later what was being advertised on the commercial they saw two minutes before. Similarly, of people who said they had recently watched the evening network news, two out of three could not recall accurately even one news story. And with respect to the 1972 Presidential campaign, "if people only watched network news, they did not come to know more than people who ignored the news media"—print and broadcast—"during the fall of 1972." Plenty of other evidence supports Anthony Smith's view that "the gentle release from the embrace of television" is a real happening, if ever we were so embraced.

On a good old educational principle these lessons bear repeating. Both the enthusiastic ad seller and the indignant intellectual have let the facts slip by them. Television today is a gigantic enterprise. The prime-time advertising rates waft ever higher, and the politicians pant after coverage. Frank Mankiewicz in *Remote Control* reports that the 1976 presidential race was "the first campaign in which both candidates virtually ignored other ways to reach the voter, and concentrated almost all of their time, energies, staff resources, and money on the ways in which they would be seen—and heard—on television." But three truths now stare us in the face. First, the impact of television news has been grossly overdrawn by the medium's friends and enemies. Second, for many millions of Americans television is the *only* source of news about the candidates. And third, there are millions more out there—their right to vote in hand—who are not even being reached by television.

Before leaping to the professor's usual conclusion, that people don't watch because the stuff is not worth watching, we might pause to notice where these truths put all of us who think of ourselves as educators. It turns out that all our national smarts and all our sophisticated machinery have as yet made a pretty modest dent in persuasion's first obstacle: getting cognized. The call for volunteers goes begging. The rattle of the civic drum, out there in the town square, cannot be heard throuh the tavern door, and when Paul Revere hoots by, down slam the windows. To get the American mule's attention, we find, is harder than we thought. To put the matter positively, there is a job to be done and the tools at hand to do it.

The Ego Strategies

The dictionary says the archaic meaning of a "lecture" is something read aloud. In olden times when books were rare and literacy more so, the lecturer proclaimed from a script positioned on his lectern—a primitive teleprompter. If he was thought to believe in what he spoke, he was a professor (from *profiteri*, to declare publicly). Time passed and status passed to the professor who wrote his own material, collecting his thoughts and facts in an original composition—a sermon (from *serere*, to join, link together). Even more impressive came to be the professor who got out and did his own research (from *circare*, to travel through, traverse) and lectured on that. And added points accrued if the professor had so mastered his material that he could throw away the script and wing it (*ad libitum*, in accordance with one's wishes).

Like badges deck today's newsmen: the reader only, for all his acting embellishment, is an announcer, a town crier braying whatever is handed him. A notch above is the professing journalist, who attests to the truth of what he says. The writer frames the message he speaks, and the reporter fares out and carries back his own reports. The commentator and the interviewer appear, at least, as spontaneous thinkers-along-with, readers from the heart.

Whichever of these stances the viewer recognizes in the face of the newsspeaker, a plausible reason for attending is to get information. Education as essentially a conveyance affecting the student's knowledge is an old and wide theme in our culture. It links with the theory of democracy through the concept of informed consent. Normatively speaking, consent from ignorance can never be genuine, no more so than conversion by the sword. Pragmatically speaking, an ignorant citizenry is dangerously unready when the time comes for choice, the key citizen choice being election. Fanatics are always available, Lippmann in *Liberty and the News* saw, and

> both in war and revolution there seem to operate a kind of Gresham's Law of the emotions, in which leadership passes by a swift degeneration from a Mirabeau to a Robespierre; and in war, from a high-minded statesmanship to the depths of virulent, hating jingoism.

How does that happen?

> The cardinal fact always is the loss of contact with objective information. Public as well as private reason depends upon it. Not what somebody says, not what somebody wishes were true, but what is beyond all our opining, constitutes the touchstone of our sanity.

If political sanity depends on voters knowing facts, a great many Americans are political neurotics. Scattered polls over the years since World War II hint at the magnitude of the remaining educational opportunity, even allowing for the fact that some respondents may say they "don't know" just to get the quiz over with. Roughly *half* or more of The People don't know *how many* U. S. Senators there are from each state, don't know that U. S. Representatives come up for reelection every two years, don't know who their Congressman is, don't know who their Senators are, don't know that the United States is a member of NATO. Roughly two-thirds to three-fourths or more don't know what the three branches of the federal government are, don't know what the Bill of Rights is, don't know what important event happened in this country in 1776, don't know the name of the national anthem. A survey published in 1974 (done by "The National Assessment of Educational Progress") showed that of people twenty-six to thirty-five years old, less than half know how to vote or knew how Presidential candidates are nominated. Half the seventeen-year-olds thought the President can appoint members of Congress. In 1976 nearly all young people knew who President Ford was—but two-thirds of the thirteen-year-olds and a quarter of the seventeen-year-olds didn't know that he was a Republican. Nor is the problem confined to wayward youth: back in the 1960s, a third of The People thought the

John Birch Society was a leftist outfit. Many another survey shows that high fractions are ignorant of who the Vice President is, who the candidates are, what they stand for, what standard political concepts like tariffs or price supports mean.

Professional reporters, perpetually marinating in the brine of politics, keep getting shocked by public ignorance. In May 1976 David Broder took a brief respite from the campaign to reflect in the July-August *Democratic Review:*

> I can remember my absolute astonishment at a Gallup Poll that was taken immediately after the Democratic convention in 1960 which showed that, at that point, more than 50% of the voters knew for the first time that John Kennedy was a Roman Catholic. That fact had been the starting point for every political discussion among Democratic Party insiders, people who were attentive to politics, for four years, going back to the Bailey-Sorensen memo about why Kennedy should be the vice-presidential nominee. You cannot exaggerate the difference between the perceptions and awareness of those who are part of the attentive public and those who are ultimately going to make the decision in the general election.

Television news puts out some corrective input, with respect to Presidential campaigning. About 40 percent of the evening news stories from September 18 to November 6, 1972, were campaign stories, according to Patterson and McClure in *The Unseeing Eye.* Earlier in the year, when voters were making their key nomination decisions, coverage was spread more thinly. But even at the fall apex, only little scraps of network time were dovted to what voters needed to know: information relevant to comparing future Presidents. Over those 18 nights, at about 22 minutes of news each program, ABC gave us a total of 19 minutes 30 seconds; CBS, 16 minutes 24 seconds; and NBC, 8 minutes and 5 seconds on "the candidates' key personal and leadership qualifications for office." There were more drops in the bucket on "key issues of the election": ABC, 35 minutes 19 seconds; CBS, 46 minutes 20 seconds; and NBC, 26 minutes 14 seconds. By contrast, each network broadcast more than two hours of news on the campaign as a horse race—rallies, motorcades, polls, strategies, and the like. At the height of the 1976 primary season—back when the race had a lot of hard runners—between the New Hampshire primary in February and the Pennsylvania primary in April, Jimmy Carter got several lions' shares of news attention: 43 percent of network coverage, according to a paper Patterson presented in 1977 to the American Political Science Association annual meeting. Jackson was next with 18 percent, and Harris, Bayh, and Shriver got 4, 3, and 2 percent, respectively. (Newspaper and magazine coverage was somewhat *more* out of balance.) Whatever the broadcasters' intentions, the predominant *operative* criteria were: winners and pictures.

The viewer tuning in for facts to guide his choice would, therefore, have to pick his political nuggets from a great gravel pile of political irrelevancy. Even then, most of what he would get would not be facts "beyond all our opining" but rather candidate opinions on issues—notoriously poor predictors of Presidential action. And television's felt duty (imposed and voluntary) to give a "balanced" account means that a clear expression of one opinion impels presentation of at least one more, subtracting yet more time from the crucial questions: who are these guys, where are they coming from, what are they likely to do to us?

Why don't the people and their educators do better? A beginning explanation focuses on the *costs* of getting and giving information. Most people have a lot of demands on their time and, more significantly, on their attention. The old image of the dozing citizenry, dawdling away its leisure while Rome burns, waiting to be tickled and poked into political life, is, in modern America, a romantic myth. So is the idea that the rich new professionals, free at last from the chains of necessity, lie around in their lawn chairs between traipses on the golf course. So is the picture of youth hippiedom wallowing away the best years of its lives. Teenagers are entering the work force 2.5 times as fast as babies are entering the American world. Close to half the grown-up women are working away from home. Men with a little time left over from their main jobs take on another one, and your average American worker changes jobs a dozen times in his career. Forty percent work overtime on the job, and, in more and more one-parent families, double-time at home (Rosabeth Moss Kanter, "Work in a New America," in *Daedalus*, Winter 1978).

In *Working* Studs Terkel quotes steelworker Mike LeFevre: "It isn't that the average working guy is dumb. He's tired, that's all." Here is how he relates to television:

> When I get home, I argue with my wife a little bit. Turn on TV, get mad at the news. (laughs.) I don't even watch the news that much. I watch Jackie Gleason. I look for any alternative to the ten o'clock news. I don't want to go to bed angry. Don't hit a man with anything heavy at five o'clock. He just can't be bothered. This is his time to relax. The heaviest thing he wants is what his wife has to tell him.

"He just can't be bothered." The cost is too high. Scholar Anthony Downs in *An Economic Theory of Democracy* puts it this way:

> In general, it is irrational to be politically well-informed because the low returns from data simply do not justify their cost in time and other scarce resources. Therefore many voters do not bother to discover their true views before voting, and most citizens are not well enough informed to influence directly the formulation of those policies that affect them.

That is not true just for the steelworkers of the world. "Ironically," notes Ben Bagdikian in *The Information Machines*, "professionalization of occupations with its high income rewards has not produced a simple expansion of daily leisure time but an increasing intrusion of career into almost every available segment of waking hours." But the same thing happens at the other end of the communications connection. Leonard Woolf sees "great mental dangers in journalism," the "most virulent" of which affects editors (and, without a doubt, television producers):

> It creates a kaleidoscopic, chaotic, perpetual motion rhythm of the mind. As soon as you have produced one number of your paper, you have to begin thinking and planning the next. Your mind gets into the habit of opening and shutting at regular intervals of 24 hours or seven days like the shells of a mussel or the shutters of a camera. . . . (*Beginning Again*)

Busy, busy, busy. Broadcaster and broadcastee rein in the reach of their temporal and spatial imaginations as the immediacies thunder through their heads. To stand back from all that, and *think* about it, costs more than it turns out to be worth.

What that means for democracy today and tomorrow is pure and simple: we have to begin where we are. Democracy's virtue is realism. It is not the best form of government; it is the best real form of government. It makes itself up out of what it has got. Nothing is to be gained by lashing the public, the educators, or the televisors with the whips of scorn—at least we know that much about educating: scorn inhibits receptivity. Defensive posturing of the "we-know-our-business" variety does not work either. Nor does the romantic dream of the Wise People as stand-ins for God, capable of alchemizing whatever dross they are handed into civic gold. When democracy works, which is far from all the time, it is essentially a learning enterprise by which the society comes to see what government can and cannot do to make life better, happier, more just for more of us. It is a second-best business, edging toward second-best values like freedom and fairness, equality and rights. There can be health in it, but no perfection; it struggles to establish *conditions* for virtue.

Journalism has, I think, contributed to perfectionistic thinking about American politics in curious ways. Polls ask people their opinions (70 percent have an opinion on anything) and thus give the impression that knowledge stands there behind. The television ratings wildly exaggerate popular cognition—it is so easy to slip over from "x" number of sets on to "x" number of people watching to "x" number obsessively glued to their tubes. But a profounder distortion may be an ironic consequence of journalism's skepticism. Network television is our first really national news facility, and it may not be accidental that public skepticism about national leaders grew up with television. But a supposition underlying the skeptical mode is that performance could be—and even usually is—much better than the individual lapse being reported. A myth of general competence is conveyed, reinforced by the apparently exceptional character of the immediate error.

Now, as anybody knows who has kicked around with professors and professionals and literati and politicians and administrators of one kind or another, the world gets by on much less competence than the innocent suppose. We have an interest in persuading clientelia that we know what we are about. They have an interest in believing that. But one has only to listen in when doctors or lawyers or journalists hold one of their hair-down humor sessions to perceive the thin ice under the snowbank. We have not read those things that we ought to have read. We subscribe to more than we can cognize. We are far less certain than we seem, all of us authorities. Insofar as it pretends otherwise—conveying a sense of competent, thoroughly informed rationality as normal—journalism brittle-izes reputations, so that one crack shatters them. Thus also the reputation of the public flashes back and forth between dumb (the fear of George Wallace's popularity) and smart (the hope that Reagan's transfer plan would laugh him out of court). Perhaps the prime example is the anchorman himself, whose years of pithy practice make him such a good conversationalist, but whose calm and knowledgeable air probably produces in his audience the habituated conviction that the right way, the true way, the competent way is *known*.

Beginning where we are would start with acknowledging the extraordinary difficulties people experience in trying to teach one another. It would develop strategies based on the actualities of the teacher's knowledge and the student's capacity to learn. Most important, it would experiment and vigorously assess the results.

An example of experimental content on television could be coverage of busing for school integration. Frank Mankiewicz and Joel Swerdlow in *Remote Control* point out a fundamental change in our social knowledge about busing. A very few years ago busing was a theory—a rather complex theory largely born by generalization from situations different in important respects from those its application would create. Since then, busing for integration has become an *experience* for millions of American children. The authors claim it works, except in Boston. If that is true (and a thorough report by the Department of Justice backs it up), television news could surely find ways to show and tell that story, including the uncertainties. For example, they could balance Boston with Rocky Mount, North Carolina, where a whole community worked through to integration in a drama featuring such highly videoable phenomena as cheerleaders, school anthems, locker mates, and Boy's State delegations. Along a wider front, television journalists could learn to cover success without sentimentality, without romanticizing The People, without pretense of finality. Considering the enormous popularity of "how to" print publications and the myriads of Americans up against tough community problems, it might work—even in the ratings. The purpose need not be charity or encouragement or moralizing, but simply the accurate representation of realities highly salient to the viewer's round of life.

An example of experimental form is already in train: slightly longer and, more importantly, more factual and thematic pieces on the evening news. When in 1963 the networks shifted from fifteen- to thirty-minute news, it was plausible to suppose individual stories would get longer, but they did not; ninety seconds became standard. Part of the reason was the need to work in more commercials; part was the broadcasters' felt duty to cover as much as possible of the day's events. A rationale from science was that viewers have short attention spans. "What men who make the study of politics a vocation cannot do," wrote Lippmann in a slower time, "the man who has an hour a day for newspapers and talk cannot possibly hope to do. He must seize catchwords and headlines or nothing." Thus the concept of television news as a "headline service," though in fact standardized story length sacrifices the precise utility of headlining: differentiation. The barrel-bottom ratings of long programs featuring candidates or social issues seemed to confirm the traditional wisdom. Thus television got stuck, or stuck itself, in a lockstep tiptoe through one little mini-story after another. Warren Mitofsky felt the constraint in 1976: "You can't put anything on the air that you have to sit there and explain. If the picture doesn't tell its own story, forget it. It's not there long enough." That tradition dies hard, but there are hints of change. Longer-story programs like "60 Minutes" have sustained popularity and spawned imitations, and it has dawned on the mind that people sit still and watch hard for many a sporting event and sitcom. The audience for "Roots" hung in there for eight straight evenings, opening to an estimated 77,868,000 pairs of eyes and closing with all-time record-smashing 99,226,000. Conceivably, the evening news might follow the development television comedy has taken: from shows jammed with one-liners, to the series of anecdotal funny stories, to Norman Lear's half-hour connected sagas.

There is nothing virtuous per se about longer news stories, but they at least open up a chance for experiment, as the "McNeil-Lehrer Report" shows. Television already has an advantage: "Television news is more *thematic* than other types of news; only the shortest items—those less than thirty seconds—lack a didactic conclusion or message.

Especially since the development of the thirty-minute newscast, television tends to offer us 'stories,' not news items." In fact, there may be a special opportunity for imitation in television ads for Presidential candidates: ordinary commercial ads are soon forgotten (though they probably have Chinese water torture effects), but, according to Patterson and McClure, Presidential ads are much more widely and accurately attended and remembered—and the cognition centers on the information they convey rather than the style of conveyance.

Nor is it eached in stone that news interviewing has to be done as it has been done. According to Mindy Nix in "The Meet the Press Game," the press panel shows miss many an opportunity for winding out strings of information because the professional culture (fostered by the print reporters asking questions) has insisted on a narrow goal: "Their major corporate purpose is to produce a story, with appropriate credit for the network, in Monday's newspaper." The producers say they "love to make news on Sunday instead of just talking about it" and aim "to make headlines in the record-breaking interviews with national and international leaders." In better pregame skull sessions, the reporters might think through sequences, beyond the single "follow-up question," that would delve into the candidate's train of thought to produce a headline perhaps, but maybe a running story.

Arlen points out that the little interviews on the regular news shows habitually concentrate on one question: "How do you feel?" Then because the person interviewed may have trouble articulating how he feels ("Fine." "Bad."), the interviewer steps in to help him, as in this question posed to "a perplexed but amiable Soviet scientist": "After the years of oppression and danger in your homeland, and after the incredible danger and difficulty of your escape, which carried you to England ten years ago—well, perhaps you can tell us about the kind of hospitality you've met with here?" As spies and psychiatrists learned long ago, there are better ways to elicit *his* story, *his* feelings. On occasion, the interpretation can overwhelm the interpreted. Michael Robinson reports on his study:

> The survey data show unambiguously that the public did not realize how serious and significant [Ford's 1976 debates slip] the "Polish blunder" was until network news told them. According to Robert Teeter, on the night of the second debate, Ford

actually held an 11-percentage point lead over Carter [as measured by responses to the question about "who won"]. Twenty-four hours later, Ford was 45 points behind Carter—a net loss of 56 percentage points!

Television on the San Francisco sidewalk asked the emerging "live" audience how they felt, how they liked it, much as later interviewers concentrated on the affective responses of Messrs. Sadat and Begin after their historic encounter.

Education means leading out of; teachers from long ago until now have struggled actively to guide their pupils to the right answers. H.S.N. McFarland in *Psychological Theory and Educational Practice* gives an example.

> Who can tell me about Shakespeare?
> Sir, there's a Shakespeare Café in the High Street.
> Yes, but this is not a lesson on cafés, is it?
> Sir, he was the author of Romeo and Juliet.
> Yes, and what is Romeo and Juliet?
> Please sir, it's a film. I saw it on television.
> Yes, but what was it before it was a film?

Here the teacher, with his "Yes, buts," is sacrificing chance after chance to capitalize on the learner's preexisting perceptual set. McFarland says new information is only likely to click into place in the learner's mind

1. if it fits into a context that the recognizes and that matters to him,
2. if he has plenty of previous experience of the kind of thing perceived, or
3. if he has received instructions which effectively direct his attention, even if the context or the thing to be perceived is unfamiliar.

Similarly with remembering: it depends on recognition, salience, experience, and instruction. Unlike controlled laboratory contexts, "The contexts of everyday life . . . play the pianoforte of attitudes which they elicit or rather interact with, thus *determining* and *organizing*—not merely *facilitating* or *inhibiting* imprinting and recall" (David

Rapaport, "The Dynamics of Remembering," in *Reflexes to Intelligence*). Thus teachers are preached at to supply contexts, to link them to those already in the students' heads, to press outward toward a larger inclusiveness. For all our effort we very often fail, and McFarland's obstacles to success will not seem strange to the televisor:

> 1. Teachers and students become so obsessed with "covering the ground" that they do not take enough time to formulate clearly what the principles of observation are. There is a reluctance to sacrifice coverage in the hope of strengthening principle. And there can be failure to distinguish even which principles are relevant to a particular group of learners—as when a young scholar obsessed by his personal research fails to present the broader perspective that a junior student needs to begin with.
>
> 2. Most teachers try to organize their material intelligibly, but, just as they may be reluctant to sacrifice detail to principle in terms of the subject itself, so they may be reluctant to sacrifice any of the subject to the psychological perspective and capacity of the learners. It may seem easier to bemoan the learners' defects than to make concessions to them—for example, by going more slowly (or quickly), recapitulating if necessary, or sacrificing expository to discussion time.
>
> 3. The time-tabling of courses must often put organizational feasibility before ideal patterns of learning practice. Solving the routine problems of the time-table can be such a major achievement that no provision is made to confirm or link the larger units of learning. It is hoped that everything will fall into place in due course. But few learners establish broader perspectives so readily. They have to be helped towards them by special discussions and exercises.

Food for thought, there. Possible experiments. A start in recognizing why we find it so hard to do it otherwise than it is done—not because we are forced by ineluctable constraints, but because we have, too often, let habit cast its wet blanket over the reflective imagination.

Unless we are going to give up on the nation's slower students, news of Presidential campaigning must be made appealing enough to convince them to volunteer attention. Normally, that will need more than links to the past; motivation points ahead. The human ego deliberates when it can see some use for it. Citizens who can be brought to see some connection between the Presidency and their lives face forward toward a vote choice. They want information they can use in vicarious experimentation before their hands are on the levers. "Deliberation," saith John Dewey "is a dramatic rehearsal (in imagination) of various competing possible lines of action"—exactly what the expectant voter is about. He is awake already, feeling already, preferring already. Television news, which moved beyond telling the citizens what their momentary collective preferences are as the next primary approaches, to telling them what they need to know—precisely on the issue of President-choosing—might yet enlist intellectual apparatus.

Superego and Id Strategies

The evening news is like a ritual. John Chancellor says, "Good evening," in a pastoral tone, inviting the faithful to the ceremony. There follows a train of abuses and cautionary tales; we experience the mini-horrors and anxious perils, but are comforted the while: nothing is so bad that the commercials are canceled or the anchormen cast emotionally adrift. The steady, regular rhythm of the liturgy lulls along. Then Howard K. Smith appears, barely restraining his ministerial rage as he Jeremiahs various distant miscreants, a spoon of bile to spice the blandness. And then at last Walter Cronkite sighs his ambiguous benediction, that all of the above has now passed away; we should go, and sin no more.

Much news consumption is that way—a familiar little arc in the round of life. Father picks up the newspaper from the stoop, brings it in, sits in his chair, opens it, and makes a quiet, private place for himself. The radio helps Mother cook; the television light colors the children's homework. Deprived of these easing events, as when the power fails, one feels vaguely anxious, like discovering at the office that you have left your belt at home.

The news ritual plugs in America's civic religion, reinforcing values thought essential to democracy. The duty to vote—the main motivator for voting, the studies show—is a prime example: anticipations of apathy are always announced in grievous accents. Attacks on free speech are satisfyingly deplored. Progressivism, liberalism, pragmatism, egalitarianism, and Constitutionalism get their licks in. In a steadily bourgeoisifying society, demographically aging, homing, and "rising," barely diverted, in our behavior, by a few literarily renascent bohemian flashers, the media tutor us in the political proprieties as they take exceptions to deviations therefrom. Mostly mild, on rare occasions the anchormen let us know, not only by their words, but by their demeanors, how revolting they find the rule-breakers. That happened late one Saturday night: John Chancellor broke out in indignation when the President had the FBI surround the Justice Department. "I heard boots!" Chancellor explains, "The Constitution was being ripped up!"

The duty to watch the news probably works among the less educated as the duty to read the *New York Times* works among the more. The utile payoffs for most are conversational. We being an opinionated people, the news helps us with the one most critical evaluative problem democrats face: linking political ethics with political experience. Much of our talk centers on that; many of our failures trace to missing that link. Gunnar Myrdal taught us that. Decade after decade we went along believing in justice for black people and acting as if they were another, lesser species.

Political values in America stay remarkably steady. From 1956 to 1972, years of formerly unbelievable change in public policy and practice in civil rights, support for school integration perked along, year by year, at about 40 percent. Everett Ladd in *Public Opinion*, March–April 1978, marshals data to show that "continuity, not change, is the most striking feature of American values today. As a society, we are being propelled by old beliefs, not by the new ones, and it is the survival of those old beliefs that is the distinguishing feature of our time." Sensitive to change, we repeatedly overestimate the degree to which party loyalties have eroded. Possibly voters are becoming somewhat more consistent in bundling issues together, but the evidence is mushy because the questions asked in the relevant polls have been changed in ways encouraging more consistent answers. So we are not in the middle of any ethical revolution, at least as far as politics is concerned. The galling old problem is not that people believe wrongly, but that they apply uncertainly. There are many examples like this one in Flanigan and Zingale's *Political Behavior of the American Elec-*

torate: in 1971, 95 percent said they were willing to support the right of their neighbors to circulate a petition—but when it is specified that the petition favors legalizing marijuana, support drops to 52 percent.

Television news has the format to address this challenge, in the sermonette and in the little hooker the reporter is supposed to attach at the end of his story. Mostly, though, those value-event connectors are far too elegant and enigmatic to get through and take hold. Years of research on such topics as anti-anti-Semitism education shows how wonderfully adroit we are at missing the point when it sticks too close to the heart. Television's devotion to balance and diverse appeal and perhaps the reporter's inhibition against sounding naive make it hard for him to say, flat out, what democratic goods and bads are tied to this and that happening. It could be tried. Tomorrow's twenty-two minutes await the attempt.

The newsmen might even find friends for this ethical adventure among their neighbors in the network—the soap opera makers. Popular romances like "As The World Turns" plod along from one sodden tragedy to another, but they do express and reinforce the value of the human care of human beings. People are portrayed as committed to one another, locked together for better or for worse in an endless round of betrayals and reconciliations. Love wins out over sex (Nancy beats Lisa), at least eventually. There is violence aplenty, but it is dramatized as awful, not easy, as in the shoot-'em-up shows. Unlike the evening comedies, the soaps do not wrap it all up at the end in a happy package; rather, this tragedy's denouement coincides with the next one's rising action. The characters are relatively complex and individualized compared to Kojak or Hawkeye or Charlie's Angels; they are moral mixtures. Children exist and are worried over. The broad human image is of flawed people struggling to cope with one damned thing after another, drawing on such faith and strength as they can muster, hoping for some happy times, discovering, now and then, a little lightening charity. In *these* respects, soap opera faces life more honestly than much "real world" political portrayal, in which slick know-it-alls prance around displaying their certainties.

There are other powerful friends of evaluative education. The *New York Times* editorial page, says its editor John Oaks, is "the soul of the newspaper," and its "guiding principle" is "to provide leadership in what we hope and believe and consider to be the public good"

(*New York*, November 3, 1975). The *Times*'s cramping sense of responsibility and restraint may occasionally restrict publication of all the fit news, but the paper is the country's preeminent chaired professor of political ethics. Yet in its direct influence, it passes right over the heads of the great national student body. If *they* are to be reached—their life-linked superego activated—television must do it.

There are those who think that television news *is* soap opera and is on the way to becoming a "Hee Haw"–style laugh show. If the public ego is otherwise occupied and the public conscience disconnected from concrete public choices, the way to get at them is Barnum's way—through the id.

Nowadays the public is pictured as bored and alienated—58 percent "alienated" in 1977, according to the Harris poll. Back in 1966, 37 percent said "yes" when asked whether or not they felt that "what you think doesn't count much anymore." By 1973 that feeling was with 61 percent. The angry alienated were far outweighed by the passive alienated, the shruggers and turners-away.

Political journalists in 1975 and 1976 largely agreed with David Brinkley (quoted by Amitai Etzioni in *Psychology Today*, April 1978); the people are "bored, sick of a government which is remote, arrogant, pushy, costly, and self-serving." In our interviews Wallace Westfeldt had them "bored with a lot of bullshit." Lou Cannon saw the people "retreating to the joys of the private garden," like Epicurus, and the candidate managers, from Reagan's Nofziger (people are "sick to death of politicians who want to be all things to all people") to Carter's Powell (people are "tired of constant yapping") agreed. The *Wall Street Journal*'s Allan Otten says, "I just have a feeling of a huge iron screen between me and everybody out there. And they are not listening or looking."

A strong old deep theme in the journalism culture is that you had better not be bored. When reportorial boredom is unavoidable, the reporters strike back; for example, by chanting along in unison with the candidate as he intones some shopworn sobriquet. But normally reporters are professionally unbored; perhaps the main journalistic custom is "Thou shalt not be bored." One says, "We *can't* be bored," another says, "Reporters shouldn't be bored. They are not to get bored." If in fact boredom starts to infect his mind, the reporter keeps it to himself. "Dull?" says one, "Relative to what? You don't report it as 'dull today' because that's a subjective judgment." Stan Cloud expresses precisely the journalist's internalization of the antiboredom rule: "I don't think journalists ought to ever say anything is boring. I just don't think things are boring, especially any story I'm working on. If I'm on it, it ain't boring!" As the national conventions approached, journalists worried that they were up against yet another "lull before the lull." When John Lindsay begins to sense the candidates as "a drab lot, slate gray, like a flotilla of United States destroyers," he can remind himself pridefully that he is "the only reporter left who is not bored by Hubert Humphrey." The norm is to see the campaign as a "great mystery," "lots of fun," "terribly exciting," "fascinating—a helluva good story."

Eleanor Roosevelt once fell asleep while being interviewed on the "Today Show." Ron Rosenbaum in *More*, March 1978, says the network evening news audience trends older, and the oldness of it gets reinforced by the extraordinary frequency of ads for Dentu-Creme, Ex-Lax, Arthritis Pain Formula, Preparation H, Sominex, Nytol, Geritol, Tums, Polident, and Pepto-Bismol. The wisdom of the 1960s was to low-key the television experience, as in NBC's principle of "Least Objectionable Programing." The rule was not to dwell unnecessarily on anything too upsetting or annoying, which is why, Ron Powers says, "Television has had to be dragged screaming by the hair into every important 'investigative' story of the past ten years." News designers worried when an authority like Jacques Ellul warned that, by always raising problems without offering solutions, the newscasters were threatening their audiences with what another critic called "psychic overload." The candidates in 1976 put their hard-hitting commercial messages back in the cans, opting instead for "Feelin' Good" (Ford) and "Down Home" (Carter) strategies.

Obviously least-objectionalism risks boredom. These days, particularly in local news broadcasts, experiments are under way to make newswatching fun. Apparently it pays. Professional consultants are felicitously feed for this kind of advice:

> Many journalists make the error of assuming that good factual reporting alone will involve typical "concerned" citizens. The truth is that there aren't too many "concerned" listeners out there. . . .

First, we suggest that the writers avoid starting a newscast with a stark fact. Begin instead with an evocative line which will catch the ear of the listener, arouse his curiosity, and begin to "pull" him into the newscast. . . .

For example, instead of beginning with the words, "Ralph Botts has been fined $10,000 for his part in an alleged . . .", you might begin with, "Is the FBI nosing in on Chicago?" or, "He'll have to cough it up . . ." or, "*Ten thousand dollars* and the poor guy is penniless. . . ."

The whole idea is to set the listener up so he becomes interested and must listen for more. (Frank Magid, quoted in *The Newcasters*)

Television did not invent the hyped lead. "You've got to lure them into it," says a print man, "get them to read the story. Give them controversy, a circus, make it funny. You're like a circus barker—'Get 'em in! Get 'em in!'" In his 1920s novel *Scoop* Evelyn Waugh had defined news as "what a chap who doesn't care much about anything wants to read," and in *Ballyhoo* (1927) Silas Bent worried over "the inflation of matter appealing to unconscious passions and hungers. . . . The news which startles, thrills and entertains . . ."

Today we have Kelly Lange, formerly known as Dawn O'Day, anchoring newsonality for the top-rated NBC-owned television station in Los Angeles. "Look," says Lange in the *Washington Post*, December 28, 1977, "you've got your boredom. You've got your misery. You've got your tragedy. You've got to have your laughs, too. You've got to have your chuckles. Otherwise you're just asking too much of viewers who've been hassled all day long." She thinks that unlike in Washington, the newscasting "people out there [in California] really care. It's a known fact that the guys and gals out there seem to be more together as far as putting things together. . . . I *care*. I care, you know? Maybe that's silly but that's the way I am." Lange credits Tom Snyder with inventing "interplay"—bits of conversation among the newsies themselves.

"In 1976," videoanalyst Ron Powers writes in *The Newscasters*, Snyder's "News Center 4" [in New York] was quite likely the best local newscast on television: the *New York Times* of TV news." In *TV Guide*, May 8, 1976, Gerry Nadel says Snyder was discovered in Los

Angeles by an NBC senior vice president whose evaluation is, "You'll believe *anything* he says. A *great* piece of talent! . . . a guy who's sooner or later going to be the biggest star we've got!" The president of NBC thinks he's "unique . . . the kind of guy you can't help noticing." Another television executive explains Snyder's appeal, his "magic": "Because he can be so abrasive, when he suddenly turns on that boyish charm of his, you're so surprised, you just fall in love with him." The president of NBC News says, "Tom has a big future with this network." Snyder's orientation toward his profession lacks ambiguity:

> I want to be *first!* I mean, when they sit down to write the history of television and they ask, "Who did the first late-late network talk show?"—it's going to be *me*. When they write about the guy who turned around the Los Angeles and New York local-news rating, it's going to be *me*. When they write about who did the first one-minute prime time news, it's going to be *me!* Give me the first, please, not some 24-year old show. . . .

If Tom Wolfe is right—that ours is "The 'Me' Decade"—Snyder's projection must ring a bell with contemporary viewers. But Snyder, brushing his long, dark hair out of his eyes, recognizes "it could all be over tomorrow. Guys like me, we're like football players or home-run hitters. We're loved for our bodies, our attractiveness. When that wears out, you're assigned to the ash heap."

Here is Tom Snyder (with anchorman Chuck Scarborough) handling the crucial news transition at 5:59 one evening:

> Snyder: You know, it's a funny thing, and we could probably spend the rest of the hour just *talking* about this and let people come in and talk about it with us. And I understand how people don't want their children to see naked bodies on television. I-I-I *guess* I understand that, a person's home is their castle. (*Pause*) But yet they go down to Forty-second Street and see it *there*, and they complain about seeing it *here*, and last night we had a picture which I thought was a little extreme, a guy in a car with five bullet holes in his *head*—and-and nobody complained about that, but they complained about seeing a woman's *breasts* on television.

Scarborough: Well, it's . . .

Snyder: (Snappishly) It's *confusing!*

Scarborough: I think we should just give 'em the option, that's all. They have the option of going to Forty-second Street.

Snyder: Exactly. Anyway, it comes on at 6:45 and, uh—that's it. It's called Sex Fantasies. (*The Newcasters*)

Kelly Lange's caring, Tom Snyder's air of barely restrained animal energy, are two modes of pitching for the youth audience. Another is the sporty bite of Howard Cosell at ABC. The leap of fiction happens with Chevy Chase whose news spoofs on "Saturday Night" were immensely popular, Here's Chevy:

And President Ford's regular weekly accident took place this week in Hartford, Connecticut, where Ford's Lincoln was hit by a Buick. Alert Secret Service agents seized the Buick and wrestled it to the ground. No one was injured in the accident, but when the President got out to see what happened, he tore his jacket sleeve on the door handle, bumped his head, and stuck his thumb in his right eye. Alert Secret Service agents seized the thumb and wrestled it to the ground. Said Mr. Ford, quote: "I just assumed that my thumb was in my pocket with the rest of my fingers. . . ." (*New York*, December 22, 1975)

The print analogue to this hard and happy talk on television is the growing fashion of gossip news. The grocery store press (e.g., *National Enquirer*) lure the pruriently curious with the endless sagas of assassination detection and Mrs. Onassis's affectional life. Great Britain's greatest gossipist, Nigel Dempster (whose byline is "Grovel"), explains the philosophy behind his line of work to Alexander Cockburn (*New York*, May 3, 1976):

I think human beings are unpleasant and they should be shown as such. In my view we live in a banana-peel society, where people are having a rotten, miserable life—as 99.9 percent of the world is—can only gain enjoyment by seeing the decline and fall of others. They only enjoy people's sordidness . . . which—but for me and other journalists around—they would not know about. They see that those who obtain riches or fame or high position are no happier than they are. It helps them get along, and frankly that is what I give them.

A milder, friendlier gossip appeal comes through in *People* magazine (circulation 1.8 million in 1976) and *Parade* (about 20 million).

What is one to make of all this? It is easy, and perhaps correct, to dismiss it as a torrent of trash, a bubbly mash of prurient indignation, secondhand licentiousness, pseudomotherly sympathy, and soul-wearing chatter, all destined, one hopes, to be washed out of public discourse by the waters of rationality. That has not happened, despite revolutionary rises in educational levels and broadcast information. Its popularity goes way back, at least to J. Fred Muggs, the dressed-up little ape on Dave Garroway's "Today Show," who won and held enormous audiences for four and a half years in the early 1950s. The realistic question then is not whether caring and bite and fun and curiosity should be walled away from the news, but rather how they might be turned to educational advantage.

We teachers have also tried to enlist student ids. In universities one of the reasons we keep insisting that professorial advancement depend on research as well as teaching ability is that the former tends to excite and enhance the latter. Simply conveying information, year after year, can make Professor Jack a dull boy, even to himself, however inventive an actor he is. But if he is engrossed in some hot truth pursuit of his own, that shows and can heat up his presentation in adjacent subject areas. The showman only, whose mind is taken up with his own act, has a comparatively short intellectual half-life and is likely to flame out as the joys of entertaining pall. More important, the researcher-teacher in his ideal incarnation communicates excitement about his *subject*, not just about himself. His affect and his intellect are coupled in tight embrace. His students see and hear his mind at work on a matter beyond himself, are lured to *it*, not to him. Alumni who will never forget old What's-his-name—that marvelous fellow who taught them chemistry (or was it English?), anyway, he was one hombre of a teacher—have missed connection with the heart of the enterprise. The Socrateses teach because they cannot help themselves; their fascination with truth-loving makes it impossible for them not to tell about it.

That analogy is useful, I think, in considering id strategies for the news. The cool commentator and the temporally undifferentiated lock-step evening news tramp through the standard story categories deprive the viewer of an educationally effective stimulus—the speaker's own reactions. In ordinary life a very large element of communication is emotional: how important does this seem to him? Does it pain or please him? Is he casual or engaged? Afraid or confident? Much of that communication is nonverbal—as in face and body language—and even more is nonliteral—as in tone of voice, accented expletives, etc. In the classroom, students are very quick to pick up signals that teacher is "really into" his subject or is "covering material" he "could care less" about. On television news cool modes of presentation, appropriate for an earlier time when audiences were cognizing the newscaster's reactions closely and continuously and were thus more vulnerable to overreacting to his emotive twitches, are out of sync with a generation gone cool to television. Struggling against hysteria, the cool newshawk may contribute to "psychic numbing"—further narcotizing an already nodding viewership, routinizing real horrors and glories into a pallid and uniform flow of current events.

The solution is not chimpanzees jumping up and down in their studio blazers. With respect to political news, what is needed are newspeople who are themselves genuinely interested in politics and who know instinctively or can learn how to get that caring curiosity through the tube. If that genuine concern is just not there, if the performer is enlivened by something short of that (such as his own ambition), over the long run it will be hard for him to fake it. The ratings may blip up for the moment with almost any novelty, but it is the excitement of politics itself which will sustain. The reporter whose fascination is so fastened to the news that he will on occasion step aside and let us see it understands that.

Anchors Aweigh?

For Jimmy Carter, says his television advisor Barry Jagoda, "Television has become a regular part of his life, as natural as anything else in his life. It's not a big deal." And thus it has become for the American millions. Its educational potential and problem is summed up in just those phrases: "a regular part of life" and "no big deal." We know far less than we might about how people connect those concepts. We do know that the trickle-out or two-step-flow idea—that highly attentive viewers will clue in the casual ones—does not work for television. The really intense electronic freaks are not widely plugged in socially and may use the medium for self-hypnosis, as does one who reports, "When I am hyper and need something to bring me down, TV is my tranquilizer. One half-hour of TV is better than a handful of Seconals." A psychological study of "heavy" television viewers found them people who "see the real world as more dangerous and more frightening than those who watch very little," and are "less trustful of their fellow citizens and more fearful of the real world" (George Gerbner and Larry Gross, "The Scary World of TV's Heavy Viewer," *Psychology Today*, April 1976)—folks hardly likely to have circles of friends or to relate to them as a source. "Television's Four Highly Attracted Audiences," by another report, are women, blacks, the poor, and the elderly—the discriminated against, not on the average those turned to for discriminating political judgments (George Comstock, "Television's Four Highly Attracted Audiences," *New York University Education Quarterly*, Winter 1978). Like every new mass medium, television cuts ground out from under extant elites, an important part of whose authority was in knowing first.

For the typical television viewer—a citizen, a voter—television news is as it is for Jimmy Carter, as natural as anything else in his life. He pays attention to the weather because he will have to cope with it tomorrow. The rest of it he can take or leave. But if Walter Cronkite says clearly and forcefully that he ought to take, he probably will, for a few minutes anyway—particularly if he can hear in the message some of the sound of the life he knows, the faith he believes, the song his heart sings.

What we have left in this country is a new elite, like it or not. They now occupy Jefferson's "higher degrees of genius," and they have a chance to impart to general America a new education, fit for the new time, a modern curriculum in the capacity for "vigilant and distrustful superintendence." They stand by at the anchor, watching and calling, lest the rest of us suddenly discover that some rogue of a pilot has run us into an enemy's port.

Like today's generation of journalist anchormen, Thomas Jefferson felt a little worm in 1795, penning that letter in Monticello; he saw himself "but as a passenger, leaving the world and its government to those who are likely to live longer in it." In 1800, he ran for President and he won.

*The way the 1980
Presidential election
was conducted and
covered by the
media illustrates the
lure of imaginary
politics and "calls
into question
whether the nation
was losing its ca-
pacity to deliberate
effectively in choos-
ing a President."*

15

Drift to Fiction

A SKEPTIC'S VIEW of democracy
begins this side of the idealist's dream of the steady citizen and the
visionary leader. Democracy to the skeptic is not a utopia but a set
of necessities in support of the opportunity for a decent life—necessities defined and developed over a long and tortuous history peren-
nially interrupted by lapses into chaos and tyranny. A key necessity
is rational discourse. That is difficult enough to sustain among learned,
dutiful elites. Among citizenries composed largely of politically ignorant and indifferent masses led by ambitious cynics, keeping the Great
Conversation rational is a never-ending challenge. From the "children's
crusades" of the thirteenth century down through modern Nazism
and Communism, history demonstrates the inadequacy of religious
conviction, intellectual sophistication, and social idealism as guaran-
tors against political madness. Absent concentrated effort, particularly
on the part of responsible participants, no automatic guarantee pro-
tects the United States of America from popular insanity.

Rational discourse in support of democracy requires debate and decision by a very wide circle of participants, conducted through media
which often subject politics to truncation, distortion, and distraction.

In the not-so-distant past, errors could be combated (if not always defeated) by proliferated structures of counsel: the otherwise preoccupied citizen would turn to the "politician" in his neighborhood or workplace for advice. Parties structured such channels. Now much of that loose-jointed "system" is gone. Citizens are more and more dependent on journalists, speaking to them through television and/or the local newspaper, for shaping the nature and content of the discussion.

Historically, journalists have contributed significantly to such maladies, fragmenting reality, touting novelty, reducing argument to linear narrative, for example. But traditionally, journalists have also contributed significantly to a strength of democracy: the test of proposals against facts. If the genius of democracy is pragmatism, the essence of pragmatism is empiricism. Democracy is about what works—not in the land of Oz, but in the real world of the here and now. Political debate can drift away from its factual base, can float out unanchored into a sea of illusion and emotion in which facts are indistinguishable from feelings.

The democratic politician may sense that drift as progress. For the reduction of politics to sentiment constitutes a leap away from the elitism of expertise toward the equality of emotion. We vary considerably in the information we possess, but all of us have feelings, and we lay claim to "the right to my opinion." Thus it is little wonder that, as democratization reaches farther toward genuine universal suffrage and brushes aside various intermediate structures, the politics of sentiment appeals to the candidate and his media managers and marketing experts.

What sentiments? In *The Pulse of Politics* I argued and tried to demonstrate that three are dominant in Presidential election campaigns.[1] The *conflict* theme appeals to the interest competition typically engenders. The primordial form is the war story—the call to arms, the romance of battle carried over into peaceful politics. Harry Truman's uphill fight in 1948 is illustrative. The *conscience* theme is typically reactive, a call for purity and dignity to counter the corruptions of politics, pejoratively defined. Eisenhower's 1952 campaign against "Communism, Korea, and Corruption" is an example. The *conciliation* theme appears after too much fighting and preaching have whetted the public appetite for solace and ease, unity and friendship. The classic conciliation election in the twentieth century is 1920, Harding's "return to normalcy." Creatively, politicians and the journalists who interpret them use these themes to attract and sustain interest in substantive politics, as devices for getting across the relevant political facts. Destructively, they cooperate in eluding the factual component, drifting past the historical realities into the realm of fiction where sentiment runs free of empirical restraint.

The drift to fiction in twentieth-century politics has followed all three of these paths. But the conciliation theme is specially suited for this perversion. Conflict directly argues comparison among candidates, which motivates a search for evidence. The conscience election features the invocation of principles, typically including honesty and responsibility. But conciliation offers a general relaxation of tension, including the strain of attention, logic, and civic virtue. Especially in the aftermath of troubled times (such as World War I or the stock market crash in 1929), the temptation to set aside calculation and go on a political vacation is powerful.

That temptation gains force when a candidate appears who offers just that appeal. It gains all the more force when such a candidate has the rhetorical skill to convey the appropriate sentiment. When other candidates lack either the conciliatory inclination or the skill to seem that way, the expert conciliator is quite likely to win out, given a reasonably propitious alignment of political forces.

Such was clearly the cast in 1920, when the American electorate chose as President a governmental moron.

The Harding Combination

Harding and the election of 1920 brought together all these factors. The configuration of political power favored the Republicans. President Wilson, chief Democrat, had collapsed in the middle of his crusade for the League of Nations, but would not release the reins of power to anyone else in his party. It took the Democrats eight days and forty-four ballots to nominate Governor James M. Cox, like Harding a virtual unknown. Harding was also a compromise candidate who, however, had behind him the force of a party hungering for a return to power following the Democratic interruption to their normal hegemony.

National sentiment, what one might call the climate of expectations, also favored a Harding, a conciliator. Only four years previously, Wilson had won reelection as the man who "kept us out of war," only to see "The Great War" follow and kill fifty thousand American men. What had felt at first like a reprise of the glorious adventure of the last war—the Spanish-American—turned into an epoch of death, anxiety, and disillusionment. Military peace brought labor war, race riots, a Red scare, soaring inflation (28 percent in 1920), tax raises, and Prohibition. More than 500 thousand Americans died in the influenza epidemic of 1918–19. The fight for the League split the country, and failed.

Harding thus came onto the Presidential scene at just the right time. He had tried his harmonizing rhetoric at the last two Republican conventions, without success. What had been out of sync in 1912 and 1916 fit the bill in 1920.

What Harding had to say was virtually impenetrable to the attentive listener, a melange of obsessively alliterative sloganeering, flag-waving, and appeals for unity. But he looked impressively Presidential: tall, solid, florid, and white-haired, with a deep and resonant voice audible in the last row of the hall. With a good deal of practice Harding had mastered the fashionable gestures of public speaking. Knowing that he knew virtually nothing of the major issues of public policy, Harding nevertheless exuded the confidence, patriotism, and hopefulness people wanted to hear. He won. Before long, his administration collapsed in scandal, registering Harding as the worst President in American history, a reputation which survived until the Nixon debacle.

The Analogy of 1980

My thesis is that 1980, the election which empowered Ronald Reagan, will go down in history as yet another 1920, an election of conciliation.

Nineteen eighty was not 1920, Reagan is not Harding. But the situational and personal similarities are too evident to miss. Like Harding, Reagan came on at a time when the opposition party was in disarray. The traumas of the pre-Reagan period did not match those of 1916–20, but comprised a series of important shocks. The candidates competing with Reagan mistook the mood, by inclination or ineptness, stepping away from the conciliation theme. As important, Reagan himself, in his character and in his political style, honed over years of practice, could hardly have suited better the opportunity 1980 handed him. What happened in that season and in the years to follow highlight in its contemporary form the ancient problem of the drift to fiction in politics.

Carter: Running as President

President Jimmy Carter approached 1980 as a wounded incumbent. Elected in 1976 after a campaign in which both he and Gerald R. Ford had concentrated on conscience politics, Carter's fortunes had declined. The electorate continued to value him highly as a person, but as a President his Gallup poll rating went down below that of Nixon. Part of that decline is no doubt traceable to Carter's awkward relations with the press, particularly his inability to move from lecturing and preaching to the kind of storymaking journalists appreciate. But Carter also suffered a largely negative "professional reputation," as Richard Neustadt defines it, based on a series of mismanaged relationships with leading Congressional figures and an apparent reluctance to develop priorities. Probably the overriding cause of his declining popularity between 1977 and 1979 was his failure to break the economic impasse: soaring inflation, rising unemployment, and energy shortages.

In July, recognizing his troubles, Carter assembled a "Camp David Domestic Summit," after which he made a national address advocating a new, comprehensive energy program. Some 100 thousand favorable letters came in and his popularity rose 11 percentage points. Then, just as unity and purpose seemed to be coming into focus, Carter suddenly fired four leading members of his Cabinet. The impression of incompetence returned.

In the fall of 1979 international crises boosted the President's popular standing in a familiar pattern. On November 4, 1979, Iranians seized the American embassy in Teheran, and captured fifty-two American hostages. Carter became "The President" as he protested on behalf of the nation and set to work to free the hostages. Near the end of December, Soviet armed forces invaded Afghanistan. Once again, Carter's unfortunate relations with Congress faded in the public mind and he emerged as the conciliator par excellence, the unifying leader speaking for the whole nation. Publicly he stepped out of political controversy, declaring himself too occupied with international crises to engage in a fight for the Democratic nomination. Behind the scenes, Carter effectively resisted his staff's pressure to conduct a "negative campaign," a combative attack on his chief rival, Senator Edward Kennedy. Back in June, Carter had let it be known that if Kennedy ran, he would "whip his ass," a message that neither dissuaded Kennedy nor advanced Carter's reputation. Carter in private did not fail to telephone his friends in the appropriate primary states, to invite politically relevant figures to the White House, to see to the politically effective distribution of federal funds to key states, and to time his announcements to political events. But in public he held to his stance as a statesman above the fray.

The Kennedy Challenge

Senator Kennedy declared his candidacy for the Democratic nomination in November 1979, shortly after the Iranian crisis broke. He, too, got off to a faltering start, beginning with a weak and wandering interview on national television. The news about a Kennedy, in that day and age, was likely to be defined around his imperfections. In the following weeks his speeches came cross as vigorous but vague. Then came a classic gaffe, at first unnoticed by the media, then picked up and headlined across the country. In an interview in San Francisco, after fourteen hours of campaigning, Kennedy said that the Shah of Iran, then America's friend (because deposed by our enemies), had ruled "one of the most violent regimes in the history of mankind" and had "stolen . . . umpteen billions of dollars" from his own people. This basically true statement stimulated candidates across the political spectrum to castigate Kennedy for interfering with

President Carter's tireless efforts to secure the release of the hostages.

Kennedy fought on, campaigning day and night in his family's hard-hitting style. In the first contest, the Iowa caucus voting, Carter defeated him, 59 to 31 percent. Misreading the signs, Kennedy lashed out even more aggressively. At Georgetown University he slammed hard and specifically at Carter policies and advanced his own definite alternatives. His partisans responded enthusiastically, but his message, delievered by the media to the public at large, fell flat.

The worse he did, the more aggressive he got, growling, "I have only just begun to fight." Kennedy kept up his hard challenge through the primaries. By the time the Democratic convention opened, Kennedy had covered no less than 300 thousand miles in thirty-nine states and Puerto Rico, Mexico, and the United Nations. At the convention itself, Kennedy combatively led a hopeless charge on the rules binding delegates to vote as instructed in the primaries. He made a strong and popular speech invoking the New Deal and the fervor of the cause, but despite Carter's troubles and his own famous name, Kennedy failed to come through as a plausible alternative. He registered in the politics of 1980 the first major rejection of a candidate who adopted the conflict mode in a conciliation election.

Rejecting the Republican Battlers

Former Governor John Connally of Texas stomped into 1980 like a cowboy at a tea party and was quickly rejected. Early in the season, his media advisers, sensing the national mood, produced commercials showing Connally playing gently with his grandchild. But he soon emerged as the Republicans' most combative candidate. As Senator Strom Thurmond said in welcoming Connally to South Carolina, "I don't know of any man of the political scene today who is more dynamic, more aggressive, and more forceful, who is as tough as this man, and we need a tough man." Connally's performances stimulated applause but few votes. Campaigning for fourteen months and spending some $11 million won him only one vote at the Republican national convention. He faded from the contest.

Other Republican aspirants barely disturbed the political atmosphere. John Anderson, at the time an independent Republican, did challenge the general serenity with his suggestion that the only way Ronald Reagan could balance the budget, cut taxes, and increase defense spending was "with mirrors." George Bush did beat Reagan in the Iowa caucuses, by six percentage points, by continuous campaigning in a state Reagan did not even visit. In New Hampshire, Reagan and Bush plodded through a televised debate which not even the *Washington Post* found interesting: "GOP Debaters Restate Basic Positions in N.H. Debate" read the headline. A second debate, in Nashua, threatened disorder when five opponents of Reagan showed up, but he managed the confusion gracefully and avuncularly, in an event the *Boston Globe* described as "A Golden Night for Reagan." In the New Hampshire primary three days later, Reagan beat Bush two to one. As Reagan left the state, the band played "Ease on Down the Road." In Illinois another debate among Philip Crane, John Anderson, George Bush, and Ronald Reagan turned into another victory for Reagan the calm and humorous elder of the clan. Anderson and Crane snapped at each other; Bush occasionally interrupted; Reagan basically sat back and let them fight, keeping his cheery and mild aura as he gently condescended to his shrill competitors. He won with nearly half the votes.

The press kept up its usual horse-race chatter on through the primary session, but in fact there was no serious challenge to Reagan.

Thus as far as the primary season was concerned, conflict was the loser. Reagan the comforting presence and Carter the steady President in crisis each blanked out their aggressive opponents.

The Lost Cause of Conscience

The conscience theme, traditionally recurrent in Presidential politics, had clearly been the dominant theme of 1976 when both Jimmy Carter and Gerald R. Ford, sensing the pulse of politics, had stressed the need for honesty and decency in Washington. Approaching 1980, some signs indicated a Carter reprise, by naming his energy policy "the moral equivalent of war," perceiving a popular "crisis of confidence," advocating "sacrifice." In a curious thematic reversal, Carter and the Democrats began to appear the cramped and confining Puritans, while Reagan and the Republicans cheerfully called for growth and freedom and progress, in a rhetoric of expansion. The loose-jointed morality of boosterism was overcoming the tightfisted morality of restriction. As the *Washington Post*'s William Greider put it, the message became "elect Ronald Reagan and let the good times roll." Carter the moralizer early faded away in the campaigns of 1980.

John Anderson, Republican Representative from Illinois, substituted in 1980 as the exemplar of the conscience theme. Anderson had emerged in the press as a Republican willing to be quoted against Nixon, as the Watergate crisis gathered. The press discovered him as an apparently hopeless but honest contender. By background, Anderson fit the conscience pattern. A fervent Christian since his conversion at a revival when he was nine, he grew up to run for state's attorney. "I prayed over this initial decision to seek public office," he wrote, "just as I have prayed over every major decision in my life." Later, as a Congressman he three times introduced a Constitutional amendment declaring that the United States "devoutly recognizes the authority and law of Jesus Christ, Savior and Ruler of nations, through whom are bestowed the blessings of Almighty God." His moral concerns guided his championing of civil rights, his opposition to the war in Vietnam, and his indignation at the Watergate scandal.

Starting in 1979, Anderson made a sincere try for the Republican Presidential nomination stressing the need for "basic moral courage," declaring that he wanted to "arouse the conscience and reason of America." He came across in the press and on television as a familiar type: the messianic politician, "running with missionary zeal," a "preachy and abstruse" speaker who "reminds too many people of an angry minister," as *Newsweek* reported. Anderson lost the primary in his home state to Californian Ronald Reagan. He went on to declare his candidacy for the Presidency as an independent. On election day, he got fewer than 7 percent of the popular votes and carried no state.

The most strident voice of conscience politics in 1980 was that of the "Moral Majority," a television following of uncertain extent led by the Reverend Jerry Falwell. The movement's genesis and impulse were plain. Sin was at the root of our problems and government was subsidizing sin; therefore, government had to be reformed. Politics had long been an arena in which the religious left had its impact— in civil rights and the peace movement, for example. Now the religious right—faithful people concerned about crime, drugs, abortion, homo-sexuality, sex education, and other perceived deviations—would mount its campaign. But the main thrust of the evidence is that the religious right made little impact in 1980. The truth seems to be that over the years Americans have become less, not more intolerant. Haynes Johnson, who has trooped the hustings as much as any professional reporter, found in 1980 that with respect to race, sex, and other personal matters, "aside from the vocal single interest groups, you simply don't hear the kinds of passion about such questions. Where once drugs, sex, and other trappings of the permissive society were issues during election campaigns, now they are largely absent." Unlike those election years in which moral concerns topped the political agenda, in 1980 the public in the main found them matters of relative indifference.

Carter's Puritanism, John Anderson's ethical emphasis, and the querulous challenge of the religious right all fell flat in 1980. What had seemed a natural agenda-topper in 1964 and 1976 felt awkwardly out of place in 1980.

The Decisive Conventions

Neither convention was decisive in terms of its major function, the choice of a Presidential nominee. But at each the winner's performance set the tone of his campaign in fateful manner.

Just when the story of politics as conflict seemed dead for 1980, Carter revived it. Having held back his political aggressions for months, as Kennedy harassed him, Carter chose to demonstrate that he too could perform as a fighting candidate. His acceptance speech matched Kennedy's intensity. *Time* reported: "Perspiration pouring from his face, his voice hoarse, his eyes coldly angry, Carter gave a shouting stump speech unlike almost any he has delivered before, in content as well as manner. It was a headlong assault on his rival."

The "assault" was mild by the standards of old-time stump politics, a toned-down-for-television translation of Theodore Roosevelt. But Carter and his strategists thought it would be easy to defeat Reagan, on the record, with a "negative" campaign. Over the years Reagan had filled the files of his enemies with a remarkably extensive collection of confidently asserted untruths and genially expressed bursts of aggression. Carter's aide Hamilton Jordan advocated hitting Reagan hard on the record, anticipating that, "Of all the elections I've been in with Jimmy Carter, this is by far the least difficult." Carter lashed out at Reagan as a "ridiculous" candidate, a man living in a world of "fantasy," a divider at home and a warmonger abroad. As the weeks wore on, Carter occasionally lapsed into hyperbole, suggesting that Reagan was a racist, or wanted war, or would as President divide "black from white, Jew from Christian, North from South, rural from urban." It was a form of rhetoric Carter had never been very good at; his aggressions often sounded shrieky and unconvincing. Worse yet, the press began to point out his "meanness." Elizabeth Drew explained, "Carter had got across to the public the idea that he was a nice man. When the idea suddenly hit that he might not be such a nice man after all, the public reacted with the sort of disillusionment about which it can be unforgiving." Not until mid-October did Carter and his staff perceive that the attack mode was a failure. In a television interview with Barbara Walters, Carter said, "Some of the issues are just burning with fervor in my mind and in my heart . . . and I get—I have gotten carried away on a couple of occasions." But by then it was too late.

Reagan's convention performance could not have been more contrasting. It too set the tone for his campaign, a tone strongly resonant with that of Warren Harding in 1920 and other conciliators in Presidential politics.

By the time the Republicans met in Detroit in July, Reagan's nomination was a foregone conclusion. The personal drama of the convention focused momentarily on a bizarre scheme, apparently developed by Henry Kissinger, to get Gerald Ford to take the Vice Presidential nomination, on the understanding that he and Reagan would eventually share a "co-Presidency." That idea quickly collapsed, despite a good deal of television hype, and Reagan, setting aside his doubts, accepted George Bush for the second spot on the ticket. Programmatic speculation centered on whether or not Reagan would come forth as a reincarnation of Barry Goldwater, whose rightist ideology he had supported in a stirring speech at the 1964 convention.

But Reagan simply transcended these concerns with a classic speech of conciliation, reaching for consensus beyond the disagreements:

I am very proud of our party tonight. This convention has shown to all America a party united, with positive programs for solving the nation's problems; a party ready to build a new consensus with all those across the land who share a community of values embodied in these words: family, work, neighborhood, peace, and freedom.

I know we have had a quarrel or two in our own party, but only as to the method of attaining a goal. There is no argument about the goal. . . .

More than anything else, I want my candidacy to unify our country, to renew the American spirit and sense of purpose. I want to carry our message to every American, regardless of party affiliation, who is a member of this community of shared values.

The substance of the speech fit nicely with the huge blue banner running across the stage: "TOGETHER—A NEW BEGINNING." Importantly for television, the manner of delivery was even more conciliatory. "The pleasant man might have been talking across the backyard fence or maybe chatting in the kitchen with the kids," said *Newsweek*. "He seemed relaxed and natural. . . . Indeed, the entire speech sounded as though it were delivered off the top of Reagan's head." At the end he asked everyone to join him in silent prayer and then, with "God bless America," he triggered the applause. *Newsweek* concluded that, "The gathering of the Republican tribes in Detroit was in fact mostly remarkable for its make-love-not-war harmonics." The *Washington Post*'s William Greider called the convention "a pivotal event of 1980" in which "the meaning of Republican has changed. In place of the party's old scolding, exclusionary style, there was a new open-armed and confident movement, one that has suppressed the nativist sentiments of its past." Reagan's manager Clifton White had told a reporter, "All we're trying to do is keep everybody happy."

The Contrasting Campaigns

Carter continued his attack, quoting Reagan's belligerent statements to paint him as a risky President. But Carter's aggression continued to come across as "mean" in both senses of the word: attacking and petty. Reagan's senior media adviser Stuart Spencer said of Carter, "The harder he gets, the softer we're going to get." When Carter lashed out at Reagan as a divider of "Jews from Christians," Reagan went on network television to say, "I can't be angry. I'm saddened that anyone, particularly someone who had held that position, could intimate such a thing, and I'm not looking for an apology from him. I know who I have to account to for my actions. But I think he owes the country an apology." Again, Reagan's calm and confident manner matched his rhetoric. Accusations that he had changed his positions over the years, confirmed in snippets of videotape, scarcely ruffled his happy demeanor. Nor was he particularly disconcerted when the media took note of his frequent gaffes, demonstrating remarkable lapses in his basic policy information.

Still, the polls were close as the election approached. Reagan's own polls showed that about 44 percent of the people agreed he was "most likely to get us into an unnecessary war," so on Sunday evening, October 19, he went on national television in the manner of Franklin Delano Roosevelt's first fireside chat, in the crisis of 1933. Reagan began, "I'd like to speak to you for a few moments now not as a candidate for the Presidency but as a citizen, a parent—in fact, a grandparent—who shares with you the deep and abiding hope for peace." Nearly quoting FDR, he said, "The only thing the cause of peace has to fear is fear itself." In this talk he spoke the word "peace" forty-seven times.

Fearing that the President might come up with some "October surprise," such as the release of the hostages or an invasion of Iran, Reagan suddenly accepted a long-standing invitation to debate Jimmy Carter on October 28, just one week before the election. Broadcast from the Cleveland Music Hall, the debate reached the largest audience in political history, some 60 million families. Reagan began, hardly pausing to notice the question he had been asked, with a comforting thought: "I'm only here to tell you that I believe with all my heart that our first priority must be world peace, and that the use of force is always and only a last resort, when everything else has failed, and then only with regard to national security." The debate continued, with reporters pressing policy questions and Jimmy Carter cutting hard at Reagan's "ridiculous" plan to cut taxes 10 percent a year over three years. Carter scored point after point. Reagan, in contrast, did not compete, he condescended: "He infused the occasion with a style, a presence, a grandfatherly sense of dignity and kindness that evoked sympathy among millions of Americans who seemed for the first time to understand what kind of a man he really is." Elizabeth Drew noted that "looking genial is what he does." Jimmy Carter's attempt to paint Ronald Reagan as a dangerous villain failed, not because Reagan had not said dangerous things, but because he did not seem a dangerous man.

As election day approached, Reagan spoke tellingly of the emotion that impels the thirst for conciliation. "Many Americans seem to be wondering, searching, feeling frustrated and perhaps a little afraid," he said. And he set the criterion of decision for 1980 in precisely appropriate terms, not of achievement or principle, but happiness: "Most importantly—quite simply—the basic question of our lives: Are you happier today than when Mr. Carter became President of the United States?"

Conciliation Triumphs

As was to be expected, the postelection polls showed that Reagan had won because the public wanted a change. Turnout was the lowest in thirty-two years. About half of the eligible electorate stayed home. Ideology played no markedly significant role. There was no conservative tide—not even a conservative trend. A careful study by Gerald Pomper and colleagues concluded, "There is no evidence that indicated a turn to the right by the nation. Reagan was not elected because of increasing conservatism in the country." "Furthermore," Pomper and his associates reported, "there is no indication that the electorate in 1980 was significantly more conservative on *specific* issues than it had been four years before." They added, "Overall, there is no reason to accept the election outcome in 1980 as indicating a conservative tide in this country, even though the elected candidate was clearly known and perceived by the electorate as a conservative."[2]

Rather, the 1980 Presidential election centered on the politics of conciliation. The public made a clear choice between a worried and combative Jimmy Carter and a calm and comforting Ronald Reagan.

As Carter adviser Patrick Caddell put it, the election was "a referendum on unhappiness." Reagan's adviser Michael Deaver placed the election exactly in the Harding context: it was "a return to normalcy." As the new administration came in, *Time* sensed that "the U.S. is famished for cheer" after too long a period of feeling "wary, worried, and waiting." Polls back in 1979 had shown 67 percent of the people picking the pollster's alternative that the country was in "deep and serious trouble," 70 percent agreeing that "things are going . . . badly." Regarding the country's future, pessimists had outnumbered optimists by three to one. Confidence in government, business, religion—indeed, the whole range of dominant institutions—was far down from the sunny days of the Eisenhower administration. Despite Carter's diagnosis of the problem as some form of alienation or "malaise," the public's troubles were real: inflation and unemployment at home, humiliation at the hands of kidnappers in Iran. Thus again, in reaction to a period of too much conflict and too much moralizing, the American public was ready for relief, for the balm of comforting reassurance. An eighty-four-year-old delegate to the Republican national convention, Terence Martin, had it right when he observed, "This is what I've been working for since 1920, when I got involved in the Harding campaign. This time, we've got the right man at the right time."

The Drift to Fiction

The election of 1980 confirmed in a clear case the dominance of a single national mood (or "climate of expectations"),[3] that of conciliation, which in varying degrees had dominated the Presidential elections of 1908, 1920, 1932, 1944, 1956, and 1968. Following on the clearly conscience-dominated election of 1976, the 1980 election once again indicated the regular sequence of alternating moods—that an election dominated by moral concerns is likely to be followed by a conciliating election. Close analysis of the 1984 campaign and election will, I believe, show a revival of the combative, conflict pattern, pointing to 1988 as a return to the conscience pattern once again. These regularities, matters of balance and dominance, not of solo characterization, point to an emotional component of elections of considerable interest to candidates and their managers as well as to scholars of the Presidential selection process. For if these rough regularities hold, candidates who fit their rhythm are likely to do better than candidates who contradict them. Such was the case with Jimmy Carter and the others who read 1980 wrongly and with Ronald Reagan who read it as rightly as any President in modern history. The hypothesis is simple: underlying the immediate particularities of Presidential campaigns and elections there is a regular (and emotively understandable) mood swing which can contribute significantly to the outcome of the election.

Fictionalizing Politics

But there is another, perhaps a more fundamental impact of the conciliation election, a danger inherent in its reaction against the calculations of politics. That is the drift to fiction. For the conciliation election tends to represent a flight from political argument, from the clash of evidence on the one hand and the clash of values on the other. The longing for happiness and harmony can lead the nation away from the realities of politics into territory beyond the reach of the facts. At the extreme, the test of policy is transformed from pragmatism to sentimentality, in which the symbolic and emotional dimension of political discourse overwhelms testing against the historical actualities.

Nineteen eighty called into question whether the nation was losing its capacity to deliberate effectively in choosing a President. The question is neither partisan nor individual. Political science has a weak record in assessing the performance of incumbent Presidents; the Reagan administration is no exception. Typical studies of incumbents concentrate on technique and/or short-term and immediate "effectiveness," postponing for history the far more significant questions of large and deep political impact. The 1980 case may well illustrate, more clearly than any modern election, how the debate over who should be the next President can degenerate into a theatrical fiction far more concerned with gestures and postures than with serious national alternatives.

Accepting the nominations of their respective conventions, both

Carter and Reagan saw the fictional beam in the eye of the other. Reagan insisted that "the Carter Administration lives in the world of make-believe." Carter in turn accused the Reagan team of inhabiting "a world of tinsel and make-believe . . . fantasy America." Both contributed to that drift, though Reagan came to exemplify it. In 1976 Carter had in an important sense run against politics itself—against the calculations by which major new political purposes gather support among the significant actors. Carter tended to reduce politics to technique, on the one hand, and to character on the other hand. The former spreads attention so thinly over a flat agenda of many items and concentration on such narrow channels of action that the major concerns get little visible definition in public debate. The latter, the reduction to character, can focus so strongly on morals and motives that fact-based calculations fade out. The politically creative contribution of a moralist like Carter is to link the achievement of values to conditions and opportunities in the real world. The pathology of moralism is the drift into a pattern in which praise and blame substitute for effective action.

Reagan exemplified a different political pathology, directly linked to the drift to fiction. In character he is a passive-positive—a President who simultaneously exerts relatively little personal energy and maintains a demeanor of smiling optimism.[4] Like Taft and Harding, also of that type, Reagan's primary personal motivation in politics is to secure the affection and encouragement of those around him. The passive-positive is essentially an "other-directed" person, in David Riesman's phrase. Reagan through the years had developed a remarkable sensitivity to small and larger audiences, learning just how to charm and divert them toward an appreciation of himself. From childhood on he had been attuned to playacting, not only in theaters but at school, at home, on the playground and beach. As a radio sports announcer and then a Hollywood actor, Reagan operated in a world in which pretending was not considered lying but performing as a professional. "So much of our profession is taken up with pretending," he wrote, "with interpretation of never-never roles, that an actor must spend at least half his waking hours in fantasy." Reagan carried those capacities over into the General Electric lecture circuit, where he quickly discovered that audiences virtually never questioned confidently asserted arguments or evidence as long as they found the speaker engaging. The transition to politics was no great leap. Extending his long-honed skills, Reagan expressed simply and convincingly, to a largely indifferent and ill-informed electorate, his anecdotal politics. His cheerful storymaking and easy eloquence on television made him a natural item of curiosity for modern journalism, much of which found him interesting, if inaccurate. Again and again, responsible journalists took note of some collosal gaffe of Reagan's, some startling revelation of ignorance directly relevant to major policy decisions, only to discover that Reagan's bland reaction was matched by that of readers and viewers. "Like any other speaker," he said, "I'd see something, and I'd say, 'Hey, that's great, and use it.'" As David Broder put it, "It is apparently President Reagan's belief that words can not only cloak reality but remake it." Reagan demonstrated the possibility that modern political rhetoric can unplug itself from the facts, provided, as in 1980, the media and the electorate accept plausibility as proof. "Politics is just like show business," Reagan told his aide Stuart Spencer. "You have a hell of an opening, coast for awhile and then have a hell of a close."

Fictional rhetoric similarly escapes the pressure for consistency over time, a pressure which can, of course, stifle rational adaptation. But political calculation depends significantly on the capacity of voters to assess the relationship between intention and performance—a necessity for rationality in the electoral process. In California and in Washington, Reagan's indifference appeared to cancel that check on actions (in economics, defense, foreign policy, etc.) markedly contradictory to what he had led voters to expect. The calculability of politics can sustain itself only to the degree that the link between words and actions is steady enough to be discerned and assessed.

Finally, fictional politics sacrifices the requirement of sincerity, that is, the voter's confidence that the politician touts values based in his life. Reagan's list of values, for example, advertised "family, work, neighborhood, freedom and peace" as his highest principles—none of which, in fact, had represented strong behavioral commitments on his part in the past. Just as Reagan apparently felt no compunction about acting in his own television commercials without knowledge of or even interest in what his producers gave him to say, so his professed political values remained largely distinct from any personal commitment.

By 1984 the climate of expectations had shifted once again, although the drift to fiction seemed still in train. Reagan fundamentally withdrew from partisan debate in 1984 as had Nixon in 1972, with a similar result: media attention focused strongly on Democratic primary races, as Walter Mondale was challenged by John Glenn, Jesse Jackson, and Gary Hart. There the usual battle and horse-race language predominated. In the general election campaign Mondale attacked the Reagan deficit, thus concentrating on a concept few voters understood and a threat to economic welfare yet to be experienced. To meet that threat, Mondale called for a rise in taxes, a threat nearly all voters could immediately understand.

But conflict in 1984 did not depend primarily on dramatic issues. To Reagan's eventual advantage, media-dominated politics concentrated on television debates. George Bush and Geraldine Ferraro traded barbs in one, Ferraro lashing out to say, "I almost resent, Vice President Bush, your patronizing attitude." Two Presidential debates formed their own drama. More than 100 million people watched. In the first, Mondale prevailed—surprisingly, given Reagan's stature as a "Great Communicator"—by combining personal geniality with pointed attacks on the President's policies and competence. Reagan appeared confused, ending with a long statistic-ridden ramble, no doubt designed to give the impression that he was well-informed. The press declared Mondale the winner. In reaction, the Reagan forces leapt into negative anti-Mondale advertising. But in the second debate, with expectations of Mondale running high, Reagan the media performer, came through, discounting attacks on his age with good humor and stressing his devotion to nuclear disarmament.

Most significant regarding the drift to fiction, however, was the fact that the conflict of 1984 was essentially a conflict of styles. The televised debates provided information on the candidates' issue stands, but such data were almost completely ignored. Instead, the fight got defined in the press as a style show, a comparison based on dramatic effectiveness in a mode of debate no President has to face in office. Image prevailed. The concreteness of empirical conditions gave way to theatrical politics in which facts were reduced to items to be assessed for their contribution to an emotional confrontation. If the contemporary election of conciliation lends itself to sentimentality, the contemporary election of conflict lends itself to theatricality. Both move away from the mundane pragmatism which has historically sustained the rationality of American democracy.[5]

Had Ronald Reagan not appeared in 1980 to perform as a Pied Piper of Presidential politics, some other experienced modern media man would surely have taken his place. Given the level of public indifference, given the complexity of the real issues, given journalism's (and especially television's) new taste for literary rather than empirical stories, not much more time could be expected to pass before either of the parties turned to a professional actor to run against an amateur. The reduction of politics to sentiment is an ancient threat. And the death of democracy, the ancients understood, results when politicians no longer even aspire to Adlai Stevenson's standard: "Talk sense to the American people."

Is journalism locked into the deterioration of political discourse? By no means. The problems are severe, but the potentialities are out there, waiting to be exploited.

16

Ways Out

LIKE HUMANS IN other ages we tend to go along with the stories current in our culture. Even the exception proves the rule: a legend strong in our mythology is the story of the maverick, the lone individual bucking the tide of society, finding his own way, attracting our interest as a prophet or a symbol or a warning. Our own history is a story we tell again and again in periodic celebrations and in pilgrimages to the shrines that mark heroic deeds. We search for present meaning in a version of the past, in our roots as we want to remember them. Even more powerfully in America, this New World, we hold to the sense that the national story continues into the adventures of the future. From the start we have been a people about to be, a nation of becomers. Whether in shock or satisfaction, Americans tune in to the new—and thus the news—to catch the sound and shape of the next episode, lest we be left behind as the country moves forward. And with an optimism absurd to the Old World sophisticates and determinists, we democrats—those who demand a return to a better past and those who insist on an advance to a better future—cling to the faith that we ourselves are the makers of our destiny. That faith falters from time to time, but then springs up again. "In God We Trust," yes, but we The People are the authors of liberty.

Yet in fact we depend, far more profoundly than we have realized, on storytellers to pluck from the chaos of experience the plot of the next adventure. From the beginning even geography had to give way to the force of myth: Columbus, flying in the face of the science of his day, believing instead in Marco Polo's tales of the Indies; the Puritans, aiming for Virginia and hitting Cape Cod, sustained by the vision of a New Zion; on down to the wildly improbable but mythically compelling idea of putting a man on the moon. The pictures in our heads conquered the ground beneath our feet. The painters of those pictures, when they can get them believed, exercise a power that is nothing less than the power to set a course of civilization. In modern politics, lacking grander visions, we make do with glimpses of possibility and shades of meaning—a kaleidoscope of fact and metaphor and judgment. Journalism, our composite Homer, delivers those partial sightings which substitute for heroic myth. If it is the default of the political parties that burdens journalism with sorting out candidates, it is the default of the contemporary intellectuals that leaves to journalists the task of composing our ruling ideas.

Being American, my purpose is improvement. But just as it seems to me quite unlikely that the pulse of politics will suddenly beat to a halt or that the basic political system now in place will change radically in the near future, so certain basics of the craft of political journalism probably have to be taken as given. Two such basics stand out: haste and drama. Journalism will continue to be history in a hurry. That is the major stumbling block in the path of improvement. Haste fights reflection, and an unreflective journalism drifts into dependence on standard and fashionable story forms. That risk can be cut to some extent by a variety of palliatives, such as alternating long and short deadlines, study leaves for reporters and editors, closer links between the more leisurely academic world and the journalistic rush to judgment, and the development of a steadier and more responsible corps of press critics. New information-retrieval technologies should make possible far quicker access to background and context data. And some journalists have already grasped the fact that it is the relevance of information, not simply its recency, that grips the reader as he tries to understand today's situation. But such changes at the edges will leave intact the main focus of journalism: current events hurrying into tomorrow.

Critics who preach against journalistic drama per se are also likely to be disappointed. The audience cannot be forced to attend; they must be attracted. Critics who urge the publication of stories no one wants to write, and they themselves would not read, deserve particular neglect. The drama can be better done. It can steer clear of fiction. It does not require brevity—as witness sustained public attention to the Army-McCarthy hearings, the Watergate saga, Theodore White's campaign books, and the like. The drama inheres in the strong, engaging narrative development that stretches the attention span. Even the quickest medium, television, has discovered that in the popular appeal of "60 Minutes." But drama itself is an inherent—essential—element of journalism. In a Presidential election year the nation is not a classroom; it is a street theater.

The main line of improvement is obvious. We need all three stories every time, to test the candidates from different angles, lest we wind up with an expert mood-reader who sails in on the tide of the dominant story of the year and then founders when it turns out he cannot handle the other challenges of the Presidency. Journalism's modern talent and enterprise and taste for variety can meet that responsibility. But the stories themselves can also stand improvement. Their promise as guides to the choice of a President has yet to be fulfilled.

The story of politics as conflict has distorted and diverted Presidential politics repeatedly. Candidates who had experienced the terrors and thrills of combat, directly or vicariously, carried over into politics an entirely inappropriate rhetoric of battle. For in a real battle the rights and wrongs are already decided. The appeal to arms cancels the appeal for deliberation. The question of arousal overwhelms the question of understanding. In each of the battle campaigns illustrated here, and as could easily be illustrated from those left out, the national debate degenerated into mere castigation, often over picayune "issues" and the thrust and parry of personal accusation. Candidates who tried to stir a debate about the major actualities of their time quickly learned that what counted with the press was not substance but difference. In Theodore Roosevelt's time, and in Truman's old-fashioned shout, the drama of attack and defense at least had the virtue of a certain visceral definiteness, the sparkle and lurch of combative action and event. But by the time Adlai Stevenson and then George McGovern entered the fray, controversy had lapsed into shadowboxing. No candidate could advance a position seriously, as a Presidential intention, without its being reduced immediately to a tactical ploy in the contest for popularity. When John Kennedy offered a different vision of what the Americans might hold themselves to, a vision of achievement considered in the light of resources, he quickly discovered how irrelevant that seemed to a press prepared to light up over Quemoy and Matsu.

The transformation of the election from an event to a saga set the stage for the appearance of new militant vocabularies, as campaign organizations maneuvered over the expanded primary terrain, month after month, exercising their logistics and strategies to build momentum and avoid erosion. Campaign maneuver itself became the featured story; the Presidential implications of what the candidates were saying faded into the distance. Horse-race imagery gave way to parcheesi politics—war against the scoreboard—a new game of expectations and scenarios and surprises played as vigorously by the candidates as by the press reporting them. By the end of the 1970s journalism, increasingly conscious of its own interpretative influence, took to reporting how the candidates were going over with the press itself. Campaign reporting became a specialty distinct from government reporting; the battle story drifted away from Washington, lost its connection with the reality the victor would encounter there. Public opinion polling, grown reliable after the 1948 fiasco, set up another dynamic: the front-runner, identified long before the first voting, emerging from the pack and fighting off the challengers. Front-runners far enough in front avoided debate like the plague: Dewey dodged debate in 1948 and nearly won; Eisenhower floated above the contest; Nixon, learning his lesson from 1960, played above it all in 1968 and 1972; Ford, to his sorrow, let himself be persuaded to debate on television in 1976. Candidates coming from behind sought to co-opt rather than confront the positions of the more popular contender.

Thus over the years inventive candidates and journalists translated the battle story into a tale of calculation and maneuver set off from the story of governing the country. We have come a long way from the Lincoln-Douglas debates. The televised debate series in 1960 and 1976 verged on deliberation—but their substance was immediately swallowed up by reporting on "who won" in the instant polls. As arousers of an apathetic citizenry, the story dragged: voting turnout drifted downward, the public turned away from the fight.

Critics of the fighting story call for "issues not personalities," for a rational debate on the candidates' programs and party platforms. But as President after President has discovered, particularly in recent years, the gap between what he wants to do in January of an election year and what he can do the following January is enormous. Pressed for specifics during the campaign, the candidate and his aides and advisers expend their intellectual energies composing tedious position papers. They are not frequently cited after inauguration day. The fundamental reason is not that the candidates lie, though some do, but that such detailed blueprints for government action are drawn up abstractly, disconnected from an as yet unknown context of forces and chances in Washington, and of necessity shaped for an immediate purpose: to win the election. It is like asking a doctor to prescribe for a patient he has yet to meet. The party platforms try to beat those uncertainties by including a little of everything. At best they become registries of access—who could marshal enough clout to nail in a plank—and at worst mere laundry lists of more or less plausible hopes. To center campaign debate on specific candidate plans is to shift the conversation away from evidence and toward opinions that cannot readily be tested, however sincerely they are advanced. The story of conflict reduces itself to a competition among assertions. Reporters closeted with the candidates on the campaign trail badger them for statements of intention, hoping for some bit of quotable idiocy, usually making do with some hypothetical clash between what A says and what B says. Their reports from the field become grist for the editorial mill; the columnists and commentators take over, producing analysis after analysis in which their own confident opinions on issues are contrasted with the uncertain and ineloquent proposals candidates make. In practice the battle between candidate and journalist supersedes the battle among the candidates themselves. Because an issue's focus must by definition highlight the hypothetical and abstract, a story told in the subjunctive language of what one would do *if* certain conditions prevailed, the way is opened for endless speculation, and theory rules the roost.

Journalism's strength is not theory but fact. And to reason toward a choice, the public's first need is to get a grip on the contemporary reality. As for candidates, each offers a picture of the facts as he sees them, a picture very likely to shape whatever he would try to do as President. A battle among *those* visions—visions of what is actually happening—could prove much more enlightening and enlivening than war stories out of New Hampshire or Wisconsin. In 1932, for example, Hoover claimed the economy was picking up, Roosevelt the opposite. Their visions of reality clashed. The facts of life were there to report—and bore directly on the task of assessing the candidates. Hoover favored local, voluntary relief. Whatever the philosophical validity of his viewpoint, it rested on a fact question: what local and private resources were available to relieve how many of the unemployed? In the 1950s Joe McCarthy's charges and threats rattled through the press, randomly ruining lives, until the facts of "Communists in government" finally smashed him. In 1960 John Kennedy charged the Eisenhower administration with allowing a dangerous "missile gap" to widen between the United States and the Soviet Union. Not until after the election did the facts blow that vision out of the water. Through the sixties, candidates posturing about the state of welfare too rarely had the facts thrown at them: how many American families lacked the money to feed their children properly? What were the actual effects of the programs in place? How typical among those aided was the able but lazy "welfare cheater"? In 1964 and beyond, Vietnam was importantly a moral issue, but what eventually turned it around was not the logic of antiwar opinion, but the revelation of what was actually happening out there in the field. Similarly, Watergate—more broadly, the corruption in government charge—barely rippled the surface of national debate until after the election of 1972. McGovern's eloquent damnations failed to convince. Two young reporters fought their way through to the facts and set in motion the fall of a President. And late in the 1970s, amid much speculation about Jimmy Carter's state of mind, the facts of an energy crisis limped late into the public consciousness.

Modern journalism clearly has the capacity to handle the battle over facts. Journalism has attracted some of the best brains in the country.

In the colleges very bright students insist on struggling their way into that overcrowded line of work. Mammoth news organizations have the requisite money and manpower. Compared to just a few years ago, today's government "secrets" are there for the reporter's asking as are the piles of scholarly studies issued by the universities. The central problem is not access but selectivity—but there journalism has just begun to exploit the incredible speed of the new information-retrieval technologies that will enable a reporter to survey a month's worth of data in an afternoon, posing question after question. A war over the facts, every four years, could help journalism break out of its losing preoccupation with the nuances of hypothetical opinion, symbolic epistemology, electoral bookie work, and the tired search for someone to quote, and do what it does best: get relevant information, quickly and accurately. Citizens, now woefully mis- and un- and under-informed on the way things work in a fast-changing world, might begin to see through the fog of rhetoric to the shape of reality. The drama of revelation might grip the public imagination a good deal more firmly than do the campaign gossip and ideological chitchat that now drone through so many eminently forgettable paragraphs.

But the main virtue of a quadrennial war about the facts would be its contribution to the central electoral task: the choice of a President. Testing potential Presidents on the facts of the national condition would test their capacity for realistic perception and judgment, their grasp of the actual shape of the situation at home and abroad. That would be an important test of a genuine Presidential ability. For time and again, in recent decades, we have seen a President cut himself off from the real world, isolate himself in the White House with his cozy crew of flattering advisers, and drift into illusion and tragedy. It happened to as cool a rationalist as John F. Kennedy when he fell for the Bay of Pigs invasion mirage, though he quickly recovered his bearings. We need a President highly curious about what in the world is happening—and ready to respond to the evidence of change. The time to assess a President's worldview is before, not after, he raises his hand on inauguration day and swears to preserve, protect, and defend the Constitution. During the campaign his fantasies should be held to the fire of fact. Whatever he may hope to do, can he bear to see the truth? Does he know what he is talking about? Presidents-to-be should never again be allowed to pass through the gate of an election without paying the admission of realism, talking sense to the American people about the realities he and they must face together.

At the heart of the story of politics as conscience is the question of character. A candidate may be in full possession of the facts of his time, but that does not determine what he makes of them, his orientation toward action. He can be counted on to present a character in the campaign, calling attention to himself as he wants to be seen. But that may be a temporary guise donned for the immediate task and shucked aside when it has served his purpose. Wilson's campaign "conservatism" is an example; Johnson's restrained reasonableness in 1964 makes the point. The problem is to get behind the mask to the man, to the permanent basics of the personality that bear on Presidential performance. That quest does not deny the possibility of fundamental change after age forty or the possibility that the candidate may be a better person than he makes himself out to be. Possible—but not likely enough to justify the risk. The "New Nixon" seduction argues caution.

Nor does the quest for character deny the relevance of ideology. The confusion that arises from the contemporary "liberal's" defense of the big government status quo and the "conservative's" demand for a radical dismantling of government does not dismiss the ideological question. For in a crude and simple sense there is an important distinction: historically Democratic Presidents have pressed for government action to relieve popular distress, while Republicans prefer free-market mechanisms. The distinction is politically important but not ultimate; it is a distinction of means, not ends. Republicans as well as Democrats aim to make people better-off; they disagree about how. And in the reality of American politics "better-off" means a grab bag of common values—security and opportunity, money and liberty, fairness and variety—not some tightly derived logical product of metaphysical demonstration.

That is where the Wilsons and Luces go wrong, wrenching the story of morals away from its American plot. Claiming that their political preferences are derived from eternal principles, they wind up investing debatable policies with the force of holy writ. Goldwaterism follows: sweeping away the conditional uncertainties of the historical present as simply irrelevant, demanding not calculation but application of received truth. That stance stops argument dead in its tracks. If it is God who prescribes the League of Nations or militant anticommunism or free enterprise, the Devil must be running the opposition—and you turn your back on the Devil, you do not argue with him. History is seen as fundamentally beside the point. Therefore, such superficially startling leaps as Wilson's shift from peace to war and such low-level contradictions as Goldwater's desire to cut federal spending while financing much stronger military forces are not so surprising. The political fundamentalist looks up the answer in his book of natural laws or divine revelations and pronounces—Q.E.D., like Euclid with his triangles. Nor is it so surprising that moralizing candidates so often wind up practicing the wily arts of public relations and psychological manipulation. Since the derivation from principle to policy is perfectly clear, the obstacles to implementation must be emotional—problems of the will, not the mind. People need selling, not convincing. That leads a Dwight Eisenhower to the commercial-making studio where, however reluctantly, he mouths little inspirational platitudes for his admen.

What is missing in this line of political philosophy is the common sense that political values are contingent. Values are not irrelevant; a politics without values reduces the democratic adventure to a dismal pull and tug among interests. But politics is not theology; there is no salvation in it. At its best it sets the conditions for a virtuous life. Its arena is a messy middle ground between the best and the probable, as philosophers from Thomas Aquinas to Reinhold Niebuhr have clearly understood. The genius of American politics operates in that territory, not above it all (Eisenhower's malady) or lost in mere manipulation (Nixon's penchant). If modern political history shows anything, it is that the right to speak for God in politics may be claimed by any sort of character—and probably will be.

The moralizing story comes up as a reaction to the battle story, which, like a war gone on too long, seems to degenerate from adventure to butchery. The moralists in journalism seek to recapture innocence in the person of an outsider who will clean up the Capitol. Each of the moralizing candidates discussed above, including Willkie and Eisenhower, was a politician in the broad sense of the word—a man of affairs already tainted with the rot of compromise. But romantic idealization sets in, beginning with the mythology of the man's upbringing in some island of innocence far from Washington and progressing to his uncanny talent for cutting through the tangles of intrigue with the sword of principle. Once that process of perfectionism takes hold it is hard to stop, short of a kind of secular deification. Criticism seems somehow blasphemous, as if one crack in the dike of personal virtue would destroy the whole. Intimations of ambition are especially dangerous; the ideal candidate should be dragged into office despite his protestations of reluctance.

This earthly elevation reflects and contributes to the popular fantasy of the President as Superman. The moralizing tales find their way into the textbooks, and movies, teaching the young to expect miracles from the White House. The regularity of disillusionment follows as the night follows the day. Instead of miracles come halting progress and/or crashed hopes, as the President discovers how short a distance his independent powers can take him. His moralizing sponsors find him disappointing, partly because they mistook his personal virtue for agreement with their particular deductions from natural law. As the country runs through that cycle of uplift and downfall again and again, the force of the story wanes and skepticism sets in. In reaction to the romantic version of the discovery of the best natural American for President, journalists turn to the equally romantic notion that every candidate is a secret crook.

The modern skeptical story of conscience fumbles after character in the Campaign Street Test—the totally unrealistic supposition that he who is good at running for President will be good at running the Presidency. Especially since the race became a marathon, campaigning, with its endless exhaustions, brief encounters, and pleadings for money and attention, tests qualities of physical endurance and superficial plausibility, but not much else. The story's prize is the gaffe. Carter's "ethnic purity" mistake and Ford's "Polish blunder" were the great gaffes of 1976, neither of which bore the slightest relationship to their public policies, much less their characters. But the story takes off and lives, sometimes for weeks of front-page attention and editorial fulmination, before it finds its rightful place in oblivion. The gaffe is our era's prime example of symbolic politics run wild. Its early retirement would make space for the story we eventually turn to for enlightenment on the question of Presidential character.

That is the life story, the biography. As the early magazine moralists discovered, that was their most appealing product. It sold far better than all the shrill denunciations and atmospheric pontifications put together. People could connect with it. Everyone lives a life history. Everyone is interested in how to do that and, through the human connection, how lives very different from their own take shape and plunge on. The poetic saga of Odysseus, the history of Moses, the parable of the life of Christ, Caesar's story, the tragedies of King Oedipus and Prince Hamlet, on down to the lives of Napoleon and Lincoln and Victoria and Churchill, to our age's fascination with the biographies of every sort of hero and villain from Gandhi to Hitler—the story of a person grips the imagination as nothing else can. The stories of "ordinary" people (each, in fact, extraordinary), told by the likes of Robert Coles or Studs Terkel, light up the contemporary scene with a clarity unmatched by any public opinion poll. For people sense that all our theoretical constructs and elaborate fantasies take their human meaning from their incarnation in the flesh and blood of persons. The theory no one lives by remains a theory only. Biography brings theory down to earth, history to focus, fantasy to reality. It is the narrative of existence, of being-in-becoming. No wonder people indifferent to mere speculation take to biography as if the life they read might be their own.

In the journalism of Presidential campaigns, biography occupies an increasingly important place. The newsmagazines in particular, but also long newspaper stories and television documentaries, have moved past the romantic "son of the soil" versions to review candidate histories from a Presidential perspective. In 1976 those stories came late in the game, but they were unusual in their thoroughness and incisiveness. Some made use of the scheme I developed in *The Presidential Character* to try to sort out the major biographical themes relevant to performance in the White House, but each developed its own focus, often explicitly stated, on the main biographical questions. Special attention went to the roots, in family, school, local culture, and early political experience, of the candidates' habits of mind and approaches to action. After Nixon and Johnson, writers were specially tuned in to evidence bearing on the character as compulsive or open to learning, self-doubting or confident, moved primarily by narrow ambition or larger values. The strength of those analyses was not only their narrative appeal but also their reach beyond the manipulatable and invariably manipulated images of the campaign to a record of performance already in place. Unsatisfied with little gaffey glimpses into character, the authors checked out candidate experiences over the years. The result was the best writing yet from the interpreters of the political meanings and values and probabilities embodied in the real men then making their way toward the Presidency. An example was set; whether it would carry forward to the next campaign and the one after that was yet to be seen.

Political observers of the "realist" school are forever underrating the problem of conciliation in American democracy. The appeal that celebrates the common hope for harmony is dismissed as mere rhetoric, masking darker purposes. Every candidate is assumed to be consumed with personal ambition and to possess an infinite capacity for meaningless blather. Conflict is real; concord is an illusion. Thus the tough-minded wordsmith, who need never bear the responsibility of action, sets out to unmask the fakers and correct the naive. In fact, of course, it is not possible for the government to move forward except by developing alliances among politicians—the politics of conciliation.

The story of that search periodically dominates the national narrative. Too often, the hunger for the relief of tension and anxiety has led us to accept the terms of a peace too fragile to last, a truce in place of a social contract. Three features of that story raise that risk.

The first is the drift toward fiction. Politics as theater, politics as a "great game," campaign politics as a story cut loose from the story of government—those themes reinforce that drift. Somehow as the Presidential election season approaches the signal goes out that a brand-new "epic struggle" is beginning in which the ordinary rules of judgment are to be set aside—the theatrical suspension of disbelief. History stops: amnesia sets in, encouraged by candidates who, unable to resolve the conflicts they inherit, invite us to forget them. People turn to the story, particularly as presented in the entertaining broadcast media, as if they were attending a spectacle, as essentially passive spectators. The question of judgment is transformed into a question of appreciation—did we like the show, or not? How did the candidate do? Did he give a good performance? Were we impressed? The typical television interviewer asks the candidate how he feels about this and that, making a connection between his feelings and the audience's feelings, defining the exchange as an emotional occasion. Harding's rhetoric, reduced to print, says nothing. Harding's performance, in person, conveyed, when the audience was ready for him, powerful feelings. Today the fragmented brevity of television news sends the message by too fast to call the mind into play. Emotion is quicker but shallower. A parade of impressions jogs gently along the edge of attention, barely disturbing the rational faculties, leaving behind a blur of affective responses. Candidates like Nixon pick up the lesson: the impression is everything. The appearance of the candidate in the watcher's emotional imagination is what counts. Politics is cut adrift from its real-world moorings and floats out into the seas of fiction.

The second risk, in a time of high anxiety, is the raising of expectations impossible to fulfill. Candidates normally overpromise and voters learn to apply a discount rate. But judging from the cases reviewed, from Bryan's silver panacea to Nixon's secret plan to end the war, there is a deeper danger: the seductiveness of a magic answer to cut through all the complexities and bring back the good old days. Even more powerfully appealing than specific magic tricks of policy may be the message that all will be well if people will just be nice to one another. That reaches the frustrated and confused citizen with an answer he can understand: Big Bill Taft's "Smile, Smile, Smile," Franklin Roosevelt's "nice jolly understanding of their problems," Eisenhower's infectious grin, Nixon's "bring us together." The hometown booster spirit is transposed to the national community; positive thinking prevails, in the hope that thinking will make it so, that acting as if one were confident will create confidence. Differences are papered over with a veneer of happy talk. The needed unity is not composed, it is assumed and celebrated. Political discussion collapses into cheerleading.

The third risk in the conciliation story springs from the direct and seemingly intimate relationship between candidate and audience, facilitated as never before by television. Harmony among the followers comes to depend almost entirely on shared allegiance to the leader. He is the celebrity. They are the fans. In between is nothing but the vibrating airwaves. When the camera moves away from him, interest evaporates. Recognizing that, the candidate and his managers seize control of his appearances and choreograph them for maximum effect. They play to a mass, undifferentiated audience, strangers to one another, focusing their friendship on the lone star on the stage. Some citizens may be brought in to pose vague and easy questions of a general nature. But throughout his varied appearances the candidate conveys the impression that he as President, backed by The People at large, will comprise the political system soon to be.

That of course is nonsense, but it points the way to a more productive path for the story of politics as conciliation to take. That story could tell of the gathering of forces and persons who might well wind up leading the nation, not just to victory at the polls but in the years thereafter. Journalists would press Presidential candidates to articulate the areas of agreement they share with actual and potential Congressmen and Senators, governors and Cabinet members, advisers and interest-group leaders—with the range of politicians preparing to join in running the country. Stories on the interesting characters running for "lesser" offices, highlighting their connnections with the Presidential candidates, would enrich the drama. Even during the primary season, now so preoccupied with conflict, emerging candidates would be asked not just what they would do with power, but with whom they might do it and what the basis for their concord could be. At and after the national convention, now a television extravaganza of doubtful instructional benefit, reporters could press the candidate for President not to name his Cabinet, but to elaborate where he and leaders of Cabinet stature come together. That challenge would test a genuine Presidential skill, because in fact the government works by an endless round of negotiation.

To attract that support committed to the long haul, the candidate would have to offer more than his person. Nor is it likely that the crew would sign on merely because they liked one another or were like one another or shared some sense of organizational neatness. They would want to work out with him a sense of purpose and direction of policy, not in unrealistic detail but in a broad outline of priorities. Together they would strain their intelligence to discover and articulate formulae of alliance, expressing those "ideas whose time has come" capable of attracting wide support before and after the election. Effort would be expected to bring in the broadest possible representation of the policy's main interests, an effort further testing the candidate's power of negotiation and formulation. Out of such experiments in purposeful unity might eventually emerge an organization lasting on into the following election. One might call it a political party.

The long-run need for such networks of cooperators between leader and followers is evident. Leader-mass politics is inherently unstable; given our Constitutional arrangements, it is governmentally unworkable. There are grave risks in proceeding as at present. John Kennedy brought his young campaign hotshots into the White House to run the show—and so did Nixon and so did Carter—a kitchen Cabinet of dependent devotees. Officers in the other Cabinet are too occupied with their departments to function as general advisers. Modern Congressmen run continuous district-oriented campaigns; Senators preen themselves for their turn at the Presidency. Governors relate to Washington as the enemy, and interest groups concentrate on their narrowly defined aims. When an incumbent President discovers, too late, that his "open administration" has gone anarchical and he seeks to force unity upon it, he winds up splintering and suppressing his official family in the name of "loyalty."

But however obvious these general malfunctions may be, pointing them out will not correct them. Reformers who urged the revival of parties as abstract good things in themselves or look to the reinvigoration of the jumbo coalitions of years gone by are marching up a blind alley. Purpose comes first, then party. In the rush of campaigning the urgent work is to discover themes of unity so compelling that they will attract allies whose allegiance might survive the selection. In the larger and longer-range picture, discerning the basic shape of the emerging future and the broad strategies that might bend it in beneficent directions is the challenging task of the intellectuals. Unless and until people who are paid to think put their minds to work on that task and learn to articulate their ideas in a language politicians and journalists can understand, the search for harmony will falter.

"Where there is no vision," Proverbs warns, "the people perish." The vision of the intellectual in America has too often in recent years been narrowly focused on technical specialties or diffused in romantic or cynical generalities. Some have done positive harm, placing their brains in the service of sinister causes. Few have ventured to look beyond the imperfections of the present to develop progressive, realistic, and humane alternatives to our current course. It is that work, if we are lucky, that might yet produce harmonies that will hold a basis for union worth its price.

The American faith is that no law of necessity bars us from molding our destiny. The story of our peculiar democracy shows how, from time to time, we have overcome old prejudices and replaced them with new visions. Sooner or later we will shuck off the myths that, in our own experience, prove to serve us ill. Those who tell the story, those who act in it, and those who think through what it yet might mean have the chance to breathe new life into our old adventure.

*Now that we know
what happened in
the Reagan Presi-
dency, we need to
understand how he
got to be President
in the first place.
The key problem:
highlighting crucial*
Presidential *charac-
teristics.*

17

Lessons from Candidate
Reagan

HOWEVER ONE RATES recent Presi-
dents, there is no denying this fact: President after President has
been picked for virtues he turned out not to have.

In 1964 we elected "Peaceable Lyndon" Johnson, who consistently
presented himself as determined to stop the war in Vietnam, constantly contrasting himself to that "warmonger" Barry Goldwater.
Johnson went on to turn a skirmish into mass slaughter.

In 1968 Richard Nixon advertised himself as a calmer of crises, an
open and delegating executive devoted to rational, empathetic politics
which would "bring us together." Instead, his behavior in office
spurred political chaos, a White House conspiracy to cut past the
Constitution, and the first sure-to-succeed effort to impeach a president in history.

In 1976 an important dimension of Jimmy Carter's image, in addition to his morality, was his competence; he seemed a political engineer, a systematic operator. From the start, the Carter White House

was a font of fumbling, especially with Congress, paving the way for the Reagan replacement.

By 1980 one might have thought the shocks of disillusionment would surely have turned observing skeptics away from campaign images to the records of the candidates—from the hopes to the facts. Ronald Reagan fit the national mood nearly perfectly. He projected precisely the confidence and warmth that an electorate battered by political anxiety needed. He also reassuringly projected realism. Like Jack Kennedy in 1960, Reagan rattled off statistics. He recounted illustrative historical incidents. He set forth specifics of his record as governor of California.

The Reagan Presidency has confirmed him as a most happy fellow. But Reagan the realist has proved a myth. From supply-side to Bitburg, from Star Wars to Grenada, from Reykjavik and Qaddafi "disinformation" down to the revelations of Iranscam, Ronald Reagan has emerged as a president whose indifference to factuality is matched only by his devotion to theatricality. Far from trivial, Reagan's factual misstatements are right in the middle of the big life-and-death crises of this age, such as nuclear proliferation, military strategy, arms control, human rights, international trade, Third World debt, domestic economics, welfare policy, public education, and the preservation of the environment. His errors have not been one-time slips of the tongue or "gaffes" but repeatedly reiterated false assertions which he continues to make after their falsity has been revealed. He gets his evidence from old movies. He has no interest in the awkward actualities of history or the complex realities of the present. He misrepresents his own life history to fit the "values" he advocates. To ask, regarding the Iran-contra scandal, what he knew and when he knew it is to suppose that knowledge is a meaningful Reagan concept.

That the United States, its position in world politics rapidly deteriorating, should have elected a President of this ilk is not only a political offense but also a journalistic mystery. For long in advance of the election of 1980 these Reagan qualities were known. (Indeed, an awareness of the man's literally fantastic character formed the basis for early Democratic misjudgments: that it would be impossible for Reagan to get nominated, and that, if by some fluke he did, it would be easy to defeat him.)

No one was in a position to bring the truth about Reagan across to the public except journalists. Charges by Reagan's political competitors—such as George Bush's claim, in the March 7, 1980, *Washington Post*, that Reagan "has no real understanding of the dangers we face in the decade of the eighties"—could not be tested by voters unless the media supplied the information needed. But a flood of information alone is little help; the reader needs to know which facts are significant. Now that party leaders and other trusted national sages have disappeared, the public has to get that guidance from columnists and editorialists. If in 1980 the voters were to be warned of Reagan's tragic flaws, they would of necessity have had to turn past the long "Campaign 80" features and the preseason candidate "profiles" to the inside pages where the familiar and profoundly attentive editorial writers and columnists would help them straighten out their thinking. And the time to get that guidance was not back in the preceding year, when few readers could summon up the necessary attention, or in the summer of 1980 after Reagan had already won the delegates necessary to nominate him, but during the primary season decision time—roughly January to June.

Reviewing the editorials and columns for this period in two leading newspapers, the *New York Times* and the *Washington Post*, the first thing one notices is that, on the few occasions when comments did focus on the candidates' qualifications, by far the most common reference was to the candidates' campaign performance rather than their records. The clear implication to curious voters was that the campaign tests Presidential qualities—which, of course, it does not. These days a Presidential campaign tests the candidate's capacity to endure the physical stress of extended travel, to deliver the same speech over and over again, to beg money from rich donors, to spin out television commercials, to announce detailed plans for government action in an unknown, yet-to-come political context, to impress crowds of recruited teenagers, and, what is perhaps most important, to puff up one's pictorial image for television news. What is tested, then, is not the candidate's actual lifetime performance—the factual historical record—held up against the requirements of the Presidential job, but rather his capacity to prance along the campaign trail, pretending, with the help of highly paid media coaches, to be what he is not. The campaign is a basket-shooting contest to pick the best poker player. As Joseph Kraft put it in a March 23 *Washington Post* column: "The personal qualities so critical to winning and losing nominations bear little relation to government."

A few editorials in the *New York Times* did take note of Reagan's "vague simplicities" (June 8), his taste for "political pabulum," and "much simplistic nonsense" (March 23). Anthony Lewis perceived Reagan's "emptiness of mind" (*Times*, March 20), and Ellen Goodman saw him as a potential world leader "unencumbered by knowledge" (*Post*, March 25). James Reston, probably the most consistent critic of Reagan's Presidential character, noted that the candidate "has a backside foremost way of saying things first and thinking about them later" (*Times*, April 16), that he "handles his formal speeches well until he's questioned about the facts" (April 11), and that "he keeps talking nonsense about foreign policy" (May 11).

But these quotations, plucked from the sprawl of spring commentary, give the false impression of sharp focus on Reagan's casual attitude toward reality. In fact, week after week went by with only a few scattered references to the topic.

An evident reason for the press's generally benign neglect of Reagan's Presidential inadequacy was that few journalists believed Reagan's candidacy could possibly succeed. As late as March 5, 1980, Meg Greenfield noted in the *Washington Post* that "most of the journalists I know and much of the Eastern world I live in find Reagan's candidacy preposterous." Later that month Anthony Lewis wrote that, to liberals, "Reagan has seemed too far-out a figure to take seriously." Why delve into the qualifications of a candidate sure to lose, if not his party's nomination, then, at least, the election?

Anxieties were allayed by confidence that the campaign itself would test his competence. On April 9, David Broder surmised that "Reagan has not yet crossed the 'credibility barrier' that stands in the way of any challenger's access to the presidency. It is the test of plausibility that makes people feel comfortable with the phrase 'President Reagan.'" Judging from the Kennedy and Carter cases, Broder thought that "Reagan will probably not be able to clear that hurdle until the American electorate sees how he handles the choice of a running mate, the conduct of his party convention and, most important, the television debates with the incumbent in the general election." In the months to come, the media would approach Reagan with increasingly "skeptical scrutiny." James Reston's hopeful perception was that Rea-

gan's "recent blunders on simple facts, and his tendency to do his research after he speaks rather than before are becoming a major issue
in this campaign" (April 13).

By focusing on the campaign—that temporary, amorphous, shifting, artificial clutch of events—commentators unplugged the essential
predictions about Reagan from the requirements of the Presidency on
the one hand and from Reagan's record on the other. Thus the way
was opened for just about any statable proposition concerning how a
President Reagan would behave. Joseph Kraft wrote in February that
"in forging to the fore . . . Reagan proved once again that he is ill-
equipped to deal with the nation's most pressing business." But there
was no clear way to challenge such wildly wrong predictions as that
of Reagan adviser Richard J. Whalen: "Reagan possesses those qualities essential to political success and effective leadership: inbred caution, an instinctive sense of priorities, a practical flexibility, a willingness to compromise on less important matters, an aversion to needless
risk-taking, and, above all, a crisp, calculating intelligence that seldom
strays for long from the issue at hand" (*Post*, March 23). Nor could
the candidate's own predictions be challenged empirically, as when
Reagan claimed that "We're going to be so respected that never again
will a dictator dare invade an American embassy and hold our people
as hostages" (Anthony Lewis, March 20). Or when he said, "If there's
one statement I'd like you to remember, it's this. . . . In my administration there will be no more betrayal of friends and allies by the
United States" (William Safire, *Times*, March 24).

What was missing was testing such prophecies against the Reagan
record. "I've been running on my record," Reagan said. But the obsession of journalism with the immediacy of the campaign meant that he
could pretend to have done what he did not do and to have been what
he never was.

He was helped along by such "experts" as the one who started his
list of Reagan executive talents with: "First of all, he's got an excellent
memory" (Ralph Goldman, *U.S. News & World Report*, July 21).

A better help to Reagan were columnists who simply took his word
for the facts, as when Tom Wicker made passing reference to Reagan's claim that "when he was governor of California, unpaid volunteers put in 117 days each, coming up with 1,800 recommendations for
reform, of which 1,600 were implemented" (*Times*, May 25). Reagan

had not only served two terms as Governor in the limelight but, as Broder had noted in February, he had been running for President for twelve years. In a long profile published in the April 26 *Washington Post*, Lou Cannon wrote of Reagan's governorship that "overall the real picture is substantially different than the one Reagan paints for his audiences," while Robert Lindsey, in a June 29 article in the *New York Times Magazine*, quoted Reagan's main Democratic ally, Bob Moretti, as observing that "the way he acted as governor didn't resemble his rhetoric."

Yet, surprisingly, his official record did not catch the sharp attention of columnists and editorialists as he approached the nomination that would win him the Presidency. A few intelligent corrections were there; Ellen Goodman's March 25 review of Reagan's record on issues of women's rights demonstrated that he was not a rigid ideologue. But only in a March 23 *New York Times* op-ed piece by Michael Calabrese does one find Reagan statements systematically assessed against the Reagan record. As Calabrese put it, "That he can now claim he accomplished his conservative goals or promises, and actually campaign on his record without serious rebuttal from the news media, is a credit to his McLuthanesque mastery of media management." Calabrese proceeded to refute with clear facts Reagan's description of his gubernatorial record on welfare reform, abortion, taxes, and the Equal Rights Amendment, drawing on precise, recorded information presented by six leading Republican legislators who had supported Reagan in his California campaigns. That fall Calabrese provided additional details in *Selecting a President: A Citizen Guide to the 1980 Election*.

Reagan himself attached the highest saliency to his performance on welfare reform. Asked in a *Washington Post* interview (April 4), "What are you proudest of in your public career?" Reagan answered, "I think the single, probably biggest achievement was the reform of welfare [in California], which turned out to be the most comprehensive and successful reform of welfare that's ever been attempted in this country."

Reagan boasted that his welfare reform cut 364,630 recipients from the welfare rolls. Calabrese demonstrated that this was simply not so. He quoted the Republican legislators as stating: "The total number of recipients on welfare in California nearly *doubled* during the Reagan years, while the state's population *growth rate* decreased from three percent to one percent per year." Reagan claimed that his reforms saved "almost $2 billion" for taxpayers. In fact, Calabrese pointed out, welfare costs tripled under his regime. Reagan claimed that his reforms increased aid to the "truly needy" by 43 percent. In fact, Calabrese wrote, the Reagan administration had fought a hard, bitter battle for four years in the California courts against implementing the federal law requiring the cost-of-living increases in welfare payments and had made the increase only when the Department of Health, Education, and Welfare threatened to cut California's federal funding by $700 million if it did not. Reagan claimed that "the various work incentive programs put more than 76,000 welfare recipients to work in fiscal 1973–74, including 47,000 through CWEP [the Community Work Experience Program]." In fact, Calabrese reported, still quoting the six California legislators, CWEP put only 4,760 recipients to work, and the 76,000 Reagan had referred to were simply the total number of welfare recipients who found work as the economy improved.

In other words, Candidate Reagan lied repeatedly about what he claimed to be his greatest achievement as governor. He lied about his lesser achievements as well. He claimed to have cut taxes and government spending, for example, when, as Calabrese pointed out, he put through the largest tax increase in California history and oversaw the highest growth rate in government spending.

Former Republican state senate leader William Bagley, who had been a close working ally of the Reagan administration in Sacramento, was on the mark when he said that Reagan's account of his record was an "absolute, total misrepresentation of the facts." His false claims were not trivial or irrelevant but rather the foundations of his justification for presenting himself as a candidate for President. And his subsequent performance in the office of President has shown the significance of Reagan's tendency to reject the facts.

When it was discovered that Reagan was purveying misinformation about the highlights of his record, the commentators should have banged the gong and flashed the lights, calling for strong and steady focus on Reagan's indifference to reality as a quality dangerous to the Presidency. Such an alarm could have triggered a hard look at his biography as a whole, in which fantasy ruled his mind at least from the time of his first main job—dreaming up the details of ball games on the radio.

Clashes between record and rhetoric are not to be taken only as moral defects but as clues to baseline Presidential qualities. The reduction of politics to morals will be a special temptation in 1988, as we head into a reprise of 1964 and 1976 when questions of conscience overpowered pragmatism. Reagan's misrepresentations in 1980 can be judged by St. Peter for their sincerity, but should have been judged by the electorate as to what it would mean to put into the White House a President unplugged from the real world.

A President's worldview is crucial: How do his convictions as to how politics work, and should work, in international and domestic affairs connect with his actual decisions? And a candidate's character is the bottom line: Can we afford another power-grabber like Nixon, another affection-seeking pretender like Reagan? These questions are not simply moral, but political. Our lives are in the President's hands. We need to know in advance in which direction he is likely to throw us. And we are nearly totally dependent on the press and television to provide us with that knowledge.

Cutting through to the key qualities is not easy but, there is no reason to suppose it cannot be done. It is not a matter of psychoanalysis on the campaign trail—a nearly impossible task, given the full-time, highly paid media consultants busily spinning the candidate's image, warping attention away from set facts to manipulable impressions. As John Sears put it when he was still running the 1980 Reagan campaign, "What we're dealing with at this level is perceptions, not facts; you can change perceptions, but you can't change facts" (*Times*, January 27).

But reporters who step off the campaign bus and away from the motel television set can get at the facts—factual answers to key Presidential questions, drawn from the candidate's past. The sources are there: interviews with people who have worked with him and can tell you what he did, news coverage from the years before the Presidential bug bit him, even biographies and histories in which he appears. In 1980, such material did begin to appear—but mainly *after* Reagan was nominated and on his way to winning. Even then, such warnings were drowned in a flood of less significant information.

The 1987 Gary Hart story illustrates the problem and the possibility. Hart's sexual peccadillo in the midst of his campaign as the leading Democrat triggered reports that he had slept around before, indeed, repeatedly. Adding in the fact that he had thrown down a gauntlet to the press, daring reporters to tail him, the episode raised serious doubts about his political realism. But long before that bimbo fiasco, columnists and editorialists should have been looking into other disturbing questions about Gary Hart as President. Had he been a loner in the Senate? Was his rhetoric too intellectual and technological for the public? Had he a serious problem in working with the press? Such explorations—not lost in massive "Campaign 88" features, but highlighted on the editorial page—should long ago have led to close examination of President Hart, not Candidate Hart. In that way, political journalism could have moved beyond process to substance, beyond campaign techniques to the Presidentially relevant facts of the life the candidate bears with him.

In June 1987 the *New York Times* took the lead in generating the needed information, asking thirteen active Presidential candidates for a very wide range of detailed background facts. Executive editor Max Frankel explained to the *Washington Post* that "when we entrust our presidents with instantaneous powers of life and death, we think we have a duty to report on the essential character and history of every contender for the office."

That is a giant step forward, to be followed, one hopes, by concentrated highlighting of *Presidential* qualifications.

Campaigning in 1980, Ronald Reagan gave us the advice we need as we move toward 1988: "What makes you think that whatever image is presented is the true image? Check me out. . . . Don't become the sucker generation."

18

Conclusion:
Reflections on the Problems of
Politics and the Science of
Solving Them

THE SKEPTICAL democrat does not
view government as an ideal but as an instrument for setting the conditions for a good life. That is the best we can hope for. But the worst
is ever at hand: governments fail. They are taken over by military or
revolutionary or corporate tyrants, or they create their own tyrannies. To suppose that the United States is invulnerable to such tragedy is naive. What prophet saw that the nation which gave us Goethe
would give us Hitler? Tyranny could happen here. So could the end of
the world through one nuclear error.

If our government goes down, the most likely route is not through
a coup d'état but through a *coup de tête*—a break of the brain. Democracy teeters on the edge of political delusion, of social neurosis,
which threatens to slide us over into political psychosis. Democracy
is closer to a mob scene than to a seminar. We try for rationality and

decency by various orderings of discourse designed to move political thinking beyond the ignorance, indifference, and prejudice of the masses and the corruptive lust for power of the elites. That is a tough task. For political thinking is easily rocked off its moorings, in times of crisis by the distortions of desperation and in easy times by the fact that politics is rather less amusing than the productions of show biz.

In times like these, when the rich are off escalating their incomes, the middle class noodling along in relative satisfaction, and the poor dispersed and disorganized in their misery, it is hard to get people to think about politics. In the 1920s as in the 1950s Americans went to sleep politically while their government drifted toward economic and then urban chaos. That trouble-ease-trouble-ease pattern is recurrent. After a world war we drop into a nap and new trouble sneaks up on us. But with every turn of that cycle the dangers jump upward in magnitude and scope. Today an American electorate bemused and distracted by the politics of sentiment stands in unprecedented need for the return of reason. Our nation was born in the Enlightenment— would that we could have called back that political mentality as a gift for our two hundredth birthday!

Thanks to political blindness at a time when we needed vision, the United States has created an economy built on sand. Internationally, we have plunged from dominance to dependency, not only in the flow of goods and money, but also in the rising threat of nuclear war. Those naive optimists who read history as showing that the "system works" need to adjust their thinking to a new dimension of threat— immediately explodable looming dangers which, if they happen only once, will ruin life. No form of rationality is harder than planning ahead when your stomach is full and your feet are warm. Yet unless we do that, our little worries will soon be over, replaced by gigantic regrets.

Planning ahead requires theory. Theory is necessary to build bridges from now to then, to link the facts of experience to the probabilities of anticipation. Which of our many wars supplies the "lessons" we need to prevent another one? That depends on which similarities are to be selected as significant, a question theory has to answer. So there is more to political reasoning than getting out the facts and debating our preferences. There is also the need to figure out what facts and preferences are worth paying attention to, and how that focus should be directed. In our culture journalists do most of the fact work and politicians expostulate preferences. Theory is, by and large, the responsibility of scholars.

Hopeful souls want to think of the university as the culture's headquarters for reason. The potential is there, to be sure, but much of the scholarly enterprise is at least as chaotic or perverse (or both) as modern politics. In this "age of analysis" scholarship shreds itself into fragments of inquiry, each with its own circle of mutually reinforcing experts who seldom think beyond the intellectual stockades they have constructed to protect themselves. Professors shrink from the wider conversation, which threatens their dignity. Instead, they retreat to their cozy campfires where they can talk their secret language with their fellow refugees. The result is a "community of scholars" in which there is, in reality, no community at all. The principle of toleration is taken—mistakenly—to prescribe silence among those who differ. As in politics, the discomforts of debate give way to the pleasures of harmony. As in politics, that pleasure of harmony drains away reason and sucks in illusion. But privatized scholars talking, teaching, and publishing within their sub-sub-fields are invisible to public discourse and thus free from challengers who might suggest that, tenured or not, they are wasting their lives.

Is political science just another "discipline," Germanically categorized in parallel rank with other boxes in the humanities and social sciences? If so, that need not be. Like politics itself, political science is essentially synthetic, not analytic. Politics concerns the common life. Politics courts alliance among tribes and genders and regions and classes and generations and vocations. Politics is worth studying because, as the long human experience demonstrates, governments can kill people or rescue people, shape happiness or misery, elevate vice or virtue. Politics counts. Therefore, knowing it counts. And while knowing it is not the same as doing it, the best of political science reflects the connecting action of politics.

The best studies concentrate on understanding political linkages, and to do that they draw on whatever methods work best to unravel the significant puzzles before them. Then they state their findings in plain language and work to get those findings into the widest and most intense political discourse available, where they can be tested not only by specialists but also by thinkers and doers in the world at large. That need not turn scholarship into polemics or journalism. It can instead turn scholarship into a developing line of understanding which can take hold and grow, not only within university departments, but also in the guidance of real political decisions. And if the results turn out to be wrong—or useless—the wider debate can make that clear and thus free the scholar to steer the inquiry into more promising waters. For as nearly all of us students (struggling to be scholars) have at last come to learn, the biggest problem of research is not answering the question but deciding what question to ask in the first place.

Great regiments of political scientists march valiantly in meaningless directions, misled by narrow, one-dimensional maps. Huge storehouses of mental resources are wasted in constructing elaborate approaches which never arrive at any useful finding. Little wonder, then, that the politicians seldom set aside their immediate struggles to ponder the pages of the *American Political Science Review*. But some political science is worth reading, and some of that gets read. The plus side is that, over the years, political science has widened and deepened its scope so that it now includes inquiries directly significant to the advancement of liberty and justice for all.

The widening is encouraging. For long years political science was stuck in legal structures and abstract ideologies. Professor Woodrow Wilson wrote his book about Congress without bothering to visit it. But then interest moved outward; researchers actually went out and got information about a widening range of political phenomena: government itself, parties and interest groups, voting behavior and public opinion, the media. Scholars ranged wherever they needed to go to discover how and why and when government worked, and they used whatever tools they could borrow from the neighboring disciplines to pry loose the truth.

Political science also turned inward, breaking into the temple of the psyche. Discerning only the simple, external surfaces of parties, regions, or ideologies proved inadequate for predicting what politicians and citizens were likely to do. Similarly, "behavioralism," in its primitive sense of stress on observable activity (like voting) rather than thoughts and feelings (like the reasons for voting), soon ran out of gas. So did institutional analysis and reform, too often caught up in the naive hope that charted relations might cancel the relevance of personal relations. Curious inquirers, prepared to look wherever they had to to get the facts, found it necessary to explore the psychology of politics.

Plumbing the human psyche to understand politics went astray in three directions. The first was cultural determinism, a malady of anthropology. To be sure, politics is rooted in culture, but how deep—and how determinative—are those roots? Does the identification of a culture-politics linkage demonstrate its necessity, its fixedness? Consider democracy. Many a link between American culture and American democracy can indeed be identified, from the Puritans of old to the Yuppies of today. But what does that teach us about the necessary foundations of democracy? Democracy exists in apparently stable form in England, Japan, Germany, India, France, Australia, Sweden, Finland, and Venezuela, for example. One would be hard put to demonstrate that these countries shared a wide range of cultural dimensions which buttressed their democracies. The same can be said for totalitarian regimes, capping cultures of very different sorts.

A second diversion from getting knowledge useful for politics fell out of psychoanalysis. Freud was a doctor; psychoanalysis has been primarily a clinical enterprise, aimed at curing individual patients suffering from mental maladies. Its first and most important step is diagnosis. For understanding political leaders, certain diagnostic patterns that psychoanalysts developed did prove useful in identifying rough patterns of political orientation—for instance, what I call Presidential character. Such rough patterns amount to generalizations applicable from one case to another. But beyond that, the clinician rightly delves far more deeply into the individual, detailed dynamics of the patient's personality because the clinical objective is to cure that person. The political objective is different: to select the right person for a political role. At the time that has to be done, we almost never have the data we would need to ferret out the innermost secrets of the candidate's mind, heart, and genitals. Years later, psychoanalytic biographies may uncover such stuff for our enlightenment and/or amusement. Even now, we need to get at each individual case as best we can, filling in the blanks left by the application of rough patterns. But as a good deal of flaky speculation about current leaders makes clear, psychoanalysis, with its emphasis on intuitive symbolism and emotional resonance, can be perverted into a diversion from the knowledge we need to understand politics.

A third wrong turn in the interior exploration of politics concerned ideology. What happened was an exaggeration of logic as tightly linking principle and practice in the world of politics, an error natural to academics who live in a world in which logic is required, a mistaken application to America of the European significance of ideology. If that tight linkage held, the content of ideology would be the key element in political analysis. But the linkage proved weak. As the research turned out, understanding the psychological dynamics of the true believer did not help much in understanding the substance of his beliefs. Fanatics are to be found on the left and on the right. So are the alienated and the apathetic. The link between ideology and political behavior is similarly weak. In the United States at least there is a lot of loose space between high commandments and the day-to-day choices of politics. In the 1980s, for example, what was a "conservative"—a Reagan Revolutionary or an advocate of hanging on to the good old New Deal?

Then how can students of politics best exploit these various pervertible modes of inquiry? By concentrating on political relevance. Politics centers on choice. What can we get from cultural anthropology to help us grasp the choice of human rights policy, or welfare reform, or fixing Congress? In choosing individual leaders, such as Presidents, how can psychoanalytic and other psychological diagnostic regularities help us to perceive and predict the main risks and promises of the selection? How can ideological analysis (or synthesis) aid in our understanding of political communication in a democracy, where good choice demands widely shared deliberation? The essential criterion becomes relevance to choice, including the choice of sustaining what is, not simply relevance to the existence of extant political phenomena.

American politics in the late 1980s confirmed the relevance of the three layers of work in this book—the person, the process, the media. Consider the Iran-contra scandal which exploded in 1987.

At its core was a person, Ronald Reagan, President of the United States. Reconstructing the story as revealed to date, the door left open for this crisis was the gap between Reagan's character and style. On the one hand, Reagan had developed over the years a rhetoric representing him as a strong, decisive, principled, independent, well-informed leader. A poll in 1984 found the most frequently mentioned reason people voted for him to be his strength of leadership. Particularly on television, Reagan came across as a straightforward, candid, responsible person. No doubt this perception contributed to the marginal choice in 1980 of Reagan over Carter, whose image had deteriorated into one of weakness and inconsistency. Like Charlton Heston playing Moses, Reagan knew how to play President.

But in private Reagan was radically different. He was and is a passive-positive. My prediction, published in the *New York Times* in September 1980, that the passive-positive type would fit Reagan in the White House was eventually confirmed even by such close friends of his as Michael Deaver and William Casey. His basic political motivation was the search for affection from those around him. In his up-close relationships Reagan wanted pleasant harmony, not disputes or bad news. Unlike in public, Reagan in the White House let his sentimentality flow and his sensitivity to personal relationships govern his behavior. His lack of appetite for candor, factuality, and logic was evident day by day. He liked banter. He could do without the complexities of national strategic calculation. Like William Howard Taft and Warren G. Harding, his passive-positive predecessors, Reagan in public seemed the essential President, while in private he was just a chuckly good old boy.

Then this contradiction between public and private Reagan, neatly compartmentalized, smashed together. Americans were taken hostage in Lebanon by allies or perhaps agents of the Iranians. To stave off the kidnappers' demands, Reagan's in-house directors scripted for him strong public statements against dealing with kidnappears for the release of hostages. Stern and determined, Reagan demanded that governments around the world follow his lead in standing firm against the temptation to provide the designated ransom. This "Operation Staunch" seemed to register, loud and clear, the President's uncompromised conviction. His adamance was reported around the world.

Meanwhile, back at the White House, the families of the hostages came to see him, pleading that he get their relatives home—a most powerful appeal to a President whose emotions are primarily attuned to the persons in the same room with him. There they were, face-to-face, with tears for those they loved. Apparently Reagan was deeply affected. Mrs. Reagan, one of his most important directors, may have hoped to lift up her husband's waning reputation by getting the hostages released. The President secretly authorized selling arms to Iranians in return for the release of hostages, in direct contradiction of his adamant public statements against just such transactions. When the arms deal was revealed, Reagan's international and domestic credibility collapsed. A poll showed that a majority of Americans thought their President was "lying."

Another scandal followed. In November 1986 a magazine in Lebanon reported that profits from selling arms to the Iranians had been used to aid the contras, guerrillas combating the government in Nicaragua, a "diversion" arranged by the staff of the National Security Council. The President claimed not to know about it. The National Security Advisor, who briefed the President every morning, testified to a Congressional committee investigating the scandal that he had held back the information in order to give the President "plausible deniability"—so that the President, if accused of such highly controversial and blatantly illegal dealings, could say he did not know about it.

That the advisor did not tell the President of this highly significant development regarding the two most sensitive areas of U.S. foreign policy—the Middle East and Central America—was shocking. The "deniability" explanation was implausible: leaving the President uninformed would—and did—set him up as looking stupid and ineffective, as well as dishonest, particularly as news of the diversion spread steadily through diplomatic and military channels around the world. A far more plausible explanation for the advisor not telling the President was available.

Anyone who had dealt with Ronald Reagan day after day had to be aware of his Harding-like incapacity to keep track of what he was hearing or to remember what was what, including such matters as which country he was in when traveling in Latin America or what "parity" meant when he was campaigning in Iowa. Reagan's press managers worked hard to shield him from unanticipated questions, for instance by virtually eliminating Presidential press conferences. Still, Reagan loved to tell stories and he could remember the good ones. And when at "photo opportunities" questions were yelled at him, he popped out answers. Reagan, the supposedly "strong leader," drifted along in a world of unreality in which the distinction between history and the movies was meaningless.

What a movie script the "diversion" would have made! NSC operative Lt. Colonel Oliver North called it "a neat idea": rescuing the Nicaraguan "freedom fighters" (the heroes) by switching funds from Iranians (the villains). To let Ronald Reagan in on that startling drama escalated the risk that he would let it out, as he regaled acquaintances or yelled back at reporters. So it is not implausible to suppose that the National Security Advisor held back from leaking the Iran-contra story to the President of the United States—that ready raconteur who could not be expected to maintain a mental barrier between secret and tellable tales.

Until the full facts of Reagan's role in this and other critically important matters become known, the scenarios are speculative. Certainly their apparent plots and scenes are consistent with Reagan's character, worldview, and style, as exemplified in his behavior and experience well before he found his way to Washington. When the complete history comes out, once again we will see that the personality of a political leader is not extraneous or exotic, but rather an essential dimension of political action.

But certainly there was more to the Iran-contra scandal than the role of Ronald Reagan. The case also illustrates the significance of process, of group politics. Beyond the White House extended an amazingly complex, secret network of unelected agents, foreign and domestic, private profiteers and weapons merchants, Swiss bank accounts in the range of millions, fraudulent fund-raisers, and officials of various nations at war, wheeling and dealing across three continents—all operating without authorization from Congress or the President. The enterprise was directed (when it was) by a tight little outfit called the National Security Council, originally set up to coordinate relations between State and Defense, not to do "covert operations." The National Security Advisor explained that the ordinary Defense and State bureaucracies had become so stiflingly complex and self-protective that they could not possibly undertake such a fast, risky enterprise. The only way to get it done was to transform an apparently powerless coordinative council into a red-hot action organization, uninhibited by the usual pluralistic constraints. Long before "Irangate," Hans Morgenthau, analyzing Watergate, explained that this mode of paralleling the regular institutions with new ones was not an American invention; Hitler had done the same. I suspect the Roman Empire was, at times, similarly supplemented. Power is drained from the regular institutions into apparently secondary or derivative ones, thus rendering the conjunction of authority and responsibility nearly impossible.

That the perceptions of their own roles and the roles of the others they deal with shape the performance of government leaders is strikingly demonstrated in the same Iran-contra case. Reagan's loose-jointed "management style" was the model for relationships among the "subordinates" arrayed beneath him, in what one skeptic called "a daisy chain of command." That lightly linked mélange of operatives was completely cut off from Congress. The National Security Advisor and his main staffer testified without the slightest hesitation to their fundamental rejection of the idea that Congress and the rule of law should govern U.S. foreign policy. Congress was to them an unfortunate obstacle to the swift and effective conduct of their work, which they "assumed" would be approved by a President elected by the people. Lying to the Congress, in their perception, was perfectly legitimate as long as it could be characterized as "misleading" or "evading" or simply leaving out information, however obviously relevant. In short, there existed inside the Reagan White House a miniculture unplugged from the federal system, dominated by the mutually supportive values of officials who considered all that yammering in the House and Senate as an asinine distraction from their patriotic endeavors. And even within the administration, the little NSC coterie held back trust from nearly every other responsible officer, including the appropriate Cabinet members. How key leaders see each other shapes what they say—and do not say—to each other, and thus structures the actual process of communication and decision-making. Whatever the organization chart looks like, what counts is how it works.

Which points directly to the third layer in this book, the media. The Iran-contra affair became a scandal when the story broke in the press. For weeks, as the congressional hearings went on, the press and television piled information and commentary onto the public. Public opinion polls, obviously reflective of the media coverage, raked in list after list of reactions to what people saw and read. The key court was not Congress or the judiciary (which would soon be involved) but the court of public opinion. The National Security Council testifiers held the media in a contempt approximating their contempt for Congress, as they explicitly declared. Indeed, a primary reason they offered for failing to inform even a few leading congressmen, even in secret, was their fear that what went in a congressman's ear would soon come out of his mouth—on camera. What they sought from the press was not a chance to tell the truth but a chance to manipulate the public.

The testimony of Lt. Colonel North, the NSC operator who exercised an amazingly latitudinous scope of actions in the Iran-contra scandal, highlighted a primary problem of contemporary journalism. North confessed, outright and without qualification, that he had lied to just about everyone, congressmen included, about the Iran-contra affair. How, then, were the people to judge what he was saying at the hearings? The initial answer reflected strongly the supposition that one's manner on television reveals one's character—the medium's shakiest assumption. Lt. Colonel North came on as a handsome, trim, bemedaled young marine, with a manner much like that of Jimmy Stewart in the movie *Mr. Smith Goes to Washington*, the innocent victim, buffeted by puffy politicians, sitting straight and talking straight while being accused of what he swore he had not done. For nearly a week Representatives and Senators lauded North for his candor. Journalists picked up and reinforced that illusion. North was featured on the cover of nearly every newsmagazine. In the public opinion polls he emerged as Mr. Honest. Only considerably later was it made public that he had not only lied as he confessed in the hearings, but had lied about what college he went to, what he majored in, and how many tours he served in Vietnam, and had claimed to be a marine company commander which, according to the Pentagon, he was not. He had covered up the fact that he had been hospitalized for an emotional disorder. But by the time the news of these fabrications came out, North's image had been set. The subsequent revelations came too late to change it. North's media victory was thus analogous to the Reagan administration's "victory" in invading Grenada, an adventure which registered with the public as a good clear win—and stayed that way in the public mind, despite later information refuting that image. Early impressions, if not first impressions, powerfully shape public perceptions.

The public's reaction to Colonel North was shaped by reporting of the public's probable reaction to Colonel North. That is, immediately after each piece of his testimony, on came a television commentator to say how he thought people would react to North. Obviously that sent a message to the audience: here's how you ought to react, unless you are some sort of oddball. Then polls were taken by telephone overnight, gathering largely favorable responses which, reported the next day, reinforced the trend again. So throughout the weeks of hearings on the Iran-contra scandal, "How People Feel" dominated the news agenda, particularly on television. Beyond the mini-minority following the facts, few people could keep up with what North said or did. He became another Per Se Celebrity, like Vanna White of the game show "Wheel of Fortune," or Donna Rice, the model famous for interrupting the Presidential candidacy of Senator Gary Hart—persons famous for being famous. In politics that phenomenon registers the ultimate disconnection between thinking and feeling.

Television journalism has helped that to happen. Television's favorite question is "How do you feel?" That resonates with and reinforces the contemporary drift of American politics away from the awkward, frightening realities of political life. Americans believe in equality, and thinking is unequal. Some think better than others. Some have far more information than others, on any given problem. Some bring to the facts much more enlightening experience than others have had. So working out our common thinking is quite difficult, quite uncomfortable. It cannot be done unless politicians put aside their feelings and concentrate on their thoughts, thus highlighting the inequalities. The reduction of politics to sentiment wipes away that problem, offering Everyman the assurance that his feelings are as good as anybody else's. Politics wafts over into the Garden of Sentiment, where relaxation of the mind sets the stage for invasion by tough-minded intruders.

If we can see the main dimensions, what fundamental problems of modern democracy call loudest for the attention of the student of human politics? The question of politics is not how to perfect it but how to keep it alive and moving forward. Politics is not morals or aesthetics or geometry, but a grubby accumulation of lessons of hard experience as to the way imperfect, insensitive, and ignorant people can nevertheless keep living and growing together.

The hard tension of democracy stretches between the necessity of leadership and the necessity of consent. Government cannot be done by the mob, especially a mob of several hundred million people. Government must not be handed over to some elite, because elites cannot be trusted to take care of the rest of us. So we have to figure out how to invest leaders with power, how to organize leadership for rational, progressive action, how to check their corruptions, how to replace them with others at least no worse than they are. We have to invent and sustain ways for an otherwise-occupied electorate to learn the lessons of humankind's long, hard struggle for life, liberty, and happiness, to understand what is happening in the real world as we choose leaders, to put enough attention and participation into politics so that when crisis arrives we will not be caught off guard and fall back into chaos or tyranny. The reason for bringing psychology to bear on these problems is not to elevate emotion over rationality or the self over the community, but to recognize that politics can slide down from the Enlightenment to the Dark Ages all over again. To elevate sanity, we have to understand political neurosis. To elevate compassion, we have to be able to hear Original Sin drumming away beneath the hymns of community.

Change compels choice. In the contemporary world the rate of political change soars ahead geometrically, while the rate of development of political capacity plods along by old arithmetic. To catch up will require new vision, and that is what scholars ought to provide.

Consider the political public. Theoretically, for two hundred years we have had a government by "we the people," but in fact it is only now that the people are in a position to run the country. The right to vote is real—for blacks, for women, for young people, as well as for the white male adults historically equated with "the people." Ill-considered reforms have virtually destroyed the political parties which used to deal between the people and the government. Polling undercuts the discretion of leaders. Quick journalism runs past the politicians who used to inform their constituents of what was happening. Taken together, these trends transform democracy from articulated federalism and representative politics to mass politics. And mass media play to the audience, working more to please than to inform them. Thus in secular politics vox populi does become vox dei. How this transition from spatially webbed and temporally developing politics to instant mass politics works is a topic many good political scientists should be devoting their minds to.

An informed, engaged, rational electorate could turn mass politics into genuine government by consent. But that is not the electorate we have, or will have any time soon. The evidence of political ignorance—of the Constitution, of where Nicaragua is, of what "deficit" means, of how many Senators each state elects—is overwhelming; taken realistically into account, that evidence would render largely meaningless the polls that gather opinions about matters the respondents know little or nothing about.

An electorate participating regularly in the process of debate, nominations, campaigns, and elections would bring to the evidence questions relevant to the choices they have to make. But the electorate in America is largely unengaged. In the "landslide" election of 1980, for example, Reagan was elected by only slightly more than a quarter of the eligible electorate. Only about half the citizenry—inheritors of the right to vote—bothered to do so. And Presidential elections are the high points of participation, far higher than Congressional and state and local elections.

As for rationality, if we had an electorate schooled in political thinking, mass politics might work well. But we do not. Thanks to various intellectual perversions, which were used to turn public education from substance to technique, the average American has not learned in school what it took to bring him to where he is in the long hard struggle for democracy. And as television concentrates on feelings and reactions, transforming journalists into drama critics and the electorate into a political audience, the very relevance of thinking about politics fades away. The drift to fiction, the relocation of political calculation from parliament to theater, eases us away from argument to sentiment. The confusion of tolerance with indifference unplugs the energy of political debate. The misinterpretation of equality as meaning that anyone's opinion is as good as any-one else's makes the comparison of alternative solutions seem unfair; instead, it is supposed, we should simply count who wants what and go with a majority composed not of convinced deliberators but of in-dividual preferers. Thus the discourse of democracy drifts off into the fandango of fiction, and matters of life and death get decided by the emotion of the day.

None of that is necessary. To get back onto the track of real-life politics means revitalizing public education—not as democratic pro-paganda, but as an account of what really happened in the history of democracy (and its alternatives) brought up to date in a way that wakes up students to the fact that the choices are theirs. That development depends significantly on the capacity of publishing and teaching intellectuals to address seriously and directly the tough reali-ties of failure and success in democracies, not to lapse into the pro-duction of Soviet-style encyclopedias, "historical" novels, docudramas, or other deviations from the test of fact, nor to burrow into the hid-den recesses of their little "disciplines" where challenge is restricted to some arcane coterie. Rescuing democratic education depends pro-foundly on the media as well, especially the mass media, where the electorate finds out what is happening.

The vocation of journalism is to make reality interesting. That can be done. Real news is a natural object of human curiosity. It need not be presented in gray, dull form. It need not be shredded into mini-fragments of print or television. It need not be confused with balanced quotations from the available extremes. It need not be Mur-doch-ized into startling headlines unconfirmed in the story. It need not put quickness ahead of rightness. None of these maladies is a necessity in any modern medium. Especially as technological flexi-bility burgeons in wire services, newspapers, magazines, radio, and television, and as all kinds of new ways of getting news become available to consumers, the media will graduate from rigid restric-tions to experiments. Combine that with the growing recognition among leading journalists that they are not walking mirrors but the philosopher kings of contemporary society and the way is opened for using that power to get the truth across. Not just out, but across. Like professors, journalists need to take a fresh interest in discerning what happens to the pearls they cast. Presenting news to the public does not mean the public gets it. Researchers ought to plumb cognition by the public, not just what is made available. Students of public opinion and voting behavior should include public knowledge and voting rationality in their agenda.

In the largest sense, then, it is clear that the public today plays an actual and potential role in democratic politics vaster, faster, and more explosive or creative than even fifty years ago. That wide and deep change links to changes in the most basic democratic decisions we make—the choice of leaders. Take Presidents. Nominees used to be chosen by the Washington elite, then by political parties, then by primary elections. Today we may be moving into an era in which the nominees are effectively chosen before the primaries start, by a combination of media events and polled reactions thereto. In 1987 about a dozen debates among various combinations of Democratic and Republican candidates were scheduled for television in the fall. Plans were under way to get immediate reactions from voters to each televised debate, in some cases by means of pro and con buttons to be pushed as the watchers watched. Thus the primary horse race in the spring would be preceded by a ghost race in the fall, doubtless moving toward the elimination of some contenders and the elevation to front-runnerdom of two others. The process is changing, rapidly and radically. How the candidates will learn to adapt to it is an open question. But what is beyond question is that the selection process itself and the criteria applied therein are contributing heavily to the irrationality of Presidential selection.

Runners for President have always been posing performers, from George Washington to Ronald Reagan. But now they pose before television cameras as they prance through the primaries. The race itself—constant travel, repeating the same speech, begging for money, blackening opponents—has little to do with being President. The myth that television displays character may have had some validity when the performers were amateurs. But now all of them get coached and rehearsed and made up in the hope of approaching the power of Reagan's television appeal. Can we judge a candidate's Presidential talents by watching him play President? Though it is in no way necessary, television coverage of candidates now encourages the public to choose the President they feel best about. Again and again, that has empowered persons who turned out to be in the White House quite different from what they seemed to be on the campaign trail.

If the television image is perilously subjective, issue debates are perilously subjunctive. Long in advance of the election and even further away from the next inauguration day, candidates are asked to say (briefly, please!) what they would get the government to do if they got in the White House. Typically each works out, from tedious papers by experts, a paragraph per issue, advertising succinctly (as in television commercials) the key they would turn to fix it. By the time one of them is actually installed in the Presidency, conditions and possibilities have changed so much that new formulas and new priorities are put together—the program of an actual as distinguished from a hypothetical administration. The candidate who had pronounced so confidently what his quick Presidential achievements would be now finds himself more nearly Daedalus than Zeus, patching together new wings he hopes will help him fly through the storms of Washington with all the help he can get. Therefore it is not surprising that we go through our ceremonial act of national amnesia when a new President is sworn in, as journalists fling the old promises into the morgue files and move on to new adventures and anticipated mysteries.

In fact, issues are seldom really debated. They are asserted. And because the assertions deal with futuristic subjunctive hypotheticals they are virtually immune to empirical challenge. Today's facts seem irrelevant as the candidates put forth their political dreams. The result is that talk which sounds on the surface as if it were realistic is not. Like the candidate's image, issue statements get evaluated as to whether or not they ring true, not whether or not they are true. Once again, the drift to fiction is enhanced by the plausible, but false, impression of serious rationality.

Candidates for President should be asked what qualifications, demonstrated in their experience, suit them to be President. Sufficiently pressed to answer, each would have to say what qualifications good and bad Presidents have had—what it has taken to succeed in that particular office, based on actual observation and study of actual Presidents. Then the candidate would have to get into the facts of his past: what talents has he proved to possess? On both fronts his contending opponents and the press could check him out. Does he know what he is talking about when he says the word "President"? Does his background (as distinguished from his ambitions) really show he has what that takes?

My studies persuade me that a President needs three main talents—in my language: rhetoric, negotiation, homework. Unlike Hoover, he needs to be able to make clear and persuasive talks to the public, these days via television. Unlike Carter, he needs to know how to deal with other politicians, particularly in Washington. Unlike Reagan, a President needs to go after the information he needs to make the right decisions. Other students of the Presidency might add a few more basic talents, such as management style, especially now that the President sits on top of his own executive bureaucracy, puffed up to many thousands more than Eisenhower had. The list of key, distinctive Presidential talents is not infinite; it should be directly, insistently, and evidentially applied to each and every aspirant for the office. Time and again, men have been elected to the Presidency lacking in even the most elementary skills the job demands.

Beyond skills are the principles which guide their use. Of course, politicians propound their principles ad infinitum—their values, their philosophies, their high beliefs. Far more significant as predictors of their behavior in office are their worldviews: the assumptions about how the world works upon which they actually base their decisions and actions. Applicants for leadership positions ought to be asked to explain what is going on in the world, how the threats and promises are developing, how their values are operating out there in the actualities of politics. Such a test—definitely empirical—would quickly weed out aspirants who live in their own mythical land of Oz, where they foster demonstrably untrue diagnoses and prescriptions for the main ills of mankind. The politicians we need are neither dreamers nor cynics, but realists who have figured out where, when, and how to get their ideals moving in the real world.

Choosing candidates rationally means testing character. The Presidency especially, as the system's least tightly defined office, permits the incumbent's character to operate across a very wide range as he picks his aides and sets his agenda. Character in the Presidency has its symptoms, its typological definitions, its limited estimations of likely tendencies. In sum, politics attracts to the top persons motivated in a few main ways. There are those for whom power is the goal, persons whose sense of personal weakness makes them yearn for the chance to prove they are strong, a self-centered need ready to take precedence over the needs of the community. There are those who love politics because it loves them—individuals who bring to the business of politics an underlying need for supportive affection to make up for the loving they have missed. Then there are those for whom politics is duty, a high calling of sacrifice and public service in which moral intent supercedes practical responsibility. And there are politicians who are in it to get things done, things beyond themselves, for the practical betterment of mankind—and who really like making that happen. These main motives are reflected in patterns of adaptation to political roles. In the Presidency, for example, it is not hard to see the recurrent significance of Presidents who keep pushing their power over the brink of public disaster, who cave in to their insistent comrades, who dodge their responsibilities by claiming political holiness, and who move out creatively to try for the best solutions. These are, I think, the commonest patterns, within which each individual President has his peculiar variations.

To get at these talents and motives, we the electorate need timely biographical accounts done by wise and ready journalists and produced well *before* election day. To derive from these observations the principles and practical lessons necessary to guide our understanding, we need incisively intelligent scholars who will devote their tenure to advancing knowledge about these critical concerns.

No President serves alone, despite the impression of one-man government the candidates portray on the campaign trail. Once one of them wins and goes to Washington, he soon discovers that while others there respect him, his wish is not their command. The White House, once just the President's home, is now a fascinating factory of political intrigue, a concentrated New World Vatican jammed with cardinals jousting for the President's power. At least since the 1960 victory of "Fighting Jack" Kennedy, Presidents have been bringing their top campaign aides into the White House as their top government aides, sometimes including persons as naive about Washington as they are about Moscow or London or Tokyo, not to mention Persian diplomacy. Bottled up in a room down the hall is the White House press corps, frustratedly dependent on the President's chief media spinner, constantly being asked to assess the mood and the anticipations of the White House household they are prevented from visiting. Across the street, wishing they were in the White House— even in the basement—staffers of the Executive Office of the President proliferate themselves. Potentates from Congress, from the State Department and exotic lands across the sea spice up the White House atmosphere. And last but far from least, there is the President's wife, now possessed not only of lots of Presidential access, but even of her own staff and headquarters to support her vice presidential work. What happens in that building and its annex cries out for research by bright political scientists, especially those with an anthropological bent.

Down the street and around the corner stands an imitation Parthenon containing the Supreme Court, where, if anywhere, the legal buck stops. There the archbishops of America are supposed to read what the Founding Fathers wrote and thought and meant, to pray hard for the power of bicentennial translation, to listen carefully to competing advocates, and then to say what the law is. But a lengthening list of trends makes it harder every year to keep the law simple, general, and stable. Often, nowadays, the justices differ one from another so that their "decisions" by votes of five to four, accompanied by markedly various explanations, are shaky. Add to that the sense of some that the law is not really the law when it is merely passed by Congress and signed by the President until the Court has ruled on it, and the idea (expressed by top-level Nixonists and Reaganites and Oliver North's secretary Fawn Hall) that the law has to be transcended when it gets in the way of the President's purpose. Throw in the incredible expansion of the volume of the law, which in practice means that everyone it applies to is ignorant of it, even if that is no legal excuse. List also that in the United States we produce approximately 10,000 new lawyers a year—about as many as there are in all of Japan—whose nourishment is complexity. Cap off the collection with statistics on crime, white collar and blue collar and no collar, showing that many break laws and few get caught. And spray over it all the fad of law as metaphor, not analogy: the literary rather than the substantive similarity between Case A and Case B. All that weaves into the contemporary scene a plausible replication of the declining Roman Empire, in which what once had been an inspiring advance—the rule of law, not the emperor's wink—

slides slowly into the bog of complication. Where are the political scientists who have delved into that recurrent human error and applied it to the legal disease of today?

Then there is Congress. Two houses for one function because the Founders could not resolve the fundamental conflict between representing persons and representing communities, except by the escape route of addition. Worse yet, modern Congress went down the escape route of division: dodging big issues by dividing them into little ones, each assigned to a mini-committee overseen by a maxi-chairman and peopled by representatives sent to Washington by the voters to deal with the guidance of the government. Instead, members of both houses spend their time ripping around from committee to committee, sampling various bits of policy and occasionally, when the bell rings, going to their chamber to vote on issues they know nothing about. In Congress, House or Senate, there is no meaningful debate. It is as if the congressman really wanted to be a judge, ensconced behind his altar at a committee hearing, glaring over his glasses at some poor benighted witness down below who, seated at a rickety card table, nervously drinks from a cracked glass of warm water. The public is deprived of the education we might get if we could see and hear the elected leaders of the nation arguing out the main directions we should take, on their way to deciding, for sure, what the law will be to shape our action. The pluralization of Congress has helped wreck the congressional parties, so that the designated party leaders are quoted as visible but not responsible. The potential of Congress as a parliament remains. The actuality, though, is the deterioration of Congress into a bureaucracy, organized by specialization. Congress means virtually nothing to the public except as it reacts to the President. Someday, one supposes, a political scientist or two will move beyond describing Congressional institutionalization or committee camaraderie and, instead, gaze hard at Congress with an eye to understanding how well it is doing what it is supposed to do. And if the answer is not well, the next study ought to move on to the question of how Congress can revitalize rationality in politics. For it is hard to imagine a lasting democracy, minus responsible debate and decision on laws.

Many more subjects suggest themselves. Political scientists who study "state and local" politics too often see themselves as lesser beings than those of us who deal with Presidents. How wrong! Presidents are derivatives of state and local politics. More fundamentally, it is here, where our neighborhoods are, that politics acquires its viscera. The cultural connection at the national level is almost completely vicarious: it is hard for most television viewers to discern a real-world difference between the realm of Ronald Reagan and the realm of Bill Cosby—invaders from Story Time, USA. Here in the home community, political reality steps in. Those few who bother with politics at home soon learn how we imperfect persons live together, how judgment strains the meaning of friendship, how money talks and power changes, how people who doubt they want to go on living rise to life when the fate of their children is in question. The frontier of culture and politics is to be found, not in Washington, but in Durham County, in White Post and Kanawha City and Boylston and Georgetown. The research of that—the visceral politics of American culture—must soon electrify the more imaginative scholars of politics.

But the gravest challenge to the advancement of life, liberty, and the pursuit of happiness is billowing up abroad. For most of our two hundred years "foreign policy" has labeled an arena extra to our regular political concerns. Foreign issues interrupted the domestic course of life, for example now and then with a military adventure. After two world wars had killed the romance of charging up San Juan Hill, we almost succeeded in institutionalizing peace through the United Nations. But that fell apart, not formally, but functionally; the UN could not prevent the tragedies of war in Korea and Vietnam, in the Mideast, in Angola or Nicaragua or Afghanistan. Now we confront a world military situation of unparalleled threat. The world is in anarchy, deluged with weapons and ammunition sold through a very busy international network of punk millionaire arms sellers who are completely indifferent to the murders they engender— an international version of handgun merchants in the United States. Military technology still produces ridiculous cases of very expensive weapons which do not work in battle, but can nevertheless be sent immediately to blast down enemies in faraway places like Libya. The extension of the arms race into outer space, following on the heels of the intelligence race already there, will, if it progresses, multiply extraordinarily the probability that accident will trigger the end of the world. The proliferation of sitting duck naval targets and their spread around the world into areas where even primitive enemy forces can get their mines and missiles to them raises the ante massively. The posting of marines in places like Beirut poses a similarly horrible vulnerability.

Our incapacity to stop terrorism, drug dealing, illegal immigration, and environmental pollution confirms the inadequacy of the international "system." Perhaps most striking is the dramatic increase in economic interdependency throughout the world. Employment in mid-America is affected by productions clear across the Pacific. Bankers in North America help wreck economies in South America. Religious machinations in the Mideast have an impact on the Texas economy and the price of gasoline in Seattle. Medicines and other products which fall short of legal standards in our country get dumped in other countries. The exchange price of a dollar bill has become an item of information immediately important to people all around the globe. Foreign investors buy up large properties in the United States that they can then shape and operate from their exotic home bases. Farmers in Iowa follow with intense interest how Soviet grain production is going these days. In short, what used to be home economics is now world economics.

Looming over all these lesser concerns is the death threat which has not yet sunk into the minds of most of us, the threat of nuclear war which will suddenly wipe away every other entry on the human agenda in favor of what to do with the bodies, where to get a safe drink of water, which roots in the forest are edible and which poisonous, how to protect yourself from your murderously desperate neighbors. To the continuing Soviet threat is added the Chinese threat, the Indian, Israeli, and Pakistani threats, and eventually the terrorist threat, as the relatively simple science of nuclear explosives is engineered into weaponry by more and more nations and groups. Given the levels of international and intertribal hatred in much of the world, and the lust for martyrdom in a few places, we confront the probability that some team of zealots will eventually set out to clean the world of their disgusting opponents by means of nuclear scrubbing. At least as likely, however, given the chaos and incompetence already demonstrated in this field, is mass death by accident, when a couple of soldiers doze off or lose track or turn the wrong key, when yet another flight of geese is mistaken for a flight of missiles, when a defective chip in the software short-circuits the computer, when a careless pilot of a too-fast jet mistakes the lights of Leningrad for the lights of Helsinki.

The political challenge, in scope and depth, is beyond any ever faced by the human race. Meeting it requires a graduation of thinking from complacency and isolation to the invention and implementation of a world politics in which we are freed from the threat of doing ourselves in by folly or intent. What we have now are old-fashioned ambassadors, appointed for their domestic political and financial contributions, settled in their embassies alongside our spy captains and covert operators, in occasional conversation with the other country's powers. Now and then a "summit" meeting between heads of state dramatizes the anarchy. Specialized conferences do continue, on such topics as arms control, but without authority. The old World Court, the UN, and various regional organizations keep trying, but lack the power to make peace, never mind justice. Within the United States every Presidential administration since World War II has left behind at least one example of bizarre, irrational military action on the international front. When international crises arise, the media habitually turn for wisdom to the failed leaders of yesteryear, as if they had surely learned from their former follies. Congress and the President continue to joust over who runs foreign policy. Thus political organization is as chaotic as the problems it is meant to address. The institutionalization of peace and justice, as they say in the theater, needs work.

That work is more than thinking. But the thinking of it is essential. In politics, ideas do not have consequences of their own, but without right thinking the consequences inevitably die or explode the wrong way. Human choice, until recently a small part of human life, is now central to human fate. Where choice is, thinking makes a difference. That is why scholars, gifted with a steady place to stand, should put their minds to work and their thoughts into print with commitment to making a world their children will want to live in.

Notes and Sources

2 Life History

1 This is not to imply that the record is any better in other political contexts; but we ought to do better in the United States, where the assumption of power is at a definite time and for a definite period via a well-defined system, than in situations where the leader himself defines anew—even creates—the office. I am indebted to Dankwart Rustow for this point.

2 I have tried to show a way of using these distinctions in *The Lawmakers: Recruitment and Adaptation to Legislative Life* (New Haven, Conn., 1965).

3 See my "Classifying and Predicting Presidential Styles: Two 'Weak' Presidents," *Journal of Social Issues* 24 (1968): 51–80.

4 Lloyd Paul Stryker, *Andrew Johnson, A Study in Courage* (New York, 1930), pp. 313–14.

5 Ibid., pp. 333–34. For bibliographic essays showing how Johnson fared with successive waves of historians, see Willard Hays, "Andrew Johnson's Reputation." *East Tennessee Historical Society Publications*, nos. 31–32 (1959); Carmen Anthony Nataro, "History of the Biographic Treatment of Andrew Johnson in the Twentieth Century," *Tennessee Historical Quarterly* 24, no. 2 (1965); Albert Castel, "Andrew Johnson: His Historiographical Rise and Fall," *Mid-America* 45, no. 3 (1963). For a sense of the poverty of basic documentation on Johnson's early years, see Leroy P. Graf and Ralph W. Haskins,

eds., *The Papers of Andrew Johnson, Vol. 1, 1822–1851* (Knoxville, Tenn., 1967).

6 It was at this point that Johnson began giving interviews to friendly reporters, defending himself vigorously against the impeachment charges. See Milton Lomask, *Andrew Johnson: President on Trial* (New York, 1960), pp. 307–10.

7 For detailed accounts of this event, see Lomask, *Andrew Johnson: President on Trial*, p. 28ff; Stryker, *Andrew Johnson, A Study in Courage*, p. 166ff; Eric L. McKitrick, *Andrew Johnson and Reconstruction* (Chicago, 1960), pp. 135–36; George F. Milton, *The Age of Hate, Andrew Johnson and the Radicals* (New York, 1930), ch. 8; Robert Winston, *Andrew Johnson, Plebeian and Patriot* (New York, 1928), pp. 264–66; Brazilla Carroll Reece, *The Courageous Commoner: A Biography of Andrew Johnson* (Charleston, S.C., 1962), pp. 51–52; Benjamin C. Truman, "Anecdotes of Andrew Johnson," *Century Magazine* 85: 435.

8 Quoted in McKitrick, *Andrew Johnson and Reconstruction*, p. 136.

9 The day before inauguration Johnson had written Stanton "to express my highest regard to you personally, and also thank you sincerely for the uniform kindness which you have been pleased to extend to me personally and officially during my service" as brigadier general and military governor of Tennessee (Milton, *The Age of Hate, Andrew Johnson and the Radicals*, p. 144).

10 Ibid., p. 147.

11 Lomask avers: "It was generally assumed that Johnson himself had asked Lincoln to exempt Tennessee from the proclamation as a means of holding in line the state's pro-Union Whigs, many of whom were slaveowners" (*Andrew Johnson: President on Trial*, pp. 24–25).

12 Ibid.

13 McKitrick, *Andrew Johnson and Reconstruction*, p. 294, quoting from the strongly pro-Johnson New York *Herald*. Johnson's words carried the drama of these speeches, even when his manner of speaking was calm. See the recollections of one of his guards, William H. Crook, *Through Five Administrations* (New York, 1907), p. 106. On the other hand, he could ignite platitudes through his style of delivery. See Howard K. Beale, *The Critical Year* (New York, 1930), pp. 362–63. Beale assesses Johnson's 1866 speeches as "disastrous," but attributes his tendency to "talk overmuch of himself" to "an inferiority complex" rather than to "egotism." Ibid., pp. 367, 11.

14 Johnson frequently spoke of himself as being, like Christ, Moses, a martyr: "In imitation of Him of old who died for the preservation of men, I exercised that mercy which I believed to be my duty" (Lomask, *Andrew Johnson: President on Trial*, p. 196). "Caesar had his Brutus, Jesus Christ his Judas, and I've had my Ed Cooper. Get thee behind me, Satan" (Stryker, *Andrew Johnson, A Study in Courage*, p. 784). And themes of blood are frequent: "If I were disposed to play the orator and deal in declamation tonight, I would imitate one of the ancient tragedies and would take William H.

Seward and bring him before you and point you to the hacks and scars upon his person. I would exhibit the bloody garments saturated with gore from his gushing wounds" (Ibid., p. 356).

15 McKitrick, *Andrew Johnson and Reconstruction*, p. 432.

16 Stryker, *Andrew Johnson, A Study in Courage*, p. 361. For an account stressing Johnson's "political ineptitude," the effects of his speeches in alienating northern moderates (such as James Russell Lowell, who wrote, "What an anti-Johnson lecturer we have in Johnson!"), and his failure to learn "that the President of the United States cannot afford to be a quarreler," see David Donald, "Why They Impeached Andrew Johnson," *American Heritage* 8, no. 1 (December 1956). For a more sympathetic account stressing the content of and the reactions to Johnson's speeches, see Gregg Phifer's series of articles in the *Tennessee Historical Quarterly* 11, nos. 1–4 (1952).

17 McKitrick, *Andrew Johnson and Reconstruction*, pp. 437–38. Of course, factors other than Johnson's speeches were at work. For broader political interpretations, see David Donald, *The Politics of Reconstruction* (Baton Rouge, La., 1965); LaWanda and John H. Cox, *Politics, Principle, and Prejudice, 1865–1866* (New York, 1963); Kenneth M. Stampp, *Andrew Johnson and the Failure of the Agrarian Dream* (Oxford, 1962), an inaugural lecture delivered before the University of Oxford on May 18, 1962.

18 Barber, *The Lawmakers*, chap. 6.

19 Variously reported with the titles *American Speaker, United States Speaker, Columbia Speaker,* Enfield's *Speaker, Standard Speaker,* but without disagreement as to its primarily British content. See Winston, *Andrew Johnson, Plebeian and Patriot,* p. 10; Stryker, *Andrew Johnson, A Study in Courage,* p. 3; John Savage, *The Life and Public Services of Andrew Johnson* (New York, 1865), p. 14. The fifth edition, published in 1818 (Philadelphia: Abraham Small) is titled *The American Speaker; A Selection of Popular, Parliamentary and Forensic Eloquence; Particularly Calculated for the Seminaries in the United States.* The name of the compiler is not given. The preface reads, in part: "Without some proficiency in Oratory, there seems to be an insurmountable barrier to the patriotic aspirations of genius—with it, the road to distinction is obvious. The many Legislative bodies in our Federal form of government, and the diversified character of our Courts, present a suitable field for every grade, from the unfledged effort of the callow young, to the mature, eagle-eyed flight in the face of the God of Day.

"It has been our aim, in making this selection, to endeavor to fire the minds of our young men, by placing in their view some of the brightest examples of Genius: to enable them 'With lips of fire to plead their country's cause!' . . . Although a great part of our selection is of an ardent and glowing character, we would not be suspected of denying the superiority of cool deliberate argument and reasoning—but how often have these failed of their effect, by a neglect of appropriate declamation? How often has truth herself been indebted to a happy appeal to the feelings, for all the impression she has made? . . . We are fully convinced of one truth—that to impress, we must feel—it is this that captivates the heart—without feeling, the electricity of Speech is never felt—with the impression which feeling produces, even ungracefulness is overlooked—and the man lost in the Orator." Ibid., pp. iii–v.

20 Stryker, *Andrew Johnson, A Study in Courage*, p. 3.

21 Milton, *The Age of Hate, Andrew Johnson and the Radicals*, p. 74.

22 Fred Greenstein's *Children and Politics* (New Haven, Conn., 1965) makes clear the significance of sequence in political learning.

23 An early biographical sketch for the *New York Times*, May 21, 1849, shows how these themes were presaged in his experience in Congress: "Whenever a member drops an expression that may be twisted into disrespect to the people, a want of confidence in their integrity or intelligence, or a hint that there are interests in society other than his which should be cared for, Mr. J. fires up; and, springing to his feet, ten to one he will, by well-put questions, extract something from the speaker either equivalent to a retraction of what has just fallen from his lips, or a bold avowal of principles and opinions tending materially to weaken him with his constituents. . . . Mr. J. will never suffer an interruption. In the course of the six years I have known him in the House, I do not recollect ever to have seen him consent to give way for an interruption. He says—'No, sir; my hour is short enough. If my facts or conclusions are not sound, obtain the floor and disprove them.' . . . Owing to the want of early advantages, of which I have written above, Mr. J. at times slashes his mother-tongue—pronouncing words of many syllables, or of recent foreign derivation, with little regard to rules laid down by Walker or Webster. More or less of his fellow-members will titter and sneer at Mr. J's many false anglicisms; yet I have rarely seen it done, save by some one smarting under the point of his oratorial bowie-knife. Though expressed in uncouth phraseology, his views are easily understood; for he talks strong thoughts and carefully culled facts in quick succession. He thrusts his opponents through and through, as with a rusty and jagged weapon, tearing a big hole and leaving something behind to fester and be remembered. Woe be unto the luckless wight who offers him a personal indignity—cast a slur upon him, in debate; for if he has to wait two years for the opportunity, when it *does* come, Mr. J. makes the best use of it. He puts no bridle upon his tongue; yet he is never guilty of a personal disrespect to a fellow-member, or even to the opposite party as a whole. Perhaps I may fairly characterize his efforts as being crushingly slashing and slashingly crushing; for he chops to mince-meat and then grinds to powder the men, measures and principles he may be contending against. He takes and maintains positions, at times, which I can hear no *other* man advocate without writing him down a demagogue. Yet no one can listen to him without feeling morally sure that the man is speaking without the least regard to the effect of his words upon his own prospects as a public man." Graf and Haskins, *The Papers of Andrew Johnson*, pp. 677–78.

24 One thinks, for example, of the critical events concentrated in Coolidge's junior year at Amherst.

25 For the list of values and an illustration of their use, see Lasswell's *Power and Personality* (New York, 1948), p. 17. Many of Lasswell's insights on political agitation apply to Johnson. See his *Psychopathology and Politics* (New York, 1960), chaps. 6–7.

26 The phrase is Alexander George's.

27 See also Erik Erikson, *Young Man Luther: A Study in Psychoanalysis and History* (New York, 1962); Alexander L. and Juliette L. George, *Woodrow Wilson and Colonel House* (New York, 1956); James Jones, *Life of Andrew Johnson* (Greeneville, Tenn., 1901); Helen Merell Lynd, *On Shame and the Search for Identity* (New York, 1961).

3 Hard Cases

1 See James David Barber, *The Lawmakers: Recruitment and Adaptation to Legislative Life* (1965); and "Leadership Strategies for Legislative Party Cohesion." David Shapiro's *Neurotic Styles* (1965) is helpful in understanding styles in general and several specific style patterns.

2 On Coolidge, I have found most useful the biographies by Fuess and White, and Coolidge's *Autobiography*. McCoy's biography, which appeared as I finished this piece, seems to confirm its interpretation. The short quotations, too numerous to attribute individually here, are from the above three books and from Cornwell's, on which I have relied for much material on presidential rhetoric. Lowry (1921) is also helpful.

3 On Hoover, the most useful sources are Irwin, Lyons, and Hoover's *Memoirs*. Here again Cornwell's chapters have supplied much material. The short quotations are too numerous to attribute individually. They are taken from the above and from Liggett, 1932; Myers, 1934; Warren, 1967; Wolf, 1956; Wood, 1932; and Hinshaw, 1950.

4 On the significance of compensation in political leadership, see Lasswell, 1930 and 1945.

5 On the interactions of motivations, resources, and opportunities in accounting for political action, see Barber (1965, pp. 10–15, 217–40).

SOURCES

Barber, James David. *The Lawmakers: Recruitment and Adaptation to Legislative Life.* New Haven, Conn.: Yale University Press, 1965.

Barber, James David. "Leadership Strategies for Legislative Party Cohesion," *Journal of Politics* (1966): 28.

Coolidge, Calvin. *The Autobiography of Calvin Coolidge.* New York: Cosmopolitan, 1929.

Cornwell, Elmer E. Jr. *Presidential Leadership of Public Opinion*. Bloomington: Indiana University Press, 1965.

Fuess, Claude M. *Calvin Coolidge: The Man from Vermont*. Hamden, Conn.: Archon Books, 1965.

Hinshaw, David. *Herbert Hoover: American Quaker*. New York: Farrar, Straus, 1950.

Hoover, Herbert. *The Memoirs of Herbert Hoover: 1874–1920: Years of Adventure*. New York: Macmillan, 1951.

Hoover, Herbert. *The Memoirs of Herbert Hoover: 1920–1933, The Cabinet and the Presidency*. New York: Macmillan, 1952.

Irwin, Will. *Herbert Hoover: A Reminiscent Biography*. New York: Century, 1928.

Joslin, Theodore G. *Hoover: Off the Record*. Garden City, N.Y.: Doubleday, Doran, 1934.

Lasswell, Harold D. *Psychopathology and Politics*. New York: Viking Press, 1960.

Lasswell, Harold D. *Power and Personality*. New York: Viking Press, 1962.

Ligget, Walter N. *The Rise of Herbert Hoover*. New York: H. K. Fly, 1932.

Lowry, Edward G. *Washington Close-ups: Intimate Views of Some Public Figures*. Boston: Houghton Mifflin, 1921.

Lyons, Eugene. *Our Unknown Ex-President: A Portrait of Herbert Hoover*. Garden City, N.Y.: Doubleday, 1948.

McCoy, Donald R. *Calvin Coolidge: The Quiet President*. New York: Macmillan, 1967.

Meyers, William Starr, ed. *The State Papers and Other Public Writings of Herbert Hoover*. Vol. 2 (October 1, 1931, to March 4, 1933). New York: Doubleday, Doran, 1934.

Schlesinger, Arthur M. Jr. *The Age of Roosevelt: The Crisis of the Old Order, 1919–1933*. Boston: Houghton Mifflin, 1957.

Shapiro, David. *Neurotic Styles*. New York: Basic Books, 1965.

Warren, Harris Gaylord. *Herbert Hoover and the Great Depression*. New York: Norton, 1967.

Wolfe, Harold. *Herbert Hoover: Public Servant and Leader of the Loyal Opposition*. New York: Exposition Press, 1965.

Wood, Clement. *Herbert Clark Hoover: An American Tragedy*. New York: Michael Swain, 1932.

4 Character and Style

Revised version of a paper prepared for delivery at the sixty-fifth annual meeting of the American Political Science Association, September 1969 under the title "The President and His Friends." A portion of the paper was later published in *The Washington Monthly* 1, no. 9 (October 1969): 33–54, under the title "Analyzing Presidents: From Passive-Positive (Taft) to Active-Negative (Nixon)." I would like to express thanks to Fred I. Greenstein and Nelson W. Polsby for comments. The version in *The Washington Monthly* also appears in *Inside the System* (New York: Praeger, 1970).

1 Harold D. Lasswell, *Power and Personality* (New York: Viking Press, 1962), pp. 32–33.

2 There is a curious periodicity in these themes historically, possibly reflecting the reactive quality of political change. The mystic could see the series politicizing-legitimizing-normalizing marching in fateful repetition beginning in 1900. Although this sequence does call for a politicizing "Big Brother" election in 1984, the pattern is too astrological to be entirely convincing.

3 "Adult Identity and Presidential Style: The Rhetorical Emphasis," *Daedalus* (Summer 1968).

4 "Classifying and Predicting Presidential Styles: Two 'Weak' Presidents," *Journal of Social Issues* 24, no. 3 (1968).

5 "Will There Be a 'Tragedy of Richard Nixon'?" Speech delivered at Stanford University, 1967.

6 For a fuller development of this typology in another context, see Barber, *The Lawmakers* (New Haven, Conn.: Yale University Press, 1965).

7 Patrick Anderson, *The President's Men* (Garden City, N.Y.: Doubleday, 1968), p. 105.

5 Strategy for Research

1 Englewood Cliffs, N.J.: Prentice-Hall, 1972.

2 George Bernard Shaw, *The Apple Cart*, in *The Complete Plays of Bernard Shaw* (London: Constable, 1931), p. 1025.

3 John A. Fairlie, "Political Developments and Tendencies," *American Political Science Review* 24 (February 1930): 7.

4 Ibid., 15.

5 "The Pragmatic Approach to Politics," *American Political Science Review* 24 (November 1930): 865.

6 "A Summary of Predictions of Richard M. Nixon as President," mimeographed, January 19, 1969, 22 pp.; "Will There Be a 'Tragedy of Richard Nixon'?" a speech delivered at Stanford University, Spring 1969, 21 pp.; "The President and His Friends," a paper presented at the 1969 annual meeting of the American Political Science Association, September 1969, published in briefer form in the October 1969 *Washington Monthly*, reprinted with its theoretical introduction restored in Fred Greenstein and Michael Lerner, *A Source Book for the Study of Personality and Politics* (Chicago: Markham, 1971). Cf. also "The Question of Presidential Character," *Saturday Review* (Society Edition), October 1972; "The Presidency After Watergate," *World*, July 31, 1973; "Tone-Deaf in the Oval Office," *Saturday Review/World*, January 12, 1974.

7 Cf. Freud: "After a close study of several patients suffering from phobias and obsessions a tentative explanation of these symptoms forced itself upon me; and as it later enabled me successfully to divine the origin of similar pathological ideas in other cases, I consider it worthy of publication and of further tests." "The Defence Neuro-Psychoses (1894)," in Philip Rieff. ed., *Early Psychoanalytic Writings* (New York: Collier Books, 1963), p. 67.

8 New Haven, Conn.: Yale University Press, 1965.

9 Chicago: Rand McNally, 1966.

10 Chicago: Markham, 1969; 2d ed., 1972. Background articles on Presidents included "Classifying and Predicting Presidential Styles: Two 'Weak' Presidents," *Journal of Social Issues* 24 (1968); and "Adult Identity and Presidential Style: The Rhetorical Emphasis," *Daedalus* 97 (Summer 1968).

11 *The Accidental President* (New York: Pyramid Books, 1968), p. 7.

12 New York: Houghton Mifflin, 1961.

13 Mimeographed, 39 pp.

14 Quoted in Hans J. and Sybil B. G. Eysenck, *Personality and Measurement* (San Diego: Knapp, 1969), p. 11.

15 Barber, *The Lawmakers*, p. 261.

16 See Henry A. Murray, "Toward a Classification of Interactions," in Talcott Parsons and Edward A. Shils, eds., *Toward a General Theory of Action* (New York: Harper and Row, 1962).

17 The ideas above extend somewhat Fred Greenstein's chapter, "Psychological Analysis of Types of Political Actors," in his *Personality and Politics*. There is one more possible step: discerning dimensions which cut across dynamic, developmental, or predictive typologies. See my "The Interplay of Presidential Character and Style: A Paradigm and Five Illustrations," *A Source Book for the Study of Personality and Politics.*

18 Act iv, scene i.

19 Act iv, scene i.

20 Act iv, scene i.

21 See my "Resonances: Presidential Style and Public Mood," a paper presented at the 1971 annual meeting of the American Psychiatric Association, mimeographed, 14 pp.; and "The Presidency: What Americans Want," *The Center Magazine* 4 (January/February 1971).

22 See Richard W. Boyd, "Electoral Trends in Postwar Politics," in James David Barber, ed., *Choosing the President* (Englewood Cliffs, N.J.: Prentice-Hall, 1974).

23 Aristotle, *Politics*, Book I, chap. 2, p. 1129, in Richard McKeon, ed., *The Basic Works of Aristotle* (New York: Random House, 1941).

24 Barber, *The Presidential Character*, p. 255.

25 *A General Introduction to Psychoanalysis* (Garden City, N.Y.: Garden City Publishing Company, 1943).

26 Arnold Rogow, *James Forrestal: A Study of Personality, Politics, and Policy* (New York: Macmillan, 1963).

27 Barber, *The Presidential Character*, p. 148.

28 Ibid., p. 401.

6 Roots of Genius

1 James MacGregor Burns, *Roosevelt: The Lion and the Fox* (New York: Harcourt, Brace and World, 1956), p. 473.

2 James MacGregor Burns and Michael R. Beschloss, "The Forgotten FDR," *New Republic*, April 7, 1982, p. 22.

3 Burns, *Roosevelt*, p. 474.

4 James David Barber, *The Pulse of Politics: Electing Presidents in the Media Age* (New York: Norton, 1980), p. 243.

5 Ibid., p. 245.

6 Paul Murray Kendall, *The Art of Biography* (New York: Norton, 1967), p. 18.

7 Adult Identity.

8 Kendall, *Art of Biography*, p. 21.

9 Sara Delano Roosevelt, *My Boy Franklin* (New York, 1933), p. 355.

10 Geoffrey C. Ward, *Before the Trumpet: Young Franklin Roosevelt* (New York: Harper and Row, 1985), p. 354.

11 Ward, *Before the Trumpet*, pictures following p. 214.

12 Ibid., p. 348.

13 Burns, *Roosevelt*, p. 8. Cf. Ward, *Before the Trumpet*, p. 31n.

14 Ibid., p. 348.

15 Roosevelt, *My Boy Franklin*.

16 Kenneth S. Davis, "FDR as a Biographer's Problem," *The American Scholar* 53.

17 Frank Freidel, *Franklin D. Roosevelt: The Apprenticeship*, vol. 1 (Boston: Little, Brown, 1952), p. 94.

18 Nathan Miller, *FDR: An Intimate History* (Garden City, N.Y.: Doubleday, 1983), p. 15.

19 Burns, *Roosevelt*, p. 9.

20 Ibid., p. 16.

21 Ibid.

22 Freidel, *Roosevelt: The Apprenticeship*, vol. 1, p. 5.

23 Ward, *Before the Trumpet*, p. 120.

24 Ibid., p. 115; Miller, *FDR*, p. 18.

25 Miller, *FDR*, pp. 20–22.

26 Ibid., p. 17.

27 Ibid., p. 12; Ward, *Before the Trumpet*, p. 121.

28 Robert W. White, *Lives In Progress*, 2d ed. (New York: Holt, Rinehart and Winston, 1966), p. 22.

29 Ibid., pp. 22–23.

30 Kendall, *Art of Biography*, p. 26.

31 John A. Garraty, *The Nature of Biography* (New York: Vintage Books, 1964), pp. 179–80.

32 Kendall, *Art of Biography*, p. 18.

33 Carl Sandburg, *Abraham Lincoln: The Prairie Years* (New York: Harcourt, Brace, 1926), vol. 2.

34 Quoted in Kendall, *Art of Biography*, p. 139.

35 Ibid., p. 136.

36 John Hersey, "The Legend on the License," *Yale Review* (Autumn 1980).

37 Kendall, *Art of Biography*, p. 17.

38 Nathan A. Scott, Jr., "The New *Trahison des Cleres*: Reflections on the Present Crisis in Humanistic Studies," *Virginia Quarterly Review* 62 (Summer 1986).

39 Ward, *Before the Trumpet*, p. 180.

40 Ibid., p. 216.

41 Frank Freidel, *Franklin D. Roosevelt: The Ordeal* (Boston: Little, Brown, 1954), vol. 2, p. 55.

42 Davis, *FDR*, pp. 155–6.

43 Ward, *Before the Trumpet*, p. 236.

44 Burns, *Roosevelt*, p. 17; Freidel, *Roosevelt: The Ordeal*, p. 55; Ward, *Before the Trumpet*, p. 239.

45 Ward, *Before the Trumpet*, pp. 232, 239; Freidel, *Roosevelt: The Ordeal*, p. 55.

46 Ward, *Before the Trumpet*, p. 239.

47 Davis, *FDR*, p. 158.

48 Burns, *Roosevelt*, p. 17.

49 Ward, *Before the Trumpet*, p. 239.

50 Ibid., p. 256.

51 Freidel, *Roosevelt: The Ordeal*, p. 52.

52 Ward, *Before the Trumpet*, pp. 239–40.

53 Freidel, *Roosevelt: The Ordeal*, p. 62.

54 Ward, *Before the Trumpet*, p. 233.

55 James David Barber, *The Presidential Character: Predicting Performance in the White House*, 3d ed. (Englewood Cliffs, N.J.: Prentice-Hall, 1985), p. 517.

56 Of course, as early as FDR's Presidency, audiotapes were significant records, and today videotapes are important historical documents. These points apply to them too.

57 On FDR, see Davis, "FDR as a Biographer's Problem," p. 102. See Miller, *FDR*, p. 303. Cf. Burns, *Roosevelt*, p. 161.

58 Barber, *The Presidential Character*, p. 218.

59 Barbara Tuchman, *Practicing History* (New York: Ballantine Books, 1981).

60 Ibid., p. 16.

61 Ibid., p. 14.

62 Ibid., p. 66.

63 Ibid., p. 35.

64 Ibid., p. 40.

65 Ibid., p. 41.

66 Ibid.

67 Burns, *Roosevelt*, p. 189.

68 Freidel, *Roosevelt: The Ordeal*, p. 62.

69 Barber, *Presidential Character*, p. 194.

70 Davis, "FDR," p. 655.

71 Burns, *Roosevelt*, p. 87.

72 Davis, "FDR," p. 659.

73 Ibid., p. 654.

74 Burns, *Roosevelt*, p. 87.

75 Freidel, *Roosevelt: The Ordeal*, p. 100.

76 John Gunther, quoted in Burns, *Roosevelt*, p. 87.

77 Freidel, *Roosevelt: The Ordeal*, p. 92.

78 Miller, *FDR*, p. 187.

79 Ibid., p. 186.

80 Quoted in Barber, *Presidential Character*, p. 198.

81 Davis, "FDR," p. 677.

82 Ibid., 678.

83 Bernard Asbell, *The FDR Memoirs* (Garden City, N.Y.: Doubleday, 1973), pp. 53–55.

84 Quoted in Marc Pachter, ed., *Telling Lives* (Washington, D.C.: New Republic Books, 1979), p. 74.

85 Freud, one supposes, would have agreed with Dostoevsky: "Every man has reminiscences which he would not tell to everyone, but only to his friends. He has other matters in his mind which he would not reveal even to his friends, but only to himself, and that is secret. But there are other things which a man is afraid to tell even to himself, and every decent man has a number of such things stored away in his mind. The more decent he is, the greater the number of such things in his mind. . . . A true biography is almost an impossibility . . . man is bound to lie about himself." From *Notes From Underground*, quoted in Pachter, *Telling Lives*.

86 Sigmund Freud, *Leonardo da Vinci and a Memory of His Childhood* (New York: Norton, 1964), p. 32.

87 *Moses and Monotheism* (New York: Vintage Books, 1967). See Parts I and II.

88 Erik Erikson, *Young Man Luther: A Study in Psychoanalysis and History* (New York: Norton, 1962).

89 Erik Erikson, *Gandhi's Truth* (New York: Norton, 1968).

90 J. P. V. D. Balsdon, *Julius Caesar and Rome* (London: English Universities Press, 1967), p. 35.

91 Gerard Walter, *Caesar: A Biography*, trans. Emma Craufurd (New York: Scribner, 1952), pp. 328–29.

92 Gaius Suetonius Tranquillus, *The Twelve Caesars*, trans. Robert Graves (New York: Penguin Books, 1979), p. 28.

93 A. H. Clough, *Plutarch's Lives: The Translation Called Dryden's* (Boston: Little, Brown, 1859), vol. 4, p. 291.

94 Much later, Shakespeare puts Caesar at an analogous decision point and has

him determined to move out, despite the danger, since "death, a necessary end, Will come when it will come." Even so, Caesar wants to know "What say the augurers?" *Julius Caesar*, Act 2, scene 2.

95 Burns, *Roosevelt*, pp. 88–90.

96 Ibid., pp. 89–90.

97 Barber, *Presidential Character*, p. 266.

SOURCES

Joseph Alsop. *FDR: 1882–1945, a Centenary Remembrance*. New York: Viking Press, 1982.

Asbell, Berard. *The FDR Memoirs*. Garden City, N.Y.: Doubleday, 1973.

Balsdon, J. P. V. D. *Julius Caesar and Rome*. London: English Universities Press, 1967.

Barber, James David. *The Presidential Character: Predicting Performance in the White House*, 3d ed. (Englewood Cliffs, N.J.: Prentice-Hall, 1985).

———. *The Pulse of Politics: Electing Presidents in the Media Age* (New York: Norton, 1980).

Burns, James MacGregor. *Roosevelt: The Lion and the Fox* (New York: Harcourt, Brace and World, 1956).

——— and Michael R. Beschloss. "The Forgotten FDR," *The New Republic*, April 7, 1982.

Clough, A. H. *Plutarch's Lives: The Translation Called Dryden's*. Boston: Little, Brown, 1859.

Davis, Kenneth S. *FDR: The Beckoning of Destiny, 1882–1928*. New York: G. P. Putnam, 1972.

———. "FDR as a Biographer's Problem." *The American Scholar* 53.

Erikson, Erik. *Young Man Luther: A Study in Psychoanalysis and History*. New York: Norton, 1962.

———. *Gandhi's Truth*. New York: Norton, 1968.

Freidel, Frank. *Franklin D. Roosevelt: The Apprenticeship*. Vol. 1. Boston: Little, Brown, 1952.

———. *Franklin D. Roosevelt: The Ordeal*. Vol. 2. Boston: Little, Brown, 1954.

Freud, Sigmund. *Moses and Monotheism*. New York: Vintage Books, 1967.

———. *Leonardo da Vinci and a Memory of His Childhood*. New York: Norton, 1964.

Garraty, John A. *The Nature of Biography*. New York: Vintage Books, 1964.

Hersey, John. "The Legend on the License." *Yale Review* (Spring 1980).

Kendall, Paul Murray. *The Art of Biography*. New York: Norton, 1967.

Miller, Nathan. *FDR: An Intimate History*. Garden City, N.Y.: Doubleday, 1983.

Novak, Michael. *The Experience of Nothingness*. New York: Harper and Row, 1971.

Pachter, Marc, ed. *Telling Lives: The Bioghapher's Art*. Washington, D.C.: New Republic Books, 1979.

Roosevelt, Sara Delano. *My Boy Franklin*. New York, 1933.

Sandburg, Carl. *Abraham Lincoln: The Prairie Years*. Vol. 2. New York: Harcourt, Brace, 1926.

Scott, Nathan A., Jr. "The New *Trahison des Cleres*: Reflections on the Present

Crisis in Humanistic Studies.' *Virginia Quarterly Review* 62 (Summer 1986).

Shakespeare, William. *Julius Caesar*, Act 2, Scene 2.

Tranquillus, Gaius Suetonius. *The Twelve Caesars*. Translated by Robert Graves. New York: Penguin Books, 1979.

Tuchman, Barbara. *Practicing History*. New York: Ballantine Books, 1981.

Walter, Gerard. *Caesar: A Biography*. Translated by Emma Craufurd. New York: Scribner, 1952.

Ward, Geoffrey C. *Before the Trumpet: Young Franklin Roosevelt*. New York: Harper and Row, 1985.

White, Robert W. *Lives In Progress*. 2d ed. New York: Holt, Rinehart and Winston, 1966.

7   Eye of the Beholder

1   Cf. Lester G. Seligman, "Political Recruitment and Party Structure: A Case Study," *American Political Science Review* 55 (1961): 77–86.

2   From 1946 to 1958, Connecticut House incumbents won 982 times and lost 219 times.

3   This is nicely illustrated by contrasting observations on the same session of Congress, as quoted by George W. Galloway, *History of the House of Representatives* (New York: Crowell, 1961), p. 35. Cf. Charles L. Clapp, *The Congressman* (Washington, D.C.: Brookings Institution, 1963), pp. 17–20.

4   David Riesman, Nathan Glazer, and Renel Denney, *The Lonely Crowd: A Study of the Changing American Character* (Garden City, N.Y.: Doubleday, 1955), p. 221.

5   For detailed analysis of conflicts underlying placidity, cf. Anna Freud, *The Ego and the Mechanisms of Defense* (New York: International Universities Press, 1946), chap. 8; Harry Stack Sullivan, *The Interpersonal Theory of Psychiatry* (New York: Norton, 1953), pp. 55–57; Otto Fenichel, *The Psychoanalytic Theory of Neurosis* (New York: Norton, 1945), pp. 185–86; Ralph Greenson, "The Psychology of Apathy," *Psychoanalytic Quarterly* 18 (1949): 290–302; Nathan Leites, "Trends in Affectlessness," in Clyde Kluckhohn and Henry A. Murray, eds., *Personality in Nature, Society, and Culture* (New York: Knopf, 1956), chap. 40.

6   For the approval-seeking person, Horney writes: "The timidity serves as a defense against exposing one's self to rebuff. The conviction of being unlovable is used as the same kind of defense. It is as if persons of this type said to themselves, 'People do not like me anyhow, so I had better stay in the corner, and thereby protect myself against any possible rejection.'" Horney, *The Neurotic Personality of Our Time* (New York: Norton, 1937), p. 137. This protective device decreases the person's chances for gaining affection, because the need remains concealed. For further evidence of the relation of concealment and low self-esteem, see Leonard I. Pearlin, "The Appeals of Anonymity in Questionnaire Response," *Public Opinion Quarterly* 25 (1961): 644.

7   On anxiety and company-seeking, cf. Stanley Schacter, *The Psychology of Affiliation: Experimental Studies of the Sources of Gregariousness* (Stanford, Calif.: Stanford University Press, 1959).

8   Cf. Alexander L. George, "Some Uses of Dynamic Psychology in Political Biography," p. 14: "The usefulness of the technical literature to the biographer will be enhanced if the distinction is kept in mind between the question of the *origins* of compulsiveness and compulsive traits, about which there are various views, and the *dynamics* of such behavior, about which there is less disagreement." Cf. Erik H. Erikson on "orinology," *Young Man Luther* (New York: Norton, 1958), pp. 18–19.

9   Cf. Karen Horney on "moving toward people," "moving against people," and "moving away from people," in *Our Inner Conflicts* (New York: Norton, 1945).

10 This is not to say, of course, that no significant changes take place after one reaches adulthood, or that personality becomes permanently fixed in the early years, though evidence of the latter appears inconclusive. See Ian Stevenson, "Is the Human Personality More Plastic in Infancy and Childhood?," *American Journal of Psychiatry* 114 (1957): 152–61. On adult consistency, E. Lowell Kelly found considerable stability in some variables (e.g. attitudes toward marriage, rearing children) among 446 subjects after twenty years of adult life: "Consistency of the Adult Personality," *American Psychologist* 10 (1955): 659–81. D. P. Morris, E. Soroker, and G. Buruss, "Follow-Up Studies of Shy, Withdrawn Children. I. Evaluation of Later Adjustment," *American Journal of Orthopsychiatry* 24 (1954): 743–54. Cf. G. W. Allport, J. S. Bruner, and E. M. Jandorf, "Personality under Social Catastrophe: Ninety Life-Histories of the Nazi Revolution," in Kluckhohn and Murray, eds., *Personality in Nature, Society and Culture*, p. 443: "Very rarely does catastrophic social change produce catastrophic alterations in personality. . . . On the contrary, perhaps the most vivid impression gained by our analysts from this case-history material is of the extraordinary continuity and sameness in the individual personality." For evidence that ability to dispense with minor habits is strongly related to childhood experience, see Charles McArthur, Helen Waldron, and John Dickinson, "The Psychology of Smoking," *Journal of Abnormal and Social Psychology* 56 (1958): 267–75. On the meaning of "habit" or "habit potential" as "the probability of evocation of the response," rather than a fixation, compulsion, or obsession of some kind, see John W. M. Whiting and Irvin L. Child, *Child Training and Personality* (New Haven, Conn.: Yale University Press, 1953), pp. 18ff.

11 Cf. Karen Horney, *Neurosis and Human Growth* (New York: Norton, 1950), pp. 185–86. Theodore M. Newcomb notes that "threat-oriented behaviors are commonly rewarding, and hence persistent, because they are perceived as defending the ego—perhaps imperfectly, but nonetheless in the best way in which the person knows how." *Social Psychology* (New York: Dryden Press, 1950), p. 462.

12 This is probably as good a place as any to assert categorically that I do not

consider the subjects of this study "psychotic," "neurotic," or even especially troubled in comparison with the theoretically normal population. Such terms represent overlapping categories. The use of clinical language implies only that certain concepts have an applicability to the generally well-adjusted as well as to those under treatment. For evidence of such continuities, see, for example, Gerald Gurin, Joseph Veroff, and Sheila Feld, *Americans View Their Mental Health* (New York: Basic Books, 1960), especially chap. 11; Raymond B. Cattell, *Personality* (New York: McGraw-Hill, 1950), especially chaps. 1 and 17; William Schofield and Lucy Balian, "A Comparative Study of the Personal Histories of Schizophrenic and Nonpsychiatric Patients," *Journal of Abnormal and Social Psychology* 59 (1959): 216–25. For a good introductory discussion of such matters, see Fenichel, *The Psychoanalytic Theory of Neurosis*, or Newcomb, *Social Psychology*, pp. 392ff.

13 "In a typically self-effacing person, feeling abused is an almost constant undercurrent in his whole attitude toward life. If we wanted to characterize him crudely and glibly in a few words, we would say that he is a person who craves affection and feels abused most of the time." Horney, *Neurosis and Human Growth*, p. 230.

14 For links between conforming behavior and personality variables, see Richard S. Crutchfield, "Conformity and Character," *American Psychologist* 10 (1955): 191–98; James E. Dittes and Harold H. Kelley, "Effects of Different Conditions of Acceptance Upon Conformity to Group Norms," *Journal of Abnormal and Social Psychology* 53 (1956): 100–107; Hans L. Zetterberg, "Compliant Actions," *Acta Sociologica* 2 (1957): 179–201; John W. Thibaut and Lloyd H. Strickland, "Psychological Set and Social Conformity," *Journal of Personality* 25 (1956): 115–29.

15 Horney, *Neurosis and Human Growth*, p. 320.

16 Cf. Samuel C. Patterson, "The Role of the Deviant in the State Legislative System: The Wisconsin Assembly," *Western Political Quarterly* 14 (1961): 463.

17 Cf. Stimson Bullitt, *To Be a Politician* (Garden City, N.Y.: Doubleday, 1959), p. 63. The ambiguity involved in such encounters is probably a general source of strain in American politics, a strain that is ameliorated in more formally conventional environments. See Matthews, *U. S. Senators*, p. 69, and Margaret Mary Wood, *Paths of Loneliness* (New York: Columbia University Press, 1953), chap. 5, "Men in Great Place." Graham Wallas describes the protective function served—"Light chatter, even among strangers, in which neither party 'gives himself away,' is very much less fatiguing than an intimacy which makes some call upon the emotions"—and notes that London clubs "are successful exactly because it is an unwritten law in almost every one of them that no member must speak to any other who is not one of his own personal acquaintances." *Human Nature in Politics*, 3d ed. (New York: F. S. Crofts, 1921), pp. 73, 71. See Georg Simmel, "The Sociology of Sociability," *American Journal of Sociology* 55 (1949): 254–61.

18 David B. Truman, *The Governmental Process* (New York: Knopf, 1960),

chap. 6; Paul F. Lazarsfeld, Bernard Berelson, and Hazel Gaudet, *The People's Choice* (New York: Columbia University Press, 1948), chaps. 6, 7, and 15.

19 The elaborateness of experimental designs for creating conflict situations gives perhaps some indication of how infrequently such situations arise in natural settings. Cf. Edward L. Walker and Roger W. Heyns, *An Anatomy for Conformity* (Englewood Cliffs, N.J.: Prentice-Hall, 1962). And there is much evidence that many people do not see their conflicting memberships or contradictory opinions as either conflicting or contradictory. Cf. Martin Kriesberg, "Cross-Pressures and Attitudes," *Public Opinion Quarterly* 13 (1949): 5–16; Leon Festinger, *A Theory of Cognitive Dissonance* (Evanston, Ill.: Row, Peterson, 1957). In an elegant article, Wilder Crane examined differences between Wisconsin representatives and their constituents on a "daylight time" issue. Ten of the fifteen whose votes were inconsistent with their constituency majorities (as later revealed in a referendum) explained that they were uncertain what their constituents felt. And "only a minority of assemblymen were faced with the problem of feeling compelled to vote contrary to their own preferences. Frequently the assemblymen could vote what were simultaneously their own opinions and majority opinions in their district. However, when there were conflicts, most assemblymen made clear that they were willing to disregard their own preferences in order to represent their constituents." "Do Representatives Represent?" *Journal of Politics* 22 (1960): 295–99. Cf. Lewis A. Dexter, "The Representative and His District," *Human Organization* 16 (1957); William C. Mitchell, *The American Polity* (New York: Free Press of Glencoe, 1962), p. 86; Warren E. Miller and Donald E. Stokes, "Constituency Influences in Congress," *American Political Science Review* 57 (March 1963): 56.

20 "The feeling of powerlessness of the other-directed character is, then, the result in part of the lack of genuine commitment to work. His life is not engaged in a direct struggle for mastery over himself and nature; he has no long-term goals since the goals must constantly be changed. At the same time, he is in competition with others for the very values they tell him are worth pursuing; in a circular process, one of these values is the approval of the competing group itself. Hence, he is apt to repress overt competitiveness both out of anxiety to be liked and out of fear of retaliation. In this situation, he is likely to lose interest in the work itself. With loss of interest, he may even find himself little more than a dilettante, not quite sure that he is really able to accomplish anything." David Riesman, *Individualism Reconsidered* (Glencoe, Ill.: Free Press, 1954), p. 110. Cf. Harold D. Lasswell, *Political Writings* (Glencoe, Ill.: Free Press, 1951), p. 499.

21 The disturbing effects of tasks on interpersonal relations has been noted in small-groups research. Cf. Robert F. Bales and Fred L. Strodtbeck, "Phases in Group Problem Solving," in Dorwin Cartwright and Alvin Zander, *Group Dynamics Research and Theory*, 2d ed. (Evanston, Ill.: Row, Peterson, 1960), p. 630.

22 Cf. William C. Mitchell, "Reduction of Tension in Legislatures," *Political Research Organization and Design* 2 (January 1959).

8   Motivated Sociology

1   There is much evidence for this in political opinion studies. See, for example, James W. Prothro and Charles M. Grigg, "Fundamental Principles of Democracy: Bases of Agreement and Disagreement," *Journal of Politics* 22 (1960): 276–94; and Samuel H. Stouffer, *Communism, Conformity, and Civil Liberties* (Garden City, N.Y.: Doubleday, 1955).

2   On relationships between self-images and perceptions, see David Krech, Richard S. Crutchfield, and Egerton L. Ballachey, *Individual in Society* (New York: McGraw-Hill, 1962), chap. 3. On vagaries involved in reports of community power, see Raymond E. Wolfinger, "Reputation and Reality in the Study of 'Community Power,'" *American Sociological Review* 25 (1960): 636–44; and Nelson W. Polsby, *Community Power and Political Theory* (New Haven, Conn.: Yale University Press, 1963), pp. 47ff.

3   Cf. Jerome S. Bruner et al., *A Study of Thinking* (New York: Wiley, 1956).

4   See Richard D. Mann, "A Review of the Relationships between Personality and Performance in Small Groups," *Psychological Bulletin* 56 (1959): 241–70; and A. Paul Hare, *Handbook of Small Group Research* (New York: Free Press of Glencoe, 1962), chap. 6.

9   Sharing Constructs

1   On the mourning process, see Otto Fenichel, *The Psychoanalytic Theory of Neurosis* (New York, 1945), pp. 395–96, and Jules Vuillemin, *Essai sur la signification de la mort* (Paris, 1948), pp. 147–52. On the reactions to the Lincoln assassination, see Carl Sandburg, *Abraham Lincoln* (New York, 1939), vol. 4, chaps. 74–76, and Theodore Roscoe, *The Web of Conspiracy* (Englewood Cliffs, N.J., 1959).

2   See Bradley S. Greenberg, "Diffusion of News of the Kennedy Assassination," *Public Opinion Quarterly* 28 (1964): 227–31.

3   On group viewing of the Kennedy-Nixon debates, see Richard F. Carter, "Some Effects of the Debates," in Sidney Kraus, ed., *The Great Debates* (Bloomington, Ind., 1962), p. 254.

4   On "the social validation of meanings," see Tamotsu Shibutani, *Society and Personality* (Englewood Cliffs, N.J., 1961), pp. 108–18. On "group absorbents of media radiation," see V. O. Key, Jr., *Public Opinion and American Democracy* (New York, 1961), pp. 366–69. Cf. S. M. Lipset, "Opinion Formation in a Crisis Situation," *Public Opinion Quarterly* 17 (1953): 20–46; Elihu Katz, "The Two-Step Flow of Communication: An Up-to-date Report on a

Hypothesis," *Public Opinion Quarterly* 21 (1957): 61–78; A. Paul Hare, *Handbook of Small Group Research* (New York, 1962), chap. 2.

5   Fred I. Greenstein, "The Benevolent Leader: Children's Images of Political Authority," *American Political Science Review* 54 (1960): 934–43, and his *Children and Politics* (New Haven, Conn.: Yale University Press, 1965).

6   See Lewis Wender, "The Dynamics of Group Psychotherapy and Its Application," in Max Rosenbaum and Milton M. Berger, eds., *Group Psychotherapy and Group Function* (New York, 1963), pp. 211–17. On the obstacles to healthy grieving in Western culture, see Robert N. Wilson, "Disaster and Mental Health," in George W. Baker and Dwight W. Chapman, eds., *Man and Society in Disaster* (New York, 1962), p. 127.

7   Research on the reactions of middle-class Americans generally would probably reveal less emotional expression than for working-class ones. See David Krech, Richard S. Crutchfield, and Egerton L. Ballachey, *Individual in Society* (New York, 1962), pp. 374–75.

8   On the persistence of conspiracy theories after the assassination, see the article by Paul B. Sheatsley and Jacob J. Feldman in Bradley S. Greenberg and Edwin B. Parker, eds., *The Kennedy Assassination and the American Public: Social Communication in Crisis* (Stanford, Calif., 1965). On the spread of "fear-justifying" rumors among those distant from a disaster, see Leon Festinger, *A Theory of Cognitive Dissonance* (Stanford, Calif., 1957), pp. 236–43.

9   On the death of another as a threat to the self, see George A. Kelly, *The Psychology of Personal Constructs* (New York, 1955), vol. 1, pp. 489ff.

10   See James E. Dittes, "Impulsive Closure as Reaction to Failure-Induced Threat," *Journal of Abnormal and Social Psychology* 63 (1961): 562–69.

11   On "morselizing and contextualizing" in political perceptions, see Robert E. Lane, *Political Ideology* (New York, 1962), pp. 350–53.

12   For evidence that this was the most frequent characterization of the suspected assassin, see Thomas J. Banta, "The Kennedy Assassination: Early Thoughts and Emotions," *Public Opinion Quarterly* 28 (1964): 220.

10   Gathering Influence

I am indebted to Fred I. Greenstein, Robert E. Lane, Duane Lockard, John Manley, Nelson W. Polsby, and Randall B. Ripley for helpful comments on a draft of this article.

1   Legislative Politics in Connecticut," *American Political Science Review* 48 (March 1954): 166–173. See also Duane Lockard, *New England State Politics* (Princeton, N.J.: Princeton University Press, 1959), chaps. 10 and 11.

2   See, for example, Donald R. Matthews, *U.S. Senators and Their World* (Chapel Hill: University of North Carolina Press, 1960), chaps. 2 and 3; Edward A. Shils, "The Legislator and His Environment," *University of Chicago Law Review* 18 (1950–51): 571–84; Corinne Silverman, "The Legisla-

tors' View of the Legislative Process," *Public Opinion Quarterly* 18 (1954): 180–90.

3   John C. Wahlke, Heinz Eulau, William Buchanan, and Leroy C. Ferguson, *The Legislative System: Explorations in Legislative Behavior* (New York: Wiley, 1962), pp. 371 and 376.

4   Ibid., table 17.4.

5   Frank J. Sorauf, *Party and Representation* (Englewood Cliffs, N.J.: Prentice-Hall, 1963), p. 145. For a clear summary of roll call studies, see Malcolm E. Jewell, *The State Legislature: Politics and Practice* (New York: Random House, 1962), chap. 3.

6   After exploratory interviews with several experienced legislators, systematic focused interviews, tape-recorded with the subjects' consent, were conducted with twenty-seven new members of the Connecticut House of Representatives. Pre-session questionnaires were returned by 204 members; the post-session response was 182. This material is analyzed from a different perspective in my book, *The Lawmakers: Recruitment and Adaptation to Legislative Life* (New Haven, Conn.: Yale University Press, 1965).

7   Although other goals may override this one occasionally. For example, leaders may work to build up a vote on the losing side to show support for a bill's sponsor, build an overwhelming vote for later campaign reference, muster special forces for supporting or overriding vetoes, etc. See Ralph K. Huitt, "Democratic Party Leadership in the Senate," *American Political Science Review* (June 1961): 338.

8   Frank J. Sorauf, "Patronage and Party," reprinted in Nelson W. Polsby, Robert A. Dentler, and Paul A. Smith, eds., *Politics and Social Life* (Boston: Houghton Mifflin, 1963), p. 449.

9   "The Representative and His District," *Human Organization* 16 (1957): 11.

10   Cf. the explanation by Fred Cina, Majority Leader of the Minnesota House: "Someone has got to be the leader, or the boss of the gang, and that's what the Majority Leader really amounts to. . . . If I want—if we want something, the group, it's up to me to see that we get it. And I have various ways of getting this. By calling in the members particularly, talking with them, telling them that we want this done, and we—we never have done this—but there are many things you could do to a member. For instance, a member could be removed from a Committee that he likes to be on . . . we can do this very quickly. . . . Some of our people have employees around here that we could discharge. Now we could make them look bad politically. We don't do these things, but these are things that they know are in the background and when I talk to them because I am the Majority Leader and have this power, they—they come around to our way of thinking easily without any threats or cajoling or whiplashing—but they always know that in the background there's something that makes them do these things."
    NBC *White Paper # 4*, "Man in the Middle: The State Legislator," available from the National Broadcasting Company, pp. 31–32. I am indebted to Duane Lockard for the comment that these expectations may have long historical

roots. On the inheritance of this kind of influence, see H. Bradford Wester-field, *Foreign Policy and Party Politics: Pearl Harbor to Korea* (New Haven, Conn.: Yale University Press, 1955), p. 85. Cf. Charles L. Clapp, *The Congressman* (Washington, D.C.: Brookings Institution, 1963), pp. 313ff.

11   On uncertainty in political decision-making see Matthews, *U.S. Senators*, p. 80; Nelson W. Polsby and Aaron B. Wildavsky, "Uncertainty and Decision-making at the National Conventions," in Polsby et al., *Politics and Social Life*. On "ambiguity of risk" as a key factor in the roles of the principal elective leaders, see David B. Truman, *The Congressional Party* (New York: Wiley, 1959), pp. 293–94, and Raymond A. Bauer, Ithiel de Sola Pool, and Lewis Anthony Dexter, *American Business and Public Policy* (New York: Atherton Press, 1963), p. 435. On the significance of anticipated rewards and punishments, see Carl J. Friedrich, *Man and His Government* (New York: McGraw-Hill, 1963), chap. 11; Robert A. Dahl, *Who Governs?* (New Haven, Conn.: Yale University Press, 1961), chap. 8; Herbert Kaufman and Victor Jones, "The Mystery of Power," *Public Administration Review* (Summer 1954): 207–8. Cf. Stanley Budner, "Intolerance of Ambiguity as a Personality Variable," *Journal of Personality* (March 1962).

12   Cf. Karl W. Deutsch, *The Nerves of Government* (New York: Free Press, 1963), pp. 116–24 and chap. 14; Talcott Parsons, "On the Concept of Influence," *Public Opinion Quarterly* 27 (1963), and "'Voting' and the Equilibrium of the American Political System," in Eugene Burdick and Arthur J. Brodbeck, eds., *American Voting Behavior* (Glencoe, Ill.: Free Press, 1959), esp. pp. 88–91.

13   On the difficulties of role choice by legislators, see Duane Lockard, *The Politics of State and Local Government* (New York: Macmillan, 1963), pp. 279–85, and Wahlke et al., *The Legislative System*, pp. 237–44. On the need for legitimating rationalizations for conformity, see Robert A. Dahl and Charles E. Lindblom, *Politics, Economics, and Welfare* (New York: Harper, 1953), pp. 262 and 230ff. On the legitimation of functional leadership roles, see Peter M. Blau, "Critical Remarks on Weber's Theory of Authority," *American Political Science Review* (June 1963): 312–13. On leader strategies "to structure a situation so that a member can select a role which will allow him to stand with the party," see Huitt, "Democratic Party Leadership," p. 339.

14   See Herbert McCloskey and Harold E. Dahlgren, "Primary Group Influence on Party Loyalty," *American Political Science Review* (September 1959): 757–76. It should be noted that reinforcement of party identification by other identifications is not the only way in which the former can be strengthened in a legislature. This may also happen when the other identifications are relatively weak or scattered in comparison to party identification.

15   For a description of similar images, see Clinton Rossiter, *Parties and Politics in America* (Ithaca, N.Y.: Cornell University Press, 1960), p. 117.

16   It is clear from several interviews that new legislators often encounter the

other party for the first time, at least in any close and intimate association, in the legislature.

17 On "interpretation" as a particularly potent persuasion technique, see Irving Sarnoff, Daniel Katz, and Charles McClintock, "Attitude-Change Procedures and Motivating Patterns," in Daniel Katz, Dorwin Cartwright, Samuel Eldersveld, and Alfred McClung Lee, eds., *Public Opinion and Propaganda* (New York: Holt, 1954).

18 On the effectiveness of isolation in Congress, see Robert A. Dahl, *Congress and Foreign Policy* (New York: Harcourt, Brace, 1950), p. 50.

19 This difficulty is increased by strong legislative norms. Members place a high value on "keeping one's word," "sticking to your promises." See Wahlke et al., *The Legislative System*, p. 144.

20 Cf. Leon Festinger, *A Theory of Cognitive Dissonance* (Evanston, Ill.: Row, Peterson, 1957), pp. 144–46.

21 For a review of small-groups literature on majority effects, see A. Paul Hare, *Handbook of Small Group Research* (New York: Free Press, 1962), chap. 2. For senatorial examples of middle-ground maneuvering, see Matthews, *U.S. Senators*, p. 127. On the flexible use of caucuses, see Jewell, *The State Legislature*, pp. 89ff.

22 See Duncan MacRae, Jr., "The Relation Between Roll Call Votes and Constituencies in the Massachusetts House of Representatives," *American Political Science Review* (December 1952). The member's *perception* of the reasons he won are probably most significant here. Cf. Warren E. Miller, "Majority Rule and the Representative System," a paper delivered at the 1962 annual meeting of the American Political Science Association, p. 28.

11 Culture and System

For helpful comments on drafts of this essay I am glad to thank Hayward Alker, Gabriel Almond, Chris Argyris, Lewis Coser, Robert Dahl, Karl Deutsch, James Fesler, William Frankena, Fred Greenstein, Albert Hirschman, Henry Kariel, Herbert Kaufman, Richard Lowenthal, Michael Maccoby, Jules Masserman, Richard Merritt, Michael Montias, Daniel P. Moynihan, Paul Mussen, Nelson Polsby, David Riesman, Bruce Russett, Harry Scoble, Charles Tilly, Meredith Wilson, Frank Young, and the members of the Working Group on American Government.

1 Many of the following propositions were suggested long ago in Robert Dahl and Charles E. Lindblom's chapter on "Bargaining: Control And Leaders," in *Politics, Economics, and Welfare* (New York: Harper and Row, 1953); they still need testing.

For an enlightening elaboration of the perils and achievements of one "multicentered" system, see Wallace S. Sayre and Herbert Kaufman, *Governing New York City* (New York: Russell Sage Foundation, 1960), pp. 716–25.

On decentralization aspects, see Irving Kristol, "Decentralization for What?" *The Public Interest* 11 (Spring 1968); Herbert Kaufman, "Administrative Decentralization and Political Power," *Public Administration Review* 29 (January/February 1969).

For examples of categorical approaches and their difficulties, see Odd Ramsoy, *Social Groups as System and Subsystem* (New York: Free Press, 1963), pp. 45–50; Peter M. Blau and W. Richard Scott, *Formal Organizations: A Comparative Approach* (San Francisco: Chandler, 1962), pp. 40ff; Andrew S. McFarland, *Power and Leadership in Pluralist Systems* (Stanford, Calif.: Stanford University Press, 1969), chap. 4, "Spurious Pluralism." On marginal time considerations in organization analysis, see S. F. Nadel, *The Theory of Social Structure* (New York: Free Press, 1957), chap. 6.

On functional interdependence, see Scott Greer, *Social Organization* (New York: Random House, 1955), pp. 19–21.

2   Cf. James W. Fesler on factors explaining "the multiplication of the bailiff's functionally specialized subordinates and the attenuation of their subordination to him" in fourteenth-century French administration. One factor was "the increase in the volume of work of the bailiffship. The other was the new ease of thinking of differentiated categories of work. Once differentiation had been conceptualized, any category could be subtracted from the bailiff's own omnicompetent role and entrusted to officials better qualified than he for performance of that specialized function." "French Field Administration: The Beginnings," *Comparative Studies in Society and History* 5 (October 1962): 103. It is harder for governments to resist pluralization than it is for industrial enterprises to do so, because the political market does not impose the degree of organizational discipline, concentration of purpose, or measurability of results found in the economic marketplace.

3   Victor A. Thompson, *Modern Organization: A General Theory* (New York: Knopf, 1961), p. 100.

4   Cf. Thomas R. Dye, Charles S. Liebman, Oliver P. Williams, and Harold Herman, "Differentiation and Cooperation in a Metropolitan Area," *Midwest Journal of Political Science* 7 (1963): 145–55, and V. Stanley Vardys, "Select Committees of the House of Representatives," *Midwest Journal of Political Science* 6 (1962): 247–65.

Some old units do die, and it would be interesting to research this carefully. Under what conditions is a unit dropped from a clearance circuit or a comprehensive budget? What happens to the personnel of disbanded units? Cf. Charles Tilly, "Clio and Minerva," mimeographed, July 1968.

5   See Thompson, *Modern Organization*, p. 105; Karl W. Deutsch, *The Nerves of Government: Models of Political Communication and Control* (New York: Free Press, 1963), pp. 225–26; Robert R. Blake and Jane Srygley Mouton, "Comprehension of Own and of Outgroup Positions Under Intergroup Competition," *Journal of Conflict Resolution* 5 (1961), 304–10.

6   For an argument that "a felt need for joint decision making, and that the existence of differences in goals or differences in perceptions or both, are

necessary for intergroup conflict," see James G. March and Herbert A. Simon, *Organizations* (New York: Wiley, 1958), p. 135. For an illustration of these tendencies, see Robert C. Wood, *1400 Governments* (Cambridge, Mass.: Harvard University Press, 1961), pp. 128–31, and Vincent Ostrom, Charles M. Tiebout, and Robert Warren, "The Organization of Government in Metropolitan Areas: A Theoretical Inquiry," *American Political Science Review* 55 (1961): 838–42.

There is a special case in which jurisdictional conflicts and other entropic results may be postponed, though, I would argue, not eliminated. This is the creation of a new unit to advance the interests of a newly mobilized clientele (that is, one whose members have been excluded from other clienteles), by providing rewards specialized to that clientele. The initial results may be encouraging. The long-term results are likely to fade as the new unit is integrated into larger organizational structures, but not as fast as in the typical case.

7   Cf. James W. Fesler, "Administration in the Federal Government," *Yale Papers in Political Science*, no. 6, 1963: "The interrelatedness of everything, and often the poor fit of long-established definitions of department functions to the kinds of policy problems that now arise, take much decision-making out of the department head's own hands. As in the national security area, many problems must be moved to the agenda of interagency committees, be referred through the Executive Office of the President to other agencies for consideration or be taken up with a presidential assistant. The department head thus becomes more an advocate, negotiator, and committee member than the master of a major segment of policy and administration."

On difficulties in feedback processes from outside the system, see especially David Easton, *A Systems Analysis of Political Life* (New York: Wiley, 1965), chap. 24.

8   This and the following two propositions are developed in a somewhat different way by James Q. Wilson, "Innovation in Organization: Notes Toward a Theory," a paper delivered at the 1963 annual meeting of the American Political Science Association. Wilson hypothesizes that the *proportion* of innovations adopted will decline as organizational diversity increases. I think the absolute number of adoptions would decline.

9   See Dean E. Mann, "The Selection of Federal Political Executives," *American Political Science Review* 58 (1964): 88; Sheldon L. Messinger, "Organizational Transformation: A Case Study of a Declining Social Movement," *American Sociological Review* 20 (1955): 3–10; Lewis A. Coser, "Social Conflict and the Theory of Social Change," *The British Journal of Sociology* 8 (1957): 199; and Herbert A. Simon, *Administrative Behavior* (New York: Macmillan, 1957), pp. 117–18.

10   The phrase is David Truman's. See *The Governmental Process* (New York: Knopf, 1960), pp. 353–62.

11   On "veto groups" in the United States, see David Riesman, *The Lonely Crowd* (Garden City, N.Y.: Doubleday, 1955), pp. 246–51. On the veto pro-

pensities of particular governmental institutions, see V. O. Key, Jr., *American State Politics* (New York: Knopf, 1956), chap. 7; Richard E. Neustadt, *Presidential Power: The Politics of Leadership* (New York: Wiley, 1960), chaps. 1–3; James MacGregor Burns, *The Deadlock of Democracy: Four-Party Politics in America* (Englewood Cliffs, N.J.: Prentice-Hall, 1963); Bertram M. Gross, *The Legislative Struggle: A Study in Social Combat* (New York: McGraw-Hill, 1953), pp. 175–79; Walter F. Murphy, "Lower Court Checks on Supreme Court Power," *American Political Science Review* 52 (1959): 1017–31; Jack W. Pelatson, *Federal Courts in the Political Process* (Garden City, N.Y.: Doubleday, 1955), p. 60; Edward C. Banfield and James Q. Wilson, *City Politics* (Cambridge, Mass.: Harvard University Press and the MIT Press, 1963), pp. 111 and 336ff.

For a suggestion that the proposal-veto sequence may be a self-reinforcing one, see Carl J. Friedrich, *Man and His Government* (New York: McGraw-Hill, 1963), p. 380. On deadlock despite the "reasonableness" of compromise, see Robert A. Dahl, *Modern Political Analysis* (Englewood Cliffs, N.J.: Prentice-Hall, 1963).

12 Wilson, "Innovation in Organization," p. 18. For a striking example, see Harry M. Scoble, "Interdisciplinary Perspectives on Poverty in America: The View from Political Science," mimeographed.

13 See William R. Dill, "The Impact of Environment on Organizational Development," in Sidney Malick and Edward H. van Ness, eds., *Concepts and Issues in Administrative Behavior* (Englewood Cliffs, N.J.: Prentice-Hall, 1962), p. 101. Cf. the invention of "non-negotiable demands" as initiations for negotiation.

14 Aaron Wildavsky summarizes the process by which executive agencies decide "how much to ask for" in the budget process as follows: "The most common conclusion resulted in some range of figures considered to be the most the agency could get; figures, however, which always bore some relationship to the agency's going base plus or minus increments involving a few programs expected to garner support or run into opposition." *The Politics of the Budgetary Process* (Boston: Little, Brown, 1964), p. 31. See also my *Power in Committees* (Chicago: Rand McNally, 1966), chap. 2.

In some cases those closest to a situation (e.g., a Peace Corpsman in the field) may develop fatalism and apathy due to first-hand awareness of the difficulties of change, in contrast to those in distant headquarters who press for action. Since energy at both points is necessary for results, the outcome is likely to be the same, but for different reasons.

15 The argument here is that incrementalism tends to be conservative in practice, not that it is inherently or inevitably so. Compare David Braybrooke and Charles E. Lindblom, *A Strategy of Decision* (New York: Free Press, 1963), pp. 106–10, with Jerome S. Bruner et al., *A Study of Thinking* (New York: Wiley, 1956), pp. 87–89, 124, 235–36, and Carl J. Friedrich, *Man and His Government*, p. 202. See John T. Lanzetta and Vera T. Kanareff, "Information Cost, Amount of Payoff, and Level of Aspiration as Determinants

of Information Seeking in Decision-Making," *Behavioral Science* 7 (1962): 459–73; Randall B. Ripley, "Interagency Committees and Incrementalism: The Case of Aid to India," *Midwest Journal of Political Science* 7 (1964): 143–65; Vernon Van Dyke, *Pride and Power: The Rationale of the Space Program* (Urbana: University of Illinois Press, 1964), chap. 16; Yehezkel Dror, Charles E. Lindblom et al., "Governmental Decision Making," *Public Administration Review*, Vol. 24 (1964): 154–65.

16 "This tendency of policies once enacted to persevere is no accident in poly-archies. It is related to the process itself. For if there is sufficient agreement on processes and policies to operate polyarchy, there is likely to be enough agreement to make for considerable stability in policy. Conversely, if alter-nating parties really do adopt widely different policies, agreement is so weak that polyarchy itself is endangered. . . . Neither party can win if its pro-gram is very much different from the other. Hence, a high degree of con-tinuity will result; there may be breaks in the continuity, if the center of public opinion shifts abruptly or if there are cumulative changes which, for some reason, neither party exploits; but these take place rather infrequently," Dahl and Lindblom, "Bargaining," p. 301. Cf. Frank W. Young, "Reactive Subsystems and Structural Differentiation," mimeographed, October 1968, p. 17. For example, teachers' strikes averaged 3.7 annually in the period 1950–1965, ranging from one to ten. In 1966 there were thirty-three and in 1967 there were an estimated seventy (*Americana Encyclopedia Annual*, p. 238). Similar contagions are seen in the student sit-ins of spring 1968, and in the New York City strikes following that of the sanitation workers.

17 See Blau and Scott, *Formal Organizations*, pp. 240ff.; Thompson, *Modern Organization*, p. 86; Michael D. Reagan, "The Political Structure of the Fed-eral Reserve System," *American Political Science Review* 55 (1961): 64–76; John A. Seiler, "Toward a Theory of Organization Congruent with Primary Group Concepts," *Behavioral Science* 8 (1963): 190–98; Talcott Parsons, *Societies: Evolutionary and Comparative Perspectives* (Englewood Cliffs, N.J.: Prentice-Hall, 1966), p. 23.

On the temptation to seek quick success with the easiest cases, see Thomas F. Pettigrew, "Complexity and Change in American Social Patterns: A So-cial Psychological View," *Daedelus* (Fall 1965), especially pp. 994–96. On the vulnerability of government to special interests, see Stanley S. Surrey, "How Special Tax Provisions Get Enacted," in Randall B. Ripley, ed., *Public Policies and Their Politics* (New York: Norton, 1966).

18 For many examples of these tendencies at work, see Henry S. Kariel, *The Decline of American Pluralism* (Stanford, Calif.: Stanford University Press, 1961), chaps. 3–7.

19 On the broadening of agency functions, see Norton Long, *The Polity* (Chi-cago: Rand McNally, 1962), chap. 6; Gideon Sjoberg, "Contradictory Func-tional Requirements and Social Systems," *Journal of Conflict Resolution* 4 (1960): 198–208.

20 Cf. Robert J. Merton, "The Environment of the Innovating Organization:

Some Conjectures and Proposals," in Gary A. Steiner, ed., *The Creative Organization* (Chicago: University of Chicago Press, 1965), p. 58. "For individual organizations, the recruitment of men of talent and the rate of innovation tend to be mutually reinforcing. The innovative organization recruits men of creative potential and helps them convert that potential into productive innovation by providing them with an effective environment *within* the organization. As the flow of innovation becomes visible to others in the environment *of* the organization, it facilitates the recruitment of new men of talent. The cycle is renewed and amplified in magnitude." Because talent is scarce many posts must be manned by persons who lack the qualities needed. Therefore, rules are proliferated to control the behavior of the semicompetent. See number 11 above.

21   The number of lawyers in government service increased from 25,621 in 1961 to 29,314 in 1964 (*American Bar Association News*, April 15, 1964). See the account of the history and powers of New York City's Board of Estimate, as described by Savre and Kaufman, *Governing New York City*, chap. 17. However, fragmentation of budgeting powers can weaken their effectiveness; see Bernard K. Gordon, "The Military Budget: Congressional Phase," *The Journal of Politics* 23 (1961): 689–710.

22   Robert A. Dahl's comments on Major Lee illustrate this. Lee "was not at the peak of a pyramid but rather at the center of intersecting circles. He rarely commanded. He negotiated, cajoled, exhorted, beguiled, charmed, pressed, appealed, reasoned, promised, insisted, demanded, even threatened, but he most needed support and acquiescence from other leaders who simply could not be commanded. . . . [T]he system was like a tire with a slow leak, and the mayor had the only air pump. Whether the executive-centered order was maintained or the system reverted to independent sovereignties depended almost entirely, then, on the relative amount of influence the mayor could succeed in extracting from his political resources." *Who Governs?* (New Haven, Conn.: Yale University Press, 1961), pp. 204–5.

23   Cf. William Kornhauser, *The Politics of Mass Society* (New York: Free Press, 1959), p. 234. On "the long-run instability of multi-polar systems," see Karl W. Deutsch and J. David Singer, "Multipolar Power Systems and International Stability," *World Politics* 16 (1964): 404–6.
   On loss of authority through inability to produce, see Chalmers Johnson, *Revolutionary Change* (Boston: Little, Brown, 1966), p. 91.

24   Herbert Kaufman, "Organizational Theory and Political Theory," *American Political Science Review* 58 (1964): 5–14. Cf. also Alvin W. Gouldner, "Metaphysical Pathos and the Theory of Democracy," in S. M. Lipset and N. J. Smelser, eds., *Sociology: The Process of a Decade* (Englewood Cliffs, N.J.: Prentice-Hall, 1961), pp. 80–89.

25   See Irving Louis Horowitz, "Sociology and Politics: The Myth of Functionalism Revisited," *The Journal of Politics* 25 (1963).

26   In the sense of Webster's definition: "Presenting themselves simultaneously and being interchangeable in the enunciation of properties. . . ." Cf. also

one of his definitions of a college: "specif., a body of clergy living in common on a foundation."

27   To begin with, one might be the Congress of the United States.

28   Chris Argyris, "Some Causes of Organizational Ineffectiveness within the Department of State," Occasional Papers, no. 2, Center for International Systems Research, Department of State. Cf. Chris Argyris, "Today's Problems with Tomorrow's Organizations," *Journal of Management Studies* 4, no. 1 (February 1967): 31–55.

13   Fighting Story

1   Hermann Hagedorn, ed., *The Works of Theodore Roosevelt* (New York: Scribner, 1926), vol. 14, chap. 12.

2   From Bryan's acceptance speech in Indianapolis, August 8, 1900, in Schlesinger et al., *History of American Presidential Elections: 1789–1968* (New York: Chelsea House, 1971), vol. 3, pp. 1943ff. Bryan had a phonograph record made of this speech.

3   *New York World*, October 22, 1900.

4   W. A. Swanberg, *Citizen Hearst* (New York: Scribner, 1961), pp. 136–37.

5   Ibid., pp. 155–56; Hearst is also celebrated, though differently, in a tedious novel by Aldous Huxley, *After Many a Summer Dies the Swan* (New York: Harper, 1939), and in the film *Citizen Kane*.

6   Charles Belmont Davis, ed., *Adventures and Letters of Richard Harding Davis* (New York: Scribner, 1917), pp. 254–55.

15   Drift to Fiction

1   *The Pulse of Politics: Electing Presidents in the Media Age* (New York: Norton, 1980).

2   Kathleen A. Frankovic, "Public Opinion Trends," in Gerald Pomper et al., *The Election of 1980: Reports and Interpretations* (Chatham, N.J.: Chatham House, 1981), pp. 113, 115.

3   See *The Presidential Character: Predicting Performance in the White House*, Englewood Cliffs, N.J.: Prentice-Hall, 3d ed., 1985.

4   See ibid., chap. 16.

5   See Gerald Pomper et al., *The Election of 1984: Reports and Interpretations* (Chatham, N.J.: Chatham House, 1985).

Index

Permission to reprint selections from the following sources is gratefully acknowledged:

1. "A Presidency with the People: Reflections upon a Unique Institution": From *A New Commitment, A New America* (New York: Duobooks, 1977 by the 1977 Inaugural Committee), pp. 9–29.

2. Reprinted by permission of *Daedalus*, Journal of the American Academy of Arts and Sciences, "Philosophers & Kings: Studies in Leadership," vol. 97, no. 3, Summer 1968, Boston, pp. 938–68.

3. "Classifying and Predicting Presidential Styles: Two Weak Presidents," from *Journal of Social Issues*, vol. 24, no. 3 (1968), pp. 51–80.

4. "The Interplay of Presidential Character and Style: A Paradigm and Five Illustrations": From *A Source Book for the Study of Personality and Politics*, ed. Fred I. Greenstein and Michael Lerner (Chicago: Markham Publishing Company, 1971), pp. 384–408.

5. "Strategies for Understanding Politicians," from *American Journal of Political Science*, vol. 18, no. 2 (May 1974), pp. 443–67.

7. "The Spectator": From *The Lawmakers: Recruitment and Adaptation to Legislative Life* (New Haven, Conn.: Yale University Press, 1965), pp. 24–66.

8. "Cognitive Dissonance and the Perception of Power": From *Power in Committees: An Experiment in the Governmental Process* (Chicago: Rand McNally & Company, 1965), pp. 72–82.

9. "Peer Group Discussion and Recovery from the Kennedy Assassination": Reprinted from *The Kennedy Assassination and the American Public: Social Communication in Crisis*, ed. Bradley S. Greenberg and Edwin B. Parker, with the permission of the publishers, Stanford University Press, copyright 1965 by the Board of Trustees of the Leland Stanford Junior University, pp. 112–29.

10. "Leadership Strategies for Legislative Party Cohesion": From *Journal of Politics*, vol. 28 (1966), pp. 347–67.

11. "Some Consequences of Pluralization in Government": From *The Future of the United States Government: Toward the Year 2000*, ed. Harvey S. Perloff (New York: George Braziller, 1971), pp. 242–66.

12. "Characters in the Campaign: The Literary Problem": From *Race for the Presidency: The Media and the Nominating Process*, ed. James David Barber (New York: The American Assembly, 1978), pp. 111–46.

13. "Theodore Roosevelt 1900": From *The Pulse of Politics: Electing Presidents in the Media Age* (New York: W. W. Norton & Company, 1980), pp. 29–46.

14. "Characters in the Campaign: The Educational Challenge": From *Race for the Presidency: The Media and the Nominating Process*, ed. James David Barber (New York: The American Assembly, 1978), pp. 173–98.

16. "A Vision Beyond the Myth": From *The Pulse of Politics: Electing Presidents in the Media Age* (New York: W. W. Norton & Company, 1980), pp. 311–22.

17. "Candidate Reagan and 'the Sucker Generation,' " from *Columbia Journalism Review* (November/December 1987), pp. 33–36.

ABOUT THE AUTHOR. James David Barber is James B. Duke Professor of Political Science and Policy Studies and Co-Director of the Center for Study of Communications, Duke University. He is the author of *The Presidential Character: Predicting Performances in the White House*, 3d ed. (Prentice-Hall, 1985), and *The Pulse of Politics: Electing Presidents in the Media Age* (Norton, 1980).